P9-DFU-534

WHERE TO STASH YOUR CASH LEGALLY

Offshore Financial Centers of the World

Robert E. Bauman JD • Ted Bauman

Ninth Edition

BANYAN HILL

Banyan Hill Publishing
P.O. Box 8378
Delray Beach, FL 33482
Tel.: 866-584-4096
Email: http://banyanhill.com/contact-us
Web: http://banyanhill.com

ISBN: 978-0-692-97403-2

Copyright (c) 2018 Sovereign Offshore Services LLC. All international and domestic rights reserved.

No part of this publication may be reproduced or transmitted in any form or by any means, electronic or mechanical, including photocopying and recording or by any information storage or retrieval system without the written permission of the publisher, Banyan Hill Publishing. Protected by U.S. copyright laws, 17 U.S.C. 101 et seq., 18 U.S.C. 2319; Violations punishable by up to five year's imprisonment and/or $250,000 in fines.

Notice: this publication is designed to provide accurate and authoritative information in regard to the subject matter covered. It is sold and distributed with the understanding that the authors, publisher and seller are not engaged in rendering legal, accounting or other professional advice or services. If legal or other expert assistance is required, the services of a competent professional advisor should be sought.

The information and recommendations contained in this brochure have been compiled from sources considered reliable. Employees, officers and directors of Banyan Hill do not receive fees or commissions for any recommendations of services or products in this publication. Investment and other recommendations carry inherent risks. As no investment recommendation can be guaranteed, Banyan Hill takes no responsibility for any loss or inconvenience if one chooses to accept them.

Banyan Hill advocates full compliance with applicable tax and financial reporting laws. U.S. law requires income taxes to be paid on all worldwide income wherever a U.S. person (citizen or resident alien) may live or have a residence. Each U.S. person who has a financial interest in, or signature authority over bank, securities, or other financial accounts in a foreign country that exceeds $10,000 in aggregate value, must report that fact on his or her federal income tax return, IRS form 1040. An additional report must be filed by April 15th of each year on an information return (FinCEN form 114) with the U.S. Treasury. IRS form 8938 also may be due on April 15th annually, depending on the total value of foreign assets. Willful noncompliance may result in criminal prosecution. You should consult a qualified attorney or accountant to ensure that you know, understand and comply with these and any other reporting requirements.

OFFSHORE FINANCIAL
CENTERS OF THE WORLD

ABOUT THE AUTHORS

Robert E. Bauman JD

Bob Bauman, legal counsel to Banyan Hill Publishing, served as a member of the U.S. House of Representatives from 1973 to 1981 representing the First District of Maryland. He is an author and lecturer on many aspects of wealth protection, offshore residence and second citizenship.

A member of the District of Columbia Bar, he received his juris doctor degree from the Law Center of Georgetown University in 1964. He has a B.S. degree in International Relations from the Georgetown University School of Foreign Service (1959) and was honored with GU's Distinguished Alumni Award.

He is the author of *The Gentleman from Maryland* (Hearst Book Publishing, NY, 1985); and the following books, all published by Banyan Hill Publishing: *The Complete Guide to Offshore Residency, Dual Citizenship and Second Passports*; *The Offshore Money Manual*; editor of *Forbidden Knowledge*; *Panama Money Secrets*; *Where to Stash Your Cash Legally: Offshore Financial Centers of the World*, 8th Edition, *Swiss Money Secrets*; *How to Lawyer-Proof Your Life*. His writings have appeared in *The Wall Street Journal*, *The New York Times*, *National Review*, and other publications.

Ted Bauman

Ted Bauman joined Banyan Hill Publishing in 2013. As an expat who has traveled to over 60 countries and lived in the Republic of South Africa for 25 years, Ted specializes in asset protection and international migration. He is the editor of *The Bauman Letter, Alpha Stock Alert,* and the *Plan B Club.* Born in Washington, D.C. and raised on Maryland's Eastern Shore, Ted migrated to South Africa as a young man. He graduated from the University of Cape Town with postgraduate degrees in Economics and History.

During his 25-year career in South Africa, Ted served a variety of executive roles in the South African non-profit sector, primarily as a fund manager for low cost housing projects. During the 2000s, he worked as a consultant, researching and writing extensively on financial, housing, and urban planning issues for clients as diverse as the United Nations, the South African government, and European grant-making agencies. He also traveled extensively, largely in Africa, Asia, and Europe.

In 2008, Ted returned to the U.S., where he served as Director of International Housing Programs for Habitat for Humanity International, based in Atlanta, Georgia. During that time, he extended his travels to Latin American and the Caribbean. He continued to research and write on a variety of topics related to international development. In 2013, Ted left Habitat to work full-time as a researcher and writer.

Ted has been published in a variety of international journals, including the *Journal of Microfinance, Small Enterprise Development, and Environment and Urbanization,* as well as the South African press, including the *Cape Times, New Internationalist, Cape Argus,* and *Mail and Guardian.*

ACKNOWLEDGEMENTS

Many people assisted in the production of this 9th Edition of *Where to Stash Your Cash Legally; Offshore Financial Centers of the World.*

Our sincere appreciation goes to Jennifer Somerville, who did the scrupulous job of proofing and updating all the contact emails, physical addresses and web sites; Jocelynn Smith for her meticulous editing; and to the many readers who made valuable suggestions that help improve the text with each revision.

Any errors of facts or interpretation remain our responsibility.

Robert E. Bauman JD
Ted Bauman

FOREWORD

Since the first edition of this book was first published two decades ago, there have been many and fundamental changes in every aspect of international life, political, economic and military. This major transformation is especially true in the world of offshore investment and finance.

The abandonment of the term "tax haven" for the now preferred "offshore financial center" (OFCs) is emblematic of these changes.

This more expansive and accurate OFC phrase recognizes the major reforms that have occurred voluntarily, as well as those imposed by new national and international rules. Nothing short of a revolution has affected every aspect of offshore banking, investing, taxes, asset protection, and financial privacy, as well as the official reporting requirements governments have imposed on these activities.

Over the last 20 years, offshore financial centers have accomplished real self-reform, bringing more openness and stricter regulation. The OFCs were successful in creating far better financial regulatory regimes than those that now exist in the City of London or in the United States, the two major financial disaster centers where the colossal global financial mess erupted in 2008.

Despite these offshore reforms and improvements, a carefully nurtured myth about the offshore world continues.

Ask any reasonably intelligent person in the United States, the United Kingdom (or many other countries) what they know about "*offshore*" financial activity. Responses are likely to be distorted, uninformed, and larded with preposterous theories promoted by biased media and tax-hungry government propaganda.

Offshore, you will be told, is an evil place populated with secret numbered bank accounts, sinister con men and fraudsters, money launderers, drug kingpins, rapacious bankers and corrupt foreign politicians grasping for briefcases full of cash bribes.

Owing to U.S. Internal Revenue Service propaganda, a complicit and lazy "news" media, too many potboiler novels, sensational Hollywood movies and TV shows, the popular notion of "offshore" is that of an international sinkhole of tax evasion, fraud, and criminal corruption.

The truth is that offshore financial centers serve as vital links in international finance, banking and investment. Most importantly, these professional centers provide much needed low tax competition for the high tax, deficit spending, hugely indebted welfare states.

For a quarter century, I have been researching and writing about offshore financial matters. That has included topics such as tax havens and asset havens, offshore banking, asset protection trusts, international business corporations, family foundations, limited liability companies, financial privacy, residence and second citizenship and about the general state of the offshore financial world.

Even though I earned a degree in international relations, a law degree, served in the Maryland State Senate and spent eight years as a member of the U.S. House of Representatives, when I began this work I quickly discovered how little I knew about the real "offshore" world.

My early and limited acquaintance with "offshore" matters had created a similarly erroneous impression that too many people have today.

For decades, tax-hungry politicians from high-tax welfare states — including the U.S. government, together with their global leftist political allies — have mounted a series of largely false attacks on the offshore financial world that continue to this day. They intentionally have smeared offshore financial centers as venues of tax evasion, drug money and terrorist cash. At one point these attacks even advanced the preposterous claim that tax havens caused the 2008 to 2012 global housing and banking recession.

Their collective motive for this massive deception is obvious: the politicians want to tax more so they can spend more, hoping to buy popular support, thus enabling them to stay in power and continue their failed policies.

Then too, many American attorneys, accountants, insurance agents and stock brokers have a vested interest in keeping their clients close to home, thus they falsely warn against going offshore. They, like the U.S. Internal Revenue Service, want to keep you and your money where they can get to it.

Don't be fooled.

Despite increased reporting requirements, it is still fully legal for Americans to bank, invest, and purchase real estate, annuities and life insurance offshore.

When this fog of manufactured lies is cleared away, the truth about "offshore" opportunities and profits is impressive.

But finding the truth for the first-time offshore adventurer can be a frustrating, discouraging task and, if you get burnt, a very short and unpleasant journey. Great care is called for because, just as domestically, there are many offshore fraudsters waiting to fleece the unwary.

Understand that the offshore world offers Americans very few tax savings, certainly not as many as slick promoters claim. That's because American citizens and U.S. resident aliens are taxed on their worldwide income, while most other nations impose "territorial" taxes, mainly on earnings within their own national borders. For those more sensible countries, taxes end at their borders.

But going offshore for Americans does offer some limited tax deferral and, most of all, in this lawsuit-happy age, their distance and laws offer far stronger asset protection.

Offshore also guarantees far more financial privacy (and yes, secrecy) than can be found in many other countries, most certainly in the United States, where the so-called PATRIOT Act has destroyed all financial privacy.

Indeed, the need for personal and financial privacy, under siege from all directions, has prompted us to include a chapter on this edition especially devoted to that topic. There we explain not just the threats, but the available solutions you can actively undertake to protect yourself and your assets in this digital electronic age.

During the 20 years since the first edition of this book appeared, U.S. politicians and government bureaucrats have become an army of control freaks when it comes to Americans' offshore financial activity. They have imposed what they hoped would be an entangling web of border controls, travel controls, currency controls, foreign investment and banking controls, all the while repeatedly implying that "going offshore" is somehow illegal (it is not) — and even unpatriotic.

The politicians shamelessly used the New York City and Washington, D.C., terror attacks on September 11, 2001, as an excuse for even greater control. The 2008 global financial crisis served as another pretext, not only to impose more financial controls, but to spend trillions of taxpayers' dollars to bail out banks and businesses, foreign and domestic, greatly increasing the ranks of those who are indebted to the existing crony system of Big Brother government.

With the support of both major political parties, counter-productive government controls and regulations stifling the American economy have grown exponentially. The invasion of every aspect of law-abiding Americans' privacy, we now know, is carried out in secret under the PATRIOT Act by the U.S. National Security Agency (NSA) and numerous federal, state and local police agencies. The record of the NSA and the FBI in the last decade is one long list of abused powers and unconstitutional acts, followed occasionally by apologies and promises to sin no more — but only when they get caught.

A few years ago, the U.S. Justice Department's Inspector General Report criticized the FBI abuse of "national security letters" (NSLs) in obtaining thousands of telephone, business and financial records without prior judicial approval. Although they cited the PATRIOT Act as their authority, the DOJ found the FBI illegally issued more than 20,000 NSLs, most having nothing to do with terrorism.

Thanks to the courageous revelations of former NSA analyst, Edward Snowden, the world now knows that the NSA, at least since 2005, has been tracking, reading, listening and recording everyone's phone calls, emails as well as our business, financial and other records, a massive violation of our privacy.

U.S. government civil asset forfeiture seizures are aimed mainly at innocent people never charged with a crime, as state and federal police agencies seek easy sources of increased income. Forfeiture federal revenue gains $4.5 billion, tripled in the five years up to 2015. In 2015 alone, the federal take soared to $6.5 billion, and that does not include millions more in state and local forfeiture income. As did the Obama administration, the Trump administration has endorsed more and expanded civil forfeiture.

So, what does all this have to do with offshore financial havens and your ability to "go offshore"?

The answer to that question should be obvious.

Wherever you live, "offshore" thankfully is a place well outside the immediate jurisdiction of your home country's government and its executive and judicial agencies.

When you move some or all your cash, assets and investments offshore, you place them on the other side of a political and legal wall that stands as a formidable obstacle. Offshore serves as far more than a speed bump to lawsuits, claims, disgruntled business partners or a spouse, family members and even to your own government.

But timing is indeed everything in life. Asset protection planning means taking steps well in advance of potential trouble to protect your assets, property, savings, investments, stocks, businesses, retirement and inheritances. Planning against unexpected threats takes on new meaning today considering events in the United States and throughout the world.

History teaches that things can and do change quickly. Don't ever think you are immune from financial and personal harm.

That's what this book is all about — strictly *legal* ways for you to protect your wealth, invest and increase your money, save on taxes and find financial privacy — and peace of mind — by "going offshore."

We will tell you the who, what, where, when and why of the offshore world — based on personal experience and due diligence. We will connect you with the many experts who are our associates across the globe; the same trusted professionals you'll find listed in these pages for your own personal use.

Bob Bauman

Robert E. Bauman JD
Delray Beach, Florida

TABLE OF CONTENTS

Where to Stash Your Cash Legally
Offshore Financial Centers of the World

CHAPTER ONE

A Safe Haven Offshore

Here we discuss the reasons and uses of an offshore haven; the ways and means of moving your assets and wealth offshore to a tax-free or low-tax jurisdiction; strategies and places where you can invest with maximum profitability, minimum taxes and greater financial privacy.

Twenty years ago, when I first began writing about the offshore world, few of the many technological changes we now have existed.

I recall the late Bob Kephart, the founder of The Sovereign Society (now Banyan Hill), returning from Switzerland in the late 1990s and saying with disgust: "Those Swiss banks don't even have email yet!"

Today, we have a technologically advanced global system that offers huge financial opportunities based on instant communications, interlinked databases, electronic commerce and digital cash flows. In many ways, this system has shifted power from the monopolistic policies of the high-tax nation state to the individual citizen, increasing personal financial freedom and the chance for profit — if you know how to navigate.

In turn, this new global freedom has caused a reaction by grasping governments everywhere, trying desperately to keep control over their citizens, eager to know what they are doing, especially with their finances.

The technology that makes these global systems available for your use, we now know also are used by governments for constant surveillance attempting to track your every move, well beyond the official reports you are required by law to file with the government.

As part of Big Brother's plans to control its citizens and their money, political leaders in major nations will use almost any excuse to attack and curb offshore financial activity. They, along with their allies in the "news" media, continue to portray "tax havens" as secretive places where crime and tax evasion is rampant.

To a degree, these big government Big Brothers have succeeded in scaring too many people about "going offshore." The political Left has so tarnished the phrase "tax haven" that these besieged offshore jurisdictions now prefer to be called "offshore financial centers," in fact, a far more accurate description of their true role.

Many people don't have a clue about what "offshore" means, while too many others have gained the worst possible impression of unjustifiably smeared offshore financial centers (OFCs).

A few clueless people even seem unaware of the major global financial revolution that has taken place. This book goes beyond the clues and reveals the secrets. It tells you the truth about offshore financial activity and OFCs, how to profit offshore and what you can do personally to reap benefits legally.

By now, most people understand the meaning of the huge advances in digital technology, satellite communications and the vast expansion of the Internet. With social networking, texting, smartphones, tweeting, iPads and iPhones, today's economic news travels fast. As of January 2018, a reported 73% of "baby boomers," ages 50 to 64, own a smartphone.

Insider information is no longer confined to Wall Street and the City of London. Waves of news and rumors ripple daily through world time zones and stock markets as 24/7 media covers events live

— an example of the irresistible technological advances that have forced a totally new operational reality on financial and banking systems — and on governments.

In many respects, all this constitutes a government bureaucrat's worst fear — hundreds of millions of instant communications devices and computers linked worldwide, electronic banking and online investment accounts, crypto-currencies, "smart card" money, easily available email encryption; free communications, even the Dark Web, much of it still unmediated by governments.

An astute observer put it this way: "You get untraceable banking and investment, a black hole where money can hide and be laundered, not just for conglomerates or drug cartels, but for anyone." (That may be true, but our advice is, "Don't try it." We will expand on that warning later.)

Understandably, government bureaucrats, especially tax collectors, are mildly frantic. The freedom of this new, world money system runs counter to all the Big Brother control freaks advocate; socialist policies that have bled taxpayers and crippled prosperity for much of the last 100 years. This official fear of losing control spurs the incessant attacks on offshore financial centers — and on those of us who use them legally to our advantage.

Many across the world now understand that government is doing all it can to stifle these liberating trends. But we believe they will fail.

Why Go Offshore?

In times past, most people thought "personal finance" meant checking and savings accounts, home mortgages and auto loans. Even now, with available international mutual and hedge funds, relatively few investors take advantage of available global diversification.

What follows are only some of the many good reasons to "go offshore."

1. Investment diversification. Not all bankers or investment and money managers are willing to do business with U.S. citizens directly. This anti-American client attitude has stiffened in reaction to U.S. government policies since the 2008 Union Bank of Switzerland (UBS) tax evasion scandal, and the adoption by the U.S. Congress in 2010 of the Foreign Account Tax Compliance Act (FATCA).

Foreigners, and many foreign banks, have made the choice that it is easier and less costly to do business with the rest of the world than it is to comply with the draconian rules of the U.S. government, especially those of the U.S. Internal Revenue Service (IRS), which now claims to have worldwide jurisdiction over every bank and financial institution that has American clients.

Nevertheless, by going offshore, you can gain direct legal access to U.S.-restricted investments unavailable in the United States.

Relatively few foreign securities are traded on U.S. stock and other markets, representing a small percentage of the securities traded on world markets. In the past the only practical way to buy these offshore shares was through an account at a foreign bank or with an offshore stock broker. In these pages you will find the names and contact information for reliable banks, brokers, investment managers, insurance and annuity advisors and attorneys, all offshore professionals who welcome American clients. We also explain how to trade globally using the Internet.

2. Higher returns. If you know where to find them, there are opportunities in traditional foreign financial markets, such as stocks sold only on foreign exchanges that offer much higher returns than generally are available in U.S. markets.

3. Currency diversification. Investors wishing to stabilize their portfolios can protect their wealth against the fluctuating U.S. dollar simply by holding currencies the experts recommend, such as the Swiss franc, the Norwegian kroner, the Australian dollar and the Singapore dollar, all good long-term currencies, when stock markets are soft.

Even past currency favorites such as the Swiss franc and the Japanese yen can pose more risk due to central bank intervention. For those interested in currency trading, consider the several Banyan Hill investment research newsletters.

While U.S. investors can purchase foreign currencies through a few U.S. banks, offshore banks generally offer higher yields, lower fees and lower minimums. Foreign currency opportunities are plentiful. In 1970, a U.S. dollar would purchase 4.5 Swiss francs but in 2017, the U.S. dollar equals less than one Swiss franc. Since 1971, the franc has appreciated nearly 400% against the U.S. dollar.

4. Safety and security. Starting in the 1980s, the United States experienced a wave of bank and savings and loans failures at a rate unmatched since the Great Depression of the 1930s. The underwriting bailout that saved U.S. thrifts and savings and loan associations by the financial industry and the American taxpayer cost a then staggering $153 billion. The disaster was a major threat to the U.S. financial system, and one of the most expensive financial sector crises the world had seen — up until that time.

But beginning in 2008, a massive government-prompted U.S. housing crisis in subprime mortgages and unregulated derivative investments, augmented by Wall Street's reckless greed, combined to produce another American banking crisis that approached the misery of that same Great Depression.

Rescuing many of the major U.S. banks from their own folly required trillions of taxpayer dollars in bailouts. The so-called Troubled Asset Relief Program (TARP) — which spent an astounding $700 billion in taxpayer' money — aimed to bail out banks in response to the financial crisis, but it was also closely dissected by both Congress and the media. There was a lot of skepticism.

Sadly, that $700 billion was just a drop in the bucket when it comes to overall amount of funds needed to support America's financial structure. And the masses paid little attention to what happened to the majority of that taxpayer money. Up to $12.8 trillion was loaned, spent or guaranteed by a variety of government agencies such as the Federal Reserve and U.S. Treasury, according to Bloomberg News. Other estimates suggest that the ultimate total for bailouts exceeded $17 trillion.

For comparison, consider the sad fact that the gross U.S. government national debt, at the end of 2017, exceeded $20 trillion. That amounts to 105% of U.S. gross domestic product, according to the Congressional Budget Office. The percentage of debt is higher than any point since World War II, and twice the percentage it was a decade ago.

In contrast to this self-induced U.S. banking morass, the offshore banks we recommend in these pages were not, and are not, exposed to risky investments, such as subprime mortgages, Third World debt and highly leveraged derivative investments.

Indeed, we at Banyan Hill take pride in the fact that since 1999 we have warned against using certain offshore banks, including by name, UBS and Credit Suisse. We have done our due diligence and the recommended banks in these pages are well-capitalized and conservatively managed — and they welcome American clients at a time when many offshore banks do not.

5. Asset protection. Lawsuits continue in epidemic proportions in America and tort reform gets nowhere in the U.S. Congress where millions of dollars in trial lawyer's political action committee contributions hold sway.

In America, if a creditor gets a judgment against you in the state where you live, that judgment may be easily enforced. In contrast, if you invest or bank in a suitable offshore jurisdiction, even Switzerland, your account can be configured financially to be essentially judgment-proof.

The prudent use of offshore havens for safekeeping some of your cash and assets provides U.S. persons with a greatly enhanced protection from the threat of lawsuits, civil forfeiture, business failure, divorce, exchange controls, repressive U.S. legislation, lengthy probate and political instability. Going offshore where privacy laws are much stricter, helps to avoid the vast U.S. asset-tracking network, which permits private or official investigators to easily identify the unencumbered assets of a potential defendant.

6. Financial privacy. Let's face the truth: since the adoption of the so-called PATRIOT Act in 2001, in so far as the government is concerned, personal and financial privacy is dead in America. In Chapter Three we explore in detail the status of financial and personal privacy.

The six advantages we described above have especially strong application when it comes to placing your cash and other assets offshore.

Offshore Legal Entities

By now the financially well-informed are comfortable with offshore bank accounts which they routinely use as investment vehicles.

But the use of some of the more complicated offshore techniques, such as the international business corporation (IBC), a foreign-based asset protection trust (APT), a private family foundation or a limited liability company (LLC) are less used.

While employing these legal entities requires more time and effort, their use can greatly enhance your choice of financial strategies and give you increased protection and investing effectiveness. In these pages we explain proven strategies and show you how to use them. You may find it difficult to believe, but each of these strategies in their basic form can cost less than $5,000 to implement, as we will explain.

One more thought: perhaps you might consider relocating your personal residence offshore in a tax haven nation that welcomes foreigners with tax exemptions and special privileges that make life easier and less complicated. We will explain which nations, such as Panama, Uruguay and Singapore, offer such incentives and suggest how you can obtain these advantages.

Investment Profits Offshore

According to a 2017 report by the Congressional Research Service, the U.S. is the largest investor abroad and also the largest recipient of direct foreign investment in the world. But the CRS reported that only 26% went to less developed countries. The majority of 74% of the accumulated $6.4 trillion U.S. foreign direct investment was concentrated in high-income developed countries, who are members of the Organization for Economic Cooperation and Development (OECD). However, the share of U.S. investment going to less developed countries has risen in recent years.

"When history books are written 200 years from now about the last two decades of the 20th Century," former U.S. Treasury secretary, Lawrence Summers, told *The New York Times*, "I am convinced that the end of the Cold War will be the second story. The first story will be about the appearance of emerging markets — about the fact that developing countries where more than three billion people live have moved toward the market and seen rapid growth in incomes."

That optimistic comment came well before the global recession of 2008 in which emerging market stock values sank along with those in other world markets. Even so, it is not a given that the U.S. economy will be who leads the world back to growth. It is the developing countries that could be the power to the future recovery.

As historian and professor Niall Ferguson noted: "The globalization of finance played a crucial role in raising growth rates in emerging markets, particularly in Asia, propelling hundreds of millions of people out of poverty."

Cross-border investments have proven profitable, despite temporary setbacks. What used to be tagged "Third World" investment funds have become the more appealing "emerging market funds." The global economy of today is very different from past times.

Offshore financial centers play a major role in world business. Included are companies in Bermuda, British Virgin Islands, Cayman

Islands, Hong Kong, Guernsey, Jersey, Isle of Man, Mauritius and Seychelles.

Coming out of a depressed time, finance and technology still dominate the world economic scene. According to the Bank for International Settlements 2016 Triennial Survey, turnover in global FX markets averaged $5.1 trillion per day in 2016. While this was down somewhat from prior years, the volume of foreign exchange trade has increased by roughly 160 times in the last 30 years.

Boom and Bust

According to www.statista.com, the U.S. mutual fund industry held more than $16.34 trillion in assets in 2016. At one time, autos, steel and grain dominated world markets, but more recently trade in stocks, bonds and currencies has replaced them.

The respected McKinsey Global Institute's report on global flows in a digital age notes that international wealth flows have been "a common thread in economic growth for centuries, since the days of the Silk Road, through the mercantilist and colonial periods and the Industrial Revolution. But today, the movement of goods, services, finance, and people has reached previously unimagined levels. Global flows are creating new degrees of connectedness among economies and playing an ever-larger role in determining the fate of nations, companies, and individuals. To be unconnected is to fall behind."

David Stockman, President Ronald Reagan's former U.S. Budget Director, underscored some disturbing stock market statistics: "Last time, global equity market inflated to a peak of $60 trillion in aggregate value before they plunged to barely $25 trillion during the post-Lehman meltdown. Now they have been pumped back to the $80 trillion mark by the sheer recklessness of the world's central bankers."

Regardless of boom or bust, what must be remembered is that wealth has become stateless, circulating wherever the owner finds the highest return and the greatest freedom. In other words, cash without a country.

From 1970 to 2010, spending by investors in industrialized nations on offshore stocks increased more than 200 times over, while national capital markets merged into one global capital market.

As stock markets close in London, they open in New York and as American exchanges end the day on the U.S. West Coast, markets in Hong Kong, Singapore and Tokyo come to life.

Unfortunately, this same interconnected global market also helps to spread economic downturns faster than the speed of the bird flu virus.

Avoiding Roadblocks to Prosperity

At a time when politicians on the Left demand more government regulation, such as the Foreign Account Tax Compliance Act of 2010 (FATCA), few realize that information about most offshore investments, profitable or otherwise, long has been denied to U.S. persons who may want to invest offshore.

Cumbersome regulations imposed decades ago by the U.S. government on foreign investment funds and banks lock out foreign fund managers. Unwilling to waste time and money on bureaucratic registrations until recently, most offshore funds declined to do business with anyone who had a U.S. mailing address.

American leftist politicians repeatedly blame "deregulation" and the excesses of the free market for every U.S. financial crisis. That creates a justification for still more regulation. But who regulates the regulators?

For investors one of the main obstacles has been restrictive U.S. securities laws. Any "investment contract" for purchase of a security sold in America must be registered with the U.S. Securities and Exchange Commission (SEC), and often with state agencies as well.

This is an expensive process. The U.S. also requires far more stock disclosure by sales entities than most foreign countries, burdening further with U.S. accounting practices that differ from those used abroad. International fund managers are practical people who calculate that operating costs in the U.S. would wipe out any profit margin.

In an effort to meet new and more stringent U.S. standards, we name offshore investment and banking associates who voluntarily, and at considerable expense, have qualified and become registered SEC investment advisers under Section 202(a)(11) of the Investment Advisers Act of 1940 (15 U.S.C. § 80b-2(a)(11)) that defines "investment advisers."

Under SEC rules this means that each person or entity must file full information on their professional activity and business. It also allows foreign advisers who register, to contact freely and visit American clients. This allows investors to access registration and other company filings using the SEC electronic system known as EDGAR.

Ironically, many foreign based mutual funds and hedge funds with top performance records are run from offices located within the U.S. by U.S. residents, but they do not accept investments from Americans. To avoid SEC red tape and registration costs, investment in these funds is available only to non-U.S. persons.

All this is changing as many foreign financial firms and banks are registering with the SEC so they can serve American clients. For your protection, within these pages we will identify SEC-registered firms such as, WHVP and ENR Asset Management that partner with Banyan Hill.

S.E.C. Goes Worldwide

In the 2007 UBS Swiss bank scandal, the IRS led the investigation of the bank's U.S. clients who evaded taxes, creating an anti-tax evasion campaign that gained major news media coverage for many months.

Much less notice was given to the fact that the U.S. Department of Justice charged that the services UBS rendered in Switzerland amounted to the bank's staff acting as unregistered investment advisers and broker-dealers. That violated the U.S. Investment Advisers Act of 1940 and SEC rules.

Using this extraterritorial approach, the SEC sought to extend its jurisdiction to include any foreign person anywhere in the world who dares to advise Americans about investing. The SEC claims that unless the adviser first qualifies and registers with them, they are engaged in illegal, even criminal conduct.

In the final 2010 settlement, UBS paid a $718 million fine to the IRS on the tax evasion charges. The financial company also paid another $200 million to the U.S. based on the SEC charges. UBS was barred permanently from acting as investment advisers or broker-dealer for American clients in Switzerland.

These successful U.S. government attacks and the fines levied against UBS caused many offshore banks to establish special, separate SEC-qualified investment banking units for American clients only. Many careful independent offshore investment advisers are now also registered with the SEC.

As part of your due diligence, check to see if the offshore bank you are considering is SEC registered. In the section on Offshore Banking in Chapter Three, we have listed some foreign financial institutions and independent investment advisers that are SEC registered.

Fortunately, there are ways for U.S. citizens to avoid government-imposed obstacles. In these pages, we explain how you can access such offshore investments, legally and safely, using offshore entities such as a trust, a limited liability company, international business corporation, or even a private family foundation, located in a low or no-tax country.

Another simple device is establishing a foreign trading account with an offshore broker. We'll have more to say about that in Chapter Three.

But, as they say: "Old habits die hard."

Despite the occasional financial excursion abroad, human nature dictates that most folks prefer to make and save money at home. We tend to be comfortable with the familiar and less-threatening domestic economy of our home nation.

In 2017, the number of Americans with a valid passport was 136,114,038. Given the size of the U.S. population, this means only approximately 42% of its citizens hold a passport. Even so, this reflects a consistent increase since the late 1980s. In 1989, for example, only 7,261,711 U.S. citizens held passports from a population of 250 million (which equals a meager 3%).

The percentage of Americans with passports has also risen since the 2007 Western Hemisphere Travel Initiative. The WHTI requires all travelers to show a valid passport or another form of approved secure document when traveling to the U.S. from areas within the Western Hemisphere. That has had a big impact, since over half of all trips by Americans are to Mexico or Canada.

Nevertheless, while the number of American citizens getting passports has been increasing, there is still a significant percentage who have not traveled outside the U.S. One report indicated one in five Americans travel abroad. The reasons range from expense to feeling everything worth visiting is in the U.S.

Taxes Drain Wealth

People who move some or all their assets offshore simply recognize the present reality — that government at all levels is engaged in the systematic control and destruction of hard-earned wealth.

It's what has been called the "Nazification" of the economy. That's certainly true in the United States, the United Kingdom and many European Union (EU) nations. Sadly, in ever greater numbers, Americans must look to a select list of foreign lands for the kind of economic freedom once guaranteed by the U.S. Constitution — and as we have shown, these "tax havens" are under constant attack by major welfare state tax collectors.

The warning flags of the attack on investing freedom include the odious Foreign Account Tax Compliance Act (FATCA), the expanded Report of Foreign Bank and Financial Accounts (FBAR) reporting, automatic tax information exchange treaties, offshore banks refusing or dumping U.S. clients, government confiscation of precious metals, police civil forfeiture of property and cash worth billions, imposition of exit taxes, passport restrictions, and still more depredations, as statist politicians fashion an American prison to confine its most productive citizens.

The tax collectors know that the most talented citizens of the U.S., U.K., EU and other welfare states are deserting, setting up financial shop where they and their capital are treated best. What has been called the "permeability of financial frontiers" now empowers investors instantly to shift vast sums of money from one nation to another, and from one currency to another. Tyrannical politicians try to thwart these wealth shifts by imposing multiple curbs on capital movements and financial freedoms.

Lovers of freedom see in these developments the potential for the liberation of "the sovereign individual" — the courageous person who declares independence from "decrepit and debilitating welfare states," as *The Wall Street Journal* described them. *The Sovereign Individual* by James Dale Davidson and Lord William Rees-Mogg [Simon & Shuster, 1997] is an excellent book that predicted and explains the mass exodus of wealthy individuals from high-tax nations.

Small wonder the U.K. Revenue and Customs, the U.S. Internal Revenue Service and other tax hounds, are worried. Research by the

Institute of Economic Affairs (IEA) concluded that Europe's shadow economy employs up to 30 million people across the European Union. Those 30 million people contribute up to 20% of the national income in Greece, Italy and Spain. That's a considerable jump from the 5% it brought in during just 40 years ago. The shadow economy provides roughly 10% of the gross domestic product (GDP) in the U.K. and approximately 20% to 30% in some southern European countries. In the somewhat freer U.S., the underground "black market" economy accounts for more than 8% of GDP. That means billions of dollars slipping through the eager hands of the taxman.

Why the growing black market? Confiscatory taxes, exorbitant labor costs, over-regulation, bailed-out banks, multiple reporting requirements with criminal penalties — all failures of big government. All things government bureaucrats love.

Action Summary

To protect your privacy and wealth, consider taking the following steps:

- Establish an offshore bank account in a low tax or tax-free, privacy-oriented, financial-friendly nation. When done correctly, your cash will be far more secure from almost all U.S.-based claims. But first, carefully investigate any foreign bank you consider using.

- As part of your overall estate plan, create your own offshore asset protection trust, limited liability company (LLC) or private family foundation to hold title to specific assets.

- Precisely document all financial transactions so that you always have ready proof that your activities are legal.

- Educate yourself about — and comply with — all laws, rules and regulations concerning reporting of your financial activities to government agencies.

- Before you act, consult an experienced professional attorney and/ or accountant and be certain you understand the U.S. and foreign tax implications of your plans.

- From professionals whom you consult, always obtain in writing a firm and reliable estimate of the cost of plans, both at the start, upon implementation and for the first few years of operation.

All the above recommendations are explained in detail in this book.

CHAPTER TWO

Privacy

"True danger is when liberty is nibbled away for expedience and by parts." — Edmund Burke

In 2013, Edward Snowden, a former contractor to the Central Intelligence Agency (CIA) and the Defense Intelligence Agency (DIA), released to news media a trove of classified information he had taken from the secret files of the National Security Agency (NSA). It was one of the most momentous leaks of top secret U.S. government information in history. Tens of thousands of documents provided evidence of years of illegal mass invasions of privacy by the NSA, both in the United States and worldwide.

A film about Snowden's courageous actions, *"Citizenfour,"* won the 2015 Academy Award for Best Documentary Feature. *Citizenfour* doesn't just expose the grave dangers of government surveillance. It makes you feel them. Seeing the film should change the way you think about the security of your own phone, email, credit card, web browser or online profile.

At one point in the film, Jacob Appelbaum, a journalist and computer security expert, observes that "privacy *is* freedom, privacy is liberty." That affirms a point that most people never fully consider: The right to privacy is essential to our personal freedom and liberty.

The threadbare argument of those who accept government surveillance of every aspect of our lives is: "If you aren't doing anything wrong, what do you have to hide?" That specious reasoning should infuriate every thinking person.

Induced fears of terrorist attacks do not justify secret government surveillance and the consequent loss of our privacy. Nor does the failed "war on drugs," alleged money laundering, or alleged tax evasion.

Privacy is an inherent human right, essential to live in dignity and respect. The choice here is liberty versus insidious control of our lives and fortunes.

True liberty requires security from government or other spying. Security requires privacy. Without privacy, we are not free to think as we wish. Widespread surveillance, whether by police, nosy bureaucrats or private businesses, in whatever form, is anathema to freedom.

Those who love liberty must champion privacy, both personal and financial, even when we have nothing to hide.

Government as Master

Well before the terror attacks of September 11, 2001, U.S. and foreign politicians mounted an organized international campaign to abolish financial privacy. They argued that governments have the right to know everything about everyone's money, accounts, property and business. Offshore "tax havens" were one of their primary targets, as we discuss elsewhere in these pages.

In America this theory first produced the Bank Secrecy Act of 1970, justified by the "war on drugs." Then came the 2001 PATRIOT Act, to counter "terrorism," and in 2009, the Foreign Account Tax Compliance Act (FATCA), to curb "tax evasion." Each of these laws entailed an unprecedented expansion of government power and reduction of your personal privacy.

The 2001 PATRIOT Act ended financial privacy in America. Under this constitutionally questionable law, government now claims the power to obtain secretly all financial information, without the search warrants required by the Fourth Amendment of the Bill of Rights — including the official power to confiscate your wealth without notice.

Congress passed the 2001 PATRIOT Act without even knowing what was in it. Less than six weeks after the 9/11 terror attacks, the Republican-controlled U.S. Congress, politically panicked to "do something," rammed through a 362-page law, sight unseen, with few members having the courage to oppose one of the worst attacks on American liberties ever enacted into law. Despite massive public opposition to the law, it was extended in 2006 and 2011, at the urging of both Presidents George Bush and Barack Obama, respectively, with majority support from both political parties in the Congress. When the NSA spying scandal was exposed in 2013, some members of Congress finally began to question some of the Act's provisions that the NSA claimed justified their illegal mass surveillance.

During the half century of the war on privacy, its advocates have demanded public and government access to all financial accounts of U.S. citizens, wherever located. They have used the open-ended, ill-defined wars on "drug money" and "terrorism" as cover for the destruction of our financial and personal privacy. Now, in addition to these dubious "wars," we know that the NSA and police engage in mass surveillance of every kind.

One of the less emphasized objectives of this war on privacy has been to allow revenue-hungry tax collectors complete access to everyone's financial lives. Anti-privacy crusaders also advocate an end to private beneficial ownership of corporations, trusts, foundations and partnerships, which they claim "...can be exploited for money laundering or terrorist financing purposes."

But abolishing financial and bank secrecy is not enough for them.

They also campaigned for an end to the privacy allowed by the tradition of lawyer-client privilege. The Organization for Economic Co-operation and Development (OECD), a group of the major heavily indebted countries, has now succeeded in promoting a global

system of automatic total tax information exchange among governments and financial institutions, known as the Common Reporting
Standard (CRS).

In America, the result of this anti-freedom onslaught has been the
abolition of personal or financial privacy, especially for those accused
or suspected of crimes of any nature. In today's America that can be
anyone, with or without probable cause. Government now has enormous power to decide who is "suspect." The list of crimes based on
paperwork rules, or failure to report, grows ever longer.

Privacy Offshore

Naturally, most people want protection from prying eyes, whether
of business partners, estranged family members or identity thieves.
Strong financial privacy can be the best protection against frivolous
lawsuits that end with big judgments. If you don't appear to have
enough assets to justify the time and expense of an attack, a plaintiff's
attorney won't see you as an easy target.

The advantage of assets placed "offshore" is that they are not only
off the domestic asset-tracking "radar screen," but also outside the
immediate jurisdiction of American state and federal courts.

The United States is one of the few nations without a law protecting bank or securities accounts from disclosure, except under defined
circumstances. Many financial disclosures that are illegal and prohibited in other countries are commonplace in America. Elsewhere,
financial privacy is protected under international agreements such as
the European Privacy Directive, or under national laws guaranteeing
financial secrecy, as in Switzerland, Singapore or Panama.

We repeat in these pages an important reminder — that the financial privacy and bank secrecy laws of many other nations are still
very much stronger than those in the United States. Privacy laws
in selected countries can be a definite advantage for you — and an
added legal shield for your financial activities. That makes the choice
of country when "going offshore" particularly important.

It's important to understand that for the average person financially active offshore, there is little to fear from reporting laws aimed principally at criminal conduct. So long as you obey the financial reporting laws and meet applicable tax obligations, you remain in the clear.

But doing so requires professional advice. In these pages we explain how to meet those obligations and give contact information for those who can assist you in doing so.

Control Through Uncertainty

As we exercise our rights to financial and personal freedom, we should realize that fear and uncertainty are very effective ways to shape peoples' behavior. If you don't know what you're allowed to do and whether the government is watching you while you do it, you'll restrict yourself — the government doesn't have to. Whether it involves finance, politics or even personal behavior, the knowledge that you may be monitored by those in positions of power has a strong inhibiting effect.

The U.S. has so many laws and regulatory agencies with enforcement and rule-making powers that it's literally impossible to know the legal definition of "wrong" in every case. That's how they control you. If you don't know what can get you into trouble, a prudent person will tend to restrict their own behavior to what they think to be "OK," especially when it comes to offshore banking and finance.

For example, the adoption of the Foreign Account Tax Compliance Act (FATCA) has prompted many people to close offshore accounts. For that reason, FATCA turns foreign banks into IRS spies — making it an excellent example of officially-induced fear. (For more on FATCA, visit http://www.irs.gov/Businesses/Corporations/Foreign-Account-Tax-Compliance-Act-FATCA.)

Yet going offshore is perfectly legal, with many little-known options available to you. The biggest obstacle to true freedom isn't always the law — it's the fear that comes with not knowing where trouble lies.

Big Brother Really Is Watching

If you think concerns about privacy are only for other people — or just tinfoil-hat paranoia — we have news for you: you are in grave danger.

The government is spying on you constantly, often using the private sector to assist in this surveillance. Let's review some of the worst cases.

- Thanks to Edward Snowden and journalist Glenn Greenwald, we all know now about the massive spying by the U.S. National Security Agency. Under the 2001 USA PATRIOT Act, the NSA claims it is authorized to demand and receive access to all the billions of call records from telephone service providers such as Verizon, AT&T or Sprint. The cellphone companies must surrender any information in their systems, both within the U.S. and between the U.S. and other countries on an "ongoing, daily basis." That includes our calls and emails. Maybe that's why the NSA has built a data storage center costing $1.5 billion at Bluffdale, Utah, five times the size of the U.S. Capitol building, with its own power plant, that reportedly will consume $40 million a year in electricity.

- Then there's greatly expanded activities of the Federal Bureau of Investigation (FBI). Also thanks to the PATRIOT Act, the FBI makes liberal use of National Security Letters (NSLs), an "administrative subpoena" that allows its agents to seek information considered "relevant" to investigations into "international terrorism or clandestine intelligence activities." NSLs usually prohibit the recipient from telling anyone, even a spouse, that the FBI has requested the information. In this way, just by accusing you of "terrorism," the FBI can learn anything it wants from anyone with whom you do business, your bank, your cell company, even your own company, and you won't know anything about it, because it is a federal crime to tell you that they've been asked. And lest you think this is a concern to just "terrorists" … an audit covering only 10% of FBI investigations between 2002 and 2007 found that agents had violated NSL rules more than a thousand times. Many NSLs involved requests for information that FBI agents aren't even allowed to obtain. NSLs have been abused for drug investigations and even banking and tax investigations.

- Our favorite snoop is the U.S. Treasury Department's Financial Intelligence Center (FinCEN) unit. FinCEN nicely illustrates why government isn't the only concern when it comes to your privacy. Its Detroit headquarters computers are filled with multi-millions of electronic records of every U.S. financial transaction of $10,000 or more. Although FinCEN can't just demand to see your other records, its arcane rules create enough uncertainty that banks will proactively surrender them if they have the slightest suspicion that you're up to no good. Under FinCEN's "Operation Choke Point," legal business activities, such as running an online business that accepts credit cards, can "flag" you as a "threat," prompting your bank to send information to FinCEN voluntarily. Everything your bank knows about you, your identity, financial history, and complete details of your banking activity, is at risk.

Of course, the uncertainty this system fosters is intentional, a feature, not a mistake. When people know that FinCEN and other government agencies can get their records easily, they avoid what the rules call "suspicious activities" that might be reported, even if these actions are fully legal.

That's the point.

What? Me Worry?

But still … why should you worry, you may ask, if you haven't done anything wrong? And doesn't the U.S. Constitution protect you?

No.

Just as we learned in secondary school, there are three branches in the U.S. government that check and balance each other: the legislative, the executive and the judicial. But the U.S. government has sprouted a fourth malignant branch: the national security state.

In 2014, the Central Intelligence Agency (CIA) was forced to admit that it deliberately hacked into the computers of U.S. Senate Intelligence Committee researchers working to compile a report on CIA torture of suspects in the years after 9/11.

The U.S. Senate is an enormously important institution, designed as a constitutional check on the executive and judicial branches of government, as well as on the House of Representatives. As representatives of the sovereign states, senators are typically accorded a great deal of deference. And yet the CIA thought it could get away with spying on the very Senate committee charged with CIA oversight.

If the hallowed Senate can't trust the U.S. security state to refrain from spying on it, Constitution or no, then we shouldn't either. We should assume that we are on our own when it comes to preserving our privacy.

And Not Just the Feds

Back in the old days, the word most often associated with government surveillance was "wiretap." It evokes images of J. Edgar Hoover's fedora-hatted G-men with old-fashioned headphones listening in on a bad guy's phone calls from a van across the street.

These days, the word "wiretap" rarely makes an appearance. That's because the government itself no longer needs to do anything technical to obtain information about you. Instead, it orders the companies that provide us with communications, banking, commercial or other services to hand over whatever they have stored on their Internet servers. All it takes is one of those FBI National Security Letters, a FinCEN directive or some other secret, extra-judicial demand, and it's all surrendered to the government.

In fact, we "wiretap" ourselves 24/7, 365 days a year. Everything we say and do, online and off line, is recorded and stored somewhere. The GPS chip in your smartphone allows for close tracking of your location, right down to the aisle you're walking down in Target. Your credit cards and loyalty cards track your specific purchases.

Amazon knows more about you than most of your friends and relatives. The thermostat in your house may be tracking your movement in the house, even when you're away.

All that digital-age convenience … and all that real risk.

Government Won't Protect You

The initial media and public reaction in 2013, after whistleblower Edward Snowden's bombshell revelations about domestic NSA spying, was widespread shock and consternation at the extent of the U.S. government's invasion of its citizens' privacy.

Five years later, however, very little has changed — except that the public debate and media coverage is now largely under control and dominated by the established powers-that-be. Predictably, once the initial flurry of indignation subsided, the mainstream press ceased reporting on the issue and the backroom deal-making began to allow continued secret surveillance.

The major players are the U.S. Congress, the White House and the very agencies responsible for these outrages — the CIA and NSA.

U.S. Rep. Jim Sensenbrenner (R-WI) was an original sponsor of the 2001 PATRIOT Act. In 2014 when he proposed PATRIOT Act "reform" legislation, the appropriately-named "USA Freedom Act," it was stalled in Congress. Sensenbrenner submitted an *amicus curia* brief in a case brought by the American Civil Liberties Union (ACLU) against the NSA. In it, he argued that Congress never intended the PATRIOT Act to permit the NSA's collection of records of every telephone call made to, from and within the United States.

In 2013, presidential candidate Donald Trump was asked whether he thought the NSA should be allowed to continue collecting masses of basic metadata of citizen's phone calls, he replied: "Yes, basic data collection is necessary to track suspected terrorists." The future president criticized Edward Snowden as a traitor who deserved execution.

Once again in 2018, a bipartisan coalition in the U.S. Congress, adopted and President Donald Trump signed into law, a six-year extension of the Foreign Intelligence Surveillance Act (FISA). FISA was not just renewed, it gave government greatly increased power over us. The original 1978 FISA prohibited all domestic surveillance, unless pursuant to warrants signed by federal judges based on probable cause — which is the constitutional guarantee of the Fourth Amendment of the Bill of Rights.

Judge Andrew P. Napolitano described the 2017 law as "a hole in the Fourth Amendment" that brings "the country full circle back to the government's use of general warrants to harass and prosecute — general warrants so odious to our forebears that they took up arms against the king's soldiers to be rid of them."

The American Civil Liberties Union best described the 2018 FISA renewal as "a bill to give the Trump administration greater authority to spy on Americans, immigrants, journalists, dissidents and everyone else." That means you and me.

Given the general ignorance and lack of respect for America's constitutional values — it's highly unlikely that the U.S. Congress will enact any of the needed NSA reforms.

Politics and Cash

How have we come to this sad state of privacy affairs?

Two intertwined processes have effectively silenced the historical voices of individual liberty in the U.S.

First, both major political parties have become increasingly "tribal," placing their own electoral fortunes above the good of the country. Leading figures of both parties are either complicit in violations or unwilling to take firm positions on civil liberty issues. Neither party has worked to rein in the NSA and various intelligence agencies, nor have they taken steps to fix the monstrous 2001 PATRIOT Act.

Republican and Democrat politicians are no longer focused on what is right for Americans but they attack our constitutional liberties. Their reluctance to oppose the "security first" terrorist fear campaign is reflected in the vast lobbying, think-tank, and activist networks supporting the two parties, those with a vested interest in fear.

Second — and more sinister — is that, to an underappreciated extent, contemporary U.S. captains of industry are an increasingly integral part of the profitable surveillance state itself. Their actions dwarf the threat of the "military industrial complex" about which President (and five-star general) Dwight Eisenhower warned when he retired in 1957.

In America, this big "security" business depends on bloated tax-payer-funded government contracts for their companies' profits and their own bonuses and stock options. For them, collaboration with a liberty-destroying government goes beyond public support for out-rageous laws; it involves massive profits, augmented at our expense as well by huge, selective congressional and presidential campaign contributions.

Indeed, the historically unprecedented feature of the current situation is the extent to which government and U.S. industry have joined forces, the former to extend its power, and the latter to profit. Consider that companies such as General Dynamics, Hewlett-Packard, AT&T, and many others provide significant intelligence-related services to the American Surveillance State, totaling more than $1 trillion annually.

That sort of money has serious sway in Washington, D.C.

Sadly, no matter how unhappy we may be at these violations of our constitutional liberties, there is little prospect that they will be addressed politically anytime soon. The bipartisan consensus in favor of the growing surveillance state is built on the solid foundation of widespread public ignorance of, manufactured fear, and/or apathy about, the destruction of our freedoms.

Did You Know?

All of us should be appalled and angry at the current behavior of the U.S. government, regardless of our political leanings. Consider some of this "official" behavior:

- The U.S. Department of Homeland Security (DHS) routinely abuses laws designed for immigration enforcement purposes to extract private information, including passwords, from U.S. residents before they officially enter or leave U.S. soil at airports and land borders. Ominously, U.S. lawyers, journalists and political activists who support the right to personal privacy and political dissent deliberately have been targeted for border searches and seizures of electronic information.

- Under Section 702 of the 2018 FISA Amendment Act (discussed above), the government, without a warrant, may collect from American companies, like AT&T and Google, the emails, texts, phone calls and other private messages of foreigners abroad even when those targets communicate with Americans.

- The NSA has routinely collected telephone, texting (SMS), email, VOIP (i.e., Skype), instant messaging and location "metadata" in order to discern the activities, interests and intentions of individual U.S. residents. To accomplish this, the NSA and FBI have forced U.S. corporate providers of email, web and cloud data-storage services to allow access to their systems, essentially by asking these private companies to "look the other way" while government agents hack into them. This has destroyed the credibility of the U.S. cloud-computing industry overseas. Fifty-six percent of 500 industry respondents in a survey said these disclosures would cause them to lose non-U.S. business, a possible cost of up to $100 billion in revenues.

- The NSA has worked for years to force purveyors of cryptographic software to build in secret "backdoor" keyholes that allow it to access encrypted data. Almost all the major encryption products developed and produced in the U.S. should now be assumed unsafe. The NSA has deliberately weakened the encryption standards developed by the National Institute of Standards and Technology (NIST) and adopted by developers around the globe. This has devastated the U.S. encryption-software industry, once the world's leader.

- According to the German daily, *Der Spiegel*, the NSA developed a system called TRACFIN to hack into VISA's credit-card transaction network to target customers in Europe, the Middle East and Africa, and has also hacked into the Society for Worldwide Interbank Financial Telecommunication (SWIFT) system. Although there are no reports TRACFIN has been deployed inside the U.S., there is no reason to think it hasn't been. In any case, it is like PRISM, a clandestine mass electronic-surveillance, data-mining program operated by the NSA since 2007.

- Edward Snowden provided documents showing how American and British intelligence agency accessed Gemalto — the world's largest maker of SIM cards. The hack handed over the encryption keys to a large swath of cellphone communication around the globe. Simply put, the U.S. and U.K. governments could easily access the day-to-day activities of your life when you used your smartphone without your permission or knowledge.

- In 2013, a spokesperson for Intel insisted there was "no basis for these highly speculative claims" that the NSA had placed embedded "back doors" inside chips produced by Intel and Advanced Micro Devices, two of the world's largest semiconductor firms, giving NSA the possibility to access and control millions of computers. In 2015, *The New York Times* reported that the NSA had in fact implanted software in nearly 100,000 computers around the world, but supposedly not in the United States, that allows the NSA to conduct surveillance on those machines. *Der Spiegel* reported that in a process called "interdiction" the NSA regularly intercepts shipments of laptops and other electronic devices to implant physical listening devices and install advanced malware.

- *The Wall Street Journal* reported that "the Justice Department was scooping up data from thousands of mobile phones through devices deployed on airplanes that mimic cellphone towers, a high-tech hunt for criminal suspects that is snagging innocent Americans." Since 2007, the U.S. Marshals Service has operated snoop equipped Cessna aircraft, flying out of five metropolitan airports, and covering most of the U.S. and its population. In 2016, the Pentagon "deployed drones to spy over U.S. territory for non-military missions over the past decade," citing a report by a Pentagon inspector general who declared that the flights are "rare and lawful."

- Typical is the attitude of former NSA Chief, Gen. Keith Alexander, the "Cowboy of the NSA," which has been described by a former intelligence official as: "Let's not worry about the law. Let's just figure out how to get the job done ... a lot of things aren't clearly legal, but that doesn't make them illegal." A generous interpretation might be that the general intends for Congress to decide when legal boundaries have been crossed. Given that both he and the former Director of National Security James Clapper have gone unpunished for perjuring themselves before Congress concerning the activities and capabilities of the NSA, this would appear naïve in the extreme.

- A 2014 review of U.S. government documents revealed that there are 72 categories of U.S. citizens and residents that are to be considered "extremists" and "potential terrorists." By far most of these categories relate to legitimate political viewpoints. Given that the

NSA's own standards require only a "reasonable suspicion" of "terroristic" intentions to prompt a privacy-invading information search, most of us now probably are eligible targets.

• If you think you've got a right to privacy when it comes to your face, you'd be wrong. Within the U.S., there is no federal regulation of biometric data. Anyone on the street with a camera can take your picture while you're in a public space. What's more, the police can use different software to match your picture against a database of pictures in the blink of an eye.

Action: What You Can Do

For all intents and purposes, you are on your own combatting what Thomas Hobbes called "the Leviathan state." What can you do to protect yourself and your privacy?

We divide possible personal responses, all of which are legal, inexpensive and relatively easy to execute into two categories: 1) privacy protection strategies and; 2) secure communications strategies.

1. Safeguard Your Privacy

Protecting your privacy essentially means limiting other parties' access to information about you. Obviously, for each of us there is a great deal of information to be protected. But with a surprisingly few steps, you can keep most of it relatively private.

One privacy protection often overlooked is the centuries-old attorney-client privilege supported by law. That simply means that once you hire an attorney, anything you discuss with him or her cannot be revealed, with few exceptions.

Privacy-protection strategies vary, depending on from whom you're trying to protect it. There is a difference between people who know you already, friends, family, business associates, companies with which you do business, and people who don't know you, but might want to for some reason.

Existing Contacts

For the former category (existing contacts), you have much more control; the key is to limit sharing of personal information to what others absolutely need to know, and to place "firewalls" between detailed facts (such as your physical address or phone number) and the information that you give to third parties.

Here is a list of examples:

- Share sensitive personal facts only with a few close, trusted family members and friends. Never discuss personal matters with casual acquaintances.

- Conceal your home address by using a mail drop — you might even consider using a forwarding mail drop in a foreign country with strict privacy laws. Have utility bills, credit cards and home deliveries made in a corporate or other entity name and do the same with motor-vehicle registration. Get an unlisted phone number and don't disclose it to anyone.

- Never discard sensitive personal correspondence in the trash unless it has been shredded and mixed. Your trash is public property and can be searched by anyone. Shred everything from receipts, credit card statements, and checks and bank statements to credit offers insurance forms, physician statements, and similar documents when you don't need them any longer. In essence, if the information is sensitive, shred it.

- Enter as little information as possible in your social media profiles — preferably just your name.

- Delete your photos from social-networking sites (especially Facebook) and dating sites. If you don't delete your photos, mark your profile as "private." Don't post photos of friends or family members online; this helps investigators reconstruct your social network. To minimize information about you available online, consider a service to remove personal information from websites that market it, such as DeleteMe at https://www.abine.com/deleteme/landing.php. From as low as $129 a year, the service will delete your personal information from some of the leading data broker sites.

- Don't accept "friend" invitations from strangers on services like Facebook, LinkedIn, Twitter or Skype. Run background and due-diligence checks on all prospective personal and business employees. Never leave sensitive information around when workers are in your home.

- Always password-protect your home PC and your cellphone.

- Keep important documents in a safe-deposit box or in a secure safe in your home.

Third Parties

To ward off privacy attacks form unknown third parties, the strategies above apply, along with several others:

- Use cash in transactions whenever possible.

- Refuse to provide your ZIP code when buying with a credit card unless absolutely necessary.

- Never use your Social Security number as an identifier if it can be avoided.

- Use one or more domestic bank accounts for minimal operating cash; bank the bulk of your cash in the name of appropriate legal entities (LLCs, trusts, family foundations) in selected offshore banks in more than one country with strong financial privacy laws and sound banking systems.

- Acquire a well-recognized second passport and use it when traveling outside the U.S. (U.S. passports must be used to leave or re-enter the U.S.) For additional information about acquiring a second passport, refer to *The Passport Book: The Complete Guide to Offshore Residence, Dual Citizenship and Second Passports* (Banyan Hill Publishing).

- Use a prepaid cellphone, not registered in your name, for most purposes. Pay in cash when purchasing prepaid calling and Internet-access cards. Activate your phone at a pay phone — not with a phone connected to you in any way. Don't give out your real phone number when you activate the phone.

- If you have a personal, permanent phone, deactivate the GPS facility unless necessary.

- Before you go out, remember to only take with you the necessary items, such as your ID, credit and/or debit card, a photo copy of your medical card (blacking out all but the last four digits of ID number), and if you are taking medication, just the amount you need for while you are out. Otherwise, leave behind items such as your Social Security card.

- Never fill in unnecessary or optional information in online forms. Use made-up information for your name, etc. (my personal favorite is "A. Lincoln"), unless it is necessary to provide accurate information. In your email-software settings, make sure the default "From" field is something other than your name.

- Only use laptops when traveling and wipe them clean when not using them.

- Ensure websites are safe and authentic before sharing information with them. Make sure all of your online accounts are properly configured to optimize their security and privacy. Read and act on those privacy notices that come with statements.

- Create passwords that are "strong" and unique. You can use a password manager that will both remember all your passwords, as well as generate ones that, with a click of the mouse, can automatically be filled into the login fields. Two recommended services are Dashlane https://www.dashlane.com and LastPass https://www.lastpass.com.

- Use two-factor authentication for Facebook, Google, Dropbox, Apple ID, Microsoft, Twitter and other accounts. Whenever you log in, you'll also need to enter a special code that the site texts to your phone.

- Set up a Google alert for your name at www.google.com/alerts. This involves telling the Google search engine to look for your name, as well as what kinds of web pages to search, how often to search and what email address the search-engine giant should use to send you notifications.

- Fabricate when setting up password-security questions, like "your mother's maiden name."

- Close old online (and offline) accounts if you are not using them.

- Opt out of marketing "cookies," using services like PrivacyFix or Opt-Out. Wipe your browser of "cookies" every time you close it.

- Use anonymous browsing windows whenever possible, preferably on Google Chrome or Firefox.

- Before you dispose of a computer or cellphone, get rid of all the personal information it stores. Use a wipe-utility program to over-write the entire hard drive.

2. Securing Your Communications

Protecting your communications is significantly more difficult than protecting personal information, such as your address, bank details and so on. If you want to communicate at a distance, you are going to have to send information through a channel or channels over which you have no, or only limited, control — including the U.S. mail. Like the spies of yesteryear, to keep things secret you are going to have to use codes and/or encryption.

Unfortunately, existing strategies for protecting electronic com-munication are currently in a state of disarray. As we now know, the NSA deliberately has built weaknesses into most publicly available encryption technologies, and we frankly do not know which of them are truly secure and which are compromised.

The shocking detention of journalist Glenn Greenwald's partner, David Miranda, by U.K. authorities using laws designed to combat terrorism is evidence that even directly delivering electronic information by hand is no longer fool proof. For the time being, we must assume that the only truly secure communication is verbal, face to face with people whom you trust. Nevertheless, there are things you can do to stop adversaries less determined than the NSA.

- Start with the obvious: Use password protected wireless in your home and office. Unplug your webcam and/or microphone when not using it. Never use the telephone for sensitive communication. Always assume someone is listening when you speak on the phone and act accordingly.

- Above all, use the strongest encryption available to you. Do not use commercial encryption software, especially from large vendors such as: Symantec or BitLocker. Most encryption products from large U.S. (and probably EU and Israeli) companies have NSA-friendly "back doors" built in. Proprietary "closed-source" software is easier for the NSA to manipulate than open-source software. Open source software using public-domain encryption must be compatible with other implementations to be effective. The NSA is far less likely to try to install secret backdoors in open-source encryption software, since it is more likely to be discovered given the many people working on it.

- Use the Tor Browser. TOR is a sophisticated service based on a browser interface that allows most users to use the web entirely anonymously. TOR is similar to a Virtual Private Network but has the advantage of being instantly available once TOR is installed.

- If you have something important to share, use an "air gap." This is a separate computer that has never been connected to the Internet that also has strong file encryption software installed. You can use such a computer to create files (documents, spreadsheets, etc.). When you want to transfer a file, you encrypt the file on the secure "air gap" computer and carry it to your Internet-connected computer, using a USB stick. To decrypt something, reverse the process. While it is true that the NSA and other government agencies can, and do, target users of the strategies above, it is difficult work for them. The harder it is for your computer to be compromised, the more work and risk it would take to do so, deterring all but the most determined adversaries.

- Use a virtual private network. There's a remarkably simple way to make it virtually impossible for police, the NSA, or any other three-letter agency to monitor your Google searches or online activities. You go "dark." You make yourself invisible — at least when it comes to what you do from the privacy of your own computer screen. All you need, to do that, is something called a "virtual private network," or VPN.

- Avoid surfing the Net while also signed in to the major social media. That includes Facebook, Google (i.e. Gmail, YouTube), LinkedIn, etc. Basically, if you're logged in, those companies will be able to track major (and many minor) sites you visit, from major news portals, to pages of a more risqué nature. For more information, visit www.nestmann.com.

The Ultimate Solution

In the end, the only lasting solution to the problem of privacy and securing communications is a change in the political conditions that have allowed our American liberties to become so compromised.

In the meantime, in this chapter we have explained how you can use tools that will provide maximum personal and financial privacy. You can keep abreast of the latest privacy information in the publications of Banyan Hill.

CHAPTER THREE

Creative Offshore Financial Strategies

In this chapter we discuss specific personal and financial strategies for offshore living, foreign residence, second citizenship, investing, bank accounts and conducting your business to achieve maximum tax savings and the greatest profit. We'll also explain U.S. government reporting requirements for offshore personal and financial activity.

After this chapter, we describe the best jurisdictions and countries that qualify as tax, asset and banking havens; the ones best suited to achieve your personal wealth and estate management goals. (*Note:* We use the phrase "jurisdictions and countries" because some places are independent nations, while others are independent regions or dependent offshore territories of the United Kingdom.)

As you read through these following sections, keep in mind the strategies described in this chapter because we name and explain the specific offshore tax and asset havens where these strategies are best suited. Afterward, you may want to match your chosen strategies to the specific jurisdictions we describe.

Before geography and places, first we consider several personal, financial and business strategies you can employ offshore now, even before you finally choose your own best tax or asset haven.

These varied strategies can be used individually or in combination, as your situation requires. But each one is fully legal, and each has been used by thousands worldwide — often with highly satisfactory results.

In later chapters, when we discuss individual jurisdictions that qualify as offshore financial centers (formerly known as "tax havens") and/or asset and banking havens, we'll suggest which havens are best suited in combination with these strategies.

One of these may be just the financial strategies you need, but be certain to obtain professional legal, tax and reporting advice, as well as cost estimates, before you act. The contacts we give you in these pages are the best places for such advice.

Part 1 — Personal Strategies

Strategy 1: Make Your Home Base in a Tax Haven

For those who choose to leave their home nation and live in a foreign country, places that qualify as tax havens can provide better living financially and greater profits because of lower taxes, or no taxes at all.

While eventually you may consider obtaining citizenship in the foreign land of your choice, the first step is to qualify for official residence approved by the government. Keep in mind that once you become a citizen of a country, you are no longer an exempt "foreigner" and you may become subject to that country's taxes and other laws, thus it may be best to remain in a foreign resident status.

Interestingly, scientists have found a link between creativity and living abroad for those who live in foreign countries for long periods. *The Economist* magazine reported on a study by academics at the Kellogg School of Management that showed "better problem-solving skills in 60% of students who were either living abroad, or had spent some time doing so, whereas only 42% of those who had not lived abroad demonstrated such skills."

Another test revealed that those who lived overseas were more likely to be creative negotiators. This valuable skill was potentially learned as part of a coping strategy. Not counting the likelihood that creative people are more likely to choose to live overseas, the correlation between creativity and living overseas continue to hold water, "…indicating that it is something from the experience of living in foreign parts that helps foster creativity."

The authors of the report supplied no details as to why living abroad should stimulate the creative juices, but their conclusion contains the most likely rationale: it may be that those critical months or years of turning cultural bewilderment into personal concrete understanding may instill the ability to "think outside the box."

Lower Taxes

The phrase "*U.S. persons*" is used in the U.S. Internal Revenue Code to designate citizens and U.S. permanent resident aliens who must pay taxes. The infamous Tax Cuts and Jobs Act of 2017 did not change that. Even though U.S. persons are taxed on their worldwide income, there are many attractive non-U.S. places where local taxes are reduced on business activities, or where business may be totally tax-exempt when conducted offshore. These hospitable places exempt foreigners who live there from taxes because they only levy taxes on income earned within their national borders, under what is known as a "territorial" tax system.

Personal income tax rates in many major countries now approach 50% of income or even higher. For example, in 2012, more than 8,000 French families' tax bills topped 100% of their income due to a one-time tax imposed by the Socialist government on those with assets of more than US$1.67 million. Courts later nullified the tax as unconstitutional. This crushing burden of combined Social Security taxes, capital gains taxes, net worth taxes, wealth taxes and inheritance taxes, has prompted many to seek low or zero tax havens where they can make a new home tax-free.

Many countries provide tax incentives to qualified foreigners who become new residents. Residence qualifications include good health, a clean record with no past criminal acts, a guaranteed sufficient income and enough assets so that you won't need a job in the local market.

However, it isn't easy to find a haven offering both low taxes and an acceptable high quality of life that also includes a wide range of amenities, excellent medical facilities, easy residence requirements and a warm climate, all within easy reach of major American or European cities.

But a few countries come close to that ideal.

For instance, the Mediterranean island nation of Malta is one of the most attractive locations for foreigners looking for a warm climate, as well as low taxes. Under a 2013 Individual Investor Program (IIP), permanent foreign residents enjoy a privileged tax status, with only a 15% tax charged on income remitted from outside of Malta, subject to a minimum tax liability of about US$6,600 per year to a maximum of US$15,000.

The Republic of Panama offers one of the most attractive locations for tax-advantaged residence in the Americas. It has a special *pensionado* program for foreign retirees providing tax-free living with substantial discounts on the price of many goods and services.

Panama also offers a fast-track "Immediate Permanent Resident" visa for foreign nationals from 50 listed countries "that maintain friendly, professional, economic, and investment relationships with the Republic of Panama." Under its territorial tax system, all residents pay no tax on income earned outside Panama. Under several other immigration programs tailored to attract them, foreigners may acquire residence as a financially independent person/retiree or as an investor.

The Central American country of Belize also offers a special program for foreign retirees much like that in Panama, with zero taxes on offshore income and other incentives. Unfortunately, it has a questionable record with its residence programs.

For people of great wealth, Austria, Switzerland and Singapore are among the nations with high cost special immigration and tax arrangements for foreigners who wish to live or retire there.

It's fair to say that there are countries in many parts of the world where individual arrangements can be made for tax-advantaged residence but be careful of possible fraud in such cases.

If you are looking for a place to do business offshore or to make a new home, the haven that will meet your needs can be found. It's out there waiting for you and we'll help you find it.

A word about personal security: in this age of random terrorism every country has safety and security issues, ranging from petty crime and scams to active terrorist groups and revolutionary movements. Each country's police and security forces operate differently — something a new resident sometimes must learn the "hard way."

For up-to-date security information on countries worldwide, check the websites listed below.

U.S. Department of State Consular Information Sheets: https://travel.state.gov/content/passports/en/country.html

U.S. Department of State Overseas Security Advisory Council (OSAC): https://www.osac.gov

Australian Department of Foreign Affairs and Trade: http://smartraveller.gov.au/countries

International Crime Threat Assessment: http://www.fas.org/irp/threat/pub45270index.html

INTERPOL Country Profiles: http://www.interpol.int

World Intelligence and Security Agencies: http://www.fas.org/irp/world

NationMaster (massive global search database including crime and terrorism): http://www.nationmaster.com/index.php

Strategy 2: Dual Citizenship

Let's say you have decided to establish a new residence in an offshore tax haven, or in any foreign country.

As a new resident, you may want to consider acquiring citizenship there and, with it, a second passport. Dual citizenship simply means that a person is officially recognized as a citizen of more than one nation. Under U.S. law, this status is fully legal, and it is legal under the laws of many other nations, although not all.

The United States government had official recognition of dual citizenship forced upon it in 1967 by a U.S. Supreme Court ruling, *Afroyim v. Rusk*, 387 U.S. 253, when a U.S. citizen successfully argued that he had no intent to end his American citizenship when he acquired the citizenship of another country. The Court ruled that Mr. Afroyim's right to keep his U.S. citizenship was guaranteed by the Citizenship Clause of the 14th Amendment to the Constitution.

Prior to that ruling it was the U.S. government's legal position that whenever a U.S. citizen acquired citizenship of another country, U.S. citizenship was automatically lost. Other acts held to end U.S. citizenship included voting in a foreign country's election or serving in an official position or in the military of a foreign government.

The *Afroyim* decision opened the way for a wider acceptance of dual or even multiple citizenships in U.S. law. A series of treaties in place between the U.S. and other nations which had limited dual citizenship following naturalization were abandoned after the U.S. government concluded the *Afroyim* ruling had rendered them unenforceable.

Since 1967, the official policy of the U.S. government is to presume a U.S. citizen does not wish to surrender their citizenship based on actions. Proof of specific intent is required before expatriation is officially recognized. The burden of proof is on the government to show intentional abandonment of U.S. citizenship.

Even though, as a matter of policy, the U.S. government now recognizes dual nationality, it still does not encourage it because of what the bureaucrats view as problems and conflicts that may result. However, the U.S. Department of State website now makes clear that dual nationality is legal for Americans. This is set forth at https://travel.state.gov/content/travel/en/legal/travel-legal-considerations/us-citizenship.html.

Although the U.S. government was forced to accept dual citizenship, it still asserts legal control based on U.S. citizenship and passports in numerous ways. For example, the law requires all U.S. citizens, including those with dual citizenship, to use only that U.S. passport to leave or enter the U.S. Until 2015, it was a crime for U.S. citizens to travel to Cuba without prior U.S. State Department permission.

Perhaps the most onerous example of these U.S. controls involves tax payments and tax reporting obligations. U.S. citizens are burdened with paying U.S. taxes no matter where in the world they live, or where their income sources are located. Countries, such as Panama, with a more reasonable territorial system of taxation, tax residents only income earned within the country's national borders, without regard to where they live or the income source.

Good Reasons

A second passport, quite literally, could save your life.

History is littered with repressive instances when a government has blocked its citizens from traveling internationally. If it becomes necessary for you to leave and you have only your home country passport, you're stuck. That's because your passport is not your property. It is the property of your government and officials can seize or suspend a passport at any time.

At the very least, having a second nationality and passport is a hedge against unexpected political and economic events at home. The dual status gives you the option of residing in another country away from your home place, which may produce tax advantages as well. But remember these tax advantages are of limited benefit to U.S. persons who are taxed on worldwide income, without regard to where they physically reside.

You may be able to acquire a second citizenship and passport based on your ancestry, by marriage or because of your religious affiliation. If you don't qualify on these grounds, your principle option for obtaining citizenship is through establishing residence in your chosen country for a required period (usually five years) or by obtaining citizenship by investment.

Citizenship by investment, also called "economic citizenship," is a euphemism for granting citizenship by a sovereign country in exchange for a financial contribution to that country, or for an investment in a business, real estate, or a government-designated, job-producing project. In recent years, the number of national economic citizenship programs has expanded, as indebted governments seek extra income to cover spending and budget deficits.

In 2013, after several years of economic difficulty, the government of Antigua and Barbuda created the National Economic and Social Transformation Plan including the introduction of a citizenship-by-investment program. See https://www.henleyglobal.com/citizenship-antigua.

Saint Kitts and Nevis and the Commonwealth of Dominica, both small island nations in the eastern Caribbean (in what used to be known as the British West Indies), were until recently the only two countries actively promoting legal citizenship by full-scale investment programs. See https://www.henleyglobal.com/citizenship-saint-kitts-nevis-citizenship.

In 2012, Ireland introduced a new economic citizenship program based on investing in what was then an economically depressed country. In Austria, it is also possible, under certain limited conditions, to obtain citizenship without prior residence based on a substantial investment (US$2 million or more), but this is done on an individual basis and is rarely granted. Each of these programs requires that applicants pass a rigorous screening process.

Other countries that have jumped aboard the economic citizenship bandwagon include Grenada, Malta, Cyprus, Bulgaria and Macedonia. If you are interested in the residence and citizenship requirements of all leading countries, you can order *The Passport Book: The Complete Guide to Offshore Residence, Dual Citizenship and Second Passports* by Robert E. Bauman JD (Banyan Hill Publishing).

Saint Kitts & Nevis

Saint Kitts and Nevis is the Western Hemisphere's smallest nation, with about 35,000 inhabitants. It's an English-speaking member of the British Commonwealth of Nations, which means its citizens have certain visa rights to the rest of the Commonwealth, as well as the right to ask for diplomatic protection from the embassy of any Commonwealth country.

Saint Kitts has the world's oldest economic citizenship program. Established in 1984, a foreigner can qualify for citizenship in Saint Kitts in two ways: with a donation to a government fund for retired sugar workers, a deal made when the government closed the sugar industry, or with an investment in an "approved" real estate project.

The economic citizenship program of Saint Kitts and Nevis enjoys an excellent reputation and it offers visa-free travel to the British Commonwealth and many other countries.

Under the citizenship-by-investment rules, to qualify for Saint Kitts and Nevis citizenship, an investment of at least US$400,000 in designated real estate, plus additional government and due diligence fees are required. Alternatively, a cash contribution can be made to the Sugar Industry Diversification Foundation in the amount of US$250,000 (for a single applicant).

Using the charitable contribution is an easier route for most applicants because it provides a set cost and avoids further expenses associated with owning real estate in a foreign country. Plus, you don't have to live in Saint Kitts and Nevis to secure your second citizenship, so buying real estate could just be an additional burden if you're not interested in spending time there.

Sugar Industry Diversification Foundation Option

Required contributions:

- Single applicant: US$250,000

- Applicant with up to three dependents (spouse, two children below the age of 18): US$300,000

- Applicant with up to five dependents: US$350,000

- Applicant with six or more dependents: US$450,000

- Additional contribution for each above seven dependents: US$50,000

- Each dependent child 18 to 25 years old and enrolled full-time as university undergraduate: US$35,000

- Each dependent parent 62 years or older living with and supported by head of household: US$35,000

Registration, application, due diligence, and processing fees:

- Registration fee (payable if application is successful):

  o Head of household: US$50,000

  o Spouse: US$25,000

  o Each child of the main applicant under 18 years of age: US$15,000

  o Each citizenship certificate of registration: US$47 (This fee is not applicable to persons investing in the SIDF.)

- Application fee: US$250 per applicant plus 17% VAT

- Due diligence background checks and processing fee (non-refundable):

o Main applicant: US$7,500

o Each dependent 16 years and over: US$4,000

- Consulting fee: US$1,200 per application

Investment in Designated Real Estate Option

Required investment:

- Minimum US$400,000, plus approximately 7% in taxes, duties, and fees.

- Alien land owner's tax, 10% to 12% of purchase price, may apply.

- Title insurance cost varies depending on the cost of the property.

Registration, application, due diligence, and processing fees:

- US$250 per applicant plus 17% VAT

- Security fee: US$3,500 per applicant

- Processing fee: US$250 per applicant

- Court fees: no additional charge

- Consulting fee: US$1,200 per application

Registration fees (after grant of approval):

- Head of household: US$35,000

- Spouse and each child under the age of 18 years: US$15,000

- Each dependent above the age of 18 (not including a spouse): US$50,000

- Each dependent child 18 to 25 years enrolled full-time as university

- Each dependent parent 62 years or older living with and supported by head of household: US$35,000

Depending on what an attorney or other professional may charge, usual legal fees can cost US$20,000 for a single applicant or applicant and spouse; US$25,000 for applicant, spouse, and up to two children; US$5,000 for each additional dependent child.

Also, 50% of the legal fee is refunded if the primary applicant is not approved. There is also a US$500 escrow fee. Due diligence fees vary from US$4,000 to US$8,000.

The real estate option requires the purchase of a condominium or villa from an approved list of developers with a minimum investment of US$400,000. Transaction costs add 10% to the purchase price (i.e., at least US$35,000, and likely US$50,000 or more) as real estate prices are at a relatively high level in Saint Kitts and Nevis and you don't get much for your money, especially in the local condo market.

Processing time for charitable contribution applications takes up to three months and dual citizenship is permitted, with no residence requirement. Using the real estate option lengthens the average processing time from four to 12 months or longer. The real estate cannot be resold until at least five years after purchase.

Commonwealth of Dominica

There are two options to acquire citizenship here:

1) **Direct Family Cash Option** (family of 4, investor, spouse, 2 children under 18 years):

- Required contribution: US$200,000

- Applicant and two minor children: US$175,000

- Applicant, spouse, and two minor children: US$200,000

- Additional children under the age of 18 years, US$15,000 per child

- Children between 18 and 21 years: US$50,000 per child (up to 2 children)

- Legal and processing fees average an additional $25,000—$30,000

2) Direct Cash Single Option

- Required contribution: US$100,000

- For both options, the cash contribution is due only after the application has been provisionally approved by the government.

Other government fees include:

- Application fee: US$1,000 per application (non-refundable)

- Processing fee: US$200 per applicant (non-refundable)

- Naturalization fee: US$550 per applicant

- Stamp fee: US$15 per applicant

Depending on what an attorney or other professional may charge, usual legal fees can cost US$20,000 for a single applicant or applicant and spouse; US$25,000 for applicant, spouse, and up to two children; US$5,000 for each additional dependent child.

Again, 50% of the legal fee is refunded if the primary applicant is not approved. There is also a $500 escrow fee. Due diligence fees vary from US$4,000 to US$8,000.

If an application is rejected or withdrawn for any reason, the government does guarantee the return of all investment funds. There is, however, a US$2,200 in processing fee that is not refundable. The government also has sole discretion in granting someone citizenship, but there is no guarantee that an application will be approved. The government has introduced more onerous due diligence requirements.

Republic of Austria

Investors of at least US$2 million in approved projects in Austria may be considered for immediate citizenship under an Austrian law seeking to attract extraordinary contributions to the nation.

This rarely granted Austrian passport offers the only possibility to obtain a "First World" (as compared to a "Third World") passport through investment, and one that offers the additional right to live, work and travel in 27 of the 28 countries of the European Union, because Austria is an EU member state. With Austrian residence, visa-free travel is possible throughout all Schengen Accord countries.

Although Austria does not have an economic citizenship program *per se*, statutory law does allow the granting of citizenship to a foreign person if he or she is judged to contribute in an extraordinary way, including economic means, to the interests of Austria. However, this is not an easy way to acquire citizenship and the process may require a year or more to complete.

Applicants are approved on a case-by-case basis and must be willing to invest at least US$2 million in an approved project in Austria. Investment proposals are submitted to the Office of Economic Development. Those that provide export stimulation or local employment receive preference.

Representation by a knowledgeable and well-connected Austrian lawyer is essential and is likely to cost considerably more than US$50,000. Fees of €250,000 (US$308,000) or more apply, depending on the case and the number of persons in an application, as each case is handled on an individual basis.

Persons of independent means with a proven minimum annual income of US$25,000, with an established home in Austria and full health insurance coverage, are eligible to apply for official Austrian residence. After five years and, in some cases, less, residents may apply for citizenship which is granted after the sixth year.

The system is based on a person's degree of integration in Austrian society rather than their duration of stay. The six-year path requires the applicant to be employed with a monthly income of €1,000 (US$1,200) or more for at least three years including, plus the last six months before application. Applicants must also have some German language ability and must pass a citizenship test.

There are also citizenship opportunities for academics, such as university professors. Both Henley & Partners and Mark Nestmann, (see the next page for contact information), can provide details on these Austrian possibilities. In special circumstances, a person who can demonstrate that their proposed residence in Austria will make a unique scientific or technological contribution that benefits the public interest will be admitted with a tax-free status. This special status is reviewed annually by the Ministry of Finance.

Since citizenship by investment remains politically controversial within each of these three countries, these programs could be changed, suspended or terminated at any time. In the event these programs are changed or abolished, those persons who already have acquired passports should be able to retain them but that is not guaranteed.

Republic of Ireland

In 2012, with its national economy in bad shape, the Irish government adopted an Immigrant Investor Program to attract both money and wealthy individuals from outside the EU. Since then the economy has improved greatly, but the program still offers special immediate residence visas to foreign individuals willing to invest in Ireland.

This investment can eventually lead to full citizenship, and Irish citizenship opens the door to full personal and commercial access to all 28 countries in the European Union.

Under this program, potential investor immigrants have these choices (all numbers are required minimums and in dollar equivalents, as of January 2018):

- Make a one-time payment of €500,000 (US$616,000) to a public project benefiting the arts, sports, health or education.

- Make a €2 million (US$2.4 million) investment in a low-interest immigrant investor bond. The investment is to be held for a minimum of five years. The bond cannot be traded, it must be held to maturity.

- Invest €1 million (US$1.23 million) in venture capital funding in an Irish business for a minimum of three years.

- Make a €1 million mixed investment in 50% property and 50% government securities. Special consideration may be given to those purchasing property owned by the National Asset Management Agency (NAMA). In such cases, a single €1 million investment in property may be sufficient.

There also is a separate Start-up Entrepreneur Program for foreigners with entrepreneurial abilities who wish to start a business in an innovation area of the economy with funding of at least €75,000 (US$92,000). They will be given a two-year residence for the purposes of developing the business.

Information is available at the Ministry of Justice at:
Email: investmentandstartup@justice.ie
Web: http://www.inis.gov.ie

For more information about each of these economic citizenship programs or for general information, contact:

The Nestmann Group, Ltd.
Mark Nestmann, LL.M., President
2303 N. 44th Street #14-1025
Phoenix, AZ 85008
Tel.: 602-688-7552
Email: service@nestmann.com
Web: https://www.nestmann.com

Mark Nestmann, a senior member of the Banyan Hill Council of Experts, is a qualified professional who assists those interested in acquiring foreign residence and citizenship.

Henley & Partners
Dr. Christian H. Kälin TEP, IMCM, Group Chairman
Henley Haus, Klosbachstrasse 110
8024 Zürich, Switzerland
Tel.: +41 44 266 22 22

Email: christian.kalin@henleyglobal.com
Web: https://www.henleyglobal.com

Henley & Partners
Jon Green, North America Partner
906 — 1112 West Pender Street
Vancouver, BC
V6E 2S1, Canada
Tel.: +1-604-239-2170
Email: jon.green@henleyglobal.com
Web: https://www.henleyglobal.com

Strategy 3: Expatriation — The Ultimate Estate Plan

Exodus Offshore Grows

Political and economic turmoil in many countries have driven a growing number of people to escape from leech-like national tax systems that prop up dying welfare states.

Historically, it was common for some of the wealthiest French or British to flee their homelands to escape excessive taxation — and wealthy Latin Americans did so to avoid political instability. These days the definition of a "sovereign individual" includes not just millionaires and billionaires, but those of more modest wealth who have joined this migratory exodus.

People in ever-greater numbers are seeking to start a new life in countries where hard work is rewarded, not punished by wealth confiscation — places where business is free to make its own decisions, without regulatory predators hovering over every attempt at free enterprise.

The numbers of U.S. persons ending their citizenship, according to U.S. Treasury figures, hit an all-time high in 2017. The tally for 2016 was up 26% from 2015. That 2016 list showed a total of 5,411, a new annual record, up from 4,279 expatriates in 2015. And 2015 had a 58% hike over 2014.

At this rate soon more than 5,000 Americans annually will relinquish their U.S. citizenship, and that dramatically undercounts the real number. Certain types of expatriations, ones in which the expat is not required to file exit-tax forms, are not reported. Given that the Exit Tax kicks in when net worth tops $2 million, or 2015 when average annual income tax exceeds $155,000 for five years running, it's easy to see how the real number of expats is higher than the official numbers indicate.

U.S. News & World Report estimated that each year an additional three million U.S. citizens and resident aliens simply leave America to make new homes in other nations. Admittedly, this surprising number of people leaving must be compared to the millions clamoring to get into the U.S., fleeing from even more restrictive nations.

But there's a huge difference in the economic status of these two groups. Those seeking admission are, by and large, poverty-stricken persons desperately trying to better their lot with new lives in what they see as the Promised Land. They'll settle for low-paying jobs, welfare, free education for their kids and U.S. government-subsidized education, housing and health care.

These new U.S. residents are not all low-income people. Chinese millionaires and billionaires are flocking to the United States in record numbers. In 2017, that U.S. Investor Visa Program was used by 7,755 Chinese citizens who sought residence. In return for a modest investment of US$500,000 to US$1 million and the creation of new jobs, this official U.S. program allows foreigners and their families' permanent U.S. residence.

Those Americans seeking to escape the growing tyranny aimed right at them by the United States government are typically middle class and wealthier people. One estimate is that the loss of three million people annually equals a loss of 2% of the national workforce and $136 billion in income. And it is this hemorrhaging of fleeing Americans who take with them the lion's share of the U.S. tax base. While many are retirees, studies show a majority are younger Americans, many with families.

These are among the very top 5% of the people who pay taxes for all those programs those new, and often illegal, immigrants covet. Increasingly, the wealthy correctly perceive that they are under attack by their own government, so they take the only rational option left open to them. They're taking their wealth and leaving.

Look back on multiple government attacks on wealth during the last decade. What you will find is U.S. congressional legislation that has abolished domestic financial privacy and reversed the burden of proof, forcing an accused to prove his or her innocence. These laws allowed billions of dollars of property confiscation by police under civil forfeiture fiat. Taken together this web of laws were all parts of the various failed wars against drugs, money laundering and anti-terrorism.

Several lawyers who represent expats told *The Wall Street Journal* that many expatriates are wealthy Americans who left due to the general anti-freedom direction taken by the nation's political leaders. "There is growing concern, particularly among the wealthy, about the future financial direction of the country," said Paul L. Caron, Professor of Law of the University of Cincinnati, College of Law.

A Case Study: Eduardo Luiz Saverin

If the last 30 years of accumulated assaults on the constitutional rights of U.S. citizens have not convinced you to make your contingency plans to escape America, perhaps a review of the reactionary political demagoguery surrounding Eduardo Saverin will do the trick.

Saverin, the billionaire Facebook co-founder, ended his U.S. citizenship in 2011 as a legal means of avoiding U.S. taxes. As we have noted, U.S. laws, unlike most other nations, impose taxes on "U.S. persons" (citizens and resident aliens), no matter where in the world they live and without regard to their income sources. Terminating citizenship is the only way to avoid U.S. taxes.

Most other national tax systems are territorial, imposing taxes only on income earned within their borders. A Canadian or British citizen, for example, can move offshore and legally leave most domestic taxes behind. A Panamanian is taxed only on income earned within his country, none offshore.

In 2012, the leading publicity hound in the U.S. Senate, Charles E. Schumer (D-NY), and his PR apparatchiks regarded the Saverin expatriation news as a great chance to make headlines and they pounced.

The "ultra-liberal" Schumer unveiled the Ex-PATRIOT Act (Expatriation Prevention by Abolishing Tax-Related Incentives for Offshore Tenancy Act). This legislative disaster would have imposed prospective 35% tax on U.S. earnings on anyone who ended U.S. citizenship during the last 10 years.

To add juice to the story, Saverin's 4% stake in the publicly traded Facebook was estimated to be worth US$3 billion to US$4 billion. This made him the perfect target for politicians — an ungrateful tax-dodging billionaire skipping out on America and all its suffering taxpayers.

Indeed, by ending U.S. citizen status, Saverin probably saved hundreds of millions in eventual estate and gift taxes. If he remained a citizen, he would not have owed U.S. capital gains tax on his income until he sold his shares. Wealthy American shareholders often borrow against their shares and live tax-free off the unrealized appreciation for years.

Anyone in Saverin's position would be insane not to act legally to save all the taxes possible, and that's just what he did. As it is, one expert estimated he paid US$350 million because of the infamous Exit Tax the U.S. imposes on expatriates.

Saverin, then 33 years old, who was born in Brazil, came to the U.S. as a teenager and became an American citizen, reportedly to avoid being kidnapped from his wealthy parents. Exercising his legal right as an American, he surrendered his U.S. citizenship in 2011, one among the 1,780 Americans who ended U.S. citizenship in that year.

He became a resident of Singapore, where, unlike the U.S., the government welcomes wealthy foreigners with low taxes and eventual citizenship. Saverin benefited from major tax savings by becoming a permanent resident of Singapore, which imposes no capital gains taxes.

Perhaps the most atrocious part of Senator Schumer's proposal was the attempt to bar re-entry into the U.S. forever. This ban would have been retroactive and applied to anyone who ended citizenship in 2002 or later. Fortunately, once he got the publicity he wanted, Schumer's proposal died a well-deserved legislative death.

The Ultimate Plan

Indeed, expatriation has been called "the ultimate estate plan."

Expatriation is nothing less than a step-by-step process that, when completed, provides the legal right to stop paying U.S. income taxes for the U.S. person (citizen or resident alien) willing to terminate that status. In sum, it requires professional consultations, careful planning, movement of assets offshore and most certainly, prior acquisition of a second citizenship. When that's done — and done exactly right — you can leave behind America as your home country and establish a new domicile, preferably in a low- or no-tax jurisdiction.

And for U.S. citizens, this unusual plan requires, as a final step toward tax freedom, the formal relinquishment of citizenship.

Obviously, expatriation is a drastic plan. And in truth, there are many other perfectly suitable offshore strategies recommended in this book that can result in some limited U.S. tax savings and that don't require anything as dramatic as expatriation.

These tax savings include purchase of international life insurance policies, annuities, and making offshore investments through retirement plans, among others.

But for U.S. citizens and long-term U.S. resident aliens ("green card holders") seeking a permanent and legal way to end their obligation to pay U.S. taxes, expatriation is the only option.

Blueprint for Ultimate Tax Avoidance

Since the dawn of humankind, individuals have been migrating away from their native lands to seek better opportunities elsewhere. But since the development of the modern nation-state and the high taxation imposed by some nations on all the worldwide income of their citizen-residents, led by the United States, this process called "expatriation" has taken on significance because of the tax freedom it allows.

One of the first tax experts to appreciate the potential tax savings of expatriation was Marshall Langer JD, a leading international tax attorney who practiced law in London and Miami. Langer is the respected author of several major international tax treatises, but also the daring creator of a now out-of-print book, *The Tax Exile Report* (1992). This title gained international notoriety when the late U.S. Senator Daniel Patrick Moynihan (D-NY), angry, red faced and emotional at a Senate hearing, denounced the book as "… a legal income tax avoidance plan." (Note that the senator said "legal" — and indeed, it is that.)

Compelling Numbers

In explaining why expatriation is so attractive to wealthy Americans (and some others), a few years ago a *Forbes* magazine article gave the compelling arithmetic: "A very rich Bahamian citizen pays zero estate taxes; rich Americans — anyone with an estate worth US$3 million or more — could pay 55%. A fairly stiff 37% marginal rate kicks in for Americans leaving as little as US$600,000 to their children."

Even though U.S. estate taxes have been reduced since then, an even more impressive part of the Langer plan is the ability to escape higher U.S. income, capital gains and other taxes.

When it comes to expatriation, however, Americans face a unique burden. Unlike almost every other nation, with one or two exceptions, U.S. citizens and long-term residents cannot escape home country taxes by moving their residence to another nation.

The only way to leave U.S. taxes behind is to end U.S. citizenship or resident alien status.

New Refugees

Becoming a "tax exile" by choosing to expatriate is not without problems. In America, expatriation to avoid taxes has been a hot political issue for 30 years.

The original source of the expatriation controversy was a sensational article in the November 24, 1994 issue of *Forbes* magazine, entitled "The New Refugees." Filled with juicy details (famous names, luxury addresses, huge tax dollar savings), the story described how clever ex-Americans who became citizens of various foreign nations, legally paid little or no U.S. federal and state income, estate and capital gains taxes.

Ever since, expatriation has periodically been a "hot button" issue kicked around by the American news media and "soak-the-rich" politicians. Indeed, Barack Obama repeatedly attacked offshore financial activity by U.S. individuals and companies during both his presidential campaigns.

It's understandable why politicians keep this political football in active play. To the average, uninformed U.S. taxpayer, expatriation seems like just another rich man's tax loophole. Before *Forbes* raised the issue, few people had even heard of the concept of formal surrender or loss of U.S. citizenship.

In 2015, *Bloomberg News* reported that $2.10 trillion in profits were held offshore by U.S. companies and their affiliates. Taken together with the fact that numerous U.S. corporations have re-incorporated offshore to avoid U.S. corporate taxes, politicians have found in expatriation a convenient straw man that they can beat unmercifully.

Former President Bill Clinton's Treasury Secretary at the time, Lawrence Summers, later President Obama's top White House economic adviser, went so far as to call tax expatriates "traitors" to America. He was forced to apologize for his hyperbole.

Right to End U.S. Citizenship

As a national political issue, expatriation is hardly new.

Following the American Civil War (1861 to 1865), Congress deliberated the status of those Americans who had formed the Confederacy. Congress resolved that any who swore allegiance could once again become U.S. citizens. As a result, the Expatriation Act of 1868 established that all Americans have the right to give up their citizenship if they decide to do so.

Approximately a hundred years later, the Foreign Investors Tax Act of 1966 tried to impose a heavy tax on wealthy Americans attempted to give up with citizenship "with the principal purpose of avoiding" U.S. taxes. Of course, that intention is nearly impossible to prove, and the IRS didn't even attempt it.

The lengths to which American politicians will go to penalize supposed tax expatriates is demonstrated by a never-enforced provision of U.S. law, sponsored by then-U.S. Representative (and later U.S. Senator) Jack Reid (D-RI) and enacted in 1996.

The Reid Amendment permits the U.S. Attorney General to bar from entering the United States anyone who renounces their U.S. citizenship to avoid taxes. Thus, Congress lumped together individuals exercising their legal right to avoid taxes by expatriating with barred narcotics traffickers, terrorists and persons suffering from communicable diseases.

Amidst the political furor, thoughtful experts question what they view as much broader and dangerous U.S. anti-expatriation precedents. They point out that these laws involve not only retaliatory government acts against resistance to high taxes, but pose possible human rights violations guaranteed by other American laws and even by the Human Rights Charter of the United Nations.

It is worth repeating that the U.S. Supreme Court has repeatedly affirmed the right of U.S. citizens to end their citizenship, as well as the right to enjoy dual citizenship.

This political frenzy probably reflects politics as usual and collective envy more than any sense of patriotism by Americans or congressional politicians. Expatriation is not as serious a problem as some pretend based on the actual numbers of Americans, rich or poor, who formally surrender their citizenship each year. Most expatriates give up their U.S. citizenship because they are returning to their native land or marrying a non-U.S. citizen, and not to avoid taxes.

Save Millions of Dollars, Legally

Amidst this controversy, until the 2008 Exit Tax, there were very substantial tax savings for wealthy U.S. citizens who were prepared to end their citizenship. While only a handful of very rich Americans legally expatriated, the list included some prominent names.

In 1964, the late billionaire mutual fund founder Sir John Templeton (knighted by Queen Elizabeth in 1987), made a controversial decision. He decided to terminate his U.S. citizenship after moving his home to The Bahamas, where there were no estate, income or investment taxes. He became both a British citizen and a Bahamian citizen and lived tax-free in The Bahamas until his death in 2008.

This move saved him more than US$100 million when he sold the well-known international investment fund that still bears his name, and many millions more in estate taxes when he died. Interestingly, Templeton's investment record improved markedly after he stopped worrying about the U.S. tax consequences of his investment decisions. Because of tax-free compounding, Templeton was worth several billion dollars and when he died he was one of the world's wealthiest men. However, Sir John did not necessarily recommend that other investors follow his lead and switch allegiance to a tax haven such as The Bahamas. (It's almost impossible for an American to become a Bahamian citizen today.) But, Templeton strongly did recommend that smart investors should take full advantage of tax-deferred vehicles such as life insurance, annuities, self-directed pension plans and offshore business.

Before Eduardo Saverin, other wealthy ex-Americans who took their formal leave from the U.S. included billionaire Campbell Soup heir John ("Ippy") Dorrance, III (Ireland); Michael Dingman, chairman of Abex and a Ford Motor director (The Bahamas); J. Mark Mobius, one of the leading emerging market investment fund managers (Germany); Kenneth Dart, heir to the billion dollar Dart container fortune (Belize); the late Ted Arison, founder of Carnival Cruise Lines (Israel); and Frederick Krieble, millionaire director of Loctite Corporation, (Turks and Caicos Islands).

The Law Today — U.S. Exit Tax

While those former U.S. citizens could escape American taxes, they did so in past years — but they might not want to do it again today.

That's because on June 17, 2008, President George W. Bush signed new anti-expatriation legislation, Public Law No. 110-245, unanimously passed by Congress under the misleading title of "The Heroes Earnings Assistance and Relief Tax Act of 2008," also called the "HEART Act." Much of this law has little to do with expatriation since it provided increased benefits for U.S. armed forces veterans.

The Act dramatically changed the former income tax rules applicable to both U.S. citizens who expatriate and long-term U.S. residents (e.g., "green card holders") who decide to end their U.S. residence status. The Act refers to both groups collectively as "covered individuals."

Because the budget rules of Congress require that all new spending programs be accompanied by a source of revenue to pay for them, the anti-expat tax crowd in Congress jumped at the chance to wrap their long-time anti-expatriate tax nostrums in the American flag.

The new expat tax was supposed to finance the hundreds of millions needed to pay for veteran's benefits, but few believed that to be true. A study by the Congressional Budget Office guessed that the law might net the government up to US$286 million over five years.

This expat Exit Tax had been the devout wish of liberal, left-wing Democrats for a decade or more. In 2008, Democrat Rep. Charles Rangel of New York, then chairman of the powerful, tax-writing House Ways and Means Committee, slipped this horrendous tax restriction into a popular military pension/pay bill (without hearings or public notice). President George W. Bush, the great "tax cutter," signed it into law without so much as a whimper.

Ironically, Rangel was later forced to resign as Ways and Means Committee chairman when he was exposed as having failed for years to pay taxes on several sources of income, failed to report offshore real estate holdings and having traded special legislative favors in return for campaign and other contributions. After 45 years in Congress he was defeated for re-election in 2016.

Totalitarian Taxes on "Covered Individuals"

In advocating an Exit Tax, Rep. Rangel and his political allies on the Left imposed expat exit restrictions very similar to those of Hitler's Nazis, apartheid South Africa and the Communist Soviet Union. Each of these totalitarian regimes in their despotic days fleeced persecuted departing citizens (Jews, gypsies, political dissidents) with similar confiscatory exit taxes.

In fact, the 2008 Exit Tax Act probably violates protections in the U.S. Constitution that guarantee the right to voluntarily end U.S. citizenship and the right to live and travel abroad freely, although we doubt seriously that any wealthy expatriate would ever waste money on a court challenge once they have escaped.

Under this law, a person described as a "covered individual" falls within the clutches of the Act if, on the date of expatriation or termination of U.S. residence, (i) the individual's average annual net U.S. income tax liability for the five-year period preceding that date is US$162,000 or more (2017 amount, adjusted annually for inflation); (ii) the individual's net worth as of that date is US$2 million or more after an exclusion of US$699,000 (for 2017); or (iii) the individual fails to certify under penalties of perjury that he or she has complied with all U.S. federal tax obligations for the preceding five years.

Of course, if you're lucky and don't fit within the above definitions, this new law may offer a very real opportunity to escape U.S. taxes as you become more prosperous in the future. (More about that, and what might be a very good no-tax deal if you qualify, later in this text.)

Exceptions

There is an exception in the Act for those who have dual citizenship and became U.S. citizens by accident of birth, either because they happened to be born in the U.S., or born to a U.S. parent and subsequently lived in the U.S. for only a limited time.

Covered individuals under items (i), (ii) or (iii) above, have two limited exceptions that avoid taxes under the Act. They won't be taxed if they certify compliance with all U.S. federal tax obligations and either: (i) were a citizen of the United States and another country at birth if, (a) they are still a citizen and tax resident of that other country and, (b) they resided in the U.S. for no more than 10 of the 15 taxable years prior to expatriation or giving up long-term residence; or (ii) they renounce U.S. citizenship before the age of 18-and-a-half if they were not residing in the U.S. for more than 10 years before the renunciation or the termination of long-term residence.

In scanning random examples of the annual official U.S. State Department expatriate lists, it seems that a large portion of those listed are probably green card holders of modest means who are returning to their country of birth. In other words, most persons who chose formally to end their American status are not very rich tax evaders, but rather folks whose assets and tax bills are well below the amounts the new Act states.

Of course, the official list of expatriates doesn't include those who simply move to another country and gradually sever their ties with the U.S. Technically, these people are still subject to U.S. taxes, but if they give up their claim to U.S. Social Security or federal pension benefits, it is difficult for the IRS to find them. This law may well increase that number.

Confiscation by Taxation

There was a time in the United States when tax rates on the top earning individuals approached 90% or more. The Reagan tax revolution brought those rates down to more reasonable, upper 30% levels.

But under the Exit Tax, covered individuals are taxed enormously under new Code Section 877A (called a "mark-to-market tax"). This vindictive tax taxes all assets as if the person's worldwide assets had been sold for their fair market value on the day before expatriation or residence termination. For 2017, the first US$699,000 in unrealized gains from a covered expatriate isn't subject to the Exit Tax, a figure that is adjusted annually for inflation.

This phantom gain will presumably be taxed as ordinary income (at rates as high as 35%) or capital gains (at either a 15%, 25%, or 28% rate), as provided under current law. In addition, any assets held by any trust or portion of a trust that the covered individual was treated as owning for U.S. income tax purposes (i.e., a grantor trust) are also subject to the mark-to-market tax.

No doubt many people caught by this tax would have to sell their assets to pay the tax, leaving them with little or nothing.

Still More Taxes

Equally as bad, the stay-at-home relatives of rich expatriate Americans who remain behind as U.S. citizens could find themselves owing tax if they receive large gifts of money or property from their expat relatives.

The Act also imposes an additional tax of a potentially far-reaching scope: gifts and bequests to U.S. persons from "covered individuals" (beyond the annual 2017 gift tax exclusion of S$16,000 per person) are subject to a U.S. "transfer tax" imposed on the U.S. transferee at the highest federal transfer tax rates then in effect (currently 47.5%).

Talk about highway robbery! Not only is wealth taxed away by the Exit Tax from a generous expatriate who gives a gift, the recipient of the gift is punished with a 45% tax on that gift.

Non-Grantor Trust Distributions

As they say on those late-night TV commercials: "But wait, there's more!" *Mucho más!*

The Act requires that trustees of certain "non-grantor" trusts (i.e., trusts in which covered individuals or others are not treated as the owners for income tax purposes) must withhold 30% of each distribution to a covered individual if that distribution would have been included in the gross income of the individual if he or she were still a U.S. taxpayer.

Defying international law, the Act says no double taxation avoidance treaty of any country with the United States may be invoked to reduce this withholding requirement. Moreover, if the trustee distributes appreciated property to a covered individual, the trust will be treated as if it sold the property to the individual at its fair market value. This treatment of distributions applies to all future distributions with no time limitation.

Retirement Plans Cut in Half

Not content with all this tax persecution, the greedy congressional politicians went after expatriates' pensions as well.

The Act forces an expatriate to pay up to a 51% tax on distributions from retirement plans. The same goes for most other forms of deferred payments. If there's a small silver lining, it's that the tax isn't due until you receive payments from the plan. Plans covered by this provision include qualified pensions, profit sharing and stock bonus plans, annuity plans, federal pensions, simplified employee pension plans and retirement accounts.

Very Select Group

For anyone who falls within the definition of a "covered individual" under the 2008 HEART expat tax law, the chance of legal avoidance of American taxes by ending citizenship is going to be a very costly endeavor. Indeed, under this confiscatory law, the richer you are, the more you stand to lose by leaving the U.S. behind.

Americans who are not "covered" by the numbers in this punitive law, but who do have good prospects of amassing future wealth, this new law may well offer you a no-tax bonanza — if you are willing to reorder your life, acquire second citizenship, move to an offshore tax haven and surrender your U.S. passport. And in this era of economic globalization and instant international communications, many enterprising entrepreneurs can do business anywhere they desire.

Let's say you paid less than US$162,000 in taxes for the last five years, your net worth is less than US$2 million and you have no problem certifying that you complied with all U.S. federal tax obligations for the preceding five years. This law says you can leave home free!

No doubt there are many ways to rearrange your finances and title your property to avoid values being assigned to your balance sheet, keeping that net worth under US$2 million. Indeed, financial obligations might reduce your net worth. And once you have left the U.S. and have become a new citizen of a tax haven such as Panama, Uruguay, Singapore, or Hong Kong, there is nothing to prevent assets being transferred to you.

In that case, it appears that the Exit Tax law allows you to end your citizenship and with that, also end your U.S. tax obligations. And the 2008 law also repealed the former 10-year claim of IRS tax jurisdiction over an expats income and assets. In fact, as a foreigner, you too can enjoy the tax breaks American tax law affords to non-U.S. investors in America.

Something to think about in your estate planning!

Green Card Holders Get Stuck

The 2008 Act not only affects U.S. citizens who expatriate, but also can financially penalize "green card" holders who return to their home country.

If a foreigner living in the U.S. has a green card and has lived in the U.S. for eight out of the most recent 15 years, they are considered a long-term permanent resident, or "permanent resident alien" (so count your years here — you may have to leave soon to avoid the tax).

Most of these individuals never intended to make the U.S. their permanent home. Now, when they do leave, if they have reached the asset/income tax threshold set in the 2008 Act, they too will be taxed as a "covered person." These people are not American tax dodgers but rather well-to-do Canadians, Brits, Indians, and other foreign residents perhaps concluding long-term business and professional assignments in the U.S.

When these foreign bankers, software engineers, chemists, teachers and others leave the U.S. to retire or transfer to a new post abroad, the Act will tax them on the unrealized capital gains of their total global assets. It includes supposedly tax-deferred U.S. retirement accounts, as well as assets like a cottage in Quebec, a share of a relative's business in Bangalore, or a great-grandmother's pearls kept in a London safe.

Here's one example: consider a Frenchman or Englishman who paid US$10,000 for a vacation home in France in 1980, came to the U.S. in 1990 when it was worth US$100,000, and left the U.S. in 2008 when the French home was worth US$1 million. That person would be subject to a capital gains tax of US$135,000 on that one asset.

Only "permanent residents" ("green card holders") will be stung. As a result, wealthy persons considering moving to the United States may increasingly select long-term visas rather than formal residence status, potentially depriving the country of wealthy immigrants.

Some developed countries, such as Canada, have so-called "exit taxes" but critics say that the Act tarnishes the image of the U.S. as a friendly place for foreign talent and capital, at a time when America needs both.

Devastating for Foreign Workers

The U.S. National Association of Manufacturers (NAM) described the proposal to tax expatriates as "potentially devastating" for American manufacturing's many long-term foreign workers. NAM argued that the rules should target U.S. citizens who expatriate to avoid taxes, not workers who return to their home countries for personal reasons and must, by U.S. law, eventually surrender their green cards.

Previously, long-term residents who surrendered their green cards could avoid taxes on their unrealized gains by spending fewer than 30 days of any year in the United States for 10 years. Even then, only U.S., not worldwide, gains were subject to tax. There is evidence that American companies have respond by sponsoring fewer green cards or filling openings with workers on less attractive long-term visas, drawing a smaller and potentially less talented pool of workers to the U.S.

Green card holders now living abroad may consider immediately giving them up under a provision of the Act that allows retroactive dating for nonresidents. But green card holders now living in the United States have no way out, lawyers say.

Unwelcome Foreigners

One other point: there is still one more vindictive punishment for any "covered individual" who dares to end U.S. citizenship. Once they are no longer U.S. citizens, they will be "foreigners" in the eyes of American immigration law.

Generally, foreigners can apply for any of the many entry visas the U.S. issues. For example, foreign tourists entering the U.S. for visits usually are granted a 90-day visa that is renewable once for a total of 180 days. If a foreigner stays in the U.S. more than 180 days in one year, they run the risk of becoming a "U.S. person" liable for U.S. taxes.

However, under the Exit Tax law, the IRS says: "...expatriated individuals will be subject to U.S. tax on their worldwide income for any of the 10 years following expatriation in which they are present in the U.S. for more than 30 days, or 60 days in the case of individuals working in the U.S. for an unrelated employer."

So, the tax-dodging U.S. Rep. Charlie Rangel and other politicians finally got their wish and enacted an exit tax on expatriates — much to the detriment of America, its economy and the nation's standing in the eyes of the world.

But don't let all this information about exit taxes scare you.

If you don't come under the Act for net worth test or for other reasons, it means you can end your American tax liability by ending your citizenship and thus permanently detach yourself from the clutches of the IRS. That possibility is something to seriously consider. Recommendations for professional tax advisors, are listed in Appendix I.

How It's Done

Long before anyone formally surrenders their U.S. citizenship, they should have reordered their financial affairs in such a way as to remove most, if not all, of their assets from possible government control and taxation.

Here are the recommended steps to take:

•   Arrange affairs so that most or all income is derived from non-U.S. sources;

•   Title property ownership so that any assets that remain in the United States are exempt from U.S. estate and gift taxes to the maximum extent;

•   Move abroad and make a new home in a no-tax foreign country so that you are no longer a "resident" for U.S. income tax purposes;

- Obtain a new alternative citizenship and passport;

- Formally surrender U.S. citizenship and change your legal "domicile" to avoid U.S. estate taxes.

One of the most important decisions is the choice of your new citizenship.

Millions of Americans already hold a second citizenship; millions more qualify almost instantly for dual citizenship due to place of birth, ancestry or marriage. At this point you may wish to review the information described above in "Strategy 2 — Dual Citizenship" at the beginning of this chapter to see if any of these faster avenues are open to you.

Part 2 — Financial Strategies

As you review this section keep in mind that when considering any investment strategy, there are five core goals. Choosing your best strategies involves balancing each of them to meet your specific needs.

1. Maximum Asset Protection: You want your financial assets to be difficult to seize. Given the litigious nature of the U.S., as well as the ever-present threat of government wealth confiscation, that is critical.

2. Optimized Estate Planning: Especially if you're preserving wealth for your family and heirs, you want a strategy that provides quick and hassle-free distribution of funds when the time comes. You also want to optimize by minimizing the tax treatment of survivor distributions.

3. Simple Compliance and Reporting: You DON'T want to have to file dozens of complex documents every year, risking big penalties if you miss one or fail to dot an "i". Hiring someone to manage this can put a big dent in your investment income ... not to mention your peace of mind.

4. Optimal Tax Treatment: Most important is tax-deferral on investment gains. Income tax-free distributions to your surviving beneficiaries would be a big plus, too.

5. Maximum Privacy: Ideally, you want more than just asset protection. You want your assets to be difficult even to identify, to discourage speculative lawsuits.

Strategy 1: An Offshore Bank Account

Until a few years ago, only the wealthiest investors could benefit from having an offshore bank account.

In the days of snail mail and trans-Atlantic Ocean travel, only the richest of the rich could afford the fees and legal advice associated with "going offshore" financially. These days with dramatic changes in international travel, banking and communications, even a modest offshore bank account can be your quick, inexpensive entry into the world of foreign investment opportunities.

Put aside the erroneous notion promoted by the IRS that foreign bank accounts are designed for shady international drug kingpins and unscrupulous wheeler-dealers avoiding taxes. For some biased people, offshore accounts will always evoke images of cloak and dagger spies, of shadowy clandestine operations and crooked officials in Third World nations.

Although these sinister images are entertaining, they hardly relate to your present practical purposes. What we want to do is build offshore financial structures that will increase your wealth legally and solidly protect your assets. Forget the intrigue and embrace the fact that an offshore bank account is a highly effective economic way to achieve your legitimate financial goals. There is nothing underhanded or sinister about protecting the wealth you have worked so hard to earn.

A foreign bank account can an effective offshore wealth strategy. It can help increase your asset value by cutting taxes and maximizing profits. It can help build a strong defensive asset protection structure. And it can be used for profitable offshore investments.

As we demonstrate in these pages, the possible variations on these important themes are nearly endless.

Offshore banking is big business worldwide. Estimates are that from US$3 trillion to US$5 trillion is stashed in nearly 40 or more offshore banking havens that impose no or low taxes, have less onerous regulations, guarantee privacy and welcome non-resident clients. Nearly a quarter of the entire world's offshore private wealth is stashed in Switzerland alone!

In high tax, deficit spending welfare system countries, led by the U.S. — the politicians howl that tax havens are engaged in "unfair tax competition" because they impose no taxes or low taxes — but these same politicians never try to imitate tax havens by lowering their own high taxes or reducing spending.

Benefits of Offshore Banking

Let us be clear about one important fact up front.

An offshore bank account is not a tool to be used illegally to evade taxes. The basic rule is that an American citizen or "green card" holder is taxed by the U.S. Internal Revenue Code on all their worldwide income.

No matter where or how you earn your money, you may owe some U.S. taxes and you must annually file with the IRS at least an IRS Form 1040 for personal income and related taxes.

An offshore bank account, located outside the immediate jurisdiction of the IRS and U.S. courts provides a "safer haven" for your money. Many thousands of sovereign individuals use their offshore bank accounts for exactly that purpose.

The International Monetary Fund (IMF) confirmed our view that "stability reasons" — and not bank secrecy — has helped foreign havens like Switzerland attract 27% (a total of US$2.3 trillion) of the world's offshore wealth.

These smart people, just as do savvy Argentineans who bank in Uruguay and smart Russians who bank in Cyprus, are using this simple, yet effective, tool to protect their wealth against a meddling government and their declining home currencies. You should consider doing the same.

Your offshore bank account is not just a place for safekeeping cash. One of the great advantages of an offshore bank account is it enhances your ability to trade freely and invest in foreign-issued stocks, bonds, mutual funds and national currencies that are not available in your home country.

Hedge Against Dollar

Another major benefit of an offshore bank account is protection against a historically long-term decline in the value of the U.S. dollar.

Since the creation of the Federal Reserve in 1913, the value of the U.S. dollar has continued to move downward. What was worth US$1.00 in 1913 is worth less than four cents today. That means the American dollar has lost more than 95% of its value during the last 100 plus years.

This demonstrates the benefit of having an offshore account, while you have assets that you can convert to more stable currencies. An offshore account gives you the ability to protect and build your wealth through currency diversification.

Opening an offshore bank account makes it easy for you to access the power of currency appreciation. Unlike most U.S. banks, offshore banks offer "multi-currency functionality." That is, they give you the ability to invest and transact business in your choice of strong currencies, such as the Swiss franc — currencies that appreciate while the U.S. dollar sinks. The bank account may also provide safe purchases of precious metals or other valuable investment items offshore.

Investment Platform

An offshore account is an excellent platform from which to diversify investments. It gives instant access to the world's best investment opportunities, including currencies and precious metals, without concern about your home nation's legal restrictions that would otherwise apply if the bank account was located within your home country.

Many offshore foreign stock, bond and mutual fund trading is not inhibited by restrictive laws such as the U.S. Securities and Exchange Act or the rules of its administrative agency, the U.S. Securities and Exchange Commission (SEC).

An offshore bank account allows the ready purchase of attractive insurance and annuity products not available in the U.S. and other nations. With such products, tax savings may result from deferred investment earnings, capital gains, or appreciation, rather than receiving ordinary income that is not only taxed by the U.S. as current income, but at a higher tax rate.

An offshore bank account provides opportunities to profit from currency fluctuations, the easy ability to purchase foreign real estate, and earnings from comparatively higher bank interest rates available only in some foreign countries. You can also trade precious metals and other tangible personal assets through most foreign accounts.

Asset Protection

Another important benefit is the relatively strong asset protection foreign bank accounts provide. The existence of your offshore account is not readily known to a possible domestic claimant considering a lawsuit or seeking to collect a judgment against your assets.

The existence of the account must be revealed on your U.S. income tax return (IRS Form 1040), but by law that is not supposed to be part of the public record. At times in a judicial proceeding you may have a legal obligation to reveal an offshore account in a full statement of your assets and liabilities. But there are times when it makes good financial sense to discourage a potential litigant and promote compromise by letting an opponent know just how difficult it will be to reach your offshore assets.

Because of defendant-friendly local laws in asset protection haven jurisdictions, domestic judgment holders often have a very difficult time enforcing a judgment obtained in their own country in another country. To reach your assets, a successful creditor must start all over using the foreign judicial process to press a claim against your offshore assets. To do that, they must bear the expense of hiring foreign lawyers and paying for travel and witness transportation.

Besides promoting compromise, the delay in such a strung-out foreign process allows ample time for a defendant to fight the action, or simply move cash or assets to an account in another country. Because of offshore laws, courts in these countries often recognize orders allowing such transfers (called "portability"), especially in civil cases. Many of these nations have one or two-year statutes of limitations accruing from the date an initial claim arises against the account holder. Since a U.S. lawsuit takes years to get through the courts, this means an American court judgment could be void under the foreign nation's one-year cutoff date. In fact, the U.S. judicial process often takes so long that time runs out in nations with five-year statutes of limitations.

Offshore Accounts More Accessible

In past times, only the wealthiest investors could benefit from any kind of offshore bank account. Now, after dramatic changes in international banking and communications, even a modest offshore account can be a quick, inexpensive entry into the world of foreign investment opportunities.

To open an offshore private investment account today, you do not always need a minimum deposit of US$1 million or more, but that is the average required amount. Some banks with which Banyan Hill has a relationship will open an investment account for lesser amounts, but with lower minimums you don't get the individual service that comes with a deposit of US$1 million or more.

Five Steps to Choosing Your Offshore Bank

With all these potential benefits and lower barriers to entry, how do you go about choosing the right country and the right financial institution for your offshore bank account?

Step #1: Carefully examine and research established financial institutions in your country of choice. This allows you to gauge banking standards and it gives you a frame of reference with which to judge individual banks and their services.

Step #2: Check Google News and local newspapers and publications for any negative mentions about a specific bank you have in mind. Google can also provide the website of the country's official bank supervisory agency, which usually lists facts about each bank, its license, its current standing and any prior complaints or official actions.

Step #3: Beware of "banks" that have only an Internet presence. Most countries have outlawed "brass plate" banks that are little more than a name on a building or lawyer's office door. Absence of bank officials' names, a physical address, and phone numbers are almost always indications of possible fraud.

Step #4: Be wary of banks you find on the Internet that offer interest rates that are unreasonably high. If the offered deal appears too good to be true, it usually is.

Step #5: Find out which offshore private banks abide by, or exceed, the minimum standards set by the international Basel Accords, the banking supervision regulations issued by the Basel Committee on Banking Supervision (BCBS). These limit risk and require minimum capital, shareholder equity, disclosed reserves, and holdings in debt and equity instruments. Bank supervisors have imposed higher capital standards on global banks. Most face both the international "Basel 3" regime and local and regional regimes. The consensus is that big global banks will need buffers of equity (or Basel's "core tier one capital") equivalent to 12% to 13% of their risk-adjusted assets, compared to about 10% for domestic firms.

Here are seven preferred banking countries, in each of which we can recommend American client-friendly banks and contact persons:

Switzerland: Historic banking center but high minimums to open accounts.

Austria: Financial privacy and access to Eastern European investments.

Singapore: Strong, Swiss-like privacy laws and a gateway to Asia.

Panama: The largest banking center in Latin America south of Miami.

Uruguay: American accounts welcome with strong privacy.

Hong Kong: Banking window to investment opportunities in China.

Liechtenstein: Much like Switzerland, but large minimums required here.

Beware of Government Digital Money

You may not have noticed, but governments in many countries are quietly and systematically imposing restrictions on the use of cash, the ultimate currency control.

When questioned, the bureaucrats claim this is done for "security reasons," to thwart criminals, terrorists, drug runners, money launderers and tax evaders, the same tired excuses used to justify abuses under the PATRIOT Act and FATCA. It is easy to understand that governments worldwide will do everything they can to discourage their citizens from using cash. After all, cash is nearly untraceable and cash transactions are private.

Rules issued under the Bank Secrecy Act consider a long list of financial activities as "suspicious activities" reportable to the U.S. government's FinCEN, the Financial Crimes Enforcement Network. In the U.S. every cash or electronic transaction of $10,000 or more is automatically reported to FinCEN.

During 2017, the momentum toward a cashless world heightened. In the EU, for example, less than 9% of the combined GDP represented cash transactions. The most impactful effort was made by the government of India. In late 2016, it withdrew all 500 and 1000-rupee notes from circulation. This made 86% of the country's cash worthless and ultimately made it almost impossible for tens of millions of Indian citizens to even pay for their daily needs.

Government snoops prefer digital forms of payment that are much easier to track. France and some other EU countries formally have banned large cash transactions. French residents are prohibited from making cash transactions of more than €1,000, (US$1,200) down from the former limit of €3,000 euros. Italy also has the same cash limit and in Spain the cash limit is €2,500.

IBM has floated the idea of turning *all* dollars and other currencies into digital form — with the central server controlled by central banks like the U.S. Federal Reserve. In fact, most of all currencies held by banks already are digital, but at least we now have the option of keeping and using cash.

There's no need to mention what would happen under IBM's monopoly system if the power goes out. Of course, the same thing can and does happen now, with so much of our transacting done by credit or debit cards.

No matter what the advantages of digital currencies, the real danger isn't power outages, but rather giving the Fed the power to turn all our money on and off. Just imagine the opportunities for official monetary mayhem: digital wealth confiscation … automatic taxation … courts issuing warrants to seize your digital money.

We are realists. We know that if governments have the power to do that, they will use it.

The slow death of cash is yet another reason to create a secure stash of gold or silver, the ultimate stores of value. So far, at least, nobody's come up with a way to turn off its power.

Payment Apps You Can Use Offshore

The wave of the future, (and of the present in much of Europe, Asia and Africa), is a hybrid system in which banks provide money-storage and credit facilities, but independent application developers provide secure, Internet-based "point-of-sale" (POS) systems that largely bypass traditional credit card processors such as Visa and MasterCard.

There are safe, simple solutions available to you that don't require complicated foreign banking arrangements and hassles. They can protect you and your wealth safely, cheaply and above all, simply. We predict that these solutions will be the norm in the U.S. itself within two to three years.

They involved cellphones and apps. (For the uninitiated, an *"app"* is a software application, typically a small, specialized program downloaded from the Internet onto mobile devices, i.e. into your cellphone). Apps can allow your cellphone to do almost anything, even obtain cash or make purchases directly using this simple and secure cellphone app.

These apps illustrate the secret to safe offshore banking: "cloud computing." That's a fancy term for large "farms" of remote servers that allow centralized data storage and processing for a variety of always available Internet-based services.

Cloud computing has created endless opportunities for innovative, competitive software companies to develop and deploy new smartphone apps for paying for goods and services, without having to own and run their own expensive server farms.

Often called "e-wallets," these financial smartphone applications allow you to avoid the obsolete card technology still used by most U.S. banks when transacting abroad. They are safer than credit cards, including the advanced chip-and-pin cards used abroad. And e-wallets have the happy side effect of often reducing or eliminating costly foreign transaction fees (for you) and credit card terminal fees (for merchants).

For generations, most retail banks around the world have stored our money and/or given us lines of credit and charged us fees and interest. They've also supplied the means by which we access our money and our credit — debit and credit cards.

This amounts to a double-dip. That's because the systems required to use debit and credit cards — such as MasterCard and Visa — were created by the banks themselves. Merchants who accept bank-issued cards must pay fees to these networks.

These payment systems still rely mainly on telephone lines because they were built before the Internet. A critical element is the "terminal" that accepts your payment card at checkout, the "point-of-sale" (POS). They are usually provided by the bank to the merchant, for a fee.

The payment processor (e.g. Visa) charges the merchant a fee every time you use a POS terminal to make a purchase. A portion of these "swipe fees" is shared with your bank and the merchant's bank. Busy merchants can generate thousands of dollars in fees every day. They're highly unpopular and have generated numerous lawsuits, but they're central to the business model of current U.S.-style retail banking systems.

There is another problem, besides the fees, with these archaic networks. With millions of terminals in use, changing technology to something safer, say chip-and-pin instead of magnetic stripe, is a wildly expensive proposition. Card processing companies expect merchants to pay for new terminals, but merchants don't want to. Resistance to mass replacement of merchant POS terminals is the main reason the U.S. lags so far behind the world. Even after a mandatory switchover deadline in October 2015, millions of U.S. merchants still ask you to swipe.

As we all know, the security weaknesses of magnetic stripe technology to store card data has been highlighted in POS system breaches at major U.S. retailers, including Neiman Marcus Group, Michaels,

Lowe's, SuperValu, Albertsons, Target and Home Depot. That's created an incentive for change.

It's this combination of unpopular fees and restrictive, insecure technology that's created a gap for alternative smartphone-based and NFC (near-field communication) payment systems that bypass the card terminals altogether and created the key to safe transacting for you. This includes purchases to a business, as well as payments directly to a person.

A merchant can acquire a generic QR Code reader and connect it to the Internet, or even use their own smartphone or tablet to accept payments. Your payment is charged to your own debit or credit card, which they set up in the payment app.

Daily, weekly or monthly, the payment app company transfers funds to the merchant, all without card swipe fees, saving the merchant, and you, lots of money. For example, an app I have used in the U.S. for food shopping, LevelUp (www.thelevelup.com), gives a 7% discount on all purchases. That really adds up.

But Is It Safe?

The question you're probably asking right now is whether this sort of system is safe, given the dangers lurking on the Internet, which is where banking has moved, after all. The answer is: it's safer than using a traditional debit or credit card — a lot safer.

That's because the payment apps we recommend here don't store your debit/credit card details on your smartphone or on their own servers. Instead, they use a sophisticated encryption technique called "tokenization."

This technique converts your Primary Account Number (your card number) into a unique, randomly and algorithmically generated sequence of numbers and/or alphanumeric characters. This "token" is then stored in your smartphone's memory. The added safeguard is that it is impossible to decode — even the phone's manufacturer can't read it.

When you make purchases with a payment app, your card information is "tokenized," encrypted and sent to businesses and banks, which decrypts it and authorizes the transaction. The token is never stored by either the merchant or the bank. This avoids exposing your real card information number to theft. You, the customer, never notice the difference in the way transactions occur.

Of course, all this encryption magic doesn't do you any good if your smartphone is lost or stolen but if you have (a) a passcode to secure the device, (b) a PIN for opening your payment app and (c) a way to "wipe" all the data from your smartphone remotely, as can be done with Apple's "Find My iPhone" app, you are as protected as you can be.

Of course, there are certain privacy risks, as distinct from financial risks, that come from using cellphones and their apps. Some apps can compromise your location and other private data, so it's important to use those that don't.

Saving You Money

Besides convenience and safety, cellphone-based transacting abroad can save you a lot of money.

Consider the fees when you use a conventional ATM card outside the U.S., or even inside it, when using another bank's ATM:

- **Flat fee from your bank:** This is a fixed fee that your bank charges for using ATMs outside of its network. These fees usually vary between $2 and $5, but even as high as $10.

- **Flat fee from the foreign bank:** You also must pay a fixed fee to the foreign bank which owns the ATM you're using. This again is usually in the range of $2 and $5.

- **International transaction fee:** Instead of a fixed fee (or in addition), your home bank may charge a percentage fee for foreign withdrawals. These range from 2% to 4%.

- **Currency exchange fee:** The ATM interbank network, like Plus (operated by Visa) or Cirrus. (MasterCard), will also take a cut, on average 1% to 3%.

Now consider this method. I bought a prepaid foreign debit card in a single transaction using my foreign credit card and paid an international transaction fee of 1%. Then loaded its information into the local payment app, and from that point on, paid no foreign transaction fees. Of course, there wouldn't have been any fees if I had used the foreign prepaid debit card directly, but then I would have lost the extra security of encrypted tokenization.

Where Offshore?

Where can you use these apps?

While cash accounts are still the leading source for global transactions, a cashless society is not only possible, but is a reality. Consumers put a premium on convenience and mobile provides it. As barriers are eliminated, any country can rapidly switch to cashless payment methodologies. The total revenue of global mobile payment reached US$780 billion in 2017 and is projected to reach over US$1 trillion by 2019.

According to Analysys International, Asia is leading in embracing mobile transactions globally, with the leading country being China. Other countries that are not far behind include Europe, Africa, and Latin America. For example, in 2016, China had a reported $9 trillion in mobile payments. "China's rapid adoption of proximity payments is in part thanks to its late-mover advantage. In effect, China has jumped directly from cash to mobile payments," market research firm eMarketer said in a report. Even looking back to 2015 percentages, Belgium's noncash payments' share of its total value of consumer payments was as high as 93%. In France, it was 92%; the U.K. and Sweden it was 89% each.

The ease with which merchants can access these payment systems — often simply by downloading them to a tablet or laptop computer — means they can accept multiple payment systems in their store or restaurant, no matter how small. And since customers can simply download the app and set it up while they're on the go, any of us can access them as needed, recharging them with local prepaid debit cards.

So, you're thinking about going abroad … and you're wondering which app you need, where to get it, and how to set it up and use it. Let's review your options. Remember, these are solutions that allow you to turn your vulnerable physical magnetic-stripe cards into virtual payment systems that require no card to be present.

Apple Pay

Globally, Apple-based payment apps are the most popular in every region of the globe. In most places, twice as many people use Apple-based apps than Android (which runs on most non-Apple smartphones). Adyen reported that 36% of global payments come from Apple iPhones. The only place where Android apps are close to Apple levels of usage is Asia. Thus, it makes sense to start with Apple Pay.

Apple Pay works only on the iPhone, Apple Watch, iPad or Mac. You register your supported credit cards in the device's Passbook app. When you want to buy something from a retailer that supports Apple Pay, you point your device at the near field communication (NFC) payment terminal, and your payment information is delivered from your iPhone over a radio frequency connection. Then scan your fingerprint on your phone's TouchID sensor to verify your identity. If everything is OK, your phone vibrates and tells you the transaction was approved.

Apple Pay also works from within other apps, such as when you wish to purchase a plane ticket using an airline's app. It also uses tokenization to keep transactions safe, storing the "token" on a chip called a Secure Element. Users of Apple phones can use the "Find My iPhone" feature, which will suspend all payments from the device if it should be lost or stolen.

There's no need to cancel your credit card, because the card information isn't stored on the device. Apple doesn't get to know what you bought, how much you paid for it or any other personal details. The guy behind the counter doesn't get to see your name or your credit card number — all of which are potential weak spots of the current system, under which cards are occasionally cloned and ripped off.

Where: Apple Pay is available in the U.S., Canada, Europe, the Middle East, and Asia-Pacific. Two things are required to use Apple Pay: the merchant must accept it and your bank must authorize use of your card abroad. Apple Pay is also making rapid inroads in Asia even with the popularity of Android smartphones there. Where Apple Pay is not as commonly utilized, you can use local payment apps in the meantime.

Pros: It's considered the safest system of all, with end-to-end tokenization and no storage of your card or personal details on Apple servers. The security built into Apple Pay also reduces costs associated with fraud. In addition, Apple Pay is widely spread across carriers, phones, and merchants.

Cons: You must upgrade to iPhone 6 or newer versions or an Apple Watch to use it. Also, not all countries allow prepaid debit cards to be loaded into Apple Pay.

Who it is for: Essentially everyone who uses an Apple iPhone, especially in the U.S., U.K. or continental Europe.

Google Wallet

Like Apple Pay, Google Wallet involves tapping your phone on a POS terminal, entering your Wallet PIN and completing your transaction as usual. And like Apple Pay, Google Wallet uses tokenization; your real 16-digit card number is never exposed to merchants. But instead of securing the token in a chip on your phone, Google uses a software called Host Card Emulation (HCE), which stores your token virtually in "the cloud." This makes Google Wallet compatible with any near field communication (NFC)-equipped Android phone.

The app also lets you store club cards and gift cards as well as credit and debit cards.

Where: Widely available in the U.S. and expanding rapidly in the U.K. and Europe.

Pros: Google Wallet is very easy to use, especially for sending money to another person. It is increasingly becoming available in the U.S., U.K. and Europe. Also, Google Wallet is potentially compatible with highly secure Android-based phones, which are experiencing dominating market share growth, such as Samsung and the "pro privacy" Blackphone from Silent Circle (although there are rumors that Blackphone is developing its own super-secure payment systems). With security always being of concern, Google has taken the necessary steps to ensure its safety.

Cons: To use Google Wallet in stores, you'll need an NFC-capable Android phone. A second drawback is that the HCE technology Google has chosen requires that your phone be connected to your cell service to use, because the phone needs to retrieve its tokens from the cloud. That could be expensive if you're traveling abroad. There is also a fee to use it with a credit cards (it's free if you use it from your bank account) and international transfers are not an option between the U.S. and the U.K. or people living in other countries. The biggest con, however, is Google's focus on Android Pay, which doesn't require using an app or a PIN and is now where users can make NFC payments and use gift cards, coupons, and receive offers.

Who it is for: For security reasons, use Google Wallet only if you are resolutely against Apple.

Android Pay

Google's newest mobile pay service, Android Pay is the next generation in mobile — "tap and pay" hands free — purchasing. It also can be used within other mobile applications. Google uses a software called Host Card Emulation (HCE), which stores your token virtually in "the cloud." This makes Android Pay compatible with any near field communication (NFC)-equipped Android phone.

Where: Widely available in the U.S. and expanding rapidly in the U.K., Europe, and the rest of the world.

Pros: You do not need an app to use Android Pay, eliminating the need for a PIN. Android Pay also is secure as it doesn't send your card number with payments, instead using a virtual account number. A bonus is the exclusive savings and offers for its users, such as a $5 Dunkin' Donuts gift card when a customer uses Android Pay three times.

Cons: The challenges are less about features and more about familiarity given this is a newer mobile payment option that is still growing worldwide. Stores also need to be able to have NFC hardware. And, Android Pay can only be used by Android users.

Who it is for: For security reasons, use Android Pay if you are resolutely against Apple.

PayPal

Like Apple Pay and Android Pay, PayPal transactions are tokenized and encrypted, and merchants never see their customer's complete identity, personal information or financial data. If your phone has a fingerprint scanner, you can use that to authorize transactions. With more than 218 million worldwide accounts, this is a practical option for both business and consumers alike, however is more of a second-choice option based on the convenience of making mobile purchases at POS.

Where: Restricted to U.S. merchants now, particularly on the West Coast.

Pros: Secure and widely accepted in the U.S. You also have the option to make purchases at credit card terminals using your phone number and a PIN code.

Cons: Because it moved in early and missed some more recent technological innovations, PayPal has struggled to get merchants to sign on to its systems and is therefore likely to be eclipsed rapidly by Apple Pay. Like Google Wallet, you need cell service in order to use PayPal.

Who it is for: People who already have PayPal accounts and for whom adding another payment option is essentially costless.

Other Apps

The reality is that in most countries outside the major markets of North America, Europe and Asia, you will need to use a local smartphone app to make payments. I was able to do this with a locally-developed app in South Africa using my Apple iPhone. It allowed me to load a local prepaid debit card into the app, which may not always be an option in every country. In such cases, you might want to stick with cash until your U.S. bank issues you the improved chip-and-pin card sometime in the coming year.

Of course, if you have a bank account in a foreign country, it is much more likely you can probably use a compatible local app with their bank cards.

When using a foreign payment app, the key is to ensure that it uses tokenization to encrypt your card details. At the moment, the only sure way to know, (other than to research the app yourself), is to see whether it is compatible with all types of smartphones. If so, it's probably not secure. Token based apps only work with iPhone 6 and recent Android phones.

Our Choice: Apple Pay

It's significantly ahead of the competition and given the iPhone's wide and deep penetration in the U.S., U.K., Europe and Asia, it will inevitably set the standard for smartphone-based payment solutions in those areas, even for non-Apple services.

U.S. SEC Goes Offshore

One important consideration is an offshore bank's status in relation to U.S. Securities and Exchange Commission (SEC) compliance and registration.

In the UBS Swiss tax evasion bank scandal (2008-2010), the U.S. Internal Revenue Service played the major role in investigating and prosecuting U.S. account holders who evaded taxes. This notorious tax evasion aspect got most of the news media coverage.

Much less notice was given to the fact that the U.S. Department of Justice also charged that the services UBS rendered to U.S. clients amounted to the bank's staff acting as "unregistered investment advisers" and "broker-dealers" in violation of the U.S. Investment Advisers Act of 1940 and of SEC rules.

Using this then novel extraterritorial approach, the SEC sought to extend its jurisdiction to include any foreign bank or person anywhere in the world who dares to advise Americans about investments. The SEC claims that unless the adviser first qualifies and registers with that agency, then they are engaging in illegal, even criminal conduct, despite the obvious fact that such activities occur outside the United States.

In the final settlement, UBS paid US$718 million to the U.S. government based on complicity in U.S. tax evasion charges. But it also paid an additional US$200 million to the U.S. based on the SEC charges. UBS was also barred permanently from acting as investment advisers or broker-dealers for American clients in Switzerland. Since then, similar SEC charges have been aimed at Credit Suisse, HSBC and other banks.

In response to the successful U.S. government attacks and the fines levied against UBS, many offshore banks have established special, separate SEC-qualified investment banking units for American clients only. Some independent offshore investment advisers have also registered with the SEC.

That SEC registration means the offshore manager is qualified and understands relevant SEC rules and regulations. It also allows him to work with an American client in a fully U.S. compliant way. That includes the U.S. investor receiving on a regular basis all investment transaction documents, as well as U.S. tax statements needed for IRS filings, all provided directly on a timely basis from the offshore custodian bank where the client's investment funds are held. As part of your due diligence, always check to see if the offshore bank you are considering is SEC registered.

Major Change in Offshore Investment Management

It is no exaggeration to observe that today when it comes to banking or other offshore financial activity, Americans have been diminished as both current and potential clients in the eyes of many foreign financial institutions. For them, the U.S. government has converted U.S. persons into potentially troublesome and costly clients.

This is so especially because of the Foreign Account Tax Compliance Act (FATCA), a legislative monstrosity enacted in 2010 by a Democrat-controlled Congress and signed into law by President Obama.

Perhaps the most damaging and unfair of all FATCA consequences is the decision of untold numbers of foreign banks, financial institutions, professionals, insurance companies and investors to avoid doing business with Americans. In the wake of U.S. Department of Justice lawsuits against UBS, Credit Suisse and many other banks, understandably many offshore banks don't want to deal with the trouble, cost and the legal threat of even accidental non-compliance with the imperial edicts of FATCA and its IRS enforcers.

FATCA also seriously hurt one important group — expat Americans living and working offshore.

FATCA has made it difficult, if not impossible, for U.S. citizens living abroad to maintain existing bank accounts or open new accounts, both in the U.S. and in their countries of residence. These

Americans find it increasingly difficult to hold bank accounts, obtain mortgages, acquire insurance coverage, and live ordinary lives that were easily taken for granted. The reality is it is easier for foreign financial institutions subject to FATCA to drop their U.S. clients than deal with the IRS.

FATCA also impedes American companies and their employees that produce much needed foreign business and trade for the U.S. We know from experience with our European, Asian and Latin American banking partners that there is a continuing alarm and resentment for claiming that U.S. tax law now covers the world and that others must conform or else.

But that is the negative side of the offshore situation. The old and often true saying is that "out of every bad situation some good results."

That is exactly what has happened in the rise of the foreign independent asset manager (IAM) as a useful and profitable link in offshore banking.

In this streamlined system, your IAM acts as the intermediary with the offshore custodial bank you choose that holds your investment funds and, within parameters you dictate and control, the IAM manages your investments for maximum profit.

Even those offshore banks and financial institutions that are willing to work with American clients, for self-protection impose limitations. Some have declined to deal directly with U.S. persons as individuals but will accept accounts opened in the name of corporations, limited liability companies or trusts controlled by U.S. persons. Others have agreed to continue only as custodians of private investment or retirement account funds but have transferred management of the investments to independent investment managers.

Banyan Hill has been fortunate, drawing on our experience and professional contacts since our founding. We have created a network of offshore banks and investment associates willing to accept our members as their banking clients, especially those with private investment accounts, notwithstanding FATCA.

Independent Asset Managers

The role of offshore independent asset managers is not new but acting as the adviser and intermediary for American clients with offshore custodial banks is an expanded role that benefits those clients in many ways.

As we do here, Banyan Hill editors consistently have recommended that part of an individual's wealth and portfolio should be held offshore. An offshore bank account offers stronger asset protection than a domestic American account. The same rule applies to offshore account holders who live in any country.

But the other major plus of an offshore account is the direct path it offers for better, more profitable and more diverse investments.

Self-management by a foreigner to produce profits from an offshore account obviously requires intimate knowledge about procedures, fees and rules in many countries. An offshore investment account also requires constant supervision and instant information, almost forcing the individual investor to become almost a day trader.

This is where an IAM can make all the difference to your investment success.

In Switzerland alone, there are about 8,000 licensed IAMs that manage an estimated US$5.3 trillion. Other leading IAMs can be found in most major financial centers such as the City of London, Copenhagen, Gibraltar, Singapore, Hong Kong, Montreal, Montevideo and the Cayman Islands.

There are good reasons why some independent asset managers attract such large investment sums; they are good at what they do and provide a vital service. Those with experience know that it is to an investor's advantage to work through your own personal IAM, rather than trying to deal directly with an impersonal foreign bank and its possibly overburdened staff.

Based on our experience, here are six reasons that recommend an IAM for successful operation of an offshore investment account:

- Most IAMs run small operations that are flexible, tailoring investments to the individual client. They don't insist on the usual bank customer investment categories of aggressive, non-aggressive or conservative, but they do offer service to fit your specific goals. They limit the total number of clients to that which their staff can assist readily without undue delay.

- A good IAM builds a personal relationship, understanding at the beginning exactly what a client is seeking and accommodating those goals on a continuous basis with periodic updating sessions.

- Working with an IAM greatly simplifies your investment life. Your manager handles opening your account at one of the leading banks with which they work. A limited power of attorney enables the manager to work with the bank on your behalf as you direct. And the IAMs we recommend work with offshore banks that welcome Americans as desired clients.

- With an IAM you don't need to devote time to monitoring your portfolio on a daily basis. A good manager stays in regular contact with his client to build on their relationship, but that does not require constant contact.

- An offshore investment manager can free you from the drag of the U.S. dollar by choosing foreign investments that do not mirror domestic U.S. investments. The IAM will take advantage of the world of investments, many not immediately available to U.S. investors; that includes foreign stocks and bonds, national currencies, commodities and precious metals.

- Having an offshore bank account will enable you to invest in all the above (and more) using one single account. An IAM and his associated foreign bank acts as your stock broker and foreign currency, commodity and precious metals trader. The IAM can also convert a domestic 401(k) or other retirement account to a foreign custodian for greater asset protection.

Once you establish your bank account all orders go from you to your IAM, as your designated manager, and through him directly to the bank. The IAM communicates via digital electronic means with the custodian bank holding your funds for quick execution of your orders. A typical IAM fee charge is 1.5% for management. You can be certain the IAM shares your mutual goal of profitable investments.

Recommended Advisers:

SEC Registered

Robert Vrijhof, President
WHVP: Weber, Hartmann, Vrijhof & Partners Ltd.
Schaffhauserstrasse 418
CH-8050 Zürich, Switzerland
Contact: Julia Fernandez
Tel.: 01141 44 315 77 77 (USA/Canada) / +41 44 315 77 77 (International)
Email: info@whvp.ch
Web: http://www.whvp.ch
Custodial banks: WHVP is associated with a variety of Swiss and other foreign banks.

Eric N. Roseman, Founder, President & Chief Investment Officer
ENR Asset Management, Inc.
1 Westmount Square, Suite 1400
Westmount Quebec
H3Z 2P9 Canada
Tel.: 1-514-989-8027
Toll-free: 1-877-989-8027
Email: eric@enrasset.com
Web: www.enrassetmanagement.com
Custodial banks: Valartis Vienna, Jyske Bank Private Banking, Vontobel Private Banking Zurich, Royal Bank of Canada (RBC)

Thomas Fischer, Lead Investment Consultant
ENR Asset Management, Inc.

1 Westmount Square, Suite 1400
Westmount Quebec
H3Z 2P9 Canada
Tel.: 1-514-989-8027
Toll-free: 1-877-989-8027
Email: thomas@enrasset.com
Web: http://www.enrassetmanagement.com
Minimum Balance: $100,000

Daniel Zurbruegg, CFA, Managing Partner & Chief Executive
Officer
BFI Infinity Inc.
Bergstrasse 21
8044 Zürich, Switzerland
Tel.: + 41 58 806 2210
Email: daniel.zurbruegg@bfiwealth.com
Web: https://www.bfiwealth.com
Minimum Balance: US$250,000 or equivalent

Dominique J. Spillmann, CEO & Partner
Swisspartners Advisors Ltd.
Am Schanzengraben 23
CH-8022 Zürich, Switzerland
Tel.: +41 58 200 0 801
Email: dominique.spillmann@swisspartners-advisors.com
Web: http://swisspartners-advisors.com
Custodial banks: Bank Julius Bär, Credit Suisse, LGT
Liechtensteinische Landesbank, Pictet & Cie, Sarasin, UBS,
Zürcher Kantonalbank

Choosing and Opening Your Offshore Bank Account

Before you choose a bank, you must pick the offshore financial
center where your banking needs will best be met. On the following
pages, you will find information designed to help you make that
decision. Different strategies offer unique benefits and we will show
you what may work best to meet your specific needs.

But first, define your goals by asking yourself your true purposes for wanting an offshore bank account. Do you want expanded investment opportunities? Increased privacy? Do you need asset protection from potential claims and creditors? All these worthy objectives can be accomplished offshore.

Once you know your objectives, your next step is to learn all about offshore banks that will fulfill your specific needs. For each bank you must determine the services it can provide. Check its reputation, financial condition and all associated costs and fees.

In many countries, banking fees are rather expensive, far more than Americans are used to paying. Often, the net benefits of an offshore account are diminished by high fees. Be practical and run a mathematical model and find out what your net profit (or loss) might be, based on bank fees alone.

This is especially important for private investment accounts where not only set fees are charged but in some cases, percentage fees are levied. Few countries tax non-resident bank accounts per se, but some, like Switzerland, do collect withholding taxes on interest earnings. In the Swiss case, as with some other countries, these taxes may be credited against your U.S. tax liability under the existing double taxation treaties, but you must apply to the IRS for this credit. See https://www.irs.gov/individuals/international-taxpayers/foreign-tax-credit.

Maximum Privacy

If you want maximum privacy and strong protection from intrusive government officials, litigation and lawyers, avoid any offshore bank with established branches or subsidiaries located within your home country, especially if you live in the United States, its territories, possessions or dependencies.

American courts have been known to threaten to shut down or confiscate accounts in U.S. branches or subsidiaries when their offshore parent bank fails to comply with a U.S. court order, as in the UBS tax evasion scandal.

Offshore retail accounts are available in some offshore banks with which we work, even if you do not live or have a business there, but usually such accounts are allowed only for in-country foreigners who are residents or have a business.

On the other hand, if you're unconcerned about creditors or personal claims and you want ease and speed in setting up and managing an offshore account, head for the U.S. branch office of a foreign bank. You might pick a major American bank that has offices and subsidiaries overseas. This latter course allows you to use offshore bank outlets when you are abroad but realize that this option offers no asset protection and no real privacy. Unfortunately, American-based international banks such as JPMorgan Chase and Citibank — both bailed out with billions from U.S. taxpayers — are hardly in the best of health.

A more convenient and more private course of action is to obtain a Barclays, Visa, MasterCard, or other international credit card issued by your offshore bank. While offshore cards are more expensive than their U.S. equivalents, the offshore bank can deduct your monthly charges from your account balance. This means you earn money offshore, incur bills offshore, make deposits into and pay with your offshore account, all outside your home country. As with offshore checks, never use that offshore credit card in your home country. Do that and your financial privacy is reduced, and the cost is prohibitive.

We now know that the U.S. National Security Agency (NSA) is spying on all our phone calls, emails and other financial information using its clandestine surveillance program, PRISM, and that FATCA requires offshore banks to report on Americans' accounts. The advice here, if followed carefully, offers some added privacy, but, in fact, financial privacy is non-existent if you become a target of the government.

Tips:

1. Never use your offshore account as a checking account for payment of home country bills. Bank fees for international check

payments are costly and, what's worse, this creates recorded links that undermine the advantages of financial privacy.

2. Under no circumstances should you attempt to hide in your offshore bank account reportable income that is taxable in your home nation.

3. Never use an offshore bank credit or ATM card as an unreported piggy bank to conceal income or personal expenses. That sort of illegal activity is tax evasion and can land you in jail. As part of their decade-long continuing campaign, the IRS has a vigorous aversion to tax cheats who use offshore credit and ATM cards to hide income.

Once you have decided which offshore financial institution is best for you, the next step is to open the account.

Opening Your Account

Except for the geography involved, opening an offshore bank account differs little from starting a domestic, home country account. As would your local domestic banker, offshore bankers want to see you in person when your relationship begins.

Just as you need to do due diligence on your offshore bank, the due diligence that banks are required to conduct on potential clients has increased greatly under "know your customer" rules now in effect worldwide.

When you apply to open an offshore bank account you will be asked to provide some or all the following:

• A notarized copy of your passport. You may also be asked to provide a notarized copy of your birth certificate or driver's license. For the U.S. State Department procedure on how to obtain a notarized passport, see https://travel.state.gov/content/travel/en/passports.html.

• A recent utility bill or equivalent document which confirms the details of your permanent home address. Make sure the bill you present is no older than three months.

- A bank reference letter on your domestic bank's letterhead, or on a form provided by the offshore bank. Your domestic bank manager must sign this letter or form stating you are a reliable customer. Most offshore private banks prefer that this reference come from a bank with which you have had at least a two-year relationship.

- A professional letter of reference from a doctor, lawyer, or accountant in your country of residence.

- A letter describing the specific source of funds you will deposit initially and your subsequent projected banking patterns. The bank will use this "profile" information to review your account activity and to determine if there is suspicious or unusual behavior that the bank must investigate.

A required minimum deposit varies with each institution and/or with type of account. The minimum preferred starting point for most offshore private investment bank accounts is US$1 million for full investment services. ENR Asset Management in Montreal, Canada, one of our recommended independent asset managers, accepts accounts for as low as US$100,000. See http://www.enrasset.com.

Retail accounts, where available offshore usually require a US$5,000 initial deposit. In some jurisdictions, such as Panama, it is traditional that a local professional must introduce a foreigner seeking a bank account. Our Panama associate, attorney Rainelda Mata Kelly, provides this service. See http://www.mata-kelly.com.

Almost all offshore banks now require that U.S. clients complete an IRS Form W-9 before they will agree to open your account. (Request for Taxpayer Identification Number and Certification: https://www.irs.gov/forms-pubs/about-form-w9.) The form allows the bank to share information with the IRS and, in some cases, acts as a waiver of the foreign country's bank secrecy laws. This form is used by a U.S. person (including a resident alien) to give their correct U.S. Taxpayer Identification Number (TIN) and to certify the TIN is correct.

10 Questions to Ask an Offshore Bank

1. What types of accounts are available to international investors?

2. Are there any restrictions on foreigners' investments, specifically on U.S. account holders?

3. What taxes, if any, will be withheld from my investment income?

4. What investments are considered part of the bank's balance sheet and available to the bank's creditors (including depositors) in the event of bank insolvency?

5. What are the fees for securities transactions and custody?

6. What other fees may apply to the account?

7. Is my account insured by law or otherwise against loss in the event of the bank's insolvency?

8. How do I transact business and with whom, and are telephone, fax, or email orders accepted?

9. Is Internet banking available and secure? If so, is this service available in English?

10. Does the bank send U.S. clients a year-end statement showing any taxable interest paid?

As we advised earlier, employing an independent asset manager is the best course to follow in opening or managing an offshore investment account. If you handle your account yourself, one-on-one banking contact should be reciprocal. When you establish your account, immediately get to know personally your contact at the bank. That person should speak your language, understand your business and be totally reliable. Always have a "back-up" contact at the bank who knows who you are, in case your usual representative is unavailable.

While selecting an offshore bank may sound exotic or even difficult, it is not that different from choosing a local domestic bank. It's important to examine closely the bank's reputation and financial condition, and to ask the right questions. What kind of fees does it require? What services does the bank provide? How much does a service cost?

But with offshore banking there is one critical extra step. Obviously, you must ensure the bank welcomes foreigners, especially those with U.S. passports. And you want to be sure they understand FATCA and IRS tax reporting requirements.

Offshore banking can be expensive, so it is important to be sure you fully understand a bank's fee structure. Make sure to crunch the numbers to find out what your net profit (or loss) might be. And once you choose a potential offshore bank, get these questions answered before you transfer the first penny.

Be sure you invest the time up front to check the bank's financial standing and perform your due diligence. This is not always an easy task. If you aren't sure where to start, first check out the bank's website to find their annual report or request a copy from the bank.

However, all the due diligence can't replace a personal visit. We recommend at least one face-to-face meeting at the bank when you open the account (often this is required by the bank) and a return visit at least every two years.

Bank Due Diligence

U.S. laws force banks and financial institutions licensed to do business in the U.S. to disclose information about transactions in other branches even if their home office is in another country. Most developed nations have similar laws.

A bank's failure to disclose information can mean the bank and its officers may be held in contempt of court, fined and/or its managers imprisoned. Indeed, U.S. courts have imposed sanctions on the American branches of a foreign bank, even when refusal is based upon a foreign court order or law that forbids production of the requested data.

The former Thomson/Polk *World Bank Directory* and the *Bankers Almanac* have now been replaced by the online services of Acuity at https://accuity.com. This is a paid service and it lists all banks worldwide, with a free listing of 50 major banks status at https://accuity.com/resources/bank-rankings. See also the website of *Banks Around the World* at https://www.relbanks.com/worlds-top-banks/market-cap. This website lists information on the world's largest banks.

You can also consult a reliable local foreign in-country professional with whom you have an established relationship. They are a valuable resource for banking advice and contacts.

Out in the Open

Here's a tip that may help you avoid unwanted scrutiny while accomplishing your offshore financial goals in relative privacy and peace.

Let's be honest: many offshore jurisdictions known for no-tax, privacy and anti-creditor banking laws are also prime suspects for certain dubious financial activities. When your name appears on a bank account in places such as The Bahamas or the Cayman Islands, it immediately raises red flags for suspicious U.S. government agents. (But then, so does the name of any tax haven.)

If privacy is your paramount goal, you do not need to use your own name when opening an offshore account. Instead, create a trust, family foundation, limited liability company or corporation under your direct or indirect control and open the account in its name. Many offshore banks now require American clients to have their accounts in the name of a legal entity. Even though this usually is not always a matter of public record, all offshore banks require full disclosure of all beneficial owners of legal entities that open accounts and this information may be shared with your home government.

Another way to obtain banking privacy is to "get lost in a crowd." You can establish your offshore account in a major banking nation where privacy is better protected than in the U.S.

A good choice might be the United Kingdom or Switzerland where there are respected private investment banks. But accept the fact that IRS agents are suspicious of accounts held in any offshore financial institution.

You might choose a country where you have family ties, or one with an active international financial role, such as Hong Kong, Singapore, Ireland or Austria. In London, Vienna or Dublin, your bank dealings will not be deemed especially noteworthy, since thousands of Americans hold accounts in these places. If you create your own "privacy haven" out in the open, instead of going to a small bank in some exotic, far-flung locale, your money, and your privacy, usually will be somewhat more secure.

Absolute Bank Secrecy — A Myth

Let us make clear that banking secrecy and financial privacy does exist in many reputable offshore financial centers.

Offshore financial centers such as Switzerland, Panama, Uruguay, Singapore, the Cook Islands and Monaco officially impose banking privacy by law, waiving this protection only in criminal situations, usually only under court order.

Unlike the U.S., where bank employees are by law surrogate government spies, many offshore nations impose fines and prison sentences on bank employees for the unauthorized violation of the privacy of account holders. A former employee of Bank Julius Baer is now serving time in a Swiss prison for just such a violation and ex-employees of Liechtenstein Landesbank and HSBC Switzerland are on the Interpol international most wanted list for secrecy violations.

But let's put one notion to rest right now — there is no such thing as a totally "secret" bank account anywhere in the world. And yes, there still are "numbered accounts" but not in the sense that the phrase used to designate an account with no name on it.

Even in nations with the strongest bank privacy laws, such as Switzerland or Austria, a bank account holder's true name is on record somewhere in an institution's files. Even if the account is in a corporate name, or the name of a trust or other legal entity, there's always a paper (or computer) trail to be traced to the beneficial owner, especially if government agents want to know about alleged criminals and their finances.

Automatic Tax Information Exchange

All major nations, especially offshore banking jurisdictions, now have in force numerous tax information exchange agreements (TIEAs) with the United States and with other nations. These agreements originally allowed each jurisdiction to share tax information with the U.S. or other governments upon a showing of probable cause that a tax violation may have occurred in the case of an account holder who is a citizen or resident of the requesting country.

This TIEA policy became well established internationally. See https://www.treasury.gov/resource-center/tax-policy/treaties/Pages/treaties.aspx. The OECD announced that as of August 2017, there were over 2000 bilateral tax information exchange relationships activated by more than 70 jurisdictions, with first exchanges scheduled to take place in September 2017.

Beginning in 2009, a major abandonment of offshore banking privacy policies occurred under a coordinated threat of "blacklisting" from major nations aimed especially as tax havens. Deserting decades of strict bank secrecy guaranteed by law, almost all offshore financial centers accepted foreign tax evasion or tax fraud as a valid basis for responding to foreign tax agency inquiries concerning foreign citizens with accounts in the OFC. Indeed, agreement to this procedure now has become a test of an OFC's good standing.

The standard for information exchange was first set by the Organization for Economic Cooperation and Development (OECD), based on Article 26 of the "OECD Model Tax Convention."

Under this OECD procedure as originally applied, foreign tax authorities wishing to take advantage of tax information exchange agreements needed to supply evidence of tax evasion (names, facts, alleged tax crimes) to the requested government. Supposedly, "fishing expeditions" were not allowed. In the absence of sufficient probable cause, the request could be denied by the foreign government, but each government varied in its policies on what constitutes probable cause. This allowed each country to apply its own rules as to whether tax information would be exchanged and on what evidence. At the time, Switzerland especially insisted it would defend its 1934 Bank Secrecy law.

That principle of each country applying its own rules was soon abandoned. The major G20 countries, in concert with the OECD, adopted what was billed as "automatic exchange" of financial information. Their motto can be summarized as: "If we ask, you tell."

By 2018, the OECD goal was the adoption by all countries of a pending multi-national treaty to fight alleged tax evasion. It mandates that upon an official request from another country, without a showing of probable cause, governments must provide information about any individual's accounts. As of January 2018, 117 countries had endorsed this "common reporting standard" pact, although implementation requires each country to approve domestic application. See http://www.oecd.org/ctp/exchange-of-tax-information/Status_ of_convention.pdf.

To say the least, this new international system amounts to another brutal nail in the coffin of financial privacy. It certainly can, and no doubt, will be used by the IRS and other tax collectors for fishing expeditions, since no probable cause supporting a charge of tax evasion will be required — only a name or even just an account number.

What is so disturbing about the purported Common Reporting Standard is its corruption of legal principles which have been at the center of constitutional and limited government. It is demanded that the domestic laws of every country on Earth should be made to conform to the edicts of a group of anonymous unaccountable bureaucrats and that ancient rights and liberties should give way to the demands of the OECD and its sponsoring bureaucrats from various national treasuries.

— *Terry Dwyer, Dwyer Lawyers, Canberra, Australia.*

In a highly suspect statement in 2015, the Swiss Bankers Association claimed that under the latest OECD standard described above: "Bank-client confidentiality will not disappear, but it is undergoing far reaching-changes, particularly in tax-related issues."

But as difficult as it may be to believe, some OFCs still do enforce tough privacy standards to protect financial confidentiality, so all is not lost. We explain this in the individual country sections.

The Imperial U.S. "External" Revenue Service

The Roman Empire's history of conquest for those countries and peoples who were conquered brought centralized control, the suppression of local laws, the imposition of a unified system of rules and general enslavement.

The question is whether the U.S. Internal Revenue Service adopted the Imperial Romans as their model, and especially, as the inspiration for the Foreign Account Tax Compliance Act (FATCA).

FATCA is a U.S. law that attempts to order all offshore banks and other foreign financial institutions to report directly to the IRS information about financial accounts held by U.S. taxpayers, or by trusts, corporations or other legal entities that have substantial U.S. ownership. Failure to follow FATCA reporting rules can impose a 30% tax, payable by non-compliant foreign banks on all their U.S.-based transactions, ultimately imposed as a cost to the U.S. account holder.

It is no secret that offshore banks were furious at being deputized as IRS agents. But if they refused to comply, the banks faced a choice of paying that punitive 30% withholding tax, or withdrawing completely from lucrative U.S. financial markets. The reaction of most foreign banks was summed up in a document title from a client of a leading Luxembourg bank: "FATCA: Turning U.S. persons into toxic liabilities."

This unprecedented American law, adopted by the U.S. Congress with little public notice or debate, follows the Imperial Roman model. It assumes that the jurisdiction of the U.S. government now extends to every bank and financial institution in the entire world. It also assumes that U.S. tax and reporting laws supersede the laws of every other nation, whether those countries like it or not.

FATCA is billed as an effort by a tax-hungry Obama administration to combat alleged rampant tax evasion by U.S. persons holding cash or investments in offshore financial accounts. In recent years, IRS Commissioners have engaged in a game of wild numbers, alleging that the U.S. government was losing annually, due to offshore tax evasion, from US$447 million to US$40 billion. They claimed also that offshore evaders number 82,000 or 505,000 or 2 million. The numbers changed with each IRS press release.

Their chosen solution was FATCA, which assumes that all U.S. persons with offshore financial accounts probably are engaged in tax evasion or other illegal conduct.

As we have noted, unlike most other countries, the U.S. government does not have a reasonable territorial tax system that ends at its borders. Americans are taxed on all their worldwide income without regard to where the individual lives or the sources of the income.

For many years, U.S. taxpayers with financial assets outside the United States have been required by law to report those assets to the IRS and to pay any taxes due — and most do so.

As successive big spending, budget deficit governments of both political parties have come and gone in Washington, D.C., politicians frantically have searched for more revenue. To finance their profligate tax-and-spend policies, they operate under the false assumption that every American engaged in offshore banking or investing probably is engaged in tax evasion. Most of a left biased news media buys this lie without question.

FATCA Basics

The Foreign Account Tax Compliance Act (FATCA) is a law, passed by Congress in 2009, that applies to all "U.S. Persons" with accounts at foreign banks and other financial institutions outside the U.S.

"U.S. Person" is government-speak for all U.S. citizens and green card holders. It also includes U.S.-based or controlled entities, such as corporations, partnerships, limited liability companies and trusts. And it applies to the estimated 8 million or more U.S. expat and dual citizens living abroad permanently, many of whom have had foreign bank accounts for years.

While FATCA is aimed specifically at Americans with bank accounts abroad, its reporting process is imposed on foreign financial institutions (FFIs) which include overseas banks, mutual funds, hedge funds, private equity funds and insurance and annuity companies.

The purpose of FATCA is to force FFIs to report the account numbers, balances, names, addresses and taxpayer identification numbers of all their U.S. person clients each year. To the IRS it makes no difference whether the FFIs don't want to do this, or even if it violates their own country's financial privacy laws.

FATCA doesn't mean that you're going to have to pay a 30% tax on any money you send offshore. That's a rumor based on a misreading of one of FATCA's enforcement techniques, which we'll explain. The point is that if you have a foreign bank account and your bank doesn't comply with the rules of FATCA, all the bank's transactions with U.S. parties can be subject to a 30% "withholding tax."

To enforce FATCA, the Obama administration invented "inter-governmental agreements" (IGAs), a treaty-like contract that the IRS claims needs no U.S. Senate approval, as treaties do. IGAs were concluded with scores of countries. Most of IGAs require foreign governments to collect information from their own banks and pass it on to the IRS. Only two countries, Japan and Switzerland, have signed agreements allowing their banks to report information directly to the IRS. See https://www.treasury.gov/resource-center/tax-policy/treaties/Pages/FATCA-Archive.aspx.

A little-known fact is that in concluding these agreements, the Obama officials promised foreign governments the U.S. government would reciprocate by providing tax information on the other country's citizens' accounts in the United States. As critics have noted, not only is there no legal authority for the U.S. government to provide such information to a foreign government, indeed there are existing legal prohibitions on such actions.

Forbes magazine reported in late 2017 that "… FATCA has been painstakingly implemented worldwide by President Obama's Treasury Department. It now spans the globe with an unparalleled network of reporting." There have been repeated calls by his supporters for President Trump to include repeal of FATCA as part of his tax reforms.

What You Need to Know

People rightly have been up in arms about FATCA and there's a lot of misinformation about it. The truth is that for most individuals, FATCA isn't really a significant additional reporting burden, compared with what's already required by law.

FATCA gathers information from the foreign banks and other FFIs in which you hold your cash and investments, but this law does impose some new reporting requirements on Americans with overseas accounts. Those covered by the law's income and asset provisions must submit, along with the annual IRS Form 1040, an IRS Form 8938 giving offshore details. That's in addition to the other reports already required concerning offshore accounts and assets which we describe at the end of this chapter.

Using FATCA, the U.S. government has forced many countries to waive or change their financial privacy laws to allow their banks to report on U.S. clients. So that they need not deal directly with the IRS, these agreements permit the foreign FFIs to report information on U.S. clients to their own national government tax collectors, which in turn relay it to the IRS. The IRS has established an International Data Exchange Service (IDES) as an electronic delivery point where FFIs and foreign country tax authorities can transmit and exchange FATCA data with the United States.

Nonetheless, if you're above board and not trying to hide anything from the IRS, your worries should be minimal, except meeting reporting requirement.

Expat Americans Suffer

FATCA presents a special problem for millions of Americans who live and work offshore, each of whom suddenly is confronted with an obligation to file all sorts of new reports which carry penalties and possible criminal indictments. Many have had established foreign bank accounts closed and been refused new ones as offshore banks have opted to stay out of this FATCA mess.

Strategy 2: The Offshore Asset Protection Trust (APT)

When it comes to protecting your assets, we'll paraphrase that old American TV show, *Gun Smoke*: "Get your assets the Hell out of Dodge." Here that means move your assets to a safe place outside the immediate jurisdiction of the U.S. government and its courts.

Frivolous litigation, expensive legal defense costs, outrageous jury awards and government privacy invasions all combine to create an urgent need to protect your family and business wealth and your privacy as well.

The United States is, far and away, the world's most litigious society. At the last count, there were more than 317 million Americans, of whom well over a million are lawyers. No other nation on earth has so many lawyers.

According to the American Bar Association, the number of U.S. lawyers increased by 300% to 1.2 million from the early 1970s to 2013. And most of those lawyers file lawsuits — about 17 million civil cases were filed in state and federal courts over the last three years.

Comparisons with other countries are telling: America now has some 361 lawyers for every 100,000 people, compared with 94 per 100,000 in the U.K., 33 per 100,000 in France and just seven per 100,000 in Japan.

In 2016, the Association of Trial Lawyers of America estimated that the total cost of civil lawsuits to the American economy at no less than $239 billion annually. That's an individual cost of $812 for every person in the country.

Consider this: Lawsuits are not filed against the poor or those with few assets; they are filed against those with "deep pockets."

But asset protection is not a necessity only for the wealthy. Working-class people with a nice home and a couple of cars are also at risk of being sued. Certain professionals — lawyers, doctors, architects and engineers — who are well-off, but far from rich, are at a higher risk, simply by the nature of their work. Let's face it, we all are targets.

You could be sued as the result of medical bills or a car accident, or so-called social-host liability, which means you could be liable if you have a party, serve alcohol, and a guest causes an accident or injury after leaving. If your business partner or employee gets in an accident, you could also be sued. And children who inherit money from parents or grandparents can also become targets for lawsuits.

A Good Solution

The offshore asset protection trust (APT) is a good solution — a legal device that shields your wealth from lawsuits, creditors, an irate ex-spouse and even the government of your home country. One of the very best methods for asset protection is to create an APT located in an offshore haven jurisdiction.

Many offshore financial centers specialize in trust creation, including Bermuda, the Isle of Man, the Channel Islands of Jersey and Guernsey, Singapore, Hong Kong and Panama.

But we recommend the Cook Islands. Here's why.

After years of direct experience with trusts and numerous trust providers in many jurisdictions, we have found the Cook Islands the best for asset protection trusts.

The Cook Islands is the home to a very modern code of offshore financial laws that provide for iron-clad asset protection and easy global banking and investing.

The islands, unlike the U.S., also enjoy very strict financial privacy laws that really do protect your personal business. The savviest individuals choose to create foreign-asset protection trusts in offshore financial centers such as the Cook Islands, because the added distance and the strict privacy laws of the land protect trust assets from claimants. Locating the trust in the Cook Islands places your assets virtually beyond the jurisdiction of the U.S. government and American courts.

The Cook Islands, although an independent country, exist in association with the government of New Zealand. The 17,390 islanders (according to the 2017 count) enjoy dual New Zealand and Cook Islands citizenship.

The Cook Islands' offshore finance regime was created by a series of legislative enactments starting in 1981. The parliament established a modern code of trusts, international companies, and limited liability partnerships, global banking, insurance and registered trustee companies — all of them covered by one of the world's strictest financial privacy laws.

This package of modern laws grew from the concept that the islands could be fashioned into an offshore financial center — and indeed they have been.

The trust business has been a major boost to the Cook Islands economy. There is a stable government and a sophisticated judiciary based on English common law with 30 years of respected case law. Cash and investment accounts, along with real estate and businesses, are typically held in the trusts, but associated trust bank accounts can be located anywhere.

None of the trust-held assets are required to be physically located in the islands and international trust business and meetings can be conducted electronically. However, titling U.S.-located real estate in an offshore trust offers little protection, because the property remains within the jurisdiction of American courts.

Low Cost

Traditionally, the cost of creating a highly complex asset protection trust in a foreign nation has exceeded US$15,000, plus several thousand dollars in annual maintenance fees. Unless the total assets to be shielded justify such costs, a foreign APT may not be practical for you.

A few years ago, a major business magazine estimated that "as a rule of thumb you should have a net worth of around US$500,000" or more to justify a foreign asset protection trust. The magazine cited expert's fees for establishing and administering such trusts running as high as US$50,000, with some demanding a percentage of the total value of assets to be transferred.

While high costs once may have been the old rule, APT costs have changed for the better. These days, offshore trusts are not just for the super-rich. Complicated trusts with many beneficiaries can cost huge amounts, but a basic Cook Islands trust, including all fees, typically costs $10,000 or more. And forget about slick promises to create a reliable trust for a few hundred dollars by filling in the blanks of some preexisting form. That guarantees disaster.

For information about Cook Islands trusts contact:

Josh N. Bennett, Esq., P.A.
440 North Andrews Avenue
Fort Lauderdale, FL 33301
Tel.: 954-779-1661
Mobile: 786-202-5674
Email: josh@joshbennett.com
Web: http://www.joshbennett.com

Puai T. Wichman, Esq., LL.B., Managing Director
Ora Fiduciary (Cook Islands) Limited
Global House, P.O. Box 92
Avarua, Rarotonga, Cook Islands
Tel.: +682 27047
USA Direct Tel.: 734-402-7047
Mobile: +682 55418
Email: puai@oratrust.com or info@oratrust.com
Web: https://www.oratrust.com

What is a Trust?

A trust is one of the most flexible, yet efficient, legal mechanisms recognized by law.

Even though the concept of a trust goes back centuries in legal history, using the offshore trust format to protect assets has gained much popularity in recent decades. A trust is highly flexible in operation. Serving as an international investment platform, it can increase wealth many times over.

A trust is a formal legal arrangement voluntarily created and funded by a person (the grantor) that directs another person (the trustee) to take legal title and control of the grantor's donated property, to be used and managed for the benefit of one or more other persons the grantor designates (the beneficiaries).

The beneficiary receives income or distributions of assets from the trust and has an enforceable equitable title to the benefits, but does not control trust assets or manage trust operation. An offshore asset protection trust may also include another party to trust operation, the protector, a person vested with certain powers to monitor the performance of the trustee.

The creation of a trust arrangement is a planned, intentional act.

A trust can serve a specific purpose or be part of a general estate plan. The trust grantor signs a written declaration describing his or her intentions, stating specific details of proposed trust operation, income distribution and the extent and limits of trustee powers. A well-drafted trust document will reflect the grantor's precise intentions.

Drafting a trust declaration as part of an overall estate plan requires expert advice based on a thorough examination of all existing arrangements that affect the grantor's estate. To create a proper estate plan, the status of all other legal documents or devices, such as a will, or jointly owned assets, must be reviewed and coordinated with the trust. Conflicts must be resolved consistent with all applicable trust and tax laws. However, a targeted trust may be drafted only to accomplish limited or even single goals, such as asset protection.

Most offshore asset protection trusts are drafted as "discretionary" trusts, a form that allows greater planning flexibility. This means the trustee is given the power to decide how much will be distributed to beneficiaries and, in some cases, who qualifies as a beneficiary.

The trust declaration may vest a trustee with the right to make payments for purposes, at times and in amounts, the trustee decides. A trustee often is given the authority to recognize beneficiaries within named classes of persons ("my children and their heirs"), or the trust may contain a right known as a "power of appointment" allowing the trustee to choose beneficiaries from a class of eligible persons.

What a Trust Can Do

Despite the onslaught of negative press, a trust can be created for nearly any legal purpose. It can be used to hold a property title or invest in things such as stocks, bonds, real estate and negotiable instruments. Trusts can be created to provide for a minor or the elderly. They can be used to expenses such as medical or educational. Financial support can be set up with a trust for retirement, marriage, divorce or even hold premarital arrangements.

While a trust may appear complicated, it is actually one of the most flexible and efficient legal instruments. In comparison to a variety of other structures, a trust can give excellent asset protection.

The APT

In recent decades, asset protection using the trust format has gained wide popularity among people of wealth who are "in the know."

The foreign asset protection trust (APT) is any trust that helps individuals protect assets from attack by creditors. It is established in an offshore jurisdiction by a grantor resident in one nation under the laws of another nation where the trust operations are based and where trust laws offer greater protection.

Because the trust is governed by the laws of the nation where it is registered and administered, this "foreignness" serves as a shield for the grantor's business and personal assets, deflecting would-be creditors, litigation and potential financial liabilities, perhaps even an ex-spouse bent on revenge.

Here are a few reasons why an offshore APT can be so effective:

Judicial Defenses: In many cases, the courts of asset protection countries often will not recognize automatically the validity of U.S. (or other nations') domestic court orders. A foreign judgment creditor seeking collection against a trust must relitigate the original claim in the foreign court after hiring local lawyers. He may have to post a bond and pay legal expenses for all parties if he loses. The legal complexity and cost of such an international collection effort is likely to stop all but the most determined adversaries or, at the very least, to promote compromise.

Minimal Needs: An offshore APT need not be complex. Creation can be little more than the signing of formal documents and opening a trust account managed by your local trustee in a bank in the foreign country of your choice. Respected offshore multi-national and local banks routinely provide experienced trust officers and staff to handle trust matters. Most international banks offer U.S. dollar or other currency denominated accounts, sometimes offering better interest rates than U.S. financial institutions.

Greater Protection: Under the laws of haven nations, assets placed in an offshore asset protection trust have far more protection than permitted under domestic U.S. trust law. The trust law in these countries is drafted specifically to provide an asset protection "safe harbor" that is unavailable in the U.S. and many other nations. With an offshore APT, foreign-held trust asset are not subject to the jurisdiction of your local or home country judicial system.

Fast Acting: Time under the statute of limitations for initiating a foreign creditor's suit varies. In many jurisdictions, the statute begins to run from the date the APT was established. Some haven nations, such as the Cook Islands, have a limit of one year for the initiation of claims. As a practical matter, it may take a creditor longer than that just to discover the existence of a foreign APT to which most assets have long since been transferred.

Better Investments: An offshore APT is an excellent platform for diversifying investments and benefiting from global tax savings. An APT allows taking advantage of the world's best investment opportunities, without being blocked by your home nation's legal restrictions on foreign investments. An offshore APT can also purchase attractive insurance and annuity products not available in the U.S. and some other nations. Tax savings may result from deferred investment earnings or capital gains, rather than ordinary income that will not only be taxed immediately but at a higher rate.

Confidentiality: The APT can provide greater privacy and confidentiality, minimization of home country inheritance taxes and the avoidance of the probate process in case of death. It provides increased flexibility in conducting affairs in case of personal disability, allows easy transfer of asset titles and avoids domestic currency controls in your home nation. An APT is also a good substitute for, or supplement to, costly professional liability insurance or even a prenuptial agreement, offering strong protection for your heirs' inheritance.

Estate Planning: An offshore APT can serve the same traditional estate planning goals achieved by U.S. domestic strategies. These include using bypass trust provisions to minimize estate taxes for a husband and wife, trusts that allow maximum use of gift tax exemptions through planned giving and trusts that provide for maintenance and tax-free income for a surviving spouse.

Asset Transfer

As a practical matter, regardless of the time of APT creation, any assets physically remaining within your home country and its courts' jurisdiction generally are not protected from domestic judgment creditors.

Simply placing title to domestic property in the name of a foreign trust is paper-thin protection at best unless the property is moved offshore. When tangible assets are transferred to the foreign jurisdiction, as when funds, stock shares, precious metals or other tangible property are moved to an offshore trust account or the trustee's safe deposit box or vault, a home country creditor will have great difficulty in reaching them, provided he even discovers the existence of the trust.

As a mandatory precaution, the APT and its trustee should always employ an offshore bank that is not a branch or affiliate of any bank within your home country. This helps insulate the offshore bank officials (and APT accounts) from foreign official or private pressure.

It gives greater legitimate protection from home country pressures or just informational snooping — whether government or otherwise.

But consider this: even with this enhanced offshore financial privacy, in some situations there can be great tactical advantage in letting a harassing party know your assets are securely placed well beyond their reach. The cost and difficulty of pursuit may well discourage any action on their part or result in a compromise.

Strategy 3: Earn US$104,100 a Year — U.S. Tax-Free

If you decide personally to follow your cash, assets and investments and make your home offshore yourself, there's a very useful provision of U.S. tax law about which you should know.

As we have noted, Americans and citizens of other nations move offshore for many reasons, to find a new or second home, to seek lower taxes, greater asset protection and more financial and personal privacy.

But there is another group of international migrants, many of them educated and professional Americans who "go offshore" to find not only a better job, but to enjoy a major tax break that U.S. law grants to those who qualify — it's called the "foreign earned income exclusion."

If you are considering moving yourself or your family to a foreign country, or if you have an offer of employment abroad, here is a definite plus that may help you decide.

A few years ago, *The New York Times* reported on a Louisiana professor with a PhD in economics who, despite being tenured at his prestigious Virginia University, left to teach at the American University in Dubai in the United Arab Emirates. Helping to tip the scales in favor of Dubai included great schools for his children, inexpensive house help, and two top-of-the-line luxury import autos he purchased, all without having to pay U.S. income tax.

The very important tax break for which the professor qualified is known as the "foreign earned income exclusion."

The U.S. Internal Revenue Code, supported by a Supreme Court decision from the 1920s, requires that U.S. citizens must pay tax on their worldwide income, no matter where they live and work. Most other countries allow their citizens who live abroad to avoid domestic taxes — but not the United States.

This foreign earned income exclusion is a legal tax break that allows a U.S. citizen who lives and works outside the U.S. to earn tax free up to a maximum of US$104,100 of foreign earned income. The stated amount is for 2018 and is adjusted annually for inflation.

If both a husband and wife work offshore, it's possible that they could earn US$208,200 tax free annually offshore, plus lower taxed housing allowances for which an offshore employer pays.

This is not a tax deduction, credit, or deferral. It's an outright exclusion of offshore earnings when calculating gross taxable income. Those who qualify pay no U.S. income tax on that excluded amount.

Qualifications

To qualify for these benefits, you must: 1) establish a "tax home" in a foreign country; 2) pass either the "foreign residence test," or the "physical presence test"; 3) have earned income; 4) live in the U.S. for no more than one month during the year, and; 5) file a U.S. income tax return for each year you live abroad claiming the exclusion.

Usually your "tax home" is where your principal place of business is located, not where you live. The term "tax home" is broader when determining eligibility for the foreign earned income exclusion. Confusion over this point stings many Americans overseas. If you work overseas and still maintain a U.S. residence, your tax home remains in the U.S.

To qualify for the foreign earned income exclusion, you must establish both your principal place of business and your actual residence outside the United States. A complicated test that determines if you get this exclusion involves counting the maximum number of days you're in or out of the U.S.A.

But the foreign residence test is easier for most taxpayers to pass. You must establish yourself as a bona fide resident of a foreign country for an uninterrupted period that includes an entire taxable year; and you must intend to stay there indefinitely. If you don't pass this test, you're considered a transient and won't qualify.

U.S. tax law defines your residence as a state of mind. It's where you intend to be domiciled indefinitely. To determine your state of mind, the IRS looks at the degree of your attachment to the country in question. Several factors, none of them decisive are examined.

Your "tax home" is the location of your regular or principal place of business, not where you live. But the definition of "tax home" is broader when determining eligibility for the foreign earned income exclusion.

Confusion over this point snags many Americans overseas who think they are earning tax-free income. If you work overseas and maintain a U.S. residence, your tax home is not outside the U.S. In other words, to qualify for the foreign earned income exclusion, you must establish both your principal place of business and your residence outside the United States.

The bottom line is that you must establish yourself clearly as a member of a foreign community. This unusual tax break is only for those who do live and earn offshore.

But consider this: suppose you base a legitimate business in an offshore tax haven such as Panama, where a territorial tax system only collects taxes on earnings from within Panama, but not from earnings outside the country. And suppose the bulk of the income comes from worldwide sources, say, for consulting or professional advice. You could cut your U.S. ties, move to Panama and charter a Panama corporation (SA) for your business. You could then pay yourself (and perhaps your spouse or significant other) a salary for services rendered, plus housing and other expenses.

Such an arrangement would have to be carefully planned with the advice of an expert U.S. tax attorney so that all requirements of the foreign earned income exclusion tests are met, and you are certain to qualify.

This is something to factor into your planning if living and working offshore beckons you.

For U.S. tax advice:

Josh N. Bennett, Esq., P.A.
440 North Andrews Avenue
Fort Lauderdale, FL 33301
Tel.: 954-779-1661
Mobile: 786-202-5674
Email: josh@joshbennett.com
Web: http://www.joshbennett.com

Strategy 4: Offshore Variable Annuities

Even though the U.S., the United Kingdom and the European Union continue to tighten the tax and financial reporting screws on wealth, there still remain private and profitable, yet strictly legal ways to protect and invest assets.

One of best of these is the offshore variable annuity because it allows you to avoid paying taxes until you withdraw funds. According to *The Wall Street Journal,* "Offshore annuities are becoming an investment vehicle of choice for those who have oodles of money they want to shelter from taxes."

This is also one of the easiest, least expensive methods to invest in offshore stocks and other funds. Another advantage is that annuity investments can be transferred from one fund manager to another with no immediate tax consequences. Plus, you achieve significant asset protection.

Annuities work very well for your children or grandchildren, because the earnings accumulated within the policy are tax-deferred until funds are paid out or withdrawn many years later when they are ready for retirement.

What really makes an offshore deferred variable annuity superior to its domestic U.S. brother is that it gives you access to a wide variety of international investment options, including foreign currencies, foreign investment funds and an entire host of offshore stocks and bonds.

Offshore variable annuity investments start around US$500,000, but more commonly exceeding US$1 million or more is preferred. In contrast, the average domestic U.S. annuity buyer's initial investment can be US$25,000 or less.

The primary objectives in purchasing annuities and life insurance offshore are asset protection, greater wealth accumulation and access to international investment opportunities.

Because they are located offshore, away from restrictive U.S. laws, foreign insurance companies can be flexible in negotiating fees. But keep in mind that, unless eliminated by a tax treaty, a one-time 1% federal U.S. excise tax is levied on all life insurance and annuity contracts issued to U.S. persons by foreign insurers.

Annuity Mechanics

A Swiss annuity, denominated in one of the world's most reliable currencies, the Swiss franc, is a good income play for smart investors. That is because, if the dollar depreciates, your annuity income appreciates. The Swiss franc generally has reflected the state of Swiss banking, strong, valuable and unaffected by inflation and monetary fads. Since 1971, the franc has appreciated nearly 400% against the U.S. dollar.

In this arrangement, the insurance company is the legal owner of the annuity bank account, and also the party that is the investor. The annuity purchaser has the right to choose initially and later change the overall investment strategy, but under U.S. law you cannot select the specific underlying investments or manage them yourself. The asset manager has the power to choose any investment he deems appropriate within the general instructions you have given, conservative, moderate or speculative.

He can pick from the entire global investment universe, without SEC restrictions or other rules that would otherwise apply to U.S. citizens. This allows him to place the deposit you made into your fixed annuity in all traded mutual funds, hedge funds, and stocks, bonds, structured products and the like.

Under this arrangement the insurer who issues the annuity is the owner of the investments. You own an annuity policy with a value linked to the underlying portfolio of investments, but you don't own the individual investments.

Swiss and other foreign insurers have established special arrangements with the successful private banks and asset managers in Switzerland and throughout the European Union, giving you assurance that there is an investment strategy available to suit your needs. You can be certain the insurer wants to make profitable investments as much as you do.

In the event of your death, the account funds will be paid to the Swiss Leader.

History shows that Switzerland and neighboring Liechtenstein are the best places for offshore annuities and life insurance. While Swiss banking often gets the world's spotlight (for reasons both bad and good), financial institutions and insurance companies located in Switzerland and Liechtenstein offer a broad range of services that, in some cases, approach the flexibility of a bank account. Indeed, many Swiss residents use their insurance company as their only financial institution.

As for integrity, in the entire history of Swiss insurers, no life insurance company ever has failed to meet its obligations or been forced to close its doors.

And Swiss insurance policies — including annuities — have important advantages:

Insurance and annuity accounts do not pay the Swiss 35% withholding tax on earned bank interest and they are exempt from all other Swiss taxes, including those on income, capital gains, and inheritance.

Swiss annuities generally offer higher interest rates than Swiss bank accounts. Swiss law gives annuities special asset protection including exemption from enforcement of foreign court judgments including bankruptcy.

However, all these special benefits are not limited to the Swiss people alone. You too can enjoy unequalled asset protection and guaranteed income at relatively low cost.

Deferred Taxes

An offshore variable annuity is a contract between you and a foreign insurance company that provides tax deferred savings. It can serve as a savings or retirement vehicle using investment structures like mutual funds, sometimes called "sub-accounts."

Here's how it works: you buy a variable annuity contract (policy) for an agreed-upon sum, often referred to as a "single premium." These monies are invested by the insurance company in one or more investments that you approve, such as an offshore hedge fund.

The annuity contract requires periodic payments by the insurance company to you representing the increased value of investments on which the annuity is based. The money compounds, tax deferred, until you withdraw part or all of it, at which time it is taxed as regular income.

This tax-deferred accumulation can continue until the contract maturity date, usually when you are 85 or older, a time when total income is lower. An annuity is not "life insurance," so you need not take a medical examination to determine "insurability."

In most cases when the annuity matures, it has to be relinquished or converted into a life annuity that pays out a specified sum annually or for some agreed upon period. Because most investors buy variable annuities for the tax-deferred savings, withdrawing funds as needed, most variable annuities never convert to a life annuity.

Strong Asset Protection

Variable insurance annuities offer significant asset protection, especially in Switzerland, shielding the cash invested and the annuity income from creditors and other claimants. Swiss law exempts annuities from foreign court judgments including bankruptcy.

Practical asset protection exists because: 1) the policies are issued by an offshore insurance company with no affiliates in the United States, and 2) the policy's underlying assets are held entirely outside your home jurisdiction. Any domestic investments are made in the name of the insurance company, not in your name.

The degree of asset protection afforded by Swiss insurance and annuities is unparalleled anywhere else in the world. Swiss law holds that simply owning Swiss life insurance or an annuity absent other evidence of business activity within the country, is not a sufficient basis for a Swiss court to honor a foreign legal judgment against you or your assets.

Swiss law offers significant asset protection for life insurance products including annuities. Neither is subject to collection remedies directed against the owner of the policy and the policies are not deemed to be a part of the bankruptcy estate of the policy owner.

If a U.S. or other foreign court authorizes the attachment or levy against a Swiss policy, whether in bankruptcy or otherwise, a Swiss court will not issue an order directing the assignment of the policy to the creditor or the bankruptcy trustee.

Because Swiss insurance companies are not subject to the jurisdiction of a U.S. court, without an order from a Swiss court the annuities are untouchable by creditors. Swiss courts repeatedly and strictly have upheld these protective rules. The law also offers special added protection for annuities naming spouses and children as beneficiaries. Recognized by the Swiss Federal Office for Private Insurance Matters, these protections apply to all life insurance policies, including annuities and those linked to mutual funds and derivatives.

Company Protection

Statutory asset protection exists in other jurisdictions for annuity contracts as well. In the Cayman Islands, a jurisdiction that is home to many insurance companies, claims by creditors can only be made through the local courts.

When a variable annuity is issued, the investment assets must be placed in a segregated account and used only to satisfy the variable annuity obligation. If the company has financial problems, these segregated assets cannot be reached by insurance company creditors or creditors of other policyholders.

The Swiss Insurance Act prevents a properly structured insurance contract from being included in a Swiss bankruptcy procedure. The law also protects the contract from foreign seizure orders or orders including them as part of foreign estate proceedings. Under Swiss law, if you are unable to pay your debts or file bankruptcy, all rights under the contract are assigned to the beneficiaries.

Other offshore jurisdictions with a well-developed insurance sector provide statutory protection against creditor claims for insurance policies.

Offshore Variable Annuities and U.S. Taxes

Section 72 of the U.S. Internal Revenue Code treats both foreign and domestic variable annuities the same. But the IRS rules must be followed by an insurance company in drafting a policy for accumulations to qualify for tax deferral. Before you buy, always obtain a copy of a reliable written legal opinion issued by the insurance company that confirms the proper U.S. tax treatment of the company's annuities. Check the opinion and policy with your U.S. tax advisors if in doubt.

To the extent that the funds you withdraw from a variable annuity represent deferred income, they are taxed at ordinary U.S. income tax rates. A loan against a variable annuity from the issuing insurance company to the annuity buyer, or a third-party loan secured by a pledge of the annuity, is a taxable distribution. Certain unsecured loans, however, may be tax-free. Also, borrowing against an annuity when it is first purchased is not taxable since no deferred income has accumulated.

Thus, you can acquire a US$2 million annuity contract and borrow up to US$1 million of the purchase price, pledging the annuity to secure the loan, with no adverse tax consequences.

Keep in mind this difference: tax deferral is available to variable annuities of U.S. investors but not to those who purchase foreign fixed annuities. A "fixed" annuity is an annuity contract guaranteeing a fixed income for a specified period of years or for life. A "variable" annuity income varies depending on the performance of the underlying investments.

Offshore Insurance is Reportable

U.S. reporting requirements relating to offshore insurance are similar to those the IRS imposed on offshore banks, such as filing the IRS Form W-9, as we discussed earlier under the offshore banking section.

Rules imposed by the U.S. Treasury agency, the Financial Crimes Enforcement Network (FinCEN), greatly expand the scope of investments that U.S. taxpayers must report annually.

U.S. persons long have been required to submit the Foreign Bank Account Report (FBAR), FinCEN Form 114, (the former U.S. Treasury Form TDF 90.22-1) by June 30 each year.

Current FBAR rules an expanded definition of the term "other financial accounts" and includes reporting "an account that is an insurance or annuity policy with a cash value." This squarely targets U.S. investors holding non-U.S. life insurance or annuity contracts. The obligation to file the FBAR in the case of life insurance or annuities rests with you as the policyholder, not with the beneficiary.

Offshore Annuities

Despite all the talk of "tax reform" in the United States, when a death occurs without prior proper planning, the combination of income tax and federal and state estate tax can consume 50% or more of a U.S. person's estate.

Such ruinous consequences can be avoided with several planning techniques, but only life insurance provides these four key benefits: 1) tax-free buildup of cash value, including dividends, interest and capital gains; 2) tax-free borrowing against cash value; 3) tax-free receipt of the death benefit; and 4) freedom from estate and generation skipping taxes.

These benefits are available in any life insurance policy designed to comply with U.S. tax laws. However, for larger estates, a U.S.-tax-compliant life insurance policy issued by a carrier outside the U.S. offers these additional benefits:

Increased asset protection. No protection against claims made on life insurance proceeds exists under federal laws. While many states have enacted laws that provide limited protection for life insurance policies, coverage varies from significant to non-existent. In contrast, many offshore jurisdictions provide statutory asset protection for the death benefit and investments held by an insurance policy. And, as a practical matter, it is much more expensive for a creditor to bring a claim before a foreign court than a domestic court.

Access to global investments. Offshore insurance policies provide tax advantaged access to international asset managers and to offshore funds that are generally not accessible to U.S. investors.

Increased privacy. Domestic assets, including life insurance policies, can easily be discovered by private investigators with access to any of the hundreds of "asset tracking" services now in existence in the U.S. In contrast, assets held offshore are off the domestic "radar screen" and cannot easily be identified in a routine asset search. The confidentiality statutes of some offshore jurisdictions are an additional barrier against frivolous claims and investigations.

Not reportable as a "foreign bank account." A life insurance policy purchased from a non-U.S. carrier is not considered a "foreign bank, securities or other financial account." This means that there is no requirement to report the existence an offshore insurance policy to any U.S. government authority. However, depending on what country from which you purchase an offshore insurance policy, it may be necessary to make a one-time excise tax payment to the IRS amounting to 1% of the policy premium.

Currency diversification. Life insurance policies are free to make investments in non-U.S. dollar assets that may gain in the event of future declines in the value of the U.S. dollar.

Obviously, the IRS is not pleased with a planning technique that simultaneously limits federal estate taxes, creates a situation where no U.S. person is subject to tax upon transfer of the assets to the beneficiaries and permits the policyholder to invest in highly lucrative offshore mutual funds without paying tax.

To this end, the IRS announced rules that would limit the tax benefits for investors in hedge funds that are setting up insurance companies in offshore jurisdictions, but that are not in fact operating as life insurance carriers. The IRS is also concerned with foreign insurance carriers that are investing in hedge funds and has promised to more aggressively enforce existing provisions in the U.S. Tax Code that prohibit life insurance investors from managing their own securities portfolio and that require adequate diversification within the policy.

However, these IRS policy changes have been "in the making" for several years. A properly planned and executed offshore insurance policy should not be affected. But it is essential that you obtain expert tax advice when considering the purchase of an offshore insurance policy.

Life insurance remains one of the few remaining opportunities for offshore estate tax planning combined with asset protection and tax deferral. And, without major changes in U.S. federal laws, these advantages will remain for the foreseeable future.

Strategy 5: Offshore Private Placement Policy

There is a relatively new form of offshore investment vehicle that combines the best aspects of both an annuity and a life insurance policy. It is called a "private placement policy."

Most of us instinctively think of life insurance as a hedging strategy, not an investment vehicle. But insurance is ultimately nothing more than an investment designed to provide a return calculated to meet the future needs of the insured. Traditional mass-market insurance does this for millions of people all at once. Private placement policies do it for an individual, tailored to his or her needs.

An offshore private placement policy is designed to maximize your offshore investment opportunities, achieve tax-deferral in investment gains, and provide for future income, either for yourself or your heirs. It offers excellent privacy and asset protection and simplifies the entire process of going offshore.

There are two types of offshore private placement policies. The distinguishing factor is whether the policy includes any actuarial "insurance" above and beyond the value of its underlying investments.

To understand the difference, it's useful to distinguish between the "cash value" of a policy and its "surrender value." The cash value is always equal to the value of the underlying investment account. It comprises your premium principal payment(s) plus any investment gains.

For one type of offshore private policy, the *Deferred Variable Annuity* (DVA), the cash value and the surrender value are the same. Whatever you pay in, plus your investment earnings, less any withdrawals you make, is what you will get back (pre-tax) when you take a final distribution.

For the other type of policy, the *Variable Universal Life policy* (VUL), there is a conventional risk insurance coverage portion in addition to the cash value underlying your policy. In this case, part of the insurance your premium payment(s) or investment gains will come out of the cash value of your policy, reducing your investment return somewhat. But in return, the surrender value of the policy will be higher, since it will combine the current value of your investment principal, any gains, and the insurance payout. Of course, the principal value at any given time can fluctuate up and down depending on the investment markets.

DVAs are for you if you're planning for retirement. VULs, on the other hand, are your best bet if a private policy is a way to provide for your heirs. Both concepts and their main advantages are combined in private placement policies.

One of the best jurisdictions for location of private placement policies is the Principality of Liechtenstein (see pg. 221). The insurance laws there offer unmatched protection to investors and maximum product and investment flexibility. Under Liechtenstein law, for example, your policy and its assets are protected from all creditors if your spouse and/or children are the beneficiaries, both during your lifetime and when the policy pays out to your heirs. If the beneficiary is a third party, such as an asset protection trust or business partner, you enjoy the same protection, as long as the designation of the beneficiary is irrevocable. Liechtenstein also uses the Swiss Franc, which means that policies based there can be denominated in that currency, which is historically far more stable than the U.S. dollar or euro.

If you are interested in learning more about annuities, life insurance or private placement policies, contact Marc-André Sola, a member of the Banyan Hill Council of Experts. Marc and his associates at NMG International in Zurich are experts in tailoring policies to each person's individual needs.

Marc-André Sola
1291 Group, Founder & Managing Partner
P.O. Box HM 1029
Hamilton HM EX, Bermuda
Tel.: +441-295-3492
Email: info@1291Americas.com
Web: http://www.1291americas.com

Strategy 6: Offshore Investing

When it comes to profitable investing, recent events have dis-abused many Americans of the false belief the U.S. was the econom-ic and political center of the world, with other countries orbiting around us. In the past, misguided U.S. investors put the greatest share of their cash into domestic markets — a phenomenon known as "home-country bias" — but that was and is a big mistake.

Impressively high foreign market returns during some periods should have convinced more American investors to trade offshore. Over-dependence on U.S. stocks is a weakness in any portfolio. Those who only invest in U.S. stocks are losing out on much larger profits abroad.

For smart investors everywhere, the message is clear: For solid prof-its, you should put some wealth to work in markets beyond America's borders. Since 2001, U.S. stocks have had nine winning years. For example, in 2003 the S&P 500 gained almost 30%. That's huge by any yardstick.

Yet, even with that huge win, U.S. stocks never cracked the top 10 list of the world's best-performing stock markets — and given the current U.S. financial situation don't expect America to move to the top of the list any time soon.

Until recently, putting money to work in overseas stock markets was largely the province of institutional investors and the super-rich, whose deep pockets attracted the interest of private bankers and exclusive U.S. brokerage firms that catered solely to the well-heeled.

That is no longer the case.

Back in 2014, there were 3,868 emerging-market investment funds managing US$300 billion in equities. Only 1,364 of these funds were U.S. based. In 2014, ETFGI, an independent U.K. research and consultancy firm, said that global assets invested in Exchange Traded Funds (ETFs) and Exchange Traded Products (ETPs) hit an all-time high of more than US$1.9 trillion.

Fast forward to June 2017; the global ETF/ETP industry had exploded to 6,889 ETFs/ETPs, with 12,970 listings, assets of US$4.103 trillion, from 313 providers listed on 68 exchanges in 55 countries. From 2004 to 2014, the compounded annual growth rate of these products globally was 26.5%.

Add to those figures the billions in multiple currencies denominated in other financial instruments and the total is impressive. International and "emerging nation" mutual funds offer a simple way for American investors to profit from the growth of foreign companies. Such funds eliminate the inconvenience associated with direct ownership of foreign shares.

American investors can also profit from American Depository Receipts (ADRs). These are listed securities traded on U.S. stock exchanges. ADRs represent shares of a foreign stock and are issued by U.S. banks that take possession of the securities. The banks convert dividend payments into dollars and deduct any foreign withholding taxes. ADRs give investors a greater guarantee of safety, as participating foreign companies must meet certain U.S. Securities and Exchange Commission (SEC) accounting and disclosure standards.

Over the past 20 years, capital markets outside the U.S. have grown rapidly in size and importance. In 1970, non-U.S. stocks accounted for 32% of the world's US$935 billion total market capitalization. By 2017, foreign stocks represented over 75% of the total value of world stock market capitalization.

In July 2017, the collective value of stocks exceeded the dollar value of the world economy for the first time in history. Bloomberg's World Exchange Market Capitalization index set global equity values at a record $76.3 trillion, a sum that topped the $75.3 trillion figure the International Monetary Fund used to value the global economy. Both figures were record highs and suggest stock values outstripped the value of the economies in which they operated for the first time.

Until the recession of 2008 to 2012, leading U.S. stocks performed well over the years; but international stock markets historically have outperformed Wall Street. The rapid growth of capital markets around the world has also created abundant opportunities for fixed-income investors.

Avoiding Roadblocks to Prosperity

International economic integration continues despite U.S. laws designed to hinder such activity by Americans. One of the main obstacles remains restrictive U.S. securities legislation. Any "investment contract" for a security sold in the United States must be registered with the SEC and similar agencies in each of the states. This is a prohibitively expensive process. The U.S. also requires far more disclosure than most foreign countries and burdens the process with different accounting practices.

International fund managers are practical people who keep an eye on the bottom line. Many correctly calculate that operating costs in the U.S. would wipe out any profit margin they could achieve. Ironically, several mutual funds and hedge funds with top performance records are run from the U.S. by U.S. residents, but do not accept investments from Americans. To avoid SEC red tape and registration costs, investment in these funds is available only to foreigners. To avoid these restrictions, as I explained earlier, some offshore investment managers have registered with the SEC.

Although you're a U.S. citizen, you may be able to qualify under the law as an "accredited investor." As such, you will have a freer hand to buy non-SEC registered foreign stocks and mutual funds directly. An accredited investor is defined by SEC rules as an individual who has a net worth of US$1 million or more, or an annual income of at least US$250,000. In other words, you must have a lot of money.

You can also buy foreign securities through a trust, family foundation or corporation you have created offshore. Properly structured foreign legal entities are not considered "U.S. residents, persons or citizens." These entities, therefore, have the unrestricted right to buy non-SEC registered securities.

Be Your Own Offshore Stock Trader

Traditionally, Americans used domestic brokers to invest in foreign markets, if the brokers offered these services. This required broker contact with a U.S.-based "market maker" or an affiliate firm located in the country where you wanted to buy shares. This was a slow, cumbersome route that didn't always guarantee timely access.

These types of opportunities, and many thousands more like them, are available right now on any number of stock exchanges around the world. And the best way to access them is through a foreign brokerage account or any brokerage firm in the U.S. that provides direct access to overseas markets, which can be started with as little as $2,000 (the typical minimum required). The rule of thumb is to invest at least as much as it costs to make your first trade.

These firms offer American investors the opportunity to trade shares directly on foreign stock exchanges — in places like Hong Kong, Germany, Japan, Australia and the United Kingdom. Some firms even offer access to smaller, emerging markets, such as Russia, South Africa and Turkey.

Forget about the big-name Wall Street brokerage firms. Firms such as Merrill Lynch and Morgan Stanley will not trade in overseas markets for individual investors, unless clients put at least US$50,000 to US$100,000 in their trading accounts.

Instead, consider the firms below. These are U.S.-based brokerage houses that not only cater to individual investors, but offer you the ability to trade directly on foreign stock exchanges:

- **EverTrade:** the St. Louis brokerage unit of Jacksonville, Florida-based EverBank (www.evertrade.com)

- **E*TRADE:** the discount online brokerage firm (www.etrade.com)

- **Fidelity:** the online brokerage, mutual funds and retirement-services giant (www.fidelity.com)

- **Interactive Brokers:** an online brokerage firm (www.interactivebrokers.com)

- **Charles Schwab:** the original discount trading firm. (www.schwab.com)

Each of these firms offer varying degrees of access to overseas markets, and each has its pros and cons. For example, with an E*TRADE domestic brokerage account you can invest in international markets with ADRs, ETFs and mutual funds. You can upgrade to an E*TRADE Global Trading Account that allows you to trade foreign stocks directly online in six global markets in five local currencies, or in 77 international markets in 35 countries in U.S. dollars.

For investors, though, the fact that a variety of foreign markets are directly available through a stateside brokerage account dramatically changes the game. It opens the world for you.

But there is another more direct route. One of the easiest ways to buy and sell offshore securities is to establish your own foreign broker account. Start by investigating brokers in a country where you would like to make investments, a broker that you can use as your base for multi-country investments.

Go to the homepage on the Internet of the foreign stock exchange of your choice. At the exchange find the web link labeled "local brokers/market makers." This will give you a list of licensed firms that trade securities for institutions and individuals in that local market.

Next, search Google for each firm's website. Then use the firm's "Contact Us" link to send an email, asking if they will accept U.S. investors as clients. You don't need to expose your financial life. Just say: "I am a U.S. investor and want to invest in shares in (name your country of choice). Can I open an account at (name of firm you're contacting)? If so, please forward the necessary applications."

That should do the trick. You'll either receive "Sorry, no can do," or, "Welcome to (name your country of choice)!" If you are accepted, you may want to use Google for due diligence to search for any news stories about the firm, either good or bad. You might also go to the country's official brokerage licensing agency to check the firm's status and history.

The IRS has a web of rules and regulations that aim to wring maximum revenue from Americans who go offshore. These tax laws are extremely complex, so move cautiously and only with expert professional advice. At every step of the way, find out exactly what the U.S. tax and reporting consequences will be before you proceed.

Move Your IRA Offshore Now

Think of the number $27.2 trillion; that's the total value of all U.S. asset funded and private pensions, more than 25% of it in personal individual retirement accounts (IRAs). Those retirement assets constituted just over one-third of all household financial assets, according to the Investment Company Institute (ICI).

The National Seniors Council warns that some politicians want radical changes in tax-deferred contributions to retirement plans like 401(k)s and IRAs, and not in a good way. They have their eye on that $27.2 trillion in private pension as source to fund their big spending plans.

As in the major 1986 tax reforms that cut deductibility of 401(k) contributions by 70%, many think the hunt for more federal tax revenue could limit or end tax deductions of retirement plan contributions, especially for upper-income earners.

One way to protect your IRA or other retirement plans from an overreaching government is by a "conversion" — moving your plan out of the immediate jurisdiction of the United States and locating your assets and their management offshore; or you can start a new plan offshore. To make this feasible you should have a minimum of $100,000 in the plan.

If your IRA is held by a U.S. custodian, (Fidelity, American Express, Entrust or T. Rowe Price), your selection of investments is unnecessarily limited because the custodian decides which funds, bonds and equities you can trade within your IRA. Most of them limit you and your money to U.S.-based opportunities.

Any U.S.-based IRA is required by law to have a U.S. custodian, and therefore to be U.S.-based. But that doesn't mean your money has to be invested in the U.S. There are selected U.S. custodians who allow your IRA to hold alternative assets, such as gold, real estate, coins and offshore investments.

IRA assets outside of the U.S. are difficult to attack or forcibly repatriate — especially if you decide to invest in real estate or land. Moving your IRA assets abroad also means your retirement cash is outside the U.S. banking system. In the event of a catastrophic banking meltdown here at home, your nest egg will be safer offshore, even if your IRA remains U.S.-based.

Once your IRA funds are successfully transferred to an offshore-friendly bank, you have multiple options. You can:

- Self-direct the account by opening a brokerage account in the name of your IRA.

- Purchase foreign real estate with the cash in your IRA.

- Purchase physical gold with the cash in your IRA and store it offshore.

- Have some or all the IRAs assets transferred to an offshore money manager.

As described earlier in this chapter, putting your money in the hands of an independent asset manager (IAM) is the most attractive option, and can give a big boost to your retirement portfolio. Foreign IAMs have insights into markets and companies that U.S. advisers usually ignore. They have experience with foreign currency diversification and can deal in strong currencies such as the Swiss franc, the Norwegian krone or the Singapore dollar.

If you decide to transfer your existing IRA to one of these alternative custodians, known as a "rollover," it's critical to work with an experienced professional, such as the U.S.-based lawyers we recommend. The IRS can regard problematic rollovers as an early distribution, triggering penalties as well as a loss of tax deferral.

Contacts for IRA conversions:

Josh N. Bennett, Esq., P.A.
440 North Andrews Avenue
Fort Lauderdale, FL 33301
Tel.: 954-779-1661
Mobile: 786-202-5674
Email: josh@joshbennett.com
Web: http://www.joshbennett.com

Robert Vrijhof, President
WHVP: Weber, Hartmann, Vrijhof & Partners Ltd.
Schaffhauserstrasse 418
CH-8050 Zürich, Switzerland
Contact: Julia Fernandez
Tel.: 01141 44 315 77 77 (USA/Canada) / +41 44 315 77 77 (International)
Email: info@whvp.ch
Web: http://www.whvp.ch

Part 3 — Offshore Business Strategies

NOTE: The Tax Cuts and Jobs Act of 2017, became Public Law No: 115-97, on December 22, 2017. This was the first comprehensive revision of U.S. personal income and corporate taxes since 1986. This law cut the corporate tax rate from 35% to 21% beginning in 2018 and made many other changes. Be certain to check with experienced tax counsel about the impact this law may have on your actions or plans.

One more word of caution: when describing the meaning and requirements of IRS reporting or other rules we may use the phrase *"appear to be."* That's because IRS requirements change with new rules and interpretations and court rulings. Always check with a qualified U.S. tax professional, tax attorney or accountant, if you have questions about IRS rules.

Throughout this book we also use the phrase *"at this writing,"* which means that our statements were accurate at the time written. With the status of so many issues constantly changing you can keep current on tax and offshore matters by subscribing to our newsletters and services. See www.banyanhill.com.

Strategy 1: International Business Corporation (IBC)

One possible vehicle for offshore tax savings is an international business corporation (IBC).

An IBC is simply a corporation registered in an international financial center or any foreign jurisdiction under its national laws. An IBC that does business offshore, but not in the nation where it is registered, usually is exempt from most local corporate and other taxes under "territorial" tax systems that end at the border. At registration there is an initial government incorporation fee and an annual maintenance fee.

An IBC can be used outside of the nation of incorporation for a variety of activities including consulting, investing, trading, finance, holding assets, or real estate ownership. Some jurisdictions permit holding companies do not produce goods or services itself but own shares of other companies to form a corporate group. In some cases, an IBC may confer a trade advantage under tax treaties or it may also be used as an integral part of a broader trust structure.

One of the main advantages of an IBC is that it can pay legitimate business expenses and be used to plough back profits for future business use. So long as these profits are used for business purposes, this avoids most immediate U.S. income tax liabilities. But even undistributed corporate income may be taxable annually to the American IBC owners.

U.S. Tax Liabilities

U.S. court decisions strictly interpret tax and reporting obligations of a U.S. person actively involved in an offshore corporation.

These cases attribute "constructive ownership" to the involved U.S. person as an individual, or they find actual control exists based on a chain of entities linking the U.S. person to the offshore corporation. The courts seek to identify the U.S. person with actual corporate control, as compared to stand-in, paper nominees with only nominal control.

Decades ago, U.S. taxpayers, corporate or individual, could defer some taxes by establishing an offshore corporation. Back then, the foreign corporation was viewed under U.S. tax laws as a "foreign entity" and shareholders had to pay U.S. income taxes only on dividends paid to the owner or others.

Now the IRS "looks through" the corporate arrangement and taxes U.S. owners annually on the offshore company's earnings as well. If corporate income is primarily "passive" income, such as income from securities or interest, the IRS may impose penalty charges on the corporate shareholders.

There are some exceptions.

First, the "look through" rule only applies to "controlled foreign corporations" (CFCs) that have passive business activities. Thus, you can defer taxes on income from non-passive activities such as real estate management, international trade, manufacturing, banking, or insurance.

A second set of IRS rules that tax offshore corporate profits apply to what is called "passive foreign investment companies" (PFICs). To avoid a PFIC classification and tax penalties, at least 30% of the corporate income must be "active" income from the categories described above, plus management fees charged by the company. (For more about this see Chapter Eleven, *The United States as an Offshore Tax Haven.*)

The Per Se Rule

For U.S. persons who control shares in an offshore IBC, there are major limitations on U.S. tax benefits that would otherwise be available to a corporation formed in the United States. This is because the offshore corporation is probably listed on what is known as the IRS "per se" list of foreign corporations, which appears in IRS regulations, section 301.7701-2(b)(8)(i). The corporations in the listed countries are barred from numerous U.S. tax benefits.

This designation means that U.S. persons cannot file an IRS Form 8832 electing to treat the corporation as a "disregarded entity" or a foreign partnership, either of which is given much more favorable U.S. tax treatment.

Under IRS rules, the per se corporation that engages in passive investments is considered a "controlled foreign corporation," which requires the filing of IRS Form 5471 describing its operations. U.S. persons also must file IRS Form 926 reporting transfers of cash or assets to the corporation.

A U.S. person who controls a foreign financial account of any nature that has in it US$10,000 or more at any time during a calendar year must report this to the U.S. Treasury IRS on (FinCEN) Form 114, (FBAR). There are serious fines and penalties for failure to file these IRS returns and criminal charges can also be imposed. As a rule, U.S. persons can be guilty of the crime of "falsifying a federal income tax return" by failing to report offshore corporate holdings.

Any eventual capital gains earned by an IRS-per se listed corporation are not taxed in the U.S. under the more favorable CGT rate of 15% to 20%, but rather as ordinary income for the corporate owners, which can be at a much higher rate up to 37%.

There is also the possibility of double taxation if the offshore IBC makes investments in the U.S., in which case there is a 30% U.S. withholding tax on the investment income. Under U.S. tax rules, no annual losses can be taken on corporate investments, which must be deferred by the U.S. owners until the IBC is liquidated.

However, compared to all these IRS restrictions, there may be offsetting considerations, such as complete exemption from foreign taxes, which may be more important in your financial planning.

As you can see, it is extremely important that U.S. persons obtain an authoritative review of the tax implications before forming an offshore international business corporation for any purpose, including holding title to personal or business real estate. A list of qualified U.S. tax attorneys and accountants can be found in Appendix I.

Certain tax havens, such as Panama, Hong Kong, the Isle of Man, the British Virgin Islands and the Cook Islands make it attractive to incorporate. When selecting a place to incorporate, here's what you need to consider:

- Legal and political attitudes of the jurisdiction toward commercial activities

- Corporate laws that facilitate incorporation and continuing management

- The level and speed of service obtainable

- The cost, both initially and for annual maintenance All IBC-friendly jurisdictions have at least two requirements: l) maintaining a local agent for the service of process, and; 2) payment of an annual franchise fee or tax.

The best offshore financial centers for IBC incorporation that we recommend are Panama and the Isle of Man, with Hong Kong a close third.

Recommended for Incorporation:

Rainelda Mata-Kelly, LL.M.
Suites 406-407, Tower B, Torres de las Americas
Punta Pacifica, Panama
Tel.: +507-216-9299
From the USA or Canada Tel.: 011 507-216-9299
Email: rmk@mata-kelly.com
Web: http://www.mata-kelly.com

Ms. Mata-Kelly, a member of the Banyan Hill Council of Experts, specializes in Panamanian law in areas of commercial, immigration, real estate, contracts and incorporation.

OCRA (Isle of Man) Ltd.
OCRA (London) Limited
3rd Floor
14 Hanover Street, Mayfair
W1S 1YH, London
United Kingdom
Email: enquiry@ocra.co.uk
Web: http://www.ocra.com/solutions/doing_business_iom.asp

Trident Corporate Services (Asia) Ltd.
14th Floor, Golden Centre
188 Des Voeux Road, Central Hong Kong
Tel.: +852-2805-2000
Email: hongkong@tridenttrust.com
Web: www.tridenttrust.com

BVI International Finance Centre
Cutlass Tower, 4th Floor
Road Town, Tortola, British Virgin Islands
Tel.: +284 468 4335
Email: info@bvifinance.vg
Web: http://bvifinance.vg

Strategy 2: Using Tax Treaties for Profit

There is at least one thing worse than paying taxes in your home country — paying taxes in two or more countries on the same income.

To avoid that "look before you leap" is good advice. Careless offshore financial arrangements can result in redundant taxes that eat up most or all profits you might make.

Bilateral (two-country) tax treaties were developed to avoid these problems. Formally known as "double tax treaties," these agreements usually allow the source of income country to tax most of the income earned within its borders, while the taxpayer's home country agrees not to tax that income, usually by giving credit for foreign taxes paid against domestic taxes owed. Those are the basic principles, but the variations within each treaty are endless.

Current U.S. tax treaties were negotiated individually over the last half-century and usually remain in effect for set time periods (20 years or more), so re-negotiation is constantly ongoing. Most U.S. treaties are with industrialized countries or nations with major commercial and banking activities. Some European countries, especially the United Kingdom and the Netherlands, have their own network of tax treaties with an extensive list of nations, including many of their former colonial possessions.

There's little point in discussing the terms of each U.S. tax treaty here, since they change periodically based on renegotiation or official reinterpretation. The information presented here is as current as possible. To be certain you are current obtain professional advice on the status and impact of any tax treaty before investing offshore. U.S. treaties are available at http://www.irs.gov/pub/irs-pdf/p901.pdf.

Tax treaty strategies are less important to someone who simply wants to use an offshore bank or investment account as personal financial tools. But treaties can be of tremendous value when doing commercial business overseas in one or more nations. Depending on your business and the way a given tax treaty is structured, taxes can be significantly lowered or avoided completely.

Tax Treaty Loophole

In theory, bilateral tax treaties are supposed to remove or reduce the burden of double taxation. That's the theory, but not always the practical result. These agreements are designed to avoid or at least minimize double taxation.

However, they have another, less publicized function — that is to facilitate information exchange between countries that helps enforcement of domestic tax laws in instances where citizens have offshore financial activity. (*More about privacy issues in Chapter Two.*)

After World War II, with the British Empire crumbling, the United States routinely agreed to extend the terms of the existing U.S.-U.K. tax treaty to newly independent nations in the British Commonwealth. As the interdependent global economy began to grow, especially in the 1970s, these new countries and creative international tax planners found tremendous profits to be made under the terms of older, existing treaties.

Former British colonies became low- or no-tax havens for certain types of exempted income earned by foreign-resident persons, trusts and corporations. Liberal local tax laws combined with the tax treaties created a bonanza in tax-free transactions. Pick the right country, the right treaty, the right business and you could enjoy tax-free profits.

The good news for U.S. taxpayers considering going offshore is that these no-tax or low-tax countries have a significant financial interest in keeping these liberal tax treaty provisions available for foreign customers. In addition, many U.S.-based multinational corporations want these favorable offshore tax provisions continued to keep their capital costs in line with those of foreign competitors.

If you are planning an offshore business, seek guidance from an attorney who knows international tax planning and tax treaties. Choosing the right country in which to incorporate your business could mean a dramatically reduced tax bill and better profits, so it's well worth checking out.

For U.S. corporate tax and reporting advice:

Josh N. Bennett, Esq., P.A.
440 North Andrews Avenue
Fort Lauderdale, FL 33301
Tel.: 954-779-1661
Mobile: 786-202-5674
Email: josh@joshbennett.com
Web: http://www.joshbennett.com

Strategy 3: Profitable "Stepping Stones"

Creative offshore tax planning often calls for business operations in more than one country. That allows you to use the most advantageous combination of available tax treaties. International tax practitioners like to call this the "stepping stone" principle. The IRS derisively calls it "treaty shopping."

Stepping stone transactions are most useful when passive interest or royalty income is involved, though some other commercial and service business structures can also be profitable.

The stepping stones work like this: a German investor naturally wants to earn the highest interest rates available. His tax advisor suggests investing through a Dutch company because the Netherlands has an extensive, ready-made tax treaty network with all other developed countries. The German could form his own Dutch corporation, but tax authorities prefer that he use an independent, pre-existing business. In effect, the German will invest money in an existing Dutch company that in turn will invest it elsewhere. The Dutch company will charge fees for its middleman role, receiving payments known as "the spread."

The tax treaty network allows a Dutch company to invest money virtually anywhere it wants. Under treaty terms, the interest it receives is not subject to withholding taxes in the countries where the money is invested. For example, the U.S.-Netherlands treaty provides for no withholding of tax by the U.S. on interest paid from the United States to a Dutch company. The Netherlands company is not required to withhold taxes when that interest, in turn, is paid to the German investor; so, no taxes all around.

The existing U.S. tax treaty network and the multiple "stepping stone" possibilities it offers to foreign investors, means the United States is a tax haven for the rest of the world, but not for its own citizens.

Many foreign businesses and investors using U.S. tax treaties as part of careful structuring make money by basing their operations in America and legally paying little or no U.S. taxes. Not surprisingly, the IRS disapproves of wholesale "treaty shopping" by Americans. In tax treaty renegotiations, the U.S. insists, not always successfully, on "anti-treaty shopping" provisions.

The actual tax terms vary, but basically the IRS wants to re-write old treaties to limit tax benefits to those who are bona fide residents of the other bilateral treaty nation. In our example, that would have ruled out the German investor.

A 2017 study by researchers at the University of Amsterdam found that nearly 40% of corporate investments moved into tax havens went to the U.K. or the Netherlands, making them the preferred option for companies wishing to utilize tax havens to safeguard their invest-ments. The Netherlands accounted for 23% of corporate investments that landed in a tax haven.

The Netherlands competes with Ireland in offering corporate tax haven facilities and the U.S. tech giants, Microsoft, Google and Facebook, use the Dutch and Irish tax rules in their drive to minimize taxes through channeling of sales revenues from other countries into Ireland and the Netherlands. About 20,000 mailbox companies are hosted in Amsterdam and prominent musicians such as Bono of U2 and Mick Jagger of the Rolling Stones avail themselves of this system.

The IRS hates such arrangements. They see this as tax evasion using phony affiliates of businesses operating within the U.S. Fortunately for astute taxpayers, if it's done right, this system is completely legal, and it works.

In the U.S. in 2017, legal tax avoidance by multinational corporations using offshore jurisdictions was estimated to be at least $130 billion a year. In 2013, the IMF said the U.S. estimate of lost taxes from tax planning by multinationals was about US$60 billion each year, about one-quarter of all revenue from the U.S. corporate income tax. But keep in mind this is not illegal tax evasion, but legal tax avoidance. Provisions in the Tax Cuts and Jobs Act of 2017 make it more attractive to U.S. companies to return offshore profits to America.

The one key requirement for successful stepping stones is strict adherence to proper form and procedures and no cutting corners. The moral: there are ways to save taxes offshore, but do it right and be sure you know what you can and cannot do. To be safe, check with the experts recommended in these pages.

I repeat, tax treaties are changing constantly and that means the end of some formerly available tax saving strategies. Internal domestic tax laws change, too. What's here today is gone tomorrow. But serious international businesspeople must pay as much attention to tax treaty developments as they do to daily weather forecasts or stock market reports. It can be that essential.

Part 4 — Required Reporting of Offshore Financial Accounts

So, you've gotten some or all your assets located offshore. Now what? Do you have to tell the U.S. government that you have opened an offshore account? The answer is a very definite "yes."

1. Annual IRS Form 1040 Income Tax

If you're a U.S. citizen or permanent resident alien and at any time during the prior year held more than US$10,000 in one or more foreign financial accounts, you must report the existence of your account, on your annual federal income tax return, IRS Form 1040 (Schedule B), Part III, Foreign Accounts and Trusts. The form asks this question: "At any time during 2014, did you have a financial interest in or signature authority over a financial account (such as a bank account, securities account, or brokerage account) located in a foreign country?"

If you had such an account, you must check the "Yes" box even if you are not required to file FinCEN Form 114, FBAR. Note that no specific amount is required, only the fact that you had a foreign account of any kind.

Form 1040 also asks at this point whether you are required to file the FBAR (URL included on the next page). If you answer "yes," you must name the countries where the account(s) were located.

2. U.S. Treasury (FinCEN) Form 114, FBAR

The 1970 U.S. Bank Secrecy Act gave the U.S. Department of Treasury the authority to collect information from U.S. persons having a financial interest in, or signature authority over, financial accounts maintained with financial institutions located outside of the U.S.

This requires that a FinCEN Form 114, *Report of Foreign Bank and Financial Accounts* (FBAR) be filed if the aggregate maximum values of the foreign financial accounts exceed $10,000 at any time during the calendar year. The FBAR must be filed before June 30 of each year and covers the previous year. Hundreds of thousands of U.S. citizens and permanent residents required to file FBARs now must do so using the IRS electronic system. See https://www.irs.gov/businesses/small-businesses-self-employed/report-of-foreign-bank-and-financial-accounts-fbar.

The penalties for non-compliance are harsh; a fine of US$10,000 for each unreported account for each year someone neglects to file the FBAR, although the sanction for a "negligent violation" is only a US$500 fine. If one "willfully" fails to comply with this obligation, the fine is up to US$500,000, imprisonment for up to five years, or both.

So who must file an FBAR? U.S. persons who have a financial interest in or signature authority over one or more financial accounts located outside of the United States and an aggregated value of foreign financial accounts exceeding $10,000 within any given year.

The FBAR definition of "U.S. person" includes: 1) a U.S. citizen, and; 2) a legal permanent resident of the U.S., and; 3) any person located "in and doing business in the U.S." It also includes, but is not limited to, corporations, partnerships, or limited liability companies, created or organized in the U.S. or under U.S. laws and trusts or estates formed under the laws of the United States.

This definition extends FBAR coverage to foreign citizens who are physically present and doing business in the United States. Previously, the definition of a "U.S. person" exempted a foreign person physically present in the U.S. for less than 180 days each year, or not a U.S. resident by treaty definition.

Instructions for (FinCEN) Form 114, read, in part: Financial Account. A financial account includes, but is not limited to, securities, brokerage, savings, demand, checking, deposit, time deposit, or other account maintained with a financial institution, (or other person performing the services of a financial institution).

A financial account also includes "commodity futures or options accounts, an insurance policy with a cash value (such as a whole life insurance policy), an annuity policy with cash value, and shares in a mutual fund or similar pooled fund (i.e., a fund that is available to the general public with a regular net asset value determination and regular redemptions)".

U.S. Treasury rules require reporting of offshore investments that include:

- A foreign account that is an insurance policy with a cash value or an annuity policy;

- A foreign account with a person that acts as a broker or dealer for futures or options transactions in any commodity on or subject to the rules of a commodity exchange or association; and

- An account with a mutual fund or similar pooled fund which issues shares available to the general public that have a regular net asset value determination and regular redemptions.

- Holdings of "foreign financial assets" outside the U.S. valued at US$50,000 or more.

The rules also say U.S. persons must report "an account with a person that is in the business of accepting deposits as a financial agency." A financial agency is defined as "a person acting for a person as a financial institution bailee, depository trustee, or agent, or acting in a similar way related to money, credit, securities, gold, or in a transaction in money, credit, securities, or gold."

On the other hand, it is clear that if you keep the gold in a non-bank private vault facility to which only you have access, the storage vault is not acting as a "financial agency" as defined above; this type of vault use is not reportable.

For maximum privacy, you should not store your precious metals in the safe deposit box that is provided by your offshore bank as a part of your account services. Use of a bank-provided safe deposit box makes precious metals reportable.

3. The Foreign Account Tax Compliance Act (FATCA)

FATCA requires, for those covered, the filing of an additional IRS Form 8938, *Statement of Specified Foreign Financial Assets*. Whether you must file is determined by the total value of all your offshore assets held during the prior year.

This form is in addition to the FBAR and does not replace it. Under this form, reportable assets include bank, brokerage or other financial accounts. See http://www.irs.gov/pub/irs-pdf/f8938.pdf. You can also find details at https://www.irs.gov/forms-pubs/form-8938-statement-of-foreign-financial-assets.

A helpful "Comparison of Form 8938 and FBAR Requirements" can be found at: http://www.irs.gov/Businesses/Comparison-of-Form-8938-and-FBAR-Requirements.

Here are the most common scenarios, with what you need to do, if anything. All of these scenarios assume you have at least one foreign bank or other financial account.

* **If you live in the U.S.** and have foreign accounts, you must file an IRS Form 8938 (Statement of Specified Foreign Financial Assets) on all your accounts, if the total value of all of them exceeds $50,000 ($100,000 for couples) on the last day of the year, or exceeded $75,000 ($150,000) at any time during the year.

* **If you live permanently abroad:** The reporting thresholds for people who pass the IRS foreign residence test are significantly higher.

To pass this test, you must live abroad most of the year, must not have made an official declaration that you are not a resident of that country, and must be subject to that country's income tax laws. The IRS Form 8938 reporting threshold for foreign-resident couples filing jointly is $400,000 on the last day of the tax year or more than $600,000 at any time during the tax year on all accounts at foreign banks. Amounts in U.S. bank accounts are excluded.

- **If you are married to a foreigner:** Americans married to a foreigner must report their spouses' foreign bank accounts under FATCA, even if the spouse isn't a U.S. resident or taxpayer. This is the case whether you live in the U.S. or live abroad.

  If you're married to a foreigner, we recommend three courses of action:

  a. Be prepared to report all of your non-U.S. bank accounts and investments for both yourself and your spouse;

  b. Make sure all the foreign banks where you and your spouse have accounts are aware of your marriage and their obligation to report on both of you under FATCA;

  c. If you haven't filed your U.S. tax returns, get ready to do so for the current year as well as previous years. This will require the assistance of a specialist legal counsel. Remember: Never approach the IRS yourself — always use an attorney.

- **If you're a dual citizen:** FATCA applies to people who hold dual citizenship, whether they live in the U.S. or not, or even whether they are aware of their U.S. citizenship status. (Remember, all it takes is to be born within the U.S., or abroad to a U.S. parent.) This has caused major problems for many individuals.

You can be a U.S. citizen even if you don't take any steps to claim it. Many Canadians, for example, were born in U.S. hospitals near the border. All of them are required to report under FATCA, as are their Canadian banks. And, of course, FATCA reporting applies to their Canadian spouses as well. This supposedly unintended situation forced the U.S. to reach a separate FATCA agreement with Canada, so strong were the thousands of protests from north of the border.

FATCA also applies to entities formed under U.S. law, such as corporations, partnerships, limited liability companies and trusts, as it does to a natural person. However, FATCA applies only to entities formed under U.S. law. FATCA has no jurisdiction over foreign-based entities, unless they are controlled in whole or in part by U.S. persons.

Adhering to these complex IRS reporting regulations is costing offshore financial institutions billions of dollars for greatly expanded compliance staffs, software programs, investigations of their U.S. clients and trying to understand and meet the IRS rules. Bank clients will pay the bill for this IRS mess in ever-higher bank fees.

For advice concerning required all offshore reports contact:

Josh N. Bennett, Esq., P.A.
440 North Andrews Avenue
Fort Lauderdale, FL 33301
Tel.: 954-779-1661
Mobile: 786-202-5674
Email: josh@joshbennett.com
Web: http://www.joshbennett.com

Trust Reporting

Accounts controlled by a trustee of an offshore trust must be reported by a trust beneficiary with a greater than 50% beneficial interest in the trust, but also by any person who "established" the trust and any "trust protector" that is appointed. A "trust protector" is defined as a person responsible for monitoring the activities of the trustee who has the authority to influence trustee decisions or to replace or recommend the replacement of the trustee.

The definition of trust "financial accounts" includes, among others, trust-owned foreign mutual funds, foreign hedge funds, foreign annuities, debit card accounts and prepaid credit card accounts.

Qualified Intermediary (QI) Rule

Years before FATCA, the U.S. Internal Revenue Service tried to force foreign banks and financial institutions into the unwelcome role of IRS informants, a.k.a. "qualified intermediaries" (QI). In effect, this was the first attempt by an agency of the U.S. government (the IRS) to impose extraterritorial tax enforcement burdens on foreign banks. The offshore banks were forced to meet IRS established anti-money laundering and "know your customer" standards in order to get the "QI" stamp of approval.

Under current QI rules, foreign banks must actively investigate, determine and report to the IRS whether U.S. investors or legal entities the U.S. person controls are the holders of foreign accounts. (As we noted before, U.S. persons already are required by law to report their offshore accounts on the annual IRS Form 1040.) The adoption and ongoing enforcement of FATCA has served as a major expansion of the original QI rules.

The IRS claims that since 2001 it has denied participation in the QI program and U.S. banking system access to about 100 foreign banks that were accused of violating QI rules. But in our observation, far fewer banks were embargoed and those few were banks located in remote places such as Vanuatu and the Solomon Islands where Russian criminal elements had established a financial presence.

Tax Information Exchange

The current standard for tax information exchange is embodied in the Organization for Economic Cooperation and Development (OECD) common reporting standard based on Article 26 of the OECD Model Tax Convention. For a discussion of this topic, refer back to Chapter Two.

Non-Reportable Foreign Investments

1. Precious Metals

Depending on the way in which titled by owners and the place of storage, precious metals held outside the U.S., at this writing, are not necessarily reportable to the U.S. government.

These are the basic current U.S. reporting rules governing offshore ownership by U.S. persons of precious metals:

a. If titled directly in an individual's name, no report to the IRS is required on the FinCEN Form 114 (FBAR). If, however, the title of the precious metals is held in the name of a legal entity, such as a corporation under your control, they must be reported.

b. No report is required under FATCA on IRS Form 8938, unless the value of the precious metals total $50,000 or more. However, the value of offshore precious metals must be included when calculating the $50,000 total threshold that triggers the annual Form 8938.

c. Gold and other precious metals if held as part of a bank account or its related services, (as in a bank-provided safety deposit box), are reportable. Precious metals held in non-bank storage vaults are not reportable.

Securities or precious metals purchased directly from an offshore bank, securities issuer, dealer, or individual are not reportable if purchased without any association with a financial account, so long as the total value of the foreign financial instruments or investment contracts doesn't exceed US$50,000. If they are worth more, they are reportable annually on as part of overall foreign assets owned. These same non-reportable rules apply to valuables such as art works, antiques, gems, jewelry, rare coins, stamps and other collectibles.

Banks are not the only places that offer safe deposit boxes. Nonbank safekeeping is available through private vaults. Since private vaults are not financial institutions, they are subject to fewer recordkeeping and disclosure requirements. Because a vault safe deposit box is not associated with a bank account, it does not constitute a financial account and it is not FBAR reportable.

Owning physical gold and silver in the form of coins and bullion will allow you to conserve your purchasing power as paper money continues to lose its value. But gold and silver should be held in a diversified way. If you are a U.S. resident, for true safety, real peace of mind and added asset protection, you should keep at least some of your gold and silver offshore.

There are many ways to invest in gold and the World Gold Council explains these in detail on its website — http://www.gold.org. If you are new to gold, you should review this information. According to industry specialists, there are 110 accredited bar manufacturers and brands in 28 countries. Between them, they produce a total of more than 500 types of standard gold bars, all of which contain a minimum of 99.5% fine gold. There are also many gold bullion coin dealers.

Offshore Vaults: The Basics

Here we refer mainly to gold and other precious metals, since these are the most common forms of physical assets held offshore. But the principles apply to certain other storable, high-value assets, valuables such as art works, antiques, gems, jewelry, rare coins, rare stamps and other collectibles.

There are a variety of non-bank services around the world that can store your physical assets. They are extremely secure; that's what they're selling, after all. All holdings are subject to regular external audits and are fully insured, typically by Lloyd's of London or another reputable international insurer. These services generally fall into two broad categories:

a. **Storage-only services** will accept and store anything of value, from coins to fleets of cars. These are typically high-end services used by seven- and eight-figure net worth individuals who have the wherewithal to arrange international asset transportation, negotiate customs, and deposit them with the vault company, to whom they pay a storage fee for strictly segregated storage (i.e., an individual vault or sub-vault). They are often used by people who have regular business in the storage country and travel there regularly.

b. **Brokerage services:** These services help you buy and sell gold (coins and bars) and other precious metals as well as store it. These services are suited to individuals who may have no reason to travel to the storage country regularly, don't have existing gold or other hard asset holdings that need to be transported there and/or who may be in the process of accumulating such assets over time. To meet the non-reporting requirement, such brokerage services must only facilitate the purchase, storage, and sale of precious metals and other assets.

They charge you for these services. The gold or other assets they store for you aren't part of their own corporate assets, so the companies can't borrow or trade against them — they are yours and yours alone always. Brokerage storage services are further subdivided into two types:

i. **Unallocated storage** means that you have an ownership interest in coins or bars that are part of a collective holding. You don't have title to specific coins or bars, but instead have fractional ownership of the total pool of metal, together with other investors. This lets you buy in smaller quantities at a more favorable price. Unallocated services usually charge lower storage fees here. Vendor reputation is critical, as the relationship is based on trust that the metal will be there should you opt to take physical possession. When you do, you'll pay a "fabrication fee" — so-called because your personal holding has to be "fabricated" from the common pool. The Perth Mint is an example of this: www.perthmint.com. au.

ii. **Allocated storage** means that you own specific coins and/or bars within a total pool of metal. They may or may not be segregated from other people's holdings, but they are certified and audited in your name. Allocated storage allows you to take delivery of your metals anytime. An allocated storage service doesn't incur delivery fabrication fees, but storage charges are higher and vary as the price of (and cost to insure) precious metals varies. The Hard Assets Alliance is an example (see pg. 183).

The best solution maximizes your financial privacy and legally eliminates the need to tell the U.S. government about physical assets that you hold offshore. In this respect, the preferred option is allocated storage. That's because, although the FATCA rules on this aren't entirely clear, it appears that unallocated storage may meet the definition of a foreign financial institution, and therefore trigger reporting requirements.

If you buy gold or other precious metals offshore on an unallocated basis, you don't own specific metal, and you can't just show up and visit it or claim it. It's not being audited in your name as owner, but in the name of whoever manages the collective pool of metal. The transaction is more about the value of the gold than the gold itself and hence could be seen as primarily a reportable financial matter.

To be absolutely secure, your goal should be to own specific metals in your own name, which are audited on your behalf, in a private vault facility to which only you or your designee (such as power of attorney) have access.

Recommended Storage Facilities:

Safe in Singapore: Singapore is a safe and political reliable jurisdiction. That's why many of the world's wealthy households are moving their gold there. But it's also the result of a deliberate strategy by the island state. Singapore's government wants to be the global leader in offshore finances, including precious metals holdings.

The best-known facility in Malca-Amit headquartered in Singapore. It also offers highly-secured, strategically located storage facilities located in free trade zones around the globe, including Bangkok, Hong Kong, London, New York, Shanghai, Singapore, Toronto and Zurich. See http://www.malca-amit.com.

Austrian Options: If completely anonymous gold storage is what you're after, the place to go is Vienna, Austria. There the most desirable option is the respected, Das Safe. However, Das Safe requires your presence to rent space initially. Under the Austrian Banking Act, Das Safe, established in 1984, is supervised by the Financial Market Authority (FMA) and the Oesterreichische National Bank (OeNB).

DAS SAFE
Auerspergstrasse 1, A-1080
Vienna, Austria
Tel.: +43 1 406 61 74
Email: info@dassafe.com
Web: http://www.dassafe.com

Hard Assets Alliance

The Hard Assets Alliance (HAA), with whom Banyan Hill has an existing relationship, offers a handy way to build a precious metals investment position directly offshore. HHA also offers secure storage with its vault partner, Malca-Amit in Singapore. HAA's Smart Metal program allows you to invest toward ownership of bullion (gold or silver) each month (minimum $250) using an online interface.

Once you've accumulated the equivalent of one troy ounce of gold (or 100 ounces of silver) you can convert it into a serial-numbered bar that sits in allocated storage under your title. (Precious metal is measured in troy ounces, unlike the avoirdupois ounces used to measure things like food; 16 ounces avoirdupois equal 14.58 troy.) At this point you can "take delivery" of the physical bullion, or simply leave it HAA's nonbank, and therefore non-reportable, Malca-Amit vaults in Singapore.

Until your account with HAA converts into a real bar of bullion, it's considered a "financial account" located inside the U.S., like any other bank or investment account. Because of this, it's not reportable as a foreign financial account (but it is traceable to you). As soon as HAA converts your account into a real piece of bullion, however, it becomes an allocated, and therefore, non-reportable physical asset located offshore.

For example, if the price of an ounce of gold is $1,250, you will own one ounce of non-reportable, fully-allocated offshore gold in five months at $250 a month with HAA. And throughout the entire process, your interest in the gold isn't reportable to the IRS or under FBAR.

It's worth mentioning that HAA has direct access to refiners, bullion banks and institutional level dealers, which helps drive its relatively lower global purchase premiums. Your order is bid out to this pool of institutions that compete for HAA's business, ensuring a great price.

Hard Assets Alliance
750 Third Avenue, Suite 702
New York, NY 10017
Toll-free: 877-727-7387
Internationally: +602-626-3022
Email: support@hardassetsalliance.com
Web: http://www.hardassetsalliance.com

For transfer of precious metals from within the U.S. and worldwide, we recommend:

Brinks Global Services
580 5th Avenue, Suite 400
New York, NY 10036 USA
Tel.: 212-869-7720 or 212-704-9500
Toll-free: 800-825-8332
Email: http://www.brinksglobal.com/contact_us/contact_form.aspx
Web: http://www.brinksglobal.com

For purchase, transport and storage outside the U.S. we also recommend:

Miles Franklin Precious Metals Investments
Andrew Schectman, President
801 Twelve Oaks Center Drive, Suite 834
Wayzata, MN 55391
Tel.: 952-929-7006
Toll-free: 800-822-8080
Email: andy@milesfranklin.com
Web: http://www.milesfranklin.com

2. Real Estate

The second major asset offshore that is not currently reportable to the U.S. IRS is direct ownership, in your own name, of foreign real property.

Income from real estate holdings, wherever located, is not reportable on FinCEN Form 114 (FBAR), but it is reportable as taxable income on IRS Form 1040.

However, real estate holdings are generally a matter of public record in the jurisdiction in which they are located, and real estate cannot be liquidated easily. If you own the real estate through a holding company or trust, that entity usually is required to file its own U.S. disclosure and tax forms.

If you wish to purchase and hold real estate in a foreign country without disclosing your ownership, this can be accomplished by placing title in an international business corporation (IBC) or a limited liability company (LLC) located incorporated in a third country such as Nevis, where beneficial ownership does not have to be disclosed except to your attorney or by court order. An IBC that holds title does not have to be registered in the same nation where the real estate is located.

Avoiding Double Taxation

Governments everywhere love taxes. The government in the nation in which an offshore bank account is located has the power to impose its own withholding taxes on any foreign owned assets and deposits and many countries do just that. For example, Switzerland levies a 35% tax on almost all interest income paid.

In many nations, the law requires that taxes be withheld by the financial institution where the account is located. That's why it's important to check the potential tax liabilities beforehand, and then make certain to locate your account in a jurisdiction with low or not taxes.

If you have a bank account in a country that has a "double taxation treaty" with your home country, you may qualify for a credit against your U.S. or other national income tax obligation in the amount of the foreign tax paid.

Average credits allowed vary from country to country according to the terms of the treaty in force at the time. In most cases, your home country tax authorities are unlikely to allow a credit of more than a fraction of the foreign tax withheld. Claiming a foreign tax credit against U.S. taxes involves much paperwork and places in IRS hands additional information.

If you are concerned about tax treaty terms obtain a copy of the U.S. tax treaty with the nation you are considering for placement of your financial business. As we mentioned earlier, treaties are published by the U.S. State Department in the *Treaties in Force* series, available online at: http://www.irs.gov/pub/irs-pdf/p901.pdf.

CHAPTER FOUR

Offshore Financial Centers Defined

*Here we name and explain jurisdictions that in the past were
called "tax havens." In keeping with political correctness and
their own consensus, they now prefer to be called "offshore
financial centers." We explain laws, procedures, and methods
to maximize your benefits and minimize your taxes. We do the
same for jurisdictions that can be called "asset havens," places
with laws that give maximum asset protection. OFCs usually
also qualify as asset havens. We examine the history of attacks
by big spending governments and their tax collectors that
altered the character of tax havens — much for the better.*

A tax haven can be defined as a country, or other "jurisdiction"
(many are colonial territories of other nations), that promotes and guarantees no taxes or low taxes for foreigners who
choose to live or do business there.

To update the record, for reasons we will explain, those places that
used to be proud to be known as "*tax havens*" now very definitely
prefer to be called "*offshore financial centers*," or "OFCs" for short.

An "*asset haven*" describes a country or jurisdiction that has adopted special laws and established a judicial system that guarantees
strong legal protection for wealth and assets placed there, plus a high
degree of financial privacy.

The same jurisdiction can be both a tax and asset haven and usually
they combine both functions. However, any given haven may qualify
in just one or the other of these two categories.

In this chapter, we explain the differences and similarities of these OFCs, how to use them and where they are located. Specific, detailed treatment of our choices of the best OFCs can be found in Chapter Five.

Understanding Offshore Financial Centers

It may be surprising to the over-taxed citizens of the world to learn that some nations can finance the operation of their governments while imposing only low taxes, almost no taxes or by offering special tax concessions to foreigners who bring in jobs, business and investments.

Indeed, theses low tax systems exist in the United States.

Seven American states of the Union have no state income tax: Alaska, Florida, Nevada, South Dakota, Texas, Washington and Wyoming. Two others, New Hampshire and Tennessee, tax only dividend and interest income. Just as these states offer their citizens a chance to escape from other states' income tax, foreign tax havens may be the solution for offshore-minded people seeking national tax relief.

And you don't have to move your residence to these offshore havens to enjoy their promised benefits — only your cash, your business operation and/or other assets.

However, despite what you may have heard, the truth is that for U.S. persons, "going offshore," using OFCs offers only very minimal tax savings.

Always keep this basic tax fact in mind: the U.S. government taxes all worldwide income wherever it is earned by Americans and wherever the U.S. person may live or have residence(s). This means U.S. citizens and resident aliens (both groups, remember, are known in tax law as "U.S. persons") must, by law, report their income to the IRS and pay U.S. taxes accordingly.

Unlike individual U.S. taxpayers, many American-owned businesses profit by establishing themselves as foreign corporations in low tax countries, since a foreign company owned by Americans pays only limited U.S. taxes on certain types of investment income. If these corporate profits are kept offshore, reinvested or ploughed back into the business, some other U.S. taxes often can be deferred indefinitely.

U.S. politicians regularly attack these beneficial corporate law provisions and attempts to change the laws failed until 2017 when the U.S. corporate tax rate was lowered from 35%, the second highest in the world, to 21%.

The U.S. Internal Revenue Code that applies to offshore business with U.S. ownership is highly complex. The very best professional tax advice is needed to assure compliance with the law if you have ownership, partial or full, in an offshore business — and to make sure you are eligible for every tax break for which you qualify.

Tax obligations differ in various nations according to their own domestic laws, so before you go offshore, check the tax status of your intended country with advice from a competent professional you trust, one located in the intended country or with a U.S. expert on foreign taxation.

Understanding Asset Havens

What characteristics qualify a given place as an "*asset haven*?"

Asset havens are countries or other jurisdictions with established laws that:

- Offer legal entities that provide asset protection, such as trusts, family foundations, limited liability companies (LLCs) and international business corporations (IBCs);

- Protect financial and personal privacy; and

- Provide and support a judicial system that consistently favors asset protection.

Most asset havens also are tax havens — meaning they do not impose income, capital gains, estate, transfer or other taxes on foreigners who choose to open bank accounts or form LLCs, IBCs or trusts registered in the country.

However, not all asset havens are tax-free for foreigners or their business operations, an important factor you should consider and be certain of in each case.

Different Havens, Different Uses

Remember, an established (OFC) "tax haven" jurisdiction does not necessarily qualify as an "asset haven."

Most nations with favorable low tax laws do offer strong asset protection laws as an added incentive to attract foreign money and investments, but such guarantees vary in quality. Here we tell you which countries or jurisdictions offer the best deals and how you can use them to your benefit.

Not all tax havens (OFCs) are independent nations. Many are colonial or territorial possessions of other nations (e.g., Bermuda is a partial self-governing overseas territory of the United Kingdom). The Cayman Islands and the British Virgin Islands hold the same status. The Isle of Man and the Channel Islands are Crown Dependencies of the United Kingdom with more independence, but still under the ultimate control of the government in London.

Historically, many OFCs have spurred economic development by fashioning themselves into both tax and asset havens. Some of these countries have never imposed an income tax. Others are countries with special tax legislation or incentives favoring certain types of business over other types, usually emphasizing job creation.

As we explain in detail in Chapter Eleven (*The United States as an Offshore Tax Haven*), the U.S. is one of the world's leading tax havens, giving special tax treatment to foreigners (but not to Americans) who invest in U.S. real estate, securities and commodities markets, the goal being to attract needed foreign capital and investment.

The United Kingdom also gives some tax breaks to foreigners, although former residential tax breaks for individuals were limited because of budget deficits. In fact, the U.S. and U.K. are both leading world tax havens, based on the calculation of total foreign-owned, tax-exempt cash and assets located and managed within each country.

One expert observed: "The two leading tax havens are indeed islands, but not in the Caribbean, rather they are Manhattan and the City of London."

Tax Havens Variety

A "tax haven" can be described as any jurisdiction whose laws, regulations, policies and treaty arrangements make it possible for a foreign national who does business there to reduce or escape entirely personal and/or corporate taxes.

This is done by bringing yourself — or your trust, foundation, LLC or corporation — within the country's jurisdiction by registration there. This general definition covers all four major types of tax haven nations discussed here, each categorized by the degree and type of taxes imposed.

It's important to understand tax haven differences because not all are equal. You must understand the tax characteristics of each haven type before making decisions and choices.

1. No-Tax Havens

In what might be called "no-tax" havens, foreign citizens who do business there pay no taxes — no income, capital gains, transfer, estate, corporate or wealth taxes.

A foreign citizen can quickly and easily incorporate and/or form a trust or LLC and register to do business immediately. There are a few minor administrative taxes, like stamp duties on incorporation documents, charges on the value of corporate shares issued, annual maintenance registration fees, or other fees not levied directly as a tax on income. In addition, there are non-governmental costs of engaging a local agent and filing annual reports.

The government in a no-tax haven jurisdiction earns considerable revenue from the sheer volume of foreign corporations and trusts that are registered within its borders, even if these entities conduct most or all their business elsewhere.

All these no-tax havens are in the Atlantic Ocean or in or near the Caribbean Basin and include Bermuda, The Bahamas, the Cayman Islands, Saint Kitts and Nevis, the Turks and Caicos Islands, Belize and St. Vincent and the Grenadines.

2. Territorial Tax Havens

The second group includes jurisdictions that enjoy a "territorial tax" system that exempts foreign-source income.

They tax only income earned within the country's boundaries. Income earned or paid from foreign sources is tax exempt, since it involves no in-country domestic business activities, apart from simple housekeeping chores. Often there is no income tax on profits from the export of locally manufactured goods, although there may be a tax on domestic manufacturing itself.

These nations include Costa Rica, Ecuador, Guatemala, Honduras, Israel, the Philippines, Thailand and Sri Lanka. Since none of these named nations qualify as full-fledged tax or asset havens, we won't discuss them further, but we encourage you to research their tax and other laws if interested.

Others in this group are full-fledged tax havens that do tax domestic business activity, while foreign business is tax-exempt. Some others impose zero business taxes.

These jurisdictions include Panama, Uruguay, the Channel Islands of Jersey and Guernsey, the Isle of Man and the United Arab Emirates.

The 2017 Tax Cuts and Jobs Act contains a change from the prior U.S. "worldwide" corporate tax system to a "territorial" system. Under the worldwide system, multinationals were taxed on foreign income earned, but they didn't pay the U.S. tax until they brought the profits home to the U.S. As a result, many corporations left untaxed billions parked overseas. Under the territorial system, they are not taxed on that foreign profit but encouraged to reinvest in the United States. The 2017 Act allows U.S. companies to repatriate $2.6 trillion they held in foreign cash stockpiles in 2018. They pay a one-time repatriation tax rate of 15.5% on cash and 8% on equipment.

3. Tax Treaty Nations

The third type of haven is called a "tax treaty nation."

While these nations impose taxes on worldwide corporate and trust income, their governments have reciprocal bilateral double taxation avoidance agreements with other nations — especially with major trading partners such as the U.S., France, Canada, Germany and the U.K.

These mutual agreements significantly reduce the withholding tax imposed on foreign income earned by domestic corporations and give credit against domestic tax liability for taxes paid by a local business to a foreign government.

Although these nations are less attractive for asset protection, they are suitable for lower taxed international corporate activity. International tax treaties permit the free exchange of information between national taxing authorities, allowing less privacy.

Among the leading tax treaty nations are Switzerland, Cyprus, the Netherlands, Belgium and Denmark. To review information on the use of tax treaties, see Chapter Three, *Creative Offshore Financial Strategies*.

4. Special Use Tax Havens

The final category of havens features several countries that impose the kind of taxes Americans and citizens of the United Kingdom know and dislike — high taxes.

However, in these jurisdictions these high taxes are tempered by a government policy of granting special tax holidays, concessions, or rebates to favored foreign business enterprises they want to attract and promote, usually aiming to increase local employment.

Concessions typically include:

• Corporate tax credits for local job creation;

• Tax exemptions for manufacturing and processing of exports;

• Tax benefits for international business or holding companies, off-shore banks, or other selected industries.

In the U.S., critics call this kind of domestic business tax break "corporate welfare," but many nations (including the United States) offer these kinds of business inducements to foreigners. Among nations that offer generous special tax concessions to foreign-owned businesses are Chile, Portugal and Barbados.

For example, Barbados grants tax exemptions to retired foreigners who settle there. Living conditions are pleasant, with high literacy rates and educational levels. Special laws favor headquarters of international companies and major banks with income tax exemptions. The government also offers generous tax breaks and subsidies for foreign-owned local companies that increase employment.

Fortunately for Chile, when the worldwide recession began in 2008, this South American country could work for its own recovery. A strong economy included banking and finance policies that meant the Chilean government did not have to spend a single peso on bank bailouts. The country also paid down foreign debt during the booming years when copper prices were high. Chile was one of the world's few creditor nations with an upgraded debt rating by Moody's Investors Service. Its economic condition has slipped since then.

Contacts:

Chile:

Pro Chile New York
866 United Nations Plaza, Suite 603
New York, NY 10017
Tel.: 212-207-3266
Web: http://www.prochile.gob.cl/importers

North American Chilean Chamber of Commerce
866 United Nations Plaza, Suite 473
New York, NY 10017
Tel.: 212-317-1959
Email: info@nacchamber.com
Web: http://www.nacchamber.com

Portugal:

Government of Portugal: https://www.portugal.gov.pt

Portugal-U.S. Chamber of Commerce
590 Fifth Avenue, 4th Floor
New York NY 10036
Email: chamber@portugal-us.com
Web: http://www.portugal-us.com

Invest in Portugal
866 Second Avenue, 8th Floor
New York, NY 10017-2905
Tel.: +1 646 723 0200
Email: aicep.newyork@portugalglobal.pt
Web: http://www.portugalglobal.pt/EN/Pages/Index.aspx

Barbados:

Barbados Government Information Service
Old Town Hall
Cheapside, Barbados
Tel.: 246-535-1900
Email: webbgis@barbados.gov.bb
Web: http://gisbarbados.gov.bb

Tax-Free Zones

Closely akin to "special use" tax havens are "tax-free zones" established in designated areas of some countries. Often these zones are used as trans-shipment points for finished goods, such as the Colón Duty Free Trade Zone (C.F.Z.) in Panama (http://www.colonfreezone.com) or the Hong Kong free zone. (For more about Panama and Hong Kong, see Chapter Five.)

Other tax-free zones, however, are major bases for industry, business and finance, complete with well-developed infrastructure and favorable laws to attract business to the zone. A good example is the Jebel Ali Free Trade Zone in the United Arab Emirates (http://www.jafza.ae). Uruguay offers such zones as well (http://fs.com.uy/media/pdf/Uruguays-Free-Trade-Zones-2013.pdf).

Offshore Financial Centers Under Attack

To understand the position in which offshore financial centers find themselves today, a review of three decades of offshore financial and political events is helpful. This historic background explains the present and how past events may affect your rights and offshore financial activities.

In the early 1990s, a coordinated international media campaign attacking tax havens was launched by the governments of major high tax and big deficit nations. Eager tax collectors, especially the U.S. Internal Revenue Service, joined the Organization for Community and Economic Development (OECD), a non-governmental, Paris-based group financed by the major nations that spearheaded this drive.

For decades leading welfare states ran up major budget deficits with a constant need for more revenue to finance growing national debts. The 2008 global recession served as an excuse for politicians to hand out trillion-dollar bailouts/stimulus plans, especially to friends at major banks. The result: even greater need for tax revenues to finance even greater debts. This fiscal insanity led to the European

Union financial crisis with indebted countries such as Greece, Ireland, Italy, Portugal, Spain and Cyprus needing bailouts of billions of euros to avoid debt defaults.

Governments of the major high tax, high debt nations, especially the United States, Germany and France, along with a coterie of allied leftist groups seeking to redistribute wealth, blamed legitimate offshore tax, business and banking havens for a host of supposed sins.

They denounced legal tax competition from low-tax nations as unfair and "harmful" to other countries. These high-tax bureaucrats wanted to abolish tax havens. They demanded an end to financial privacy offshore, especially in nations that historically have had strict bank secrecy laws, such as Switzerland, Austria and Panama. OFCs were pressured to sign tax information exchange agreements (TIEAs) or face possible financial "sanctions" and "blacklisting" from major countries.

Sad to say, but the attack on offshore financial centers did curb many freedoms and did limit privacy. There was a very positive result, as well, largely ignored by critics.

Offshore financial centers accomplished real self-reform, bringing more transparency and stricter regulation. They were so successful that the OFCs created far better financial regulatory regimes compared to those in the City of London or in the United States, the two financial disaster centers where the colossal 2008 global financial mess originated.

What This Means for You

For those with existing offshore investments and banking arrangements, and those considering going offshore, history favored expansion of traditional financial freedoms.

Those offshore freedoms remain in place for Americans, although opponents have done much legislatively to curb offshore financial liberties. Similar restrictions were adopted in the United Kingdom, Germany and other major high-tax nations.

The current situation in America and other nations makes it imperative that you keep abreast of offshore developments. You can do that with information from Banyan Hill.

There remain many attractive legal opportunities for offshore asset protection, business, investing, banking, currency trading, even making a new home offshore.

- It is legal to have and use an offshore bank account.

- It is legal to invest offshore in stocks, bonds and other investment properties and have an offshore brokerage account.

- It is legal to create and donate assets to an offshore asset protection trust (APT) or family foundation.

- It is legal to form and operate an international business corporation (IBC).

- It is legal to purchase offshore life insurance and annuities that may allow deferred U.S. taxes.

- It is legal to invest in offshore mutual and hedge funds, precious metals and real estate.

- It is legal to acquire dual citizenship and a second passport.

- It is legal to voluntarily end U.S. citizenship and thus remove oneself from the U.S. tax system.

The truth is that, despite the continued attempts at political strangulation of financial and personal freedom in the United States and other nations, offshore wealth preservation and prudent asset protection planning remain an option to be considered.

CHAPTER FIVE

Offshore Financial Centers

In prior editions of this book, our Banyan Hill colleagues and associates formed a consensus on what we believed to be the leading offshore financial centers in the world.

However, the revolution in laws, rules and policies governing what used to be called "tax havens," especially in financial privacy and bank secrecy, now requires a broader approach. Offshore opportunities are not confined to leading OFCs but are available in many places.

Here we analyze offshore financial centers based on their individual best uses for you, without attempting to rank them in an artificial numeric world order.

Random Opportunities Offshore

- Some of the best SEC-registered independent wealth management experts are in Switzerland, Denmark and Canada.

- For superior personal investment banking services, add Austria to Switzerland, with the Swiss also offering a link to banks in neighboring Liechtenstein where the Swiss franc is the official currency.

- If you want to open your own regional Asian brokerage/investment accounts, Singapore and Hong Kong are close rivals for best place.

- Gibraltar is a good brokerage and investment base for all European business.

- Both Panama and Uruguay welcome foreigners and specialize in immediate residence and eventual citizenship.

- For your offshore asset protection trust the Cook Islands is a world leader.

- Nevis provides limited liability companies overnight, backed by 30 years of strong asset protection laws.

- Some of the most well-crafted investment vehicles and funds can be found in the United Kingdom's overseas territories (Cayman Islands, Bermuda) and the Crown dependencies (Isle of Man, the Channel Islands).

FINANCIAL PRIVACY: In this chapter and throughout the book, when we speak about individual financial privacy and privacy laws, keep in mind that virtually every country now applies the standard for tax information exchange set by the Organization for Economic Co-operation and Development (OECD), based on Article 26 of the "OECD Model Tax Convention." Most countries have agreed to the expanded OECD "Common Reporting Standard" that imposes automatic tax information exchange as an international rule. Also understand that each country applies Article 26 exchanges within its own procedural framework, and some are more restrictive than others in protecting privacy. For more about this see *Automatic Tax Information Exchange* in Chapter Three.

As you read, you will discover how each offshore financial center can best fit your needs. Where appropriate, we provide professional and official contacts.

In considering the usefulness of individual offshore financial centers (OFCs), we constantly review the laws, political stability, economic climate, tax regime and the overall financial standing of each jurisdiction.

Applying these and other important criteria, we start with six selected offshore financial centers that stand out from others — Switzerland, Liechtenstein, Panama, Uruguay, Hong Kong and Singapore. They are grouped geographically, and their list position does not necessarily indicate our opinion of their comparative rank.

As with all other jurisdictions, we evaluate five factors for each, rating on a scale of 1 to 5 based on the following considerations:

Government/political stability: How long has the current system of government been in place? Is the jurisdiction politically stable?

Favorable laws, judicial system: Is there a well-established legal tradition and judicial system with a solid reputation for "fair play" with regard to foreign investors?

Available legal entities: Does the jurisdiction offer a variety of legal entities that meet the needs of foreign persons seeking estate planning, asset protection and/or business solutions?

Financial privacy/banking secrecy: Does the jurisdiction have and enforce financial privacy laws? How strictly are they applied? Are there exceptions to these laws and, if so, how extensive are they?

Taxes: Does the OFC impose taxes on foreigners that invest and do business there, and if so, to what degree? Are there tax treaties or tax information exchange agreements in effect?

Switzerland
Historic World Leader

Even considering its many international difficulties and attendant bad publicity, Switzerland remains as one of the best all-around asset and financial havens in the world.

For centuries, the Swiss have acted as banker to the world. In that role Switzerland acquired a deserved reputation for integrity and financial privacy, although both have been tarnished in recent years.

It is also an attractive place for wealthy people to reside, which may explain why Switzerland is home to 9.5% of all world millionaires. In 2016, ranking seventh in the world, the number of millionaires rose by 4.5% to 358,500, millionaire households in Switzerland. Out of every thousand Swiss households, 127 were home to millionaires.

Switzerland may be said to be neutral in international politics, but it's far from bland or flavorless.

The fusion of German, French and Italian influences has formed a robust national culture. The country's alpine landscapes have more than enough zing to reinvigorate even the most jaded traveler. The German, Johann Wolfgang von Goethe, summed up Switzerland succinctly as a combination of "the colossal and the well-ordered." You can be certain that trains will run meticulously on schedule and provide you with breathtakingly magnificent views from your railcar window.

The tidy, "just-so" precision of Swiss towns is tempered by the lofty splendor of the landscapes that surround them. But there's a lot more here than just trillions of dollars and euros.

Reputation to Uphold

A global survey of private banks published by PricewaterhouseCoopers (PwC) found that the major attraction for a bank's new customers is its reputation.

Switzerland's financial reputation is central to the claim that this alpine nation serves as "banker to the world." Indeed, in these turbulent days, good judgment and reliability are banking traits more sought after than ever before — and difficult to find.

For more than 250 years, as European empires and nations rose and fell, Swiss topography, geography and determination have combined to defend their mountainous redoubt from external attack. All the while, the Swiss people have prided themselves for their neutral attitudes and policies toward other nations.

FACTORS	FINDINGS	RATING
Government/ political stability	"Swiss" and "stability" have long been synonymous	5
Favorable laws, judicial system	Very protective of personal wealth	5
Available legal entities	All major legal entities available or recognized	5
Taxes	35% on interest paid, reduced under bilateral tax treaties; income taxes negotiable for resident foreigners	3.5
Financial privacy Bank secrecy	World's oldest bank secrecy law now significantly weakened	3
Final Rating		**21.5**

World Financial Refuge

In 1945, after the 20th century's second "war to end all wars," Swiss voters overwhelmingly rejected membership in the United Nations. It was not until 2002 that a slim majority backed U.N. membership. In 1992 and 2001 national polls, Swiss voters also rejected membership in the European Union, rightly fearing EU bureaucratic interference with Swiss privacy and banking laws. A 2014 national ballot soundly rejected a proposal to ease Swiss bank secrecy laws and recent opinion polls reconfirm that position.

After each of these national referenda and during wars, world crises and recessions, ever-greater amounts of foreign cash flowed into Swiss banks, confirming the widespread notion that Switzerland is the place to safeguard cash and other personal assets in troubled times. As a haven for cash, Switzerland has become a modern cliché.

The numbers continue to support the confidence the world historically places in Switzerland.

Today, Switzerland is the world's leader in offshore private banking. It is still considered the best place for the world's wealthy to keep their riches, even after the tax evasion and bank secrecy scandals were exposed.

In 2018, Switzerland maintained its position as leading world wealth management center, with 34% of the $8.15 trillion in total global wealth. Of that amount, Swiss banks held $2 trillion of offshore wealth, according to financial consulting firm Deloitte. Switzerland was a prime location for cross-border wealth management, ahead of both Britain and the United States, representing $1.7 trillion and $1.4 trillion respectively.

It is no accident that the governments of both of its competitors have been among Switzerland's chief critics, pushing for an end to Swiss bank secrecy laws.

The fate of the non-euro Swiss economy is tightly linked to that of its neighbors who are in the euro zone, which purchases half of all Swiss exports. After the 2008 global financial crisis, the Swiss National Bank (SNB) implemented a zero-interest rate policy, which in turn boosted the economy and its recovery.

This SNB policy continued in the sovereign debt crises in neighboring euro zone as countries such as Greece posed a major risk to Switzerland's financial stability and drove up demand for the Swiss franc by investors seeking a safe-haven currency. The independent SNB upheld its zero-interest rate policy and conducted major market interventions to prevent further appreciation of the Swiss franc. The franc soared 20% against the euro when the SNB abandoned its euro peg in 2015.

Switzerland has one of the highest per capita GDPs in the world (US$61,400, 2017 est.) with inflation rates below 1% or zero in recent years (0.5%, 2017 est.). Its location in the center of Europe, a favorable tax regime, high standard of living and low crime rate makes Switzerland an attractive place to live and work for expatriates.

Very Special Swiss Franc

The Swiss franc is referred to as a "safe haven" currency. It is a currency that investors buy when other currencies, such as the euro and dollar, are struggling. A "safe haven" currency also equates to a strong economy, stable government and enough liquidity to deal with strong bouts of international trading. Neutral Switzerland, with its conservative economic policy and a strong financial sector, has been a classic haven currency for many decades, especially during the two World Wars as remains today.

Switzerland's currency, the Swiss franc, generally has reflected the state of Swiss banking — strong, valuable and unaffected by inflation and stylish monetary fads. Since 1971, the franc has appreciated nearly 330% against the U.S. dollar. U.S. owners of Swiss franc-denominated assets usually have profited as a result. That profit came despite traditionally low Swiss interest rates and the bothersome 35% withholding tax on bank interest.

The 2013 sovereign debt crises in Greece, Cyprus and other euro zone countries posed a significant risk to Switzerland's financial stability and drove up demand for the Swiss franc by foreign investors seeking a haven currency. The independent Swiss National Bank upheld its zero-interest rate policy and conducted major market interventions to prevent further appreciation of the Swiss franc. The franc's strength had driven up real estate prices, made Swiss exports less competitive and weakened the country's economic growth outlook, which is one reason the GDP growth slipped to 1.3% in 2016.

Despite its reputation for bank secrecy, in 1990, Switzerland was one of the first European countries to make money laundering a criminal offense. That law resulted in the demise of the famous Swiss *"compte anonyme"*, as the French-speaking Swiss termed it — universally known as a "numbered account." Previously, it was possible to open a nominee account in which the identity of the account holder could be concealed from almost everyone except the highest bank officials.

Since 1994, a central office in Bern has been devoted exclusively to fighting organized crime. Mandatory "know your customer" guidelines are used by Swiss banks to investigate potential clients.

This strict anti-money laundering law has transformed Swiss banking in a fundamental way. Previously, bankers had the option of reporting suspicious transactions to police authorities. Now, under pressure from world governments pursuing corruption, drug cartels and organized crime, the government requires banks to report suspicious transactions. Failure to report is a crime and bankers can now go to prison for keeping secret the names and records of suspected clients. Not so long ago, they faced imprisonment for failing to reveal such information.

The Swiss government also has proven willing to freeze assets before an individual is even charged with a crime if a foreign government can demonstrate "reasonable suspicion" that the accused engaged in criminal conduct. This is especially the case in high-profile drug or political corruption cases, such as those involving Swiss bank accounts of someone such as the late dictator of the Philippines, Ferdinand Marcos.

World-Class Banking System

Although Swiss banking privacy was legendary, secrecy is not the most important reason for Switzerland's success.

Of far greater significance are the country's political, financial and economic stability and strength. Most of the world's largest companies and hundreds of thousands of honest, law-abiding foreigners bank with the Swiss. Traditionally, Swiss banks have managed close to 40% of the world's private wealth, or more than US$3 trillion in assets.

It is no coincidence that the official international intermediary banking institution, the Bank for International Settlements, is in Basel, Switzerland.

Switzerland is home to several hundred banks ranging from small private and regional banks to the two giants, UBS AG and Credit Suisse. These major Swiss banks have branch offices in most of the world's financial centers, from New York to Panama to Singapore.

Swiss banks combine traditional banking with international brokerage and financial management. To guard against inflation or devaluation, Swiss bank accounts can be denominated in the currency you choose — Swiss francs, U.S. dollars, Euros or any other major currency. An account opened in one currency can be switched to another denomination when the time is right for short-term profits or long-term gains and safety.

You can invest in certificates of deposit, U.S. and other national stocks, bonds, mutual funds and commodities; buy, store and sell gold, silver and other precious metals; and buy insurance and annuities. Swiss banks can act as your agent to buy and hold other types of assets. Of course, Swiss banks also issue international credit and ATM bank cards. Bank officers speak English as well as many other languages. Swiss banks are equipped for fax, wire, email, or telex and instructions are carried out immediately. Or, just phone your own personal banker who handles your account.

To some extent, "know your customer" rules have complicated the process of opening a bank account in Switzerland and proof of identity and references are required. But, the biggest downside is the high minimum deposit required by most Swiss private investment banks.

A few years ago, many banks were content with initial deposits of only a few thousand dollars. Now Switzerland's popularity with foreign investors, along with the cost of administering "know your customer" laws and FATCA, has led to sharp increases in deposit minimums, the lowest now being US$500,000. Most private investment accounts require a minimum of US$1 million.

An alternative can be found in banks run by the various Swiss cantons. These banks offer full services, have relatively lower minimum deposits and each cantonal government insures the deposits.

Swiss banks usually require that foreigners applying to open a new account do so in person. Because of U.S. government lawsuits against Swiss banks and onerous U.S. government regulations and reporting requirements involving Americans, such as that imposed by FATCA, many Swiss banks now refuse to do business with U.S. persons.

Strict Control, High Quality

Swiss banks have attained their unique position with financial expertise, global capabilities and the high percentage and quality of their reserves, much of it in gold and Swiss francs. The Swiss financial industry is tightly regulated, with banks strictly supervised by the Federal Banking Commission (FBC).

Swiss law imposes stiff liquidity and capital requirements on banks. The complicated official liquidity formula results in some private banks maintaining liquidity at or near 100%, unheard of in other national banking systems. The Swiss reputation also rests on the fact that some banks traditionally hold substantial unreported, hidden reserves. Every month, Swiss banks with securities investments must adjust the book value of their holdings to current market price or actual cost, whichever is lower. This assures no Swiss banks will have unrealized paper losses, as often happens in other countries.

Swiss banks are also subject to two regular audits. The first audit is to ensure compliance with Swiss corporate law. The second is the banking audit, conducted by one of 17 audit firms specially approved by the FBC. These exacting audits provide the primary guarantee for Swiss bank depositors. Supervision and regulation of Swiss banking surpasses that of any other nation. Plus, the banks have comprehensive insurance to cover deposits, transfers, theft, or abnormal losses. This means that your funds are insured in the event of a bank failure — but that hasn't happened in Switzerland in many decades.

Fiduciary Investment Account

One popular Swiss account for foreign investors is the fiduciary account. A Swiss bank investment manager oversees the account, but all its investments are placed outside Switzerland, as the account holder directs. Funds that pass through the account are therefore not subject to Swiss taxes.

The fiduciary account comes in two forms: (1) an investment account and (2) a fiduciary loan account. With the investment account, the bank places the client's funds as loans to foreign banks in the form of fixed-term deposits. In the loan account, the customer designates the commercial borrower. Although the bank assumes no risk, it provides an important service by conducting a thorough investigation of the prospective borrower's credit credentials.

Many international companies use fiduciary loans to finance subsidiaries. There is an element of risk in making such loans, though. In the event of currency devaluation, or the bankruptcy of the borrower, the lender can lose.

Discretionary Accounts

With more than 250 years in the international portfolio management business, Swiss banks are among the world leaders in investment management.

Experienced money managers constantly analyze world markets, choosing investments with the greatest potential and minimal risk. Swiss banks offer a broad selection of investment plans diversified by industry, country, international, or emerging markets. Outside financial managers can be employed to invest deposited funds and bank loans can be arranged for investment purposes. These accounts are best managed by a private Swiss bank or by an independent asset manager (IAM). (For more about IAMs, see Chapter Three.)

The Swiss invented what has come to be called "private banking." They honed private banking to a fine edge many centuries before U.S. cookie-cutter banks discovered the concept. With an independent asset manager working with a private bank, you get personal contact and individual service.

However, most private banks require a high initial minimum investment of at least US$1 million and a personal introduction from a well-known source.

Swiss Investment Alternatives

Switzerland is also a world-renowned center for insurance and reinsurance. Many Swiss insurance companies offer a broad range of financial services that, in some cases, approach the flexibility of a bank account. Indeed, many Swiss residents use their insurance company as their only financial institution. (See Chapter Three, *Part 2 — Financial Strategies.*)

Swiss insurance policies offer other important advantages, including:

• Generally higher interest rates than bank accounts.

• Policies may be configured to offer significant asset protection, unlike a bank account.

• Insurance accounts are not subject to the Swiss 35% withholding tax on earned bank interest.

U.S. tax law ended the tax deferral previously allowed on fixed annuity contracts issued by foreign insurance companies. All such annuity income must now be reported as part of taxable annual income. However, income from properly structured foreign variable annuities, life insurance and private placement contracts generally remains U.S. tax deferred. There is a one-time U.S. 1% excise tax on Swiss life insurance and annuities due at the time of purchase.

Taxes

Switzerland is not a low-tax country for Swiss residents or companies, although tax rates are lower than in the surrounding EU nations. But foreign investors can avoid many local taxes by choosing certain types of investments that avoid taxes.

By law, Swiss banks collect a withholding tax of 35% on all interest and dividends paid by Swiss companies, banks, the government or other sources. Foreign investors to whom this tax applies may be eligible for refunds of all or part of the tax under the terms of Switzerland's network of more than 80 tax treaties with other nations.

In addition, there are many legal ways to avoid Swiss taxes by investing in accounts especially structured for foreign investors. These include non-Swiss money market and bond funds, fiduciary precious metal accounts and other instruments. For instance, Switzerland imposes no taxes on dividends or interest from securities that originate outside Switzerland. For this reason, many Swiss banks offer investment funds with at least 80% of earnings in foreign investments or, even better, in money market funds located in Luxembourg or Ireland where they are tax exempt.

Companies are welcome in Switzerland and are established in the form of a corporation (*Aktiengesellschaft; AG*). Shareholders are not personally liable for company debts and a corporation can be formed by one or more individuals or legal entities. Nominees may act as founders. There are no restrictions as to the nationality or the domicile of the founders or the shareholders.

Holding companies enjoy an effective income tax rate of 7.83%, while dividend income is practically tax exempt. In addition, principle companies, intellectual property (IP) companies, and financing and international trading activities can see effective tax rates between 8% and 11%. However, the overall effective tax rate of 12.6% to 24% comes into play for operating companies in other sectors.

These are federal taxes and there may be additional cantonal taxes.

Tax Treaties Abound

To reduce the possibility that Swiss citizens or companies might be subject to double taxation, the Swiss government has created a global network of about 80 tax treaties.

Tax treaties, however, have the unfortunate side effect of reducing financial secrecy. It is not possible to claim a tax credit under a tax treaty without also revealing the income that was taxed. In addition, tax treaties have a second purpose: they exist not only to help individuals and companies investing or doing business internationally to avoid double taxation, but also to facilitate information exchange between tax authorities.

The 1997 U.S.-Swiss tax treaty, still in effect, is a case in point.

While non-payment of taxes is not a crime in Switzerland, Article 26 of the U.S.-Swiss treaty permits the two governments to exchange information about alleged "tax fraud and the like." In addition, it also allows authorities to transfer information that may help in the "prevention of tax fraud and the like in relation to taxes."

In 2013, the Swiss parliament rejected a new tax treaty with the U.S. because it would violate what little remains of the Swiss Bank Secrecy Law of 1934. Swiss banks very much wanted the agreement because it would have granted a limited amnesty for all banks and protected them and some of their employees from U.S. prosecution. For several years ratification of a new Swiss-U.S. tax treaty has remained in political limbo, stalled in the U.S. Senate by Senator Rand Paul (R-KY) who opposes it because it destroys the financial privacy rights of Americans.

Tax-Advantaged Swiss Residence

For the very wealthy foreign immigrant, Switzerland's cantonal tax system allows a unique personalized income tax plan that calls for annual lump-sum tax payments.

Foreign citizens who fulfill certain local requirements may be eligible for this special tax arrangement in which Swiss taxes are levied based on a person's personal expenditures and standard of living in Switzerland, rather than on worldwide income and assets. This lump sum taxation (called *forfait fiscal* in French, *Pauschalbesteuerung* in German) is available in 20 of 26 cantons, but not in the cantons of Zurich, Schaffhausen, Appenzell Ausserrhoden, Basel Landschaft and Basel Stadt. The system was originally introduced by the canton of Vaud in the 1860s to get wealthy British residents to pay for local services.

This unique lump-sum taxation effectively caps the income and net wealth tax for qualifying foreign citizens. Switzerland is also attractive because it imposes no federal inheritance or gift taxes. But the cantons do levy inheritance and gift taxes, which means that there are 25 different inheritance and gift tax regimes. In the 26th canton, Schwyz, there is neither inheritance nor gift taxes.

Remember that we said that in 2016, there were 385,000 millionaire households in Switzerland. Now you know one of the main reasons.

Under the forfeit deal, foreigners pay an average CHF75,000 Swiss francs (US$80,000) in annual taxes, producing more than US$710 million per year in revenue. The system allows resident foreign citizens to negotiate a fixed tax rate based on their Swiss property factors, excluding income earned outside Switzerland.

Forfeits have caused resentment among Swiss because top rates of income tax exceed 40% in cantons such as Geneva. Since 2009, five of the 26 Swiss cantons have repealed the scheme, while another five have kept the tax break but raised the bar for beneficiaries. However, in a national referendum in 2014, the Swiss people decided by a clear majority to maintain the lump sum *forfait fiscal* tax break for foreigners resident in the country.

A 2016 federal law on lump sum taxation makes these changes to the system: a) the lump sum income should amount to at least seven times (instead of the current five times) the rental value or the annual rent of the person's Swiss residence; b) at federal level the lump sum amount shall not be lower than CHF 400,000 (US$428,000); c) each canton has the right to fix a cantonal minimum lump sum amount. All existing lump sum taxpayers in 2014 were 'grandfathered' for period of five years and the 2016 law will not apply to them until tax year 2021.

Ordinary federal and cantonal tax rates are applied to this figure and there is no obligation to declare worldwide income or assets, and no tax is paid on income from securities holdings. Deals vary widely among the 26 cantons that allow it. (Many nations entice foreigners as individual or corporate residents by exempting them from all or most taxes, including the United Kingdom, Monaco, Luxembourg, Austria and Ireland.)

The Swiss may be conservative in many ways, but they do welcome foreigners. A proposal to limit — constitutionally — the number of foreigners allowed to enter the country was rejected. The proposed limit was a max of 18% of the population of approximately 7.2 million at that time (the population has increased to a reported 8.2 million in 2017). There are now a reported 2.1 million foreigners (about 25% of the population) living in Switzerland.

People come from all over the world to live here. In fact, 86.5% of Switzerland's permanent foreign resident population is of European origin, two-thirds of whom are nationals of an EU country.

Swiss Bank Secrecy

In recent years, Switzerland's image as "bankers to the world's rich" has taken some serious and deserved hits, along with the much-vaunted Swiss Bank Secrecy Law of 1934, now in tatters.

The decline of Swiss strict adherence to its bank secrecy can be traced to 1998 and initial pressure from the U.S. Federal Reserve System.

In that year, Swiss Bank Corporation and Union Bank of Switzerland merged creating UBS AG. Hungry for American business, UBS applied for a license for banking in America. The U.S. Federal Reserve approved UBS, but with an eye on possible American client tax evasion, the Fed demanded and got a guarantee that the banking giant would provide U.S. regulators all information "necessary to determine and enforce compliance with [U.S.] federal law."

As events have shown, that certainly meant UBS compliance with U.S. tax laws. In 1998, rather than defend their potential U.S. clients' privacy rights, the bank compromised with the Fed and, in effect, ignored the strong privacy guarantees of the Swiss Bank Secrecy Law of 1934.

Because of this UBS capitulation on financial privacy, many who advocated maximum legal financial privacy, publicly advised potential U.S. depositors considering Swiss banks to avoid UBS AG, and any other Swiss bank with U.S.-based branches, affiliates or banking operations, other than a mere "representative office." These warnings predated the subsequent UBS tax evasion scandal that erupted in 2008.

From its U.S. start, UBS did business in America under threat of U.S. regulators shutting down UBS's extensive U.S. operations. (UBS now has about 80,000 employees worldwide, 30,000 in the United States.)

After the Fed's 1998 approval, UBS secretly assisted at least 4,500 American clients to engage in illegal evasion of U.S. taxes. UBS later admitted its private banking managers conspired from 2001 to 2006 to defraud the IRS. The bank was forced to pay a US$780 million fine to the U.S. government to settle a federal tax investigation, and an additional $200 million for SEC violations.

A suit by the U.S. Department of Justice (DOJ) against UBS seeking the names of an alleged 55,000 Americans that had UBS accounts was settled in 2010 with the UBS surrender of 4,500 names, many of whom have been prosecuted by the IRS. Since then some

Swiss bankers individually have been prosecuted successfully by the U.S. government for assisting U.S. tax evasion and some have been acquitted. The same fate has met many of their former U.S. clients.

Bank Secrecy Ends

The Swiss Bank Secrecy Law of 1934 continues to hold majority support among the Swiss. The law was originally created to guard the assets of Jews and others hunted by Adolf Hitler's Nazis. But the law created a level of privacy was a major draw for the trillions of dollars the country manages for investors around the globe.

In 2012, the Swiss government did the once-inconceivable — in effect they repealed the 1934 Bank Secrecy Law as it applied to U.S. persons with Swiss financial accounts. A respected law that defeated the Nazis could not stop the combined political power of the seemingly disparate interests of the tax-hungry U.S. IRS and nervous Swiss bankers willing to surrender secrecy to avoid indictment by the U.S. Department of Justice.

This historic surrender of Swiss bank secrecy result resulted from the immense political and financial pressure from Swiss banks under investigation for U.S. tax evasion. The Swiss government desperately tried to get the U.S. to drop tax investigations against 11 banks, including Credit Suisse and Julius Baer. In exchange for a general amnesty and payment of fines they offered to surrender of U.S. client names. The politicians also wanted to shield the other 300-plus Swiss banks and financial institutions from possible U.S. prosecution.

Looming over the surrender was the 2009 debacle when UBS was forced to pay the U.S. a $780 million fine and release the names of 4,500 clients to the IRS. They acted to settle a lawsuit that threatened to shut down UBS American operations with more than 30,000 employees. That 2009 deal was the first major crack in the 1934 Bank Secrecy Law.

In 2009, the Swiss government was forced to seek, and got, parliamentary approval for the UBS-IRS settlement after the Swiss Federal

Administrative Court twice ruled that the deal was illegal because it violated the 1934 Bank Secrecy Law. Officials cited the U.S. Foreign Account Tax Compliance Act, (FATCA) as the reason for the Swiss-IRS agreement.

Switzerland's State Secretariat for International Financial Matters claimed in a questionable statement that a Swiss refusal to implement FATCA would cause "major disadvantages" for Swiss banks.

To save face, the ever-efficient Swiss opted for a streamlined procedure that allows individual Swiss banks to hand over data about American clients directly to the IRS. The FATCA procedure of the U.K., France, Germany, Spain and Italy uses government-to-IRS conduits.

The New York Times reported: "This better takes into account the particular characteristics of the Swiss financial center, crowed the Swiss Bankers Association that welcomed the sellout of traditional Swiss bank secrecy."

In the famous legend of William Tell that every Swiss knows and respects, Tell represents the common man, who respects authority but is quick to fight for his rights once authority turns despotic; thus a modest peasant became a national hero.

The governing Swiss Federal Counsel chose not to emulate Tell's modest peasant courage. While the politicians ignored the noble example of William Tell, they certainly did not ignore their friends at UBS, Credit Suisse and other Swiss banks.

Follow the Money

The explanation here, as in the United States, is: "Follow the money!"

It can be argued that, over time, Swiss bank secrecy would have been relaxed to some degree anyway — but the villain in this historic defeat was, of course — UBS — that mismanaged, greedy, tax evading behemoth bank that demanded and got a multi-billion bailout package by the Swiss government, when it posted record losses in the 2008 world recession.

For the usual anti-privacy, anti-tax haven crowd who habitually bash any offshore financial activity, Switzerland has always been a special target and the UBS-IRS scandal was a godsend for them.

These leftists hated the Swiss Bank Secrecy Law because they believe that the privacy rights of the individual must be subordinated to government and that all offshore accounts probably are used for tax evasion.

Rob Vrijhof, is a leading Zurich investment manager and a trusted partner of Banyan Hill since our founding. He has spoken at our events and points out: "Many of the attacks on Swiss bank secrecy in the name of 'justice' are, in truth, attempts to eliminate cross-border banking competition, to impose an international tax cartel, or to undermine Switzerland's recognized status as a world financial center that easily competes with the City of London and Wall Street."

Contacts:

Embassy of Switzerland

2900 Cathedral Avenue NW
Washington, D.C. 20008
Tel.: 202-745-7900
Email: was.information@eda.admin.ch
Web: https://www.eda.admin.ch/washington

Consulates General are in Atlanta, Los Angeles, New York and San Francisco. For more details, visit https://www.eda.admin.ch/countries/usa/en/home.html.

United States Embassy

Sulgeneckstrasse 19
CH-3007 Bern, Switzerland
Tel.: +031 357 70 11
Email: https://ch.usembassy.gov/u-s-citizen-services/contact-us-acs
Web: https://ch.usembassy.gov

U.S. Consular Agency Zürich
Dufourstrasse 101
CH-8008 Zürich, Switzerland
Tel.: +41 43 499 29 60
Web: https://ch.usembassy.gov/u-s-citizen-services/ca-zrh-contact

Recommended U.S. SEC-Registered Investment Advisors:

Robert Vrijhof, President
WHVP: Weber, Hartmann, Vrijhof & Partners Ltd.
Schaffhauserstrasse 418
CH-8050 Zürich, Switzerland
Contact: Julia Fernandez
Tel.: 01141 44 315 77 77 (USA/Canada) / +41 44 315 77 77
(International)
Email: info@whvp.ch
Web: http://www.whvp.ch
Custodial banks: WHVP is associated with a variety of Swiss and other foreign banks.

Daniel Zurbruegg, CFA, Managing Partner & Chief Executive
Officer
BFI Infinity Inc.
Bergstrasse 21
8044 Zürich, Switzerland
Tel.: + 41 58 806 2210
Email: daniel.zurbruegg@bfiwealth.com
Web: https://www.bfiwealth.com
Minimum Balance: US$250,000 or equivalent

Dominique J. Spillmann, CEO & Partner
Swisspartners Advisors Ltd.
Am Schanzengraben 23
CH-8022 Zürich, Switzerland
Tel.: +41 58 200 0 801
Email: dominique.spillmann@swisspartners-advisors.com

Web: http://swisspartners-advisors.com
Custodial banks: Bank Julius Bär, Credit Suisse, LGT
Liechtensteinische Landesbank, Pictet & Cie, Sarasin, UBS,
Zürcher Kantonalbank

Residence & Citizenship Services:

Henley & Partners
Dr. Christian H. Kälin TEP, IMCM, Group Chairman
Henley Haus, Klosbachstrasse 110
8024 Zürich, Switzerland
Tel.: +41 44 266 22 22
Email: christian.kalin@henleyglobal.com
Web: https://www.henleyglobal.com

Henley & Partners
Jon Green, Partner
906 — 1112 West Pender Street
Vancouver, BC
V6E 2S1, Canada
Tel.: +1-604-239-2170
Email: jon.green@henleyglobal.com
Web: https://www.henleyglobal.com

Principality of Liechtenstein

This tiny principality, the world's sixth smallest country in territory, is a constitutional monarchy that has graced the map of Europe since 1719. Within the last century it has transformed itself into a major offshore financial center. Among all the world's OFCs, Liechtenstein has adopted some of the most drastic changes, abolishing near absolute financial privacy and ending their past refusal to share client information with any other government.

Major Changes in Oldest Tax Haven

Tiny Liechtenstein (16 miles long and 3.5 miles wide with a population of 37,922) is nestled in the mountains between Switzerland and Austria. It has existed in its present form since January 23, 1719, when the Holy Roman Emperor, Charles VI, granted it independent status.

In the past, the world's wealthy could do business here quietly, protected by near absolute secrecy and financial privacy laws. It also offered global banking and investment direct access through its cooperative neighbor, Switzerland. The Swiss franc is the local currency and, in many respects, except for political independence, Liechtenstein's status is that of a de facto province integrated within Switzerland.

With asset protection laws dating from the 1920s, a host of excellent legal entities designed for wealth preservation and bank secrecy guaranteed by law, at one time this tiny principality had it all. But that secrecy made it a prime target for outside pressure from the OECD, the U.S. and other major high tax countries.

Under pressure, Liechtenstein more than blinked, it folded.

In the not too distant past, one had to be a philatelist to know the Principality of Liechtenstein even existed. In those days, the nation's major export was exquisitely produced postage stamps, highly prized by collectors. Until the 1960s, the tiny principality subsisted on income from tourism, postage stamp sales and the export of false teeth.

In the last 60 years, its tax free financial privacy propelled Liechtenstein to top rank among the world's wealthiest nations. This historic Rhine Valley principality grew into a major world tax and asset haven, posting the highest per capita income level in the world, US$169,492, according to United Nations figures for 2015, higher than Germany, France and the United Kingdom.

FACTORS	FINDINGS	RATING
Government/political stability	Popular absolute monarchy, dictates subject only to national referenda	5
Favorable laws, judicial system	Well-established, respected rule of law	5
Available legal entities	All major legal entities available or recognized	5
Taxes	Foreign-owned entities mostly tax-exempt, but TIEAs with the UK and others	3.5
Financial privacy/ Bank secrecy	Weakened by law and TIEAs	3
Final Rating		**21.5**

Absolute Monarchy

The Prince of Liechtenstein, Johannes "Hans" Adam Ferdinand Alois Josef Maria Marco d'Aviano Pius Fürst von und zu Liechtenstein, rules the government in a constitutional monarchy as head of state. In a 2003 referendum, Hans-Adam II won an overwhelming majority in favor of changing the constitution to give him powers greater than any other European monarch. The Prince ("*Fürst*" in German) is one of the wealthiest monarchs, as well, owning the banking group

LGT, a family fortune of $7.6 billion, and his own personal fortune of $4.0 billion.

Liechtenstein's ruling Prince has the right to dismiss governments and approve judicial nominees. The Prince may also veto laws simply by refusing to sign them within a six-month period. Tempering this authority is the fact that the signature of 1,500 Liechtenstein citizens on a petition is sufficient to force a referendum on the abolition of the monarchy, or any other change in the law.

In 2004 Prince Hans-Adam II ceded day-to-day rule of the country to his son, Prince Alois, now 53, while he remains the official head of state. This was viewed as the first step towards the eventual full succession of power to Prince Alois.

Financial Center

Liechtenstein's economy is well-diversified, and it is, for its small size, one of the most heavily industrialized countries in Europe.

Still, financial services provide a third of GDP. Its 16 locally owned banks, 60 law firms and 250 trust companies employ 16% of the workforce. Its licensed fiduciary companies and lawyers serve as nominees for, or manage, more than 80,000 legal entities, most of them owned and controlled by nonresidents of Liechtenstein.

Although only 16% of workers are in the financial sector, financial services account for 30% of the gross national product, with industry and manufacturing trade (4%), general services (25%) and agriculture and households (5%). Forty-six percent of the workforce is employed in the industrial sector and 40% of employees work in other service activities, such as trade, hotels and restaurants, transport and public administration. About 12,000 workers commute daily from Austria and Switzerland. GDP has grown as much as 10% annually in recent years and unemployment stays below 3%.

Liechtenstein has positioned itself as "an oasis of political and economic stability" amidst the chaos of European debt crisis and despite significant pressure to tighten control over tax evaders. Leaders of this nation have distanced themselves from the "tax haven" label.

Liechtenstein was one of the first nations in the world to adopt specific offshore asset protection laws, as far back as the 1920s. Indeed, Liechtenstein's unique role in international circles was not so much as a banking center, but as — that hated phrase — a tax haven.

The nation still acts as a base of operations for foreign holding companies, private foundations, family foundations and a unique entity called the *Anstalt* (i.e., establishment). The banks and a host of specialized trust companies provide management services for thousands of such entities. Personal and company tax rates are low, generally under 12% for residents.

Any company domiciled in Liechtenstein is granted total exemption from income tax if it generates no income from local sources. As much as 30% of the state's revenue comes from companies that have established nominal offices there, with the biggest attractions being the low business tax rate (a max of 20%) and the easy incorporation rules. Foreign-owned holding companies are a major presence in Liechtenstein, with many maintaining their accounts in Swiss banks.

Liechtenstein is independent, but closely tied to Switzerland in a customs union. The Swiss franc is the local currency and Liechtenstein's status is that of a de facto province operating within Switzerland. Liechtenstein banks are integrated into Switzerland's banking system and capital markets. Many cross-border investments clear in or through Swiss banks.

Reputation

For the most part, Liechtenstein had an impeccable reputation with government regulators stressing the professional qualifications and local accountability of its well-trained financial managers. Liechtenstein's reaction to outside demands for stronger anti-money laundering laws and combatting foreign tax evasion has been in keeping with its conservative history.

In 2001, Liechtenstein was removed from the Financial Action Task Force (FATF) blacklist after it adopted tough anti-money laundering laws that covered "all crimes;" created a Financial Intelligence Unit (FIU); imposed much stricter "know-your-customer" and suspicious activity reporting laws; eased its historic, strict financial secrecy; and abolished the rights of trustees and lawyers not to disclose the identity of their clients to banks where funds are invested.

Liechtenstein's longstanding tax haven status was the source of criticism by the OECD, which placed the principality on its questionable, 41-nation FATF "harmful tax practices" blacklist because of its low taxes.

Stolen Names

Until 2008, Liechtenstein managed to stay on the good side of the self-appointed international busybodies who make it their duty to attack tax havens and, most especially, demand an end to bank secrecy.

It was then revealed that the German government illegally had bribed a disgruntled former Liechtenstein bank employee, Heinrich Kieber, to gain confidential bank information he had stolen from LGT Bank in Liechtenstein with 1,400 names of foreigners with LGT accounts.

The German secret police paid Kieber €5 million (US$6.1 million) for the stolen data, containing about 1,400 "client relationships," 600 of them Germans, a major haul for German tax collectors. Germany shared the information with the governments of Britain, France, Italy, Spain, Norway, Ireland, Netherlands, Sweden, Canada, the U.S., Australia and New Zealand.

Liechtenstein's billionaire royal family manages and controls LGT Bank and LGT Group. Banking secrecy and the government's refusal to share financial information, except in criminal cases, used to be one of Liechtenstein's leading selling points. LGT Bank and Liechtenstein authorities rightfully advanced the theory that high tax governments were using the stolen DVD and misinformation to scare people away from the principality and from its banks, which is what indeed happened.

After this highly publicized incident, the high tax governments of the G-20, assisted by the OECD, began a coordinated year-long "surrender now" phase in their decade long anti-tax haven campaign.

The worldwide publicity about the stolen bank list and the pressure from neighboring Germany, the G-20 countries and the OECD, seriously hurt the principality's financial bottom line. Liechtenstein's banking industry suffered a 60% drop in profits in 2009, in part due to the global economic downturn, but also because of questions about its future as a leading tax haven. Assets under management by the principality's 15 banks were down 22%. (Unlike in most other countries, Liechtenstein's banks did not ask for or require any government bailout support.)

Liechtenstein was removed from the OECD black list of uncooperative tax havens in 2009 after it agreed to reveal foreign tax dodgers. Yielding to the pressure, the country all but eliminated its banking secrecy laws. That scandal plus tough markets and a rise in value of the Swiss franc, Liechtenstein's official currency since 1924, greatly reduced the amount of assets managed in the country. Ratings agency Standard & Poor's confirmed its AAA rating for Liechtenstein, citing "stable and conservative policies ... which we expect to continue."

Less Secrecy Guaranteed by Law

Bloomberg News reported: "Liechtenstein, a principality once fabled for its banking secrecy laws, is losing its perch as one of the world's top tax havens for the richest people on Earth."

The reason was and is clear: the principality has abandoned its strict bank secrecy laws, the main attraction for many foreigners in decades past. Until 2009, there was a near-total absence of any international treaties governing double taxation or exchange of information, with the one exception of a double tax agreement with neighboring Austria, primarily to cover taxes on people who commute across the border for work.

In 2009, Liechtenstein was one of the first acknowledged tax havens to adopt OECD tax information exchange standards that cover alleged foreign income tax evasion. As part of that major change in policy, the principality began negotiating tax information exchange treaties with other nations. In 2008, Liechtenstein and the United States signed a tax information exchange agreement (TIEA) that provides for direct cooperation between the two countries tax and judicial authorities. By 2015, Liechtenstein had signed 85 tax information exchange agreements, including one with the U.S.

Liechtenstein's financial secrecy statutes historically were considered even stronger than those in Switzerland. In almost every case of lawsuits or official requests it refused to divulge client information. The adoption of the OECD tax information exchange standard ended that tradition. Nevertheless, Liechtenstein claimed that it still would enforce its strict confidentiality law, with criminal penalties for unauthorized information release. In its promotional advertising, Liechtenstein keeps up the pretense of having strict bank secrecy.

Banks keep "know your customers" records of clients' identities, but supposedly these may not be made public except by judicial or official government order. Financial secrecy is also said to extend to trustees, lawyers, accountants and to anyone connected to the banking industry. All involved are subject to the disciplinary powers of Liechtenstein's Upper Court. A court order or an officially approved request showing cause from a foreign government still is required to release an account holder's bank records. Creditors seeking bank records face a time-consuming and costly process.

Big Bucks Banking

Liechtenstein's banks have no official minimum deposit requirements, but their stated goal is to lure high-net-worth individuals as clients. Opening a discretionary portfolio management account generally requires a minimum of CHF1 million (US$1.1 million).

Trusts and limited companies registered here must pay an annual government fee of 0.1% of capital. Most banks also charge an annual management fee of 0.5% of total assets under their supervision. Bank, investment and professional fees here are at the top of the world scale.

If you're considering opening an offshore bank or investment account, Liechtenstein may be worth a comparative look if the level of your wealth permits it. The principality has benefits many other OFCs lack, including a strong economy, rock-solid (Swiss) currency, political stability and ease of access, plus a few added attractions of its own. The government guarantees all bank deposits against loss, regardless of the amount involved, even though there have been no recent bank failures.

Rob Vrijhof, senior partner in a leading Swiss investment firm and a senior member of the Banyan Hill Council of Experts, for years has done considerable business in Liechtenstein on behalf of international investors. He has witnessed a noticeable cleaning up of suspect practices, together with a new willingness to accommodate legitimate foreign banking and investment. He says: "I recommend Liechtenstein unreservedly — if you can afford it."

Foundation/Trust/Corporation Options

Liechtenstein is known worldwide among lawyers for its highly original and innovative legal entities created by statute, some of them copies of other countries' laws.

Liechtenstein law allows limited liability companies (LLCs), but does not provide for formation of international business corporations (IBCs) as they are known elsewhere. Over the years, the country's legislators have been highly inventive when it comes to unusual and useful legal entities fashioned to serve special financial needs.

Government regulation of the *Anstalt*, foundations, companies and trusts is extremely strict. This is primarily accomplished through training and regulation of managers, not by prying into the internal affairs of the entity or its holdings. As a result, business management services available in Liechtenstein are excellent in terms of quality, if somewhat slow in execution.

The *Anstalt*

Liechtenstein is perhaps best known for the *Anstalt*, sometimes described in English as an "establishment" (the German word's closest English equivalent). The *Anstalt* is a legal entity unique to Liechtenstein and is something of a hybrid somewhere between the trust and the corporation with which Americans are familiar.

The *Anstalt* may or may not have member shares. Control usually rests solely with the founder, or with surviving members of his or her family. Both have the power to allocate the profits as they see fit.

The law regulating *Anstalt* formation is extremely flexible, allowing nearly any kind of charter to be drafted. Depending on the desired result, *Anstalts* can take on any number of trust or corporation characteristics. They can be tailored to meet specific U.S. tax criteria, the basis for an IRS private letter ruling recognizing your *Anstalt* as either a trust or corporation.

Only limited information about those involved with an individual *Anstalt* or company appears on public records. The beneficial owners of a company do not appear by name in any register and their identity need not be disclosed to the Liechtenstein authorities.

On the other hand, diligent inquisitors may discover members of the board of directors by searching the Commercial Register. At least one member of the board must reside in Liechtenstein. Unlike U.S. corporations, the shares of a Liechtenstein company do not have to disclose the names of shareholders.

The Family Foundation

Liechtenstein's concept of a "foundation" is unique. Although Americans associate a foundation with a non-profit, tax-exempt organization, in Liechtenstein a foundation is an autonomous fund consisting of assets endowed by its founder for a specific, non-commercial purpose. The purpose can be very broad in scope, including religious and charitable goals.

One of the more common uses is as a so-called "pure family foundation." These vehicles are dedicated to the financial management and personal welfare of one or more particular families as beneficiaries. The foundation has no shareholders, partners, owners, or members — only beneficiaries. It can be either limited in time or perpetual.

The foundation and a beneficiary's interest therein cannot be assigned, sold, or attached by personal creditors. Only foundation assets are liable for its debts. If engaged in commercial activities, the foundation's activities must support noncommercial purposes, such as support of the family. Unless the foundation is active commercially, it can be created through an intermediary. The founder's name need not be made public. Foundations may be created by deed, under the terms of a will, or by a common agreement among family members.

A family foundation can sometimes be more useful than a trust, since it avoids many restrictive trust rules that limit control by the trust creator. On the issue of cost, a simple family foundation located here may cost US$30,000, while the same entity in Panama, where the law was copied in 1995, can cost as little as $15,000. (See Panama section below in this chapter.)

If you are interested in exploring the creation of a foundation, I recommend you obtain top-quality tax and legal advice, both in your home country and in Liechtenstein.

Hybrid Trusts

You can use a Liechtenstein trust to control a family fortune, with the trust assets represented as shares in holding companies that control each of the relevant businesses that may be owned by the family. This legal strategy brings together various family holdings under one trust umbrella, which, in turn, serves as a legal conduit for wealth transfer to named heirs and beneficiaries.

Liechtenstein's trust laws are practical and interesting due to the country's unusual combination of civil law and common-law concepts. In 1926, the Liechtenstein Diet adopted a statutory reproduction of the English-American trust system. They even allow trust grantors to choose governing law from any common law country.

This puts the Liechtenstein judiciary in the unique position of applying trust law from England, Bermuda, or Delaware (U.S.A.) when addressing a controversy regarding a particular trust instrument.

Even though it is a civil law nation, a trust located in Liechtenstein can be useful in lowering taxes, sheltering foreign income and safeguarding assets from American estate taxes. The law allows quick portability of trusts to another jurisdiction and accepts foreign trusts that wish to re-register as local entities. The trust instrument must be deposited with the Commercial Registry, but is not subject to public examination.

In 2009, revisions and updates of existing 70-year-old statutes by Parliament produced a new Foundations Act and amendments to the Law on Persons and Companies.

It is worth noting that some of the best life insurance, annuities and private placement polices are issued by companies in Liechtenstein, although they are usually purchased through Swiss-based companies. (See Chapter Three, *Part 2 — Financial Strategies.*)

Taxes

In 2011, Liechtenstein adopted a first ever flat annual tax of 12.5% on the net earnings, including earnings from interest, of family foundations, trusts and corporations. The result of this new tax has been the redomiciling of many Liechtenstein trusts, foundations and companies to Panama and other financial centers where no tax is imposed.

Low business taxes — the maximum tax rate is 20% — and easy incorporation rules have induced many holding or so-called letter box companies to establish nominal offices in Liechtenstein, providing 30% of state revenues.

The principality participates in a customs union with Switzerland and uses the Swiss franc as its national currency. It imports more than 90% of its energy requirements. Liechtenstein is a member of the European Economic Area, an organization that serves as a bridge between the European Free Trade Association and the EU.

Contacts:

Embassy of Liechtenstein
2900 K Street NW, Suite 602-B
Washington, D.C. 20007
Tel.: 202-331-0590
Web: www.liechtensteinusa.org

The U.S. has no Embassy in Liechtenstein. The U.S. Ambassador to Switzerland is accredited to Liechtenstein.

United States Embassy
Sulgeneckstrasse 19
CH-3007 Bern, Switzerland
Tel.: +031 357 70 11
Email: https://ch.usembassy.gov/u-s-citizen-services/contact-us-acs
Web: https://ch.usembassy.gov

U.S. Consular Agency Zürich
Dufourstrasse 101
CH-8008 Zürich, Switzerland
Tel.: +41 43 499 29 60
Web: https://ch.usembassy.gov/u-s-citizen-services/ca-zrh-contact

Recommended Attorneys & Trust Company:

First Advisory Group
Wuhrstrasse 6
LI-9490 Vaduz
Tel.: +423 236 30 00
Web: https://www.firstadvisorygroup.com

Recommended U.S. SEC-Registered Financial Advisor:

Robert Vrijhof, President
WHVP: Weber, Hartmann, Vrijhof & Partners Ltd.
Schaffhauserstrasse 418
CH-8050 Zürich, Switzerland
Contact: Julia Fernandez
Tel.: 01141 44 315 77 77 (USA/Canada) / +41 44 315 77 77
(International)
Email: info@whvp.ch
Web: http://www.whvp.ch

Mr. Vrijhof and his staff can arrange Liechtenstein and Swiss bank accounts for Banyan Hill members.

Republic of Panama

We recommend the Republic of Panama as a leading offshore financial center. In an unusual intentional triple play among countries, Panama combines no taxes on offshore income, strong asset protection laws and quick residence programs that welcome foreigners.

Only a few hours by air from the United States, Panama offers a variety of lifestyles and geographic diversity with a century-long history of working with Americans. The real estate boom of a few years ago has cooled, replaced by an infrastructure surge with government spending on transportation, airports and highway expansion.

A US$6 billion modernization of the century-old Panama Canal, a long-thriving banking and offshore sector, plus incoming capital flight driven by unrest in Venezuela, Bolivia and other Latin countries has helped provide Panama with one of the highest economic growth rates in all Latin America.

GDP growth in Panama averaged 8.73% from 2010 until 2014, reaching an all-time high of 12.20% in 2011. While rates aren't that high now, GDP growth is continuing, averaging 7.54% from 2010 to 2017. Panama will continue to be a fastest-growing country in Central America.

Alone among current offshore financial centers, Panama combines maximum financial privacy, a long history of judicial enforcement of asset protection-friendly laws, a strong anti-money laundering law, plus tax exemptions for foreign income. Thanks to its unique historic and often contentious relationship with the United States government, it also exercises a high degree of independence from outside pressures, including those from official Washington.

FACTORS	FINDINGS	RATING
Government/ political stability	Politics are volatile but democracy is stable	4
Favorable laws, judicial system	Favorable laws but significant court delays, political and judicial corruption	3
Available legal entities	All major legal entities available or recognized	5
Taxes	Territorial tax system taxes only in-country earnings, Outside income exempt from taxes	4
Financial privacy/ Bank secrecy	Strong, but TIEAs signed with US and other nations	4
Final Rating		**20**

Panama Revisited

To appreciate where modern Panama stands today, historic perspective helps to understand the country's 50-year economic and political revolution.

Prior to the implementation of the Torrijos-Carter Treaties of 1975 that ceded U.S. control of the Panama Canal, Panama was little more than an American colony where widespread domestic poverty contrasted with the wealth of the U.S. government-run Panama Canal Zone.

A visitor to Panama City today finds a city in constant transition; huge cranes topping off new high-rise condominiums, office towers, banks and hotels. The city's Pacific waterfront *Cinta Costera* highway has helped reduce some downtown traffic bottlenecks, but traffic congestion can be terrible.

On the south side of the Panama Canal, just across the Bridge of the Americas, the former Howard U.S. Air Force Base is now a mixed-use residential, corporate and industrial park, called Panama Pacifico. Leading international firms, including Dell, 3M, Procter & Gamble and Caterpillar are here. In 2014, another new giant shopping mall was built, the fourth in recent years. More than 10,000 new hotel rooms recently constructed have produced a surplus and room price competition.

Modern Panama has excellent digital Internet and other international communications. Downtown Panama City, the balmy, tropical capital on the southern, Pacific Ocean end of the Canal, suggests Los Angeles or Miami, except arguably more locals speak English here than in some parts of South Florida or LA.

Panama City also offers first-class hotels and restaurants, including the inevitable Trump Tower. Night clubbing and fine dining can be local delights. For first time visitors, the Panama Canal is a must-see tour. For those who want to combine business with pleasure and real estate shopping, there are multiple gated retirement and vacation retreats on the Pacific side, in Bocas del Toro on the Atlantic side and in the cooler, less humid Boquete in Chiriquí province in the western mountains on the Costa Rican border.

Image of Panama

When most people think of "Panama," they think — Panama Canal!

But the country is less well-known for what it has become in the last 60 years — second only to Miami, serving as Latin America's major international banking and business center, with strong ties to Asia, Europe and a special relationship with the United States that, however contentious, serves both countries well.

Panama's historic change came at midnight, December 31, 1999, when 96 years of official United States presence in the Republic of Panama ended. Panama finally got what its nationalistic politicians long had demanded — full sovereign Panamanian control over its famous inter-oceanic canal.

New Era

Indeed, in many respects — financial privacy, solid asset protection and freedom from outside political pressures — Panama has moved into the top rank of world OFCs.

There are historic reasons for Panama's enviable standing as a leading offshore financial center, including:

• A territorial tax system that taxes only earnings from within the country;

• Continuously modernized asset protection laws, dating from 1927;

• An array of useful legal entities (trusts, corporations, private foundations);

• A solid community of qualified offshore professionals and bankers;

• Some of the strongest financial privacy laws anywhere; and,

• Considering its history, a remarkable degree of political stability in a viable democratic system that works fairly well.

That stability was confirmed again in 2014 with the election as president for a five-year term of the country's sitting vice president, Juan Carlos Varela, an American educated businessman and head of Panama's most conservative political party, the *Panameñistas*.

Foreign Cash Welcome

The prior administration of President Ricardo Martinelli adopted an open-door policy for both foreign direct investment and skilled international professionals. Panama's pro-growth policies are aimed at designated strategic sectors such as logistics, tourism, banking and bolstering Panama's role as a regional hub for 110 multinational companies based there.

New job creation lowered unemployment to 5.5% in 2017 and GDP grew by 5.3% in 2017.

Panama is winning its struggle to emerge from the status as a "Third World" country where much of its population lived in poverty. About 30% of the population lives in poverty; however, from 2006 to 2012 poverty was reduced by more than 10%.

The Panama economy is in much better shape financially than its Central American neighbors to the north, or Colombia to the south. Since the 1990s, inflation barely has exceeded 1% per year. Annual inflation has averaged 1.4% for the past 30 years, much lower than in the United States.

Foreign investment, at around 10% of GDP in recent years, has continued to be a source of growth. The Ministry of Economy and Finance reported that direct foreign investment was $11.5 billion in 2017.

Then, there is the enormous wealth represented by the canal, generating over US$1 billion in annual revenues. While much of this income must be plowed back into maintenance, profits from the canal represent Panama's largest single source of income. And in an historic improvement that increased flow of 14,000 annual ship transits, the Panama Canal in 2016 completed a modernization at a cost of US$5.3 billion financed by the Canal and foreign investors.

The world-famous waterway now has wider locks that accommodate the largest ships now afloat, such as oil supertankers. The work, 104 years after the canal's 1914 opening, is providing a major boost to Panama's already thriving national economy.

The thousands of acres of land from former U.S. military installations, prized real estate with an estimated value of US$4 billion has been distributed and privatized. Development of this property brought significant benefits to Panama.

Privacy, Profits, No Taxes

The Republic of Panama is ideally suited for the foreign offshore investor who wants to enjoy the increasingly rare privilege of guaranteed financial privacy, (or as much privacy as is available anywhere these days), and no taxes on offshore corporate or personal income.

According to the annual *Economic Freedom of the World* ratings that measure countries' economic freedom, co-published by the Cato Institute, the Fraser Institute in Canada and more than 70 think tanks around the world, Panama ranked No. 30 among approximately 160 countries in the latest 2017 report.

Panama has adopted more than 40 laws protecting foreigners financial and investment rights, including the Investment Stability Law (Law No. 54), that guarantees foreign and local investors equal rights. The country's central, world crossroads geographic location makes it a natural base for global business operations. Importantly, Panama isn't directly under the political thumb of the United States. And unlike the British Overseas Territories of Bermuda and the Cayman Islands, London has no control here.

Among the 77 licensed banks in Panama, the major players are the 29 multinational banks representing 26 countries that primarily conduct offshore business. In 2018, Panamanian banks held an official US$169 billion in total assets, with liquidity impressively high at 58%, more than required by law. The banks had virtually no exposure to the kinds of bad investments that undermined U.S., U.K. and other national banking systems. Banking accounts for about 11% of Panama's GNP. Nearly every one of the world's major banks has a full-service branch office in Panama, with representation from Japan, Germany, Brazil and the United States.

Financial Privacy

Panama also is one of the world's oldest offshore financial centers. A 1924 company incorporation law was patterned after the corporate laws of the State of Delaware and has been updated continuously.

Central to this tax haven tradition has been statutory guarantees of financial privacy and confidentiality. Violators can suffer civil and criminal penalties for unauthorized disclosure. In the past, Panama pointedly refused to commit to exchanging information with tax authorities in other countries.

In 2010, Panama signed a tax information agreement with the U.S. government — an act that prior Panama leaders had resisted for 20 years. It followed a Panama-Mexico TIEA and many more TIEAs other countries have followed since. A revision of its previously strict bank secrecy realists was an inevitable move, given the state of international financial and tax information exchange policies.

Panama has a sensible "territorial tax system" that does not tax earnings outside its borders, so its tax collectors had no need to know what Panamanians or foreign nationals earn elsewhere in the world. All information under the U.S. treaty will flow one way, from Panama to the United States, negating benefits for foreigners from the country's financial privacy laws.

Speculation at the time held that the U.S. pushed Panama to agree to the 2009 tax treaty as a pre-condition for the Obama administration to submit a George Bush 2007 free trade agreement (FTA) with Panama to the U.S. Senate, where it was opposed by U.S. labor unions. As it was, the FTA submission was delayed, and approval came in 2011.

The Yankee Dollar

While "dollarization" has been debated as a novel concept elsewhere in Latin America, since 1904 the U.S. dollar has been Panama's official paper currency.

In 1904, the government of Panama, largely out of convenience, adopted the U.S. dollar as its official currency. However, as a matter of national pride, the country has another official currency, known as the *balboa*, pegged to the US $ at a rate of 1:1. Panamanian coins are issued in the same denominations as U.S. coins and both circulate freely. In 2011, the government began circulating a 1-balboa coin, equal in value to US$1. Forty million coins were minted and issued at a cost of roughly 25 cents each, netting the government US$30 million in the process, not a trivial sum. Now, 2-balboa coins ($2) are being considered.

Panama has no central bank to print money. And as Juan Luis Moreno-Villalaz, former economic advisor to Panama's Ministry of Economy and Finance, noted: "In Panama... there has never been a systemic banking crisis; indeed, in several instances international banks have acted as the system's lender of last resort. The Panamanian system provides relatively low interest rates on mortgages and commercial loans. Credit is ample, with 30-year mortgages readily available. These are unusual conditions for a developing country and are largely achieved because there is no exchange rate risk, a low risk of financial crises and ample flow of funds from abroad."

What if the U.S. dollar sinks? How will that impact Panama? This is a common question. While it isn't likely to happen any time soon, if the U.S. dollar collapsed completely one day, then Panama could simply expand and adopt its own currency as the official replacement for the dollar.

As does the strength of any national currency, the strength of that currency would depend on the health of Panama's national economy, which as we have indicated, is excellent.

Because of the U.S. government and policies, the U.S. dollar value has weakened consistently over decades, resulting in a loss of respect as a world-reserve currency.

At any time, Panama could expand the issuance of its own currency if it wished. The value of that currency would be judged by economic factors that apply within Panama, without regard to the status of the U.S. dollar.

Fitch and S&P have given Panama's government debt a desirable "investment-grade" rating., This rating is an indicator that the country's fiscal and tax policies are seemingly moving in the right direction. As we have noted, Panama's unemployment rate is 5.5% with lots of job opportunities. In fact, Panama has one of the fastest

GDP growths in all Latin America. The country even managed to dodge the effects if the 2008 — 2010 global downturns. Banks in Panama have an average liquidity of 30%, which is well above that of the bailed-out U.S. banks.

This separate and distinct economic existence has been demonstrated over decades as Panama has enjoyed very low inflation, while U.S. inflation at times soared to double-digit levels. Should the dollar ever tank beyond repair, Panama can issue its own currency backed by its own strong domestic economic fundamentals. If the dollar was abandoned, a new official Panamanian balboa currency would likely have as much or more value and respect than the U.S. dollar.

Welcome Bankers

Panama grew as an international financial center after the enactment of Decree No. 238 of July 2, 1970, a liberal banking law that also abolished all currency controls. The law exempts offshore business in Panama from income tax and from taxes on interest earned in domestic savings accounts and offshore transactions.

Panama has adopted significant reforms in its banking system to minimize corruption and ensure that banking secrecy can be lifted in criminal investigations, especially when money laundering is alleged.

In 1999, a comprehensive new banking law was enacted that accelerated Panama's growth as a leading world offshore finance center. That law uses the guidelines of the Basel Committee on Banking Supervision, the international oversight group that sets banking standards, requiring all banks with unrestricted domestic or international commercial banking licenses to maintain currently capital equivalent to at least 30% of total assets. (In fact, Panama banks have far exceeded that minimal percentage requirement.)

Government investigative powers and tighter general controls bring Panama in line with regulatory standards found in European and North American banking centers. Under this law, a prima facie case of illicit financial conduct can launch an investigation of possible criminal conduct. The law also permits foreign bank regulators to make inspection visits to any of their domestic banks with branches in Panama.

Panamanian banks are very reluctant to open new accounts for Americans and other foreigners, unless the applicant has a home or an active business or investment in Panama. In most cases, foreigners need a personal local introduction to a bank, and that can be obtained by arrangement with the professional contact listed at the end of this section.

Panama's financial sector also includes an active, but small, stock exchange, captive insurance and re-insurance companies and financial and leasing companies. Another major business and financial attraction at the Atlantic end of the canal is the booming Colón Free Trade Zone (http://colonfreezone.com), a major tax-free transshipment facility, the second-largest free trade zone in the world, after Hong Kong, and currently under major expansion.

IBCs and Foundations

Panama has liberal laws favoring trusts, international business companies and holding companies. Law No. 25 (1995), a private interest foundation statute as modeled after the popular *Stiftung* family wealth protection and estate planning vehicle long used in Liechtenstein.

Law 25 allows the tax-free family foundation to be used for investment, tax sheltering, ownership (but not management) of commercial businesses and private activity, with the founder retaining lifetime control. Foundation assets are not counted as part of the founder's estate for local death tax purposes and Panama does not recognize the often-restrictive inheritance laws of other nations.

Some argue that the Panamanian private foundation law is only a clone of the Liechtenstein law. It is true that the Panamanian law is newer, but the costs of creating and operating a Panama foundation are half that in Liechtenstein where it can cost as much as $30,000.

For South American clients and others from civil law countries who are unfamiliar with the concept of an Anglo-American common law trust, a Panamanian private foundation often represents an ideal estate planning solution, even if just for the estate tax savings it may allow.

Panama's international business corporation (IBC) Law 32 (adopted in 1927) was modeled after the U.S. state of Delaware's corporation-friendly statutes. There are about 350,000 IBCs registered in Panama, second only to Hong Kong's 400,000. A Panamanian IBC can maintain its own corporate bank account and credit cards for global management of investments, mutual funds, precious metals, real estate and trade. Non-Panama tax-free corporate income can be spent for business purposes worldwide and using the Panama IBC allows avoidance of home country zoning, labor, manufacturing, warranty, environmental and other restrictions.

Americans should consult a U.S. tax expert before forming a Panama IBC, since there can be some severe and costly U.S. tax consequences when using offshore corporations. Corporations in Panama, as in other countries that employ the civil law (as compared to common law) system, designate companies as "S.A." standing for *Sociedad Anónima*, the equivalent of the U.S. "Inc." for incorporated.

Leading Retirement Haven

Despite its relatively advanced industrial and financial infrastructure compared to other Latin nations, Panama remains an affordable place in which to live. A live-in maid earns about US$300 per month; first-run movies cost US$4. Unlike much of Central America, Panama boasts a first-class health care system with low costs compared to the United States — a doctor's office visit costs about US$45.

Because of Panama's geographical diversity, there is considerable variation in the climate. Panama City, the historical and financial center, has a year-round tropical climate, warm and humid. Yet, only a few hundred miles to the West near the Costa Rican border are sub-tropical forests, with cascading waterfalls, mountainsides covered with flowers and spring-like weather year-round. There are also many good buys on condominiums and other real estate, particularly in Panama City and the surrounding areas, a byproduct of over-building during the now-slowed housing building boom.

There is a wide variety of programs in Panama for foreigners who wish to make a home there, the best known of these being the *pensionado* program. All resident visa applications must be made through a Panamanian attorney. There is no minimum or maximum age requirement, except that those less than 18 years old, the legal age of emancipation in Panama, will qualify as dependents of their parents. None of these visas automatically grants the right to work. Work permits must be applied for and obtained separately.

For many years the Republic of Panama deliberately has positioned itself as a first-class retirement haven, with some of the most appealing programs of special benefits for foreign residents and retirees anywhere in the world. In addition to the "Immediate Permanent Resident" visa, Panama also offers a variety of other visas for investors, persons of high net worth, wealthy retirees, small business and agricultural business investors and entrepreneurs, and those who simply want to immigrate and become Panamanian citizens.

The government makes retirement in Panama easy and laws provide important tax advantages for foreigners who wish to become residents. The only significant requirements are good health and a verifiable monthly income of at least US$500. There are no local taxes on foreign income and you can import your household goods tax-free.

Fast Track Residence

In 2012, Executive Order 343 created a new category of "Immediate Permanent Resident" for foreign nationals from 24 listed countries "that maintain friendly, professional, economic, and investment relationships with the Republic of Panama," including the United States and the United Kingdom.

A labor shortage, especially for skilled workers, was said to be a major reason for the new rules. This new permit grants permanent residence immediately, unlike current investor visas that grant only temporary residence at first. There will be no need to renew the permit several times as current visas require.

Under this immediate immigration category, qualified applicants can engage in professional and economic activities, establish businesses and have the right to work in Panama, permissions that in the past have been difficult to obtain. After five years they will be eligible to apply for full citizenship, as is the case with most of the country's visa programs.

The law grants immediate residence and a "*cédula*," the national identification card issued to all Panamanians, and will not only include qualified foreign individuals, but also dependent spouses, children under 18, family members with disabilities and dependent parents. Children aged 18 to 25 can be included if they are students.

To qualify for Immediate Permanent Resident status the foreign applicant must submit one or more of the following:

1) proof of ownership of real estate in Panama; 2) an employment letter and work contract issued by a company registered in Panama; 3) evidence of ownership of a registered Panamanian corporation which has a valid business license.

Applications must be made to the National Immigration Service (NIS). Work permits are governed by Panamanian commercial and labor laws issued by the Ministry of Labor. Experience shows you will need to be represented by a qualified Panamanian attorney.

Rainelda Mata-Kelly JD, a leading Panama attorney and Banyan Hill associate, can assist applicants who qualify for this quick-residence category (see the contacts section on pg. 249).

The Panama Papers

In 2016, someone at the major Panamanian law firm, Mossack Fonseca, stole and leaked 11.5 million digital documents, violating the privacy and revealing details of the legal offshore structures used by thousands of individuals in dozens of countries.

Media outlets worldwide covered these leaks as if the "Panama Papers," (as they were quickly named), revealed details of horrific crimes; corruption, money laundering and tax evasion. Few reports noted that having an offshore company, trust, bank account or other vehicle is not illegal.

Biased news media coverage created the impression that the only real reason to operate an offshore structure was criminal. The major news angle were names of numerous foreign politicians and officials revealed as having "secret" offshore accounts.

There are many reasons to open a bank account or a corporate structure, or a limited liability company (LLC), in an offshore jurisdiction, especially if you are in a lawsuit-prone profession like medicine. One of the valid reasons for operating offshore is if you just feel like it. It's your right as a human being.

The official and media hypocrisy surrounding the "offshore issue" is unlimited.

The United States is the world's No. 1 tax evasion and money laundering haven. The U.S. government does not practice any of the things it preaches to other countries through stupid laws like the Foreign Account Tax Compliance Act (FATCA). It hasn't even signed the Common Reporting Standards for tax information adopted by the rest of the world. Foreigners who want to create a trust or corporation in the U.S. to avoid taxes in their home country are perfectly free to do so, and there is no mechanism by which the U.S. government can report them. With some exceptions, foreigners are also free to buy real estate for cash and register it in the name of a U.S. LLC that is virtually untraceable. That's the reason places like Miami and Manhattan have such stratospheric real estate markets.

Corruption and tax evasion indeed are crimes — in the jurisdictions where they occur. Although law firms like Mossack Fonseca are accountable to the governments and bar associations where they have offices, it's not their job to enforce other nation's laws. In this case, Mossack Fonseca may have knowingly violated Panamanian and other laws, but that's no reason to regard all their clients, or the clients of similar offshore firms, as likely criminals.

The Panama Papers were only one of the several journalistic smear campaigns against offshore financial activity and privacy, implying that any offshore financial activities are inherently corrupt.

The thieves responsible for this intentional stealing and public exposition of personal information without consent sanctimoniously cloak themselves in terms of investigative journalism and freedom of the press. These arrogant thieves who stole this mass of private information pompously call themselves the "International Consortium of Investigative Journalists," a confessed group of more than 380 journalists from over 90 media organizations in 67 countries seeking to sell their lurid stories.

This is the same ICIJ gang that in 2013, stole 2.5 million records of over 120,000 companies and trusts from two offshore companies, Commonwealth Trust Ltd. in the British Virgin Islands and Portcullis TrustNet in the Cook Islands, and in 2015 published "Swiss Leaks" from a private Swiss bank office in Paris. In 2017, came the "Paradise Papers", where ICIJ trumpeted the theft of more than 13.4 million documents from the respected, 119-year-old Bermuda law firm Appleby, which specializes in serving corporations and wealthy people.

These concerted attacks have been ongoing for three decades. As I stated earlier, in the 1990s, a coordinated international media campaign attacking tax havens was launched by the governments of major high tax and big deficit nations. Eager tax collectors, especially the U.S. Internal Revenue Service, were joined by the Organization for Community and Economic Development (OECD), a Paris-based group financed by the major nations.

Governments of the major high tax, high debt nations, especially the U.S., Germany and France, along with a coterie of allied leftist groups seeking to redistribute wealth, will continue to blame legitimate offshore tax, business and banking havens for a host of supposed sins. Your knowledge of these facts arms you against the next ICJL fraud.

Contacts:

Embassy of Panama
2862 McGill Terrace NW
Washington, D.C. 20008
Tel.: 202-483-1407
Email: info@embassyofpanama.org
Web: www.embassyofpanama.org
Consulates located in New York, Philadelphia, Atlanta, Chicago, Houston, Los Angeles, Miami, New Orleans, and Tampa.

United States Embassy
Building 783, Demetrio Basilio Lakas Avenue
Clayton, Panama
Tel.: +507-317-5000
Email: panamaweb@state.gov
Web: https://pa.usembassy.gov

Recommended Professionals:

Rainelda Mata-Kelly, Esq.
Suite 406-407, Tower B, Torres de las Americas
Punta Pacifica, Panama
Tel.: +507-216-9299
From the USA or Canada Tel.: 011 507-216-9299
Email: rmk@mata-kelly.com
Web: http://www.mata-kelly.com

Ms. Mata-Kelly specializes in administrative, commercial and maritime law and assists clients with immigration, real estate, contracts, incorporation, and other legal issues. She is a senior member of Banyan Hill's Council of Experts.

Banks:

Banvivienda
Banco Panameño de la Vivienda, S.A.
Headquarters: Ave. La Rotonda & Boulevard Costa del Este, Republic of Panama
Tel.: +507-800-7500 / +507-306-7500 (from cell)
Web: https://www.banvivienda.com/en

Multibank Inc.
Headquarters: Vía España, Edif Prosperidad Building #127, Apdo 0823-05627, Republic of Panama
Tel.: +507-294-3500 ext. 1530 / +507-800-3500
Web: https://www.multibank.com.pa/en

UniBank
Local Branch: Building Grand Bay Tower, PB Panama City, Republic of Panama
Tel.: +507-297-6000 / +507-297-6006
Web: https://www.unibank.com.pa/en

Scotiabank
Main Office: Ave. Federico Boyd and Calle 51, Scotia Plaza Building, Bella Vista, Republic of Panama
Tel.: 1-800-472-6842 / +507-208-7700
Web: http://www.scotiabank.com/gls/en

Republic of Uruguay

The Oriental Republic of Uruguay is one of the few remaining countries that still offer a sound banking system, welcomes Americans and their money, provides far greater financial privacy than the United States, as well as many attractive investment possibilities — and qualifies as a place where people seem genuinely happy.

Spend a few days in Uruguay, as we have many times, and you will be impressed by the friendly citizens; you may soon realize that this is a place you might want to make your home.

FACTORS	FINDINGS	RATING
Government/political stability	Stable democracy with right of center politics	5
Favorable laws, judicial system	Modern offshore laws, clean judicial system, full transparency, minimal corruption	5
Available legal entities	All major legal entities available or recognized	5
Taxes	Residents and foreign investors exempt from most taxes on income earned offshore	5
Financial privacy/ Bank secrecy	Strong, honors TIEAs with other nations; no TIEA with the US or Canada	5
Final Rating		**25**

Three important points to keep in mind:

1. Unlike many Latin countries, Uruguay has been egalitarian for a long time, and has a strong democratic culture. There is no large landowning class and no landless rural population. Uruguay has

escaped the rigid class society ("us vs. them") attitude that exists in much of South America.

2. The population is homogenous; an estimated 88% of the people here are of European descent, principally Italian and Spanish. Other immigrant groups include Portuguese, Armenians, Basque, Germans, and Irish, making the country somewhat like the ethnic melting pot the U.S. once was. This ethnic unity has helped Uruguay avoid the politics of racial division.

3. The Uruguayan economy has evolved in such a way that most of the people benefit from economic freedom and an export orientation. Unlike Argentina, there have been no failed government-driven attempts to develop domestic industry. When the economy does well here, everyone benefits.

High Rankings and Happiness

The official name of the country is the "Oriental Republic of Uruguay." "Oriental" in this case means "eastern" because all of Uruguay's territory (about the size of the American State of Washington) lies east of both the Uruguay River, separating it from Paraguay, and the huge, 137-miles wide estuary of the Río de la Plata, that here meets the Atlantic and forms the boundary with Argentina.

Uruguay in 2017 ranked 54th in Best Countries Overall by *US News & World Report* and ranked No. 1 in quality of life/human development in Latin America. Uruguay ranked No. 9 in *Reader's Digest* as the "most livable and greenest" country in the world and first in all the Americas. According to Transparency International, in 2016, out of 176 countries, Uruguay ranked No. 21 in the world and was the least corrupt country in Latin America.

It was the highest rated country in Latin America (and No. 28 in the world) on the Legatum 2016 Prosperity Index, based on factors that help drive economic growth and create happy citizens. *International Living* rated it one of the 10 best places to retire in 2017.

Besides these accolades, Uruguay has much more to make it what might be the best offshore residence for you. For one, it is still a tax haven ... and in that sense Uruguay has now definitely earned its long-time nickname — the "Switzerland of Latin America," in the best sense of that title.

Moderate Politics

Tabare Vazquez, previously president from 2005 to 2010, was elected again in 2015. He continues the ruling left-center coalition in parliament that supports capitalism, free-market and free-trade policies — and welcomes foreigners who want to make a home in Uruguay with its liberal, open-minded social policies and low or no taxes.

In his first term as president, Vazquez was popular for his mix of strong social welfare programs with pro-business economic policies. He replaced the widely respected former president Jose "Pepe" Mujica Cordano. In Uruguay, presidents constitutionally are barred from a second consecutive term, perhaps an idea the United States should consider.

Based on a conservative-libertarian political philosophy and our extensive visits to Uruguay in the last three years, we judge Uruguay's government to be far more moderate and far less socialist than the Obama U.S. administration — and far more open and clean.

Investor-Friendly

Uruguay's economy is largely supported by the export agricultural sector, educated work force, and high amounts of social spending. Political and labor conditions are among the freest in Latin America.

The Uruguayan economy is ideal for foreign expatriates even if they are retired. That is because there are low levels of poverty, a relatively high standard of living and a large middle class. It has one of most equitable income distributions in Latin America. The result is lower crime rates and a very livable society. And if you do want to invest actively, start a company, or do business, Uruguay offers a very good environment.

If you had packed up and moved to Uruguay a decade ago you would have missed a lot — including the U.S. housing bubble and the property market crash — even as property values in Uruguay appreciated substantially, some even dramatically.

You would also have missed the world recession — which mercifully passed Uruguay by, the only Latin American country that escaped unscathed.

Strong, Growing Economy

Unlike the faltering economic powerhouses of the America's, U.S., Brazil, Mexico, and Argentina, the Uruguayan economy expanded during the global recession. In 2017, Uruguay's gross domestic product (GDP) was $78.41 billion , with growth at 3.5%. The per capita GDP was $22,400, the highest in South America.

Uruguay is also a South American leader in direct foreign investment, US$24.5 billion at the start of 2017. In fact, in 2009, Uruguay was the first nation in the world to provide every school child with a free laptop and wireless Internet access.

Uruguay is not a country where you should look for a cheap retirement.

Its first world living standards come with first world prices. If you plan to be in Uruguay for a few months every year, the beauty and stability of the place make this requirement easy to meet, and one should consider investing in local property. Foreigners are not required be residents of the country to own real estate or to establish a corporation or to do business in Uruguay.

For this first-time visitor Montevideo, an attractive, modern capital city, among the safest in the World, impresses with its relatively clean, charming mix of old and new architecture, winding streets, busy people and leisurely traffic. The skyline is punctuated by a relatively few skyscrapers, and it has charming small shops, museums, and a lively *Ciudad Vieja* (Old City). There is much to be said for this city of 1.3 million souls — about half of Uruguay's total population.

South America's premier, world-famous beach resort is here, Punta del Este. It's a town with miles of blue Atlantic water and sandy beaches. It also is a country known for its nightlife, casinos, fine restaurants, and a world-renowned property market.

And one other very important point: Uruguay offers not only financial, but also physical security — you feel and are safe walking the streets and byways in Montevideo, Punta del Este or anywhere else in this unusual country.

Investing

Among the many profitable investment opportunities, real estate is a leader. Many foreigners purchase second or vacation homes that can return strong rental income when not in personal use. One of the easiest ways to invest directly for profit is farmland ownership, a safe, turn-key investment, easy to operate with appreciation potential and good returns.

Uruguayan property, including farmland, is plentiful and relatively inexpensive. The country has far more land than its residents "need," and foreigners have long been able to buy residential or commercial property, including farmland, without restriction. Uruguayan farmland is considered among the world's best and is particularly well-suited to livestock, which can subsist almost entirely on the land's abundant and well-watered grass, requiring no additional feed grain.

Principal crops include soybeans, wheat, rice, cattle and sheep ranches and dairy farms. Forestry includes growing eucalyptus and pine and there are many vineyards, olive groves and fruit orchards. Uruguay is perfect cattle and grain country — long prized for its output since the 19th century, when Uruguay became a key player in the supply of beef products to Europe through venerable companies such as Fray Bentos.

Foreign investors may farm the land directly or have a farm management company handle all aspects of operation. There is also an active market for cropland rental.

Uruguayan farmland itself is one of the 21st century's hottest real estate commodities with steady annual returns from 4% to 12% possible. In the last 15 years, 18.5 million acres of Uruguayan farmland has changed hands, for more than US$10 billion in sales. That's 44% of Uruguay's total arable farmland.

That is because Uruguay has 42 million acres of arable farmland — enough to meet the needs of more than 50 million people, 16 times Uruguay's own population. There is land to spare, making agricultural exports a natural growth sector for the country. That's why this little country is the world's fourth largest exporter of rice, fifth largest exporter of dairy products, sixth largest exporter of soybeans, and responsible for 5% of global beef exports.

Banking

Sixty-four years ago, in the wake of World War II, Uruguay was described as the "Switzerland of the Americas" in a 1951 *New York Times* article. It earned that name because of its popularity as a haven for capital and precious metals fleeing Europe at the time, and for its adoption of Swiss-inspired banking laws and customs.

Foreign and local investors are treated equally under the law, there are no limitations on business ownership by foreigners and no currency exchange controls or forced currency conversion.

Foreign currencies are used freely including dollars and Euros. Most bank accounts are denominated in U.S. dollars, which are also used for pricing and in real estate and major business deals.

Uruguay is the financial center for the region, serving Brazil, Argentina and Chile's needs. Rated investment grade by Moody's S&P and Fitch, Uruguay's banks treat foreign and local investors equally. In fact, 25% of bank accounts belong to non-residents. Uruguay's banking system is solid, appealing to investors and depositors from around the world who seek a haven that also offers tax advantages.

Unlike many offshore banks in other parts of the world, banks in Uruguay do welcome American clients. Cities with main banking options available include Montevideo, Punta del Este and Colonia. Most banks offer e-banking.

Uruguay's financial reputation has made it an important financial center for the entire southern continent. There are 10 private banks, plus the government central bank, *Banco de la República* (BROU) that strictly supervises all the banks. BROU has a general policy against authorizing new banks.

The 10 private banks are totally or partially owned by leading American or European financial institutions. *Banco Itaú* in Montevideo usually will accept non-resident American clients in their retail banking branches. In addition, attesting to its regional banking role, there are more than 30 representative offices of foreign banks.

Financial Privacy Guaranteed by Law

Unlike the United States, where the PATRIOT Act has destroyed financial privacy, Uruguay protection is based on a bank secrecy statute (Law #15,322, 1982) that forbids banks to share information with anyone; that includes the government of Uruguay and foreign governments.

The only exceptions are allowed in cases involving issues of alimony, child support, or alleged crimes, including foreign tax evasion and fraud; even then information can be shared only after obtaining a local court order.

The country now allows automatic exchange of tax or bank account information with other government under the Common Reporting Standard (CRS) and Article 26 of the Organization for Economic Co-operation and Development. That is, banks may exchange information upon proof of foreign tax evasion or tax fraud. (See *Automatic Tax Information Exchange* in Chapter Three.)

Currently, Uruguay limits such exchanges to countries with which it has signed tax information exchange agreements (TIEAs), specifically excluding both neighboring Brazil and Argentina. The Uruguayan government now has TIEAs with Germany, Mexico, Portugal, Spain, France, Korea, Finland, Malta, Switzerland, Liechtenstein, India, Belgium, Hungary, Malaysia, Chile and Luxembourg. It does not have a TIEA with either the United States or Canada.

One-third of all banks accounts in Uruguay are held by foreigners, including many thousands of Brazilians and Argentineans. Most accounts are denominated in U.S. dollars, which is also used for pricing of real estate and major business deals. The local UYU peso and the euro are also available.

There are no exchange controls or capital restrictions and unlike neighboring Argentina, Uruguay has no political need for, and no history of, forced conversion of currencies or of freezing or confiscation of deposits. The government guarantees bank insurance on deposits only to a maximum of US$2,500 — but bank failure is unknown here in recent years.

Bank financing is available to foreign residents, with proof of income. A first or second mortgage on U.S. property is often accepted to finance local bank loans. A bonus is the country's interest rates, which are around 7.5%. Banks offer up to 4.5% on various types of accounts. That means your money may earn 18 times more than it does sitting in a U.S. bank account where minimum interest is about 0.25%.

Still a Tax Haven

In keeping with current international "political correctness" Uruguay's government does not want the country labeled as a "tax haven." Nevertheless, Uruguay is, in fact, an offshore tax haven that imposes very few taxes on foreign residents living here.

Uruguay, as does Panama, has a territorial tax system; personal income tax only applies to Uruguayan-source income, including rental income of properties in Uruguay. There is a flat tax of 12% on interest and dividend income from abroad, which may apply to both Uruguayan citizens and foreign residents living in Uruguay. However, resident foreigners are credited with any income tax paid to other countries.

Otherwise, income from abroad is not taxed, even if the foreign-source money is received by a bank in Uruguay. However, if a resident foreigner already pays tax on income in another country, which Americans must do, Uruguay does not impose double taxation and credit is given on taxes already paid to the IRS or to other national tax collectors.

Free Trade Zones

Uruguay has several free trade zones in the country where foreign companies operate free of corporate and import taxes. In recent tours, we visited Uruguay's main free zone, Zonamerica, near Montevideo's international airport. It is an impressive, privately owned modern commercial home to 7,000 workers including many global companies, such as Sabre, RCI, Tata, Merk, with extensive global and regional offices.

These areas are used for imported product storage, assembly and distribution for introduction into Uruguay or for export to other regional countries. These zones also are home to financial services, such as Merrill Lynch, KPMG, Deloitte, as well as many other types of services, all tax free.

Quick, Easy Residence

The immigration law of Uruguay states that residence is granted to those "who show intent to reside in Uruguay." That intent is evidence in the first instance by coming to the country and establishing a new home there.

Uruguay has a foreigner-friendly, open immigration policy, although, as with any official bureaucracy, it takes time — usually 12 to 18 months on average to obtain permanent resident status after coming to the country and applying. After three to five years, one can apply for citizenship and a passport.

Most foreigners enter Uruguay as a tourist for 90 days (extendable for another 90 days), find a living place and later a permanent home. Official residence status is not required to own real estate.

Once you file for residence status with the National Migration Office you receive a temporary identity card, the *cédula de identidad*. From that time forward you are considered a temporary "resident in process" and can stay in Uruguay indefinitely.

When permanent residence is granted you receive a new *cédula* that enables you to travel within the Mercosur countries, Argentina, Paraguay and Uruguay (except Brazil) without using your U.S. or other national passport.

The government requires that a temporary resident working towards citizenship must log a significant amount of physical presence time within Uruguay, at least six months during each year.

Citizenship

The law in Uruguay, as in the United States, allows its citizens to hold dual or multiple citizenships. New citizens are not required to surrender their home country passport and no notice is sent to the home country government.

While all this appears to be complicated, professional assistance will handle all these matters making certain you meet the legal requirements. We recommend Fischer & Schickendantz, a full-service law firm that specializes in immigration law and arranges bank accounts.

Juan Federico Fischer, Esq., Managing Partner
Fischer & Schickendantz
Rincón 487, Piso 4 – C.P: 11.000
Montevideo, Uruguay

Tel.: +598 2915 7468 ext. 130
Email: jfischer@fs.com.uy or info@fs.com.uy
Web: www.fs.com.uy

Contacts:

Embassy of Uruguay
1913 I (Eye) Street NW
Washington, D.C. 20006
Tel.: 202-331-1313
Email: urueeuu@mrree.gub.uy
Web: www.mrree.gub.uy
Uruguayan Consulates: Chicago, Miami, Los Angeles, New York
and San Juan, Puerto Rico.

United States Embassy
Lauro Muller 1776
Montevideo 11200, Uruguay
Mailing Address: UNIT 4500, APO AA 3403
Tel.: +598 2 1770-2000
Email: MontevideoACS@state.gov
Web: https://uy.usembassy.go

Bank:

Banco Itaú
Pedro Berro 1039
11300 Montevideo, Uruguay
Tel.: +598 2916 0127 x 505
Web: https://www.itau.com.uy/inst
Retail banking only - Minimum Balance: US$2,500

Hong Kong

Special Administrative Region of
the People's Republic of China

The economy of Hong Kong remains one of the freest in the world, even if its people are not freed. This major offshore financial center has a strong common law-based legal system governing banking and finance, even though this city-state is controlled, ultimately, by a Communist Party government in Beijing. The question is how long Hong Kong will remain free.

Free and Not Free

In the 2017 *Economic Freedom of the World Index*, published by the conservative U.S. think tank, the Heritage Foundation, Hong Kong was rated the world's freest economy with a rating of 89.8 out of a possible 100. The libertarian Cato Institute also gave Hong Kong the highest rating for economic freedom, with a score of 8.98 out of 10, a first-place rating it has held for several years.

Hong Kong's freedom is now in question.

Beijing's Communists took control in 1997 with the end of British colonial rule. The economy of semi-democratic Hong Kong has remained remarkably free, an economic reflection of Beijing's need for this historic city-state as a financial conduit for China's business with the world. But gradually since 1997, and with far greater pressure in the last five years, Beijing has tightened official control and lessened individual political freedom.

Hong Kong has never known true democracy. In the wake of the First Opium War of 1839, the British Empire transformed a sleepy fishing village into an imperial *entrepôt* that served as a staging ground for its exploitation of the Chinese mainland. For the next 156 years,

Hong Kong was governed as a British Crown Colony. Only in the 1980s did indigenous Hong Kongers obtain significant rights to political participation.

Since the territory's transfer to China in 1997, Hong Kong has been governed under a Basic Law negotiated between Chinese Communists and British diplomats, with behind-the-scenes input from powerful local financial interests who still play a major rule in government. It provided for greater democracy than the British ever allowed.

Hong Kong's Legislative Council (LegCo) is comprised of 40 representatives elected directly by the people and 30 elected by "functional" constituencies such as industrial, labor and finance associations, the 30 heavily weighted with Beijing's wealthy HK allies. Candidates for Chief Executive are selected by an electoral college comprised of representatives of these constituencies. The final selection, however, is made by the Communists in Beijing.

The continuing dispute pits Hong Kong citizens who want both the LegCo and the Chief Executive to be elected by direct universal suffrage as promised in 1997, without interference from Beijing, against the Communist Party of China (CPC) which insists that it retain the right to make the final selection.

In 2014, the CPC officially determined that the next chief executive of Hong Kong would be chosen by Beijing, reneging on a 1997 pledge that the city-state would be given full suffrage. In other words, the Communist Party of China — heir to Mao Zedong's glorious peasant revolution, architect of the Cultural Revolution, vanguard of the Chinese Proletariat — opposes true democracy in Hong Kong to protect the interests of Hong Kong's capitalist elite with which they are allied.

Indeed, the interests of Hong Kong's tycoons are identical to those in China itself. China has the highest number of billionaires in Asia — 319 in 2017, second only to the U.S. Most of those achieved their status via connections to the CPC. Many are family members of leading CPC figures.

In truth, the rulers in Beijing are not "communist." If anything, they are watered-down fascists. Fascism combines totalitarianism, a single-party state, nationalism and a mixed economy. The ruling party is motivated by the desire for power and to harness capitalism's power to create wealth. Like communism, fascism is inherently anti-democratic. Power must be retained by the Party that claims it knows best what's good for the nation.

Selfish, unprincipled capitalists support fascism because it protects their short-term interests. So long as the CPC keeps the masses in thrall and allows Hong Kong and Chinese tycoons to get and stay rich, they will support Beijing's stance curbing democracy. If Beijing does crack down on Hong Kong, it will probably not harm their long-term interests, even if their short-term profits take a knock.

This isn't just speculation on our part. We have heard directly from wealthy individuals in Hong Kong who strongly oppose the pro-democracy forces and support Beijing unreservedly. They fear democracy much more than totalitarianism.

Let us be clear: we don't think Hong Kong is in any danger of losing its status as Asia's leading offshore banking, asset protection and stock-trading hub. It is far too valuable for Beijing to allow that to happen. Wealth remains safe there.

Street Protests

In 2003, Beijing had plans to require adoption of Hong Kong laws banning acts of "treason, secession, sedition and subversion", but they were dropped after half a million took to the streets.

In 2012, Beijing experienced a large-scale protest for its proposal of a "patriotic and national education" system. Critics felt the government was trying to brainwash children. A very large crowd, estimated at 120,000 by organizers besieged his headquarters and caused Hong Kong's chief executive, Leung Chun-ying, to back down and revoke a 2015 deadline for every school to start teaching the subjects.

Huge demonstrations against mainland control have been held annually. In 2014, new and much larger demonstrations protested the murders and assaults on leading Hong Kong editors and journalist who supported faster reforms, rallying for press and speech freedoms, as well as the announced Beijing delay of full voting rights. The protests in Hong Kong were like the much larger Tiananmen Square protests in Beijing in 1989.

For months, large numbers of Hong Kong students gathered in front of government buildings, staging sit-ins and hunger strikes. This 2014 wave of popular sit-in protests involved mass civil disobedience in what became known as the "Umbrella Revolution." Protests were aimed at Beijing's announced rejection of electoral reforms that were tantamount to Communist Party control over which candidates would be allowed to present themselves to the Hong Kong electorate.

Hong Kong students were also protesting corruption and the perception that government officials had become too close to the city's business tycoons, accepting bribes while in office, including discounted apartments, yacht trips, and highly paid jobs after retirement.

Students led strikes and demonstrations occurred outside the Government headquarters, and protesters occupied major city intersections, blocking major arterial routes for weeks. Police tactics, including the use of tear gas, and attacks on protesters by opponents that included triad members, triggered more citizens to join the protests. The number of protesters peaked at more than 100,000 at any given time, at times overwhelming the police.

Perhaps wisely from Communist Beijing's viewpoint, the protests continued until the students were worn down and weary. Then police dismantled their barricades and cleared streets, arresting student leaders. Beijing won, and promised democracy lost.

More recently, Beijing has cracked down on Hong Kong, arresting and jailing student protest leaders, refusing to seat validly elected pro-democracy legislators, even kidnapping journalists and publishers critical of the Chinese Communist rule. With his consolidation of power in 2017, President Xi Jinping and his suppression of democracy in Hong Kong can be expected to continue, as it has in mainland China.

FACTORS	FINDINGS	RATING
Government/ political stability	Political freedom limited, ultimate control in Beijing, free market economics	3
Favorable laws, judicial system	Rule of law in theory; courts susceptible to pressure from Beijing	3
Available legal entities	All major legal entities available or recognized	5
Taxes	Foreign investors can avoid most local taxes; corporate taxes low	5
Financial privacy/ Bank secrecy	OECD automatic tax information exchange	4
Final Rating		**20**

Gateway to China

By almost any measure, Hong Kong is one of the world's leading financial and economic powerhouses. In total cash and assets, it is the world's third wealthiest financial center, after New York and London. It has a very strong banking, business and investment infrastructure that rivals any place in the world.

Although it offers no natural resources with the notable exception of a world-renown deep-water port, Hong Kong is considered a world-class city. It also boasts a highly educated population of more than 7 million regarded for its productivity and creativity. There is a Chinese phrase that describes Hong Kong well, *Zhong Si He Bing*, literally meaning "combination of East and West."

If you're doing business in China (or anywhere in Asia) you should consider Hong Kong as your base of operations. It's a place where you can obtain financing, do your banking, create the corporate or trust entities you may need to succeed in a very tough market — especially in China.

Keep in mind that Hong Kong has a major competitor for the role of leading Asian OFC — Singapore. And both well-developed financial centers are competing against a growing mainland Chinese rival in Shanghai.

There is no question that China is an attractive market and Hong Kong is the gateway to the Mainland. Until recently the huge mass of 1.382 billion people in China were experiencing some of the most rapid, although highly uneven, economic growth in world history. For some, living standards had improved dramatically, yet political controls remain tight.

Since the late 1970s, China has advanced to a more market-oriented system, compared to a closed one that plays a major global market role. In 2010, China became the world's largest exporter and continues to be to this day. The country's changes started with the gradual removal of agriculture as a collective and grew to include a free-market price movement. Financial power was removed from a central group and more state enterprises were able to take control of their future. In addition, there was expansion of the private sector, creation of stock markets, the growth of a modern banking system, and a welcome for foreign trade and investment.

In addition to better living conditions, following restructuring of the economy, China boasted impressive results and efficiency that produced a tenfold increase in GDP since 1978. However, China's economy is cooling with an estimated GDP of $23.12 trillion and per-capita GDP of US$16,600 in 2017. While the per capita income is below the world average, this still makes China the second-largest economy in the world after the U.S. It is the world leader in manufacturing and agricultural, exceeding the U.S., but is second to the U.S. in the value of services it produces.

With a growing financial system consisting of banks, stock markets and financial exchanges controlled by the Communist government and the military, the Chinese domestic economy still lacks the experience and controls Western nations take for granted. Indeed, many of the existing financial institutions in China are loaded with billions in non-performing, politically allocated loans, thousands of shaky investments, permeated with official corruption.

To add to this uncertainty there is no "rule of law" or reliable judicial system in China, in the sense the Western world understands such basic safeguards. This means doing business in China lacks the legal protection foreign investors take for granted elsewhere.

This mainland financial situation has served to accentuate and expand the role that Hong Kong has played with great success since the Communist revolution took control of mainland China in 1949 — that of China's financial window and conduit to the rest of world.

Hong Kong is ideally situated — legally a part of, but also different and somewhat apart from, China. In Hong Kong, you can find what struggling mainland China sorely lacks — the legal, financial and investment expertise and experience that can provide you with a sensible approach to investing and doing business in China.

And that's where the profits will be — if you are prudent and careful in your approach. If you want to deal in China, unless you have longstanding family or business ties there, you are best served working with a Hong Kong-based partner who has firsthand knowledge of the Chinese market. China, a long-time trading partner for Hong Kong, accounts for about half of HK exports by value.

Hong Kong is a very easy place in which to reside and do business. It has easy access to the mainland by air, train or ferry. If you become a Hong Kong resident, you can get a six-month, multiple-entry visa to China with little difficulty. From one of the most modern airports in the world there are multiple flights daily to all major centers in China, as well as in the U.S., Europe, the Middle East, Africa and Asia.

Economy

Hong Kong is proof that "money talks." China has too much invested in Hong Kong to destroy it because of rigid political ideology. Today, 30% of Hong Kong's bank deposits are Chinese. China accounts for 47.8% of all Hong Kong imports (including cross-border trade), and 54.2% of exports, 20% of the insurance business and more than 12% of all construction.

Hong Kong has also established itself as the premier stock market for Chinese firms seeking to list abroad. The HK Stock Exchange is Asia's third largest stock exchange in terms of market capitalization behind the Japan Exchange Group, and the seventh largest in the world. In 2016, mainland Chinese companies accounted for 51% of the list on the Hong Kong Stock Exchange and accounted for about 62.1% of the exchange's market capitalization. In 2016, the HK Exchange had 1,955 listed companies, 989 from mainland China, 856 from Hong Kong and 110 from abroad. In an historic move, the HK Stock Exchange merged with the Shanghai Exchange, making easier cross border investing.

Hong Kong serves as the Chinese banker, investment broker and go-between in what is now a multi-billion annual trade flows. In 2017, direct foreign investment in China was $1.514 trillion and in the past 20 years most of this FDI that has flooded into China; 60% came from, or through, Hong Kong.

As reported by the *CIA World Factbook*, "Hong Kong has a free market economy, highly dependent on international trade and finance — the value of goods and services trade, including the sizable share of re-exports, is about four times the GDP." Since 1997 when China took over control from Britain, Hong Kong has thrived under the Beijing promise of "one country, two systems" approach. The socialist economic policies of the mainland are not imposed on Hong Kong, even though Beijing's political rule is. The HK government now promotes the HK Special Administrative Region (SAR) as the site for Chinese renminbi (RMB) currency internationalization.

Twenty years after the handover to Beijing, there's no doubt protests were inspired by Hong Kong's many challenges — political corruption; property prices at highest levels since 1997; the gap between rich and poor, already the worst in Asia and the greatest in over

40 years; worsening air pollution; and the denial of a clear path to a system allowing public election of leaders as promised.

But the HK quasi-capitalist elites are quick to insist that street protests have not and will not affected Hong Kong's world business standing.

Prosperity, Low Taxes

In a strange twist of world economic fate, the clampdown by the European Union and the OECD on tax havens in the West created a benefit for far-removed offshore financial centers, such as Hong Kong and Singapore.

Wealthy people from the Middle East shifted cash toward Asia and away from Europe and the United States as a response to EU and U.S. tax evasion investigations and more stringent bank and financial reporting rules. When much of the world was mired in a major recession in 2008, Asian banks, many based in Hong Kong, were sitting on more than US$2 trillion of reserves. Funds had been continuously pouring money into emerging markets and Hong Kong was a major beneficiary of this global trend. No leading Asian banks were caught in collapses, so no bailouts were needed.

Economists attribute the strong Hong Kong economy to a series of factors: tight limits on senior citizen and other welfare spending, no military spending and an economy that continues to expand, 3.5% in 2017. Mostly Hong Kong has cashed in on China's economic boom. The 2017 per capita GDP was $61,000. That impressive GDP figure is higher than that enjoyed by the citizens of Germany, Japan, the United Kingdom, Canada or Australia.

Hong Kong's total population is close to 7.2 million, with a work-force close to four million and an impressive 2017 unemployment rate of 2.6%.

Mainland Chinese investors have flocked to real estate, pushing housing prices higher, in hopes of achieving political stability and possibly even protection from tax collectors and fraud investigators.

The government has raked in higher tax revenue on real estate sales thanks to higher apartment prices and the sale of government land for new construction projects.

Because of China's easing of travel restrictions, the number of mainland tourists to the territory jumped to 42.8 million in 2016, up from 4.5 million in 2001. They account for approximately 76% of all arrivals to Hong Kong.

Retail sales have surged because of this influx. More than 100,000 mainland visitors a day come to Hong Kong and most head straight for retail stores.

Tax breaks and allowances are so generous that only about 1.5 million people pay income tax. A single person starts paying income tax at HK$108,000 a year (US$14,000) and above. A married person with a dependent spouse can earn HK$216,000 (US$28,000) tax-free. The maximum income tax rate is 17% and most pay less. There are no sales or no capital gains taxes, no VAT and no tax on dividend income.

By comparison in mainland China, the top tax rate for high-come earners is 45%, though corporate taxes there are relatively low.

The main draw for Hong Kong has been a safe haven status against the 17% value-added tax in mainland China, as well as import and consumption taxes, which can tack on an additional 10% to 50%.

Business, Banking

Hong Kong's financial services sector is a mainstay of the economy. It accounts for 13% of gross domestic product and provided 230,000 jobs in 2017 in a population of 7.1 million, according to the government.

Hong Kong continues to link its currency to the U.S. dollar, maintaining an arrangement established in 1983 that pegs: US$1 = 7.75000 HKD. However, the government is promoting Hong Kong as the site for Chinese *renminbi* (RMB) internationalization. Hong

Kong residents can open RMB-denominated savings accounts. Both RMB-denominated corporate and Chinese government bonds are sold and RMB trade settlement is permitted.

The clearest sign of Hong Kong's economic assimilation with the mainland can be seen in the banking and financial sector. The Hong Kong-Shanghai Stock Connect, the Hong Kong Shanghai Gold Connect, and the Mutual Recognition of Funds, all mark key steps toward expanding the mainland's capital markets and strengthens Hong Kong's position as a leader in China's offshore RMB market. Hong Kong authorities are also examining additional RMB products in areas from bonds to commodities.

It is relatively easy and quick to register a company and/or open bank accounts, although a local address is needed for either. This is simple to arrange with the help of any of the many businesses offering real or virtual offices for rent. However, most local banks reject accounts held directly in the name of American clients, although they may consider them if opened by a U.S.-person-owned trust, LLC or IBC.

Hong Kong maintains a three-tier system of deposit-taking institutions, namely licensed banks, restricted licensed banks and deposit-taking companies collectively known as "authorized institutions." The territory has one of the highest concentrations of banking institutions in the world. More than 70 of the 100 largest world banks operate in Hong Kong.

The Hong Kong Monetary Authority actively supports policies for the maintenance and the development of the status of city-state as an international financial center and for the stability and integrity of the financial system.

Hong Kong ranks No. 4 among the world's largest banking centers (after New York, London and Singapore), No. 6 as the largest foreign exchange center, No. 11 as the largest trading economy, busiest container port and is Asia's second-biggest stock market. With low taxes and a usually trustworthy common law legal system, international banking and business flows in and out, assured of stability and a high degree of financial privacy.

Hong Kong is regarded by foreign firms as a highly advantageous regional location from which to do business. Almost 80% of foreign firms based in Hong Kong surveyed said they felt that it was the best location for them, due to advanced telecommunications networks, a free trade environment, low taxes and effective regulation. On an industry basis, according to the survey results, the financial services sector was the most positive overall.

Hong Kong's status as one of the world's top trading centers for stocks, bonds, commodities, metals, futures, currencies and personal and business financial operations means that such transactions are conducted there with a high degree of sophistication.

Business Tax

A major attraction for offshore business is Hong Kong's relatively low 16.5% business tax rate. Hong Kong has a territorial tax system that applies to "territoriality of profits." If profits originate in or are derived from Hong Kong, then they are subject to local tax. Otherwise, they are tax-free, regardless of whether the company is incorporated or registered there. Interestingly, IBCs and all other foreign corporations generally may open a Hong Kong bank account without prior registration under the local business statute.

This can save charges for auditing and annual report filing and removes the annoyance of having to argue with the Inland Revenue Department about the territoriality of the business.

On the other hand, one must be careful not to transact any taxable local business, because doing that without local registration is against the law. In cases where local business does occur, tax authorities generally are lenient, usually requiring local registration and payment of unpaid tax. But in some cases, IBCs have been forced to register as a listed public company at considerable expense.

Corporations

There are more companies — more than 500,000 — registered in Hong Kong than anywhere else in the world. (Here, they are called "private limited companies" and are identified with a "Ltd.," not an "Inc.") Hong Kong is also home to the largest community of multinational firms in Asia. The reasons are first, the territory's colonial roots spanning over 150 years, making it a natural hub for British companies. The second reason is its consistent reputation for openness, simplicity of operation and institutional familiarity.

In Hong Kong, there is no specific legal recognition of an international business company (IBC) per se, as there are in some offshore financial havens. The law recognizes only the one corporate "Ltd." form. Companies must have a minimum of one director and one shareholder. Shareholders or directors do not have to be residents of Hong Kong and they can be individual persons or corporations.

Company incorporation does require a registered office in Hong Kong and a Hong Kong resident individual or Hong Kong corporation to act as the secretary. Hong Kong companies must be audited each year.

Hong Kong offshore companies require by law a local resident company secretary, who usually charges about US$500 per year for filing a few documents with the Company Registry. Annual auditing by a CPA starts from about US$500 for companies with few transactions and can easily reach ten times as much for a mid-size operational offshore trading company.

Financial Privacy

Until recently, Hong Kong's laws did not permit bank regulators to give information about an individual customer's affairs to foreign government authorities, except in cases involving fraud. Hong Kong never has had specific banking secrecy laws as have many other OFCs such as Switzerland, Panama or Austria.

Hong Kong now allows automatic exchange of tax and bank account information with other governments under the Common Reporting Standard (CRS) and Article 26 of the Organization for Economic Co-operation and Development. That is, banks may exchange information upon proof of foreign tax evasion or tax fraud. (See *Automatic Tax Information Exchange* in Chapter Three.)

Hong Kong also exchanges tax information under a network of nearly 30 income tax treaties (TIEAs). Hong Kong's willingness to embrace greater transparency, after years of resistance, underscored their fear of being tarred as "*bei sui tin tong*" or "tax evasion havens," as tax havens are known in Cantonese.

In 2014, native Hong Kong, leaders in the city-state's important financial sector organized against trends and denounced money laundering by mainland government officials and their families as official corruption. The anti-Beijing financial group said they feared the destruction of Hong Kong's reputation as a clean and desirable offshore financial center. They demanded a political wake-up among bankers, stockbrokers and financial traders who might have become entangled in mainland China's cash and influence. This came at a time when the mainland government was first cracking down on financial corruption with major show trials of accused officials. These trials continued in 2018.

Hong Kong also has a mutual legal assistance treaty (MLAT) with the United States. Anti-money laundering laws and "know-your-customer" rules have made the opening of bank accounts for IBCs more difficult, but no more so than other countries. Account applicants must declare to the bank the "true beneficial owner" of an IBC or a trust with supporting documentation. Proof must be shown for all corporate directors and shareholders of the registering entity and any other entities that share in the ownership.

Basics

If you intend to pursue business investments in Asia, keep in mind lessons other foreigners have learned the hard way. Pick your Asian business partners (and business investments) carefully, avoiding the inefficient mainland Chinese state-owned enterprises. Stick with solid basics like marketing, distribution and service. Be sure to guard carefully your technology from theft.

And remember, a series of small ventures gets less government attention and red tape than big showcase projects that often produce demands for graft. Many foreign business investors have been burned by crooked bookkeeping, few shareholder controls, sudden government rule changes and systemic corruption.

Only recently, as China's economy became more westernized, did Beijing finally begin to address the need for laws guaranteeing the right for citizens and foreigners to own and transfer private property.

Most importantly, keep a sharp eye not on the Chinese government hype, but on what's really happening in China. Uncertainty means that offshore financial activities by foreign citizens can prosper, but without immediate assurance of success. Unless the "New China" is your sphere of intended business activity, you may want to look elsewhere for your Asian financial base of operations in places such as Singapore or Malaysia.

Contacts:

Hong Kong Immigration:
http://www.immd.gov.hk/eng/index.html

Hong Kong Monetary Authority: www.hkma.gov.hk

Hong Kong Trade Development Council:
http://www.hktdc.com/en-buyer

Economic and Trade Offices
Washington, D.C.:
http://www.hketowashington.gov.hk/dc/index.htm

New York, NY: http://www.hketony.gov.hk/ny/index.htm
San Francisco, CA: http://www.hketosf.gov.hk/sf/index.htm

United States Consulate General
26 Garden Road
Central, Hong Kong
Tel.: +852 2523-9011
Email for American Citizen Services: acshk@state.gov
Web: https://hk.usconsulate.gov

Residence & Citizenship Services:

Henley & Partners
1002A, Tower 1, Admiralty Center
18 Harcourt Road
Admiralty, Hong Kong
Tel.: + 852 3101 4100
Web: https://www.henleyglobal.com/residence-hong-kong-overview

Jeffrey Y.F. Chen, Esq.
3A, Yunhai Garden Office Tower
118 Qinghai Road, Shanghai, 200041, China
Tel.: +86 21 52281952
Mobile: +86 13916089368
Email: lawyer_chen@lawyers.cn

Banks in mainland China do not accept account applications from foreign individuals nor from corporations unless the foreign company has registered subsidiaries located in China. Mr. Chen advises on investments, business or other legal matters concerning China.

Republic of Singapore

Singapore has fashioned itself into a major international financial center — but it's not exactly an offshore tax haven. It has traded its ancient Oriental image for towers of concrete and glass and rickshaws have been replaced by high-tech industry. Singapore appears shockingly modern, but this is an Asian city with Chinese, Malay and Indian traditions from feng shui to ancestor worship as part of daily life. These contrasts bring the city to life, but foreigners may want to avoid talking about local politics.

FACTORS	FINDINGS	RATING
Government/ political stability	Stabile but political opposition restricted; strict libel laws, Draconian punishments, paternalistic free market economics	3
Favorable laws, judicial system	Rule of law in theory tempered by executive policies	3
Available legal entities	All major legal entities available or recognized	5
Taxes	Territorial tax system; 17% corporate tax rate, 15% on interest; 20% maximum income tax; offshore income mostly tax exempt	5
Financial privacy/ Bank secrecy	OECD automatic tax information exchange honors TIEAs; no TIEAs with US or Canada	4
Final Rating		**20**

The Republic of Singapore (population 5.9 million) has the distinction of its 277-square miles being a small island, a state and a city — all in one. Located just a few steamy miles north of the Equator, it has Malaysia and Indonesia as close and sometimes uneasy neighbors.

The climate is hot and humid, with rainfall of more than two meters (about seven feet) annually.

Colonial Singapore gained its independence from Great Britain in 1965. Lee Kuan Yew became its autocratic leader and served until 1990, when his son, Lee Hsien Loong, now in office, replaced him in his official capacities. Until his death at the age of 91 in 2015, the father remained the power behind his son's throne and their one-party state does not tolerate dissent or opposition. There are no jury trials. Civil matters, such as alleged libel or slander, can escalate into criminal issues with serious consequences, especially for political opponents. It has been called "a utopian police state." But as *The Economist* observed: "Under him Singapore, with no natural resources, was transformed from a tiny struggling island into one of the world's richest countries."

Draconian laws keep crime (and freedom) to a minimum, but the enforced stability attracts massive foreign investment. Moreover, as visitors can attest, the streets are very clean, since spitting or littering can land you in jail. Clean streets are a tradeoff for individual political freedom. And as election results suggest, opposition to such restrictions is increasing. With the death of Lee Kuan Yew in 2015, greater freedom may be in order.

Offshore Financial Center

Singapore continues to be a top draw. The Global Financial Center Index ranked Singapore third in 2017, while PricewaterhouseCoopers stated that it was the best city for transportation and infrastructure. *The Economist* Intelligence Unit ranked Singapore as "the best place in the world to do business."

But as the *Salon* news website said: "If money is free in Singapore, people are not. Speech, expression and assembly are all tightly controlled; the justice system is notoriously harsh. Migrant workers are treated poorly; labor organizers are deported. There is no minimum wage, and the Gini co-efficient for inequality is among the highest in the developed world."

"Singapore is improving," its defenders insist. But *Reporters Without Borders* in 2017 ranked it 151 of 180 nations in press freedoms. *The Economist* magazine's rigorous Democracy Index ranked it with Liberia, Palestine and Haiti.

Nevertheless, Singapore has grown into a world offshore financial haven, certainly comparable to Hong Kong and way ahead of its neighbor, fledgling Labuan in nearby Malaysia. Singapore has cultivated a sophisticated private banking sector, offering discreet financial services aimed at luring wealthy clients. Many Swiss banks have been here for several years with BNP, Credit Suisse, Morgan Stanley and UBS all expanding in Singapore to service wealthy mainland Chinese clients. Along with Hong Kong, it sees itself as a financial gateway to expanding China, the eventual colossus of the East.

While free trade and export zones weren't invented in Singapore, they have been perfected there. It is a prime location in East Asia for attracting industries and multinational corporations looking for tax incentives and low labor costs.

Singapore has emerged as the financial service center for African and Middle Eastern sovereign wealth funds that want to put oil and natural resource money to work in Asia, and for Western money seeking investments in Southeast Asia.

Modern infrastructure, developed capital markets, an educated workforce, comparatively stable political institutions and a low crime rate are attractions. Singapore is viewed as highly developed with some of the best investment potential in Asia and some of the lowest levels of economic corruption. It attracts investors seeking profits as well as those seeking safety outside the U.S. dollar.

Singapore is reportedly the world's fourth-largest foreign exchange center after London, New York and Tokyo, and is home to many businesses, multinational corporations, banks and financial investment companies. It holds the world's ninth-largest foreign exchange reserves, impressive for a small country. The currency is the Singapore dollar and it has become a haven currency, like the Swiss franc.

Singapore also provides investors the ability to access other regional markets. Many companies with direct ties to Myanmar, Vietnam, Thailand and other neighboring economies are listed on the Singapore Exchange, providing a convenient way to invest in regional growth.

Singapore has become a financial melting pot attracting foreign corporate operatives and investors. That benefits key Singapore industries, such as banking, as well as tourism and real estate. Regional business travelers and tourists now visit for shopping, casinos and finance.

Singapore has also attracted major investments in medical technology and pharmaceuticals. It is aiming to establish itself as the financial and high-tech hub for Southeast Asia.

It has a highly developed and successful free-market economy. Despite political repression, it enjoys a remarkably open and corruption-free environment, stable prices, and a per capita GDP ($90,500 in 2017) higher than most developed countries. The economy depends heavily on exports, particularly in consumer electronics, information technology products, pharmaceuticals, and on a growing financial services sector.

The common language is English. Most Singaporeans are Asian, with commerce dominated by 74.3% ethnic Chinese. Malays make up 13%, with a mix of Indians, Thais, Vietnamese, Laotians and a very small number of Europeans. Europeans hold most management positions and are generally well regarded. In Singapore, state regulation has created a paradise, if you like high-rise buildings, crass materialism and minimal personal freedom.

Many Swiss banks, such as Bank Julius Baer, have expanded their operations in Singapore to capitalize on the new business opportunities. The Swiss National Bank opened a branch in Singapore, being the first non-Asian official central bank to do so. The number of private banks operating in Singapore has increased to 26 in the past nine seven years. The Singapore Monetary Authority estimates that assets held by banks in Singapore has grown 20% each year since 2000 to more than US$6.9 billion in 2017.

Taxes

Singapore is not necessarily a tax haven. But as competitors, the two Asian financial hubs of Singapore and Hong Kong have kept personal and corporate taxes among the lowest globally to attract more foreign investment. As reported in *The Wall Street Journal*, "The tax codes are more transparent, making it easier for small businesses to not need a tax consultant or advisor. Top individual income tax rates are 22% in Singapore and 17% in Hong Kong, compared with 37% at the federal level in the United States."

The two Asian financial centers also have simpler taxation systems compared to the U.S. and other countries. Businesses make an average of three tax payments per year in Hong Kong and five in Singapore, compared with 11 in the U.S. and a global average of 28.5 per year.

Singapore has a corporate tax rate of 17%, while the GST (goods and services or VAT) tax kicks in only after annual sales jump above SGD$1 million (US$755,000). Dividends and capital gains earned from foreign subsidiaries/branches benefit from tax-exempt status. Dividend distributions by Singapore-based companies have zero tax withholding, while interest has a 15% tax withholding and royalties have a 10% withholding.

Singapore doesn't have a capital gains or inheritance tax. Only income earned in Singapore is taxable, while offshore income sources are exempt. Non-residents see a 15% tax for employment income after expenses while director and consultant fees are taxed at 20%.

Foreigners can incorporate with one shareholder, one resident director (with a local address), and a minimum capital of SGD$1 paid within 48 hours. Self-registration isn't permitted, but for foreign individuals or entities, professional firms can provide company formation and nominee local directors. Work visas are available for foreigners for employment, entrepreneurs or short-term for attending to business.

Modern infrastructure, developed capital markets, an educated workforce, comparatively stable political institutions and a low crime rate are added attractions. Negatives are a high cost of living for employees, (the city's cost of living index is the highest in the world), mandatory filing of audited accounts of a foreign parent company, and mandatory designation of an active local secretary.

We visited Singapore for a legal conference and personally saw how local trust laws have been updated on a par with leading offshore trust nations, such as Bermuda or Panama. Singapore strengthened its bank secrecy laws, originally patterned after the strict privacy laws in Switzerland.

Singapore now allows automatic exchange of tax and bank account information with other governments under the Common Reporting Standard (CRS) and Article 26 of the Organization for Economic Co-operation and Development. That is, banks may exchange information upon proof of foreign tax evasion or tax fraud. (See *Automatic Tax Information Exchange* in Chapter Three.) Instead of signing separate TIEAs, it amended existing double tax agreements with other countries to include information exchange provisions and Singapore is now officially on to the OECD "white list."

Immigration

The government actively recruits wealthy businesspersons as residents. For those active in offshore finance, the island city-state wants to establish itself as Asia's newest private banking hub by luring the super-wealthy away from places such as Hong Kong and even Switzerland.

The government allows foreigners, especially Europeans, who meet its wealth requirements, to buy land and become permanent residents. The goal is to attract private wealth from across Asia, as well as riches that Europeans and other Westerners are moving out of Switzerland and European Union nations to avoid new tax and reporting laws there.

Singapore, which occupies an area about half the size of the city of Houston, Texas, has added about one million people since 2004 with government encouragement to make up for a declining birth rate. This has contributed to crowded transportation and more competition for jobs, housing and places in schools, fueling voter anger that led to the ruling party's smallest electoral win in 2011 since independence in 1965.

Foreigners and permanent residents make up more than a third of the island's 5.9 million population. Most new citizens come from countries other than China, nearly half from Southeast Asia. The surge of new arrivals from China was part of a government immigration push that almost doubled Singapore's population since 1990.

The government has made it more expensive for companies to hire overseas workers by raising taxes and in 2012 it increased salary thresholds and required better educational qualifications for some categories of foreigners.

Tensions over immigration are problems in many nations, but most of Singapore's population was already ethnic Chinese, many born of earlier Chinese immigrants. Some locals now blame mainland Chinese for driving up real-estate prices, stealing the best jobs and clogging the roads with flashy European sports cars.

The government reacted by adjusting immigration downward. New permanent residents have decreased two-thirds since 2008, when 80,000 applications were accepted. The number of people granted citizenship has remained level at about 18,500 a year. But despite the growing complaints, Singapore remains the third-most desirable immigration destination for affluent Chinese after the United States and Canada, according to a survey by the Bank of China.

Political Change

The year 2012 saw an increased civic activism sweeping this highly politically controlled island. Many of the loudest vocal activists are young, wired and cynical about the government's argument that it alone can maintain the prosperity and social harmony that has transformed this resource-starved island into one of the most advanced economies.

Activists say some opposition started in the 1990s but was seen in 2011 when the governing People's Action Party lost six seats in the 87-member Parliament. The PAP has dominated politics since 1959 and is headed by Prime Minister Lee Hsien Loong, the son of the late Lee Kuan Yew, Singapore's founding father. The PAP support in the most recent 2011 election dropped to a historic low of 60%, down 6 points from the previous election, but the PAP got more than 90% of the seats. The next elections will be held in late 2017.

Public rallies have demanded repeal of the anti-subversion law coinciding with the 25th anniversary of Operation Spectrum, a crackdown on activists that led to the arrest of 22 student leaders, lawyers and teachers grabbed in nighttime raids and forced, in what they alleged were harsh interrogations, to confess to an anti-government plot.

Over the years, legal advocates here claim more than 2,600 people have been arrested under the Internal Security Act, which allows the authorities to imprison suspects without trial.

In 2017, in accordance with the strict criteria in the national constitution requiring as president a candidate from the minority Malay community, Halimah Yacob, a member of the PAP, was declared to be the only eligible presidential candidate and she was inaugurated as the eighth president, a largely figurehead position.

Prime Minister Lee Hsien Loong, the son of Singapore's founding Prime Minister, Lee Kuan Yew, heads the People's Action Party (PAP), which has run Singapore since 1959. It controls 83 of the 89 elective seats in Parliament.

Based on the past 50 years of local history, no one is predicting any huge public agitation or the end of Singapore's one-party rule, but political types do say increasingly people are dropping traditional reluctance to challenge Singapore's paternalistic leaders and their "autocratic light" style of governance.

Contacts:

Government of Singapore: http://www.gov.sg

Monetary Authority of Singapore: http://www.mas.gov.sg

Embassy of the Republic of Singapore
3501 International Place NW
Washington, D.C. 20008
Tel.: 202-537-3100
Email: singemb_was@mfa.sg
Web: http://www.mfa.gov.sg/content/mfa/overseasmission/
washington.html

United States Embassy
27 Napier Road
Singapore 258508
Tel.: +65 6476-9100
Email: singaporeacs@state.gov
Web: https://sg.usembassy.gov

Professional Assistance:

Singapore & Hong Kong

Banks in Singapore & Hong Kong usually do not accept accounts directly from individual U.S. persons, but require an intermediary to submit account applications. The banks may require account applicants to appear personally at their offices as part of the application process.

Below is contact information for our designated intermediary, Josh Bennett JD, an expert attorney in offshore asset protection, U.S. offshore taxes and reporting requirements. He also acts as contact for Trident Corporate Services that provides incorporation, trust creation and related business and banking services in both Hong Kong and Singapore and in many other OFCs worldwide.

Josh N. Bennett, Esq., P.A.
440 North Andrews Avenue
Fort Lauderdale, FL 33301
Tel.: 954-779-1661
Mobile: 786-202-5674
Email: josh@joshbennett.com
Web: http://www.joshbennett.com

CHAPTER SIX

The United Kingdom

London remains one of the leading financial centers of the world, but the U.K. is not a tax haven in any sense. The "City of London," (the country's equivalent of Wall Street), is the world's second leading financial center in asset size and trade volume, second only to New York City.

The U.K. is home to a dwindling number of private banks, but they offer possibilities for careful investors. Despite its 20th century decline from empire status, the U.K. still has a few service-oriented exclusive financial institutions that originated and perfected private family banking. These banks cater to the wealthy, experienced investor and are worth considering. Indeed, the U.K. provides 17% of the global market in offshore financial services.

We don't advocate use of the subsidized U.K. banks that were rescued from financial ruin, propped up by trillions of pounds sterling in Labor government bailouts at the taxpayers' considerable expense. An estimated £1.2 trillion (US$1.6 trillion) was spent bailing out the Royal Bank of Scotland, HBOS/Lloyds and Northern Rock.

But for personal service and true privacy, a precious few remaining small British banking houses have not been swallowed in mergers and bailouts. Some have been purchased by larger banks but retain their separate identities and traditional practices. These banking survivors far exceed in personal service anything offered in U.S. banks.

Traditionally, the Bank of England, the nation's official central bank, for centuries was a relative pillar of economic stability, although the British economic downturn that began in 2008, plus years of government deficit-spending, weakened the stabilizing powers of the "Old Lady of Threadneedle Street," (the central bank's London location since 1734).

For Americans, banking in the U.K. always has been just one step away from home. Since the founding in 1607 of the Jamestown Colony in Virginia, America has been linked inextricably with England — politically and financially. The shared colonial experience, the American Revolution, two world wars, the Cold War and more recent military conflicts, all formed bonds between America and its parent nation that remain strong.

And while the United States clearly surpassed Mother England in both military and financial power, the U.K. remains an ally with which the United States continues to maintain its much-vaunted "special relationship."

British Economy

Even in decline, the United Kingdom remains one of the world's great trading and financial powers centered within the area known as "The City of London" or just, "The City."

In the medieval period, The City of London Corporation was most of what was then London, but now is a small enclave in central London. It holds distinct legal status, as a separate county headed by a ceremonial Lord Mayor who heads the world's oldest continuous municipal democracy, at least ten centuries old.

With its relatively small size and limited resources, the U.K. economy still ranks among the four largest in Western Europe. At this writing the economy is in improved condition. In early 2018, the national debt, excluding the bailed-out banks, was at a new record high of £1.79 trillion, (US$2.3 trillion), 87.2% of GDP, but the budget deficit was at the lowest level in a decade.

During 18 years of Tory rule, (1979-1997), successive Conservative Party governments reversed the worst of the socialist trends that began under the Labor Party in 1945. Labor returned to power in 1997 under a moderate prime minister, Tony Blair, by co-opting much of the Tory platform and emphasizing political change. But Labor lost in 2007, after running up massive deficits and imposing high taxes that drove individuals and companies to tax havens in Ireland and Switzerland.

In 2015 elections, Prime Minister David Cameron led the Conservative Party to a major victory. For the first time since 1992 the Tories won an absolute majority ending the first coalition government since World War II.

Brexit

The 2015 election lighted a burning fuse on a political time bomb; "Brexit," the word coined to describe a British exit from the European Union after 44 years as a member state.

PM Cameron promised a national referendum on whether the U.K. should leave or stay in the European Union they joined in 1973. On June 23, 2016, England voted for Brexit, 53.4% to 46.6%. Wales also voted for Brexit, 52.5% to 47.5%. Scotland and Northern Ireland both backed staying in the EU. The vote's result upset global markets, causing the British pound to fall to its lowest level against the dollar in years.

David Cameron, who had opposed U.K. withdrawal from the EU, resigned as PM, replaced by Theresa May, a member of the cabinet. She faced the difficult task of negotiating with the EU the terms of departure amid a storm of criticism from the 27 other member EU countries.

May called a surprised election in June 2017 to strengthen her hand in Brexit negotiations with EU leaders. In was a major mistake; May did not increase her party's seats in the Commons and lost the

Conservative's majority. She held on with support from the 10 MPs from Northern Ireland's Democratic Unionist Party.

The U.K. has been one of the fastest growing economies in the G7, but economists were concerned about the negative impact of Brexit and what would happen to extensive U.K. trade relationship with other EU members through its single economic market membership.

Important to those to those considering future business, banking or investments in the U.K., expert economic observers warned Brexit could jeopardize London's position as the central location for European and world financial services.

The U.K. enjoyed several years of controlled economic growth before the 2008 world crash. Until the recession hit, the British mostly had remained loyal to the free market traditions that made them one of the world's most prosperous nations. Central to that success has been a high level of service and privacy offered by their banks, financial and investment institutions, but that could be in jeopardy.

Andrew Bailey, the U.K. Financial Conduct Authority chief executive, told MPs that British banks might make irreversible moves to transfer staff from London to rival cities in the EU unless there was clarity over Brexit. The BBC reported that the Bank of England believed up to 75,000 U.K. financial services jobs could be at risk. Goldman Sachs contingency plans included leasing the top eight floors of a 37-story building in Frankfurt, Germany, although it built a new European headquarters in London.

Equally serious is the future the unity of the British-led United Kingdom itself, with Scotland seeking greater devolution of powers and another vote on independence. In 2014, with the highest turnout in history (84.6%), a majority of 55.3% voted against Scottish independence, with 44.7% voted in favor. A new referendum is being considered.

David Cameron and many other senior figures who opposed Brexit predicted an immediate economic crisis if the U.K. voted to leave. They were wrong. The pound slumped after the referendum but in 2017 remained only 10% lower against the dollar and 15% down against the euro.

Contrary to economic doomsayers, the U.K. economy grew an estimated 1.8% in 2016, second only to Germany's 1.9%, among the world's G-7 leading industrialized nations. The U.K. economy grow at almost the same rate in 2017. In late 2017, inflation was a low 3%, and unemployment continued to fall, to a 42-year-low of 4.3%.

That Conservative-Liberal Democrat government had adopted an austerity program, continued under the Conservative majority. Gradually the U.K. recovered from a years-long recession, but now the major economic policy question remains: "On what terms will the U.K. participate in the financial and economic integration of the European Union?"

The outcome of two years of tough UK-EU negotiations, scheduled to end in 2019 or before, will answer that question.

U.K. Banks

For Americans one major advantage of banking in the United Kingdom is language.

English now has become the de facto international language of banking — and almost every other global endeavor. Language facility is certainly a big plus when banking offshore, where local customs and rules can be confusing enough without having to cultivate multilingual capabilities.

For those seeking an offshore bank account with a reasonable degree of privacy and freedom from U.S. withholding taxes, London may be the place.

Despite growing government intervention and demands for financial information, as a foreigner, it is easy to get lost in the crowd of other foreigners who bank in London. There is an advantage to banking in a major world financial capital where you are only one among many.

IRS bureaucrats don't raise eyebrows nearly so high when an American reports a London bank account, as they might for an account in the Cayman Islands or The Bahamas.

While client confidence with a bank comes only after time, a new U.K. client can benefit from one of the oldest and most efficient private banking systems in the world. The government guarantees bank accounts against losses of up to £85,000 (US$119,000).

U.K. Bank Privacy

A 1922 judicial decision declared four situations in which an English banker legally could compromise a client's banking secrecy: 1) by an order pursuant to law; 2) when a duty to the public exists; 3) in the interests of the bank; and 4) with a client's express or implied permission. Until a few years ago, these principles continued to guide the English banking system's privacy policies.

The former general rule was that U.K. Custom and Revenue agents had no right to seek the identities of the true owners of shares of stock. In cases where a bank account holder was discovered not to be a British resident, agents ended their ownership inquiry as a matter of policy.

Today, anti-money laundering laws, tax reporting requirements, FATCA and U.S. and other governments' pressures seriously has diminished banking privacy in England as they have everywhere else. The U.K. government, in partnership with the U.S., has been in the forefront pushing anti-money laundering "all crimes" reporting laws on the British Overseas Territories, Crown dependencies and British Commonwealth nations. "All crimes" refers to the expansion of the application of money laundering as a crime to any financial offense, but it also recognizes foreign tax evasion as a reportable U.K. crime.

The U.K. is one of the countries that applies the standard for tax information exchange set by the Organization for Economic Cooperation and Development (OECD), based on Article 26 of the OECD Model Tax Convention. The U.K. has joined most countries agreeing to the OECD "Common Reporting Standard" that imposes automatic tax information exchange as an international rule. Understand that each country applies Article 26 exchanges within its own procedural framework, and some are more restrictive than others in protecting privacy. (For more about this see *Automatic Tax Information Exchange* in Chapter Three.)

British FATCA

In Chapters Three and Seven, we explain that the U.K. has ultimate sovereignty and control over a network of largely self-governing British jurisdictions around the world, remnants of its colonial empire. These include the Crown Dependencies of Jersey, Guernsey and Isle of Man, and the Overseas Territories of Gibraltar, the Cayman Islands, Bermuda, Montserrat, the Turks and Caicos Islands, the British Virgin Islands and Anguilla. To some degree, all are established offshore financial centers, some of them major OFCs.

In 2014, the U.K. adopted CDOT (informally called the "U.K. FATCA" because it is patterned after the U.S. law). "CDOT" is an acronym for the constitutional status for the 10 British offshore financial centers to which it applies, notably the three Crown Dependencies and the 14 Overseas Territories. Though these jurisdictions have a measure of independence on internal political matters, Britain supports and controls them.

The U.K. government now requires British OFCs make FATCA-like disclosures to U.K. tax authorities about all U.K. account holders doing business in these areas.

Under the CDOT rules, information is provided automatically to HM Revenue and Customs (HMRC) about offshore bank accounts and non-U.K. structures with U.K. resident owners, or U.K. resident settlors, beneficiaries and protectors of trust structures. That is so even where there is no U.K. tax payable, no assets are in the U.K., and even where all covered U.K. persons are compliant with U.K. tax requirements. Non-domiciled persons without a U.K. residence are able to limit the information passed to HMRC, but some information must be provided.

The reaction to CDOT was justified anger on the part of those caught in this worldwide reporting net, especially those who were and are tax compliant, rightfully concerned for privacy and security reasons about their personal information.

In 2013, when Edward Snowden revealed that the U.S. National Security Agency for years had spied on millions of U.S. and foreign people, it became clear that the NSA was cooperating with the U.K. and the U.S. government was funding British surveillance operations, with the two countries sharing data in real time.

The Bank of England supervised all British banks until 1997 when the Labor government made sweeping changes, creating the Financial Services Agency (FSA). Many criticized the FSA as a muscle-bound giant with too many duties and not enough practical sense.

When the Conservative-Liberal coalition government took office in 2010, it abolished the FSA and moved its responsibilities to new agencies and back to the Bank of England. A new Financial Conduct Authority was made responsible for policing the City and the banking system. The Prudential Regulatory Authority regulates financial firms, including banks, investment banks, building societies and insurance companies. All other responsibilities are exercised by the Bank of England and its Financial Policy Committee.

Money Laundering Laws

The 2002 Proceeds of Crime Act gives U.K. police plenary powers to seek financial information related to money laundering, terrorism and many other alleged crimes. The Act imposes a positive duty on bankers, solicitors (lawyers) and other professionals to report any financial "suspicious activities" to the police. This means that financial privacy is diminished to a great degree for anyone who is the subject of police interest.

As in the U.S., Britain's anti-money laundering laws place the burden of detection on individual banks, their managers and even clerks and tellers. If a bank fails to establish and carry out detection procedures, it may be fined, and uncooperative bank officials face a two-year prison sentence. British bankers are forced to spy on their own customers, just as their American counterparts are required to act as spies under the U.S. Bank Secrecy Act and the PATRIOT Act.

U.S.-Style Forfeiture

Forfeiture began in medieval England as a power of the monarch. When the Labor government was in power it adopted American-style civil forfeiture laws with broad police powers. HM Customs and Revenue and the National Criminal Investigation Service (NCIS) have a free hand to rummage through tax files at will. The official policy line is that tax inspections only target individuals suspected of crimes.

This allows police "fishing expeditions" looking for evidence to build civil forfeiture cases. An important House of Lords decision held that anyone investigated for suspected U.K. tax offenses at least must first be given a warning and an explanation of their rights.

As in the U.S., U.K. government forfeiture policy calls for cash confiscation from individuals suspected of criminal activity, even if insufficient evidence exists to convict them in a court of law. In theory, if a suspect is judged to be "living beyond his visible means," the police can ask a court to freeze his or her assets immediately, pending investigation.

Future of Banking

The Labor Party government was a leader in the global attack on tax havens mounted by the high-tax G-20 countries and the OECD in the 1990s. The major goal was to force all countries to agree to a system of automatic exchange of tax information between governments, a goal that now is being imposed at the expense of financial and personal privacy.

Since 1975, a tax information exchange treaty between the U.K. and the U.S. has allowed great latitude in its application. While British courts may legally compromise your financial privacy in response to a foreign judicial subpoena, in the past they did so only occasionally, usually under diplomatic pressure. Now it is likely that the British system will reveal your bank records if substantial probable cause is shown by your home government.

The U.S. Treasury and the IRS maintain large staffs at the American Embassy in London's Grosvenor Square. All things considered, your money may be only marginally safer in the U.K. than in the U.S. if the Feds come knocking.

Home of Private Banking

Many English "private banks" offer a measure of discretion that American institutions will not (or cannot) approach. But some added privacy is not the only advantage of private banking in the U.K. Some English bankers work hard to provide excellent service in addition to financial security.

Americans love convenience and speed, usually at the expense of civility and dignity in everyday life. The British are more willing to provide personalized traditional services. While it's not easy to find such care, banking with small, private British banks provides a welcome reminder of gentler, more civilized times. Of course, such service does not come cheap.

There are some trade-offs involved to obtain this kind of personal service. First, without a formal introduction from a prominent British person or a respected American bank manager, you won't be able to open an account with C. Hoare & Co. or Child & Co. or at Rothschild's, for instance.

C. Hoare & Co. is England's oldest, privately owned banking house. Founded in 1672 by Sir Richard Hoare, it remains family owned and is currently managed by the 11th generation of direct descendants. It provides private banking, financial planning and investment management services that include loans, mortgages, savings accounts and investment advisory services as well as tax and estate planning services. The bank's clients typically are high-net-worth individuals and families.

37 Fleet Street
London EC4P 4DQ
Tel.: +44 (0)20 7353 4522
Email: info@hoaresbank.co.uk
Web: http://www.hoaresbank.co.uk

Child & Co. was founded in 1664. It is now a subsidiary of the **Royal Bank of Scotland (RBS)**. It specializes in private banking and wealth management. Coutts & Co. founded in 1692, also manages private wealth and it too is now a subsidiary of the RBS.

If either private bank interests you, first check the status of the Edinburgh-based RBS. The 71% U.K. taxpayer-owned bank, in 2017 suffered the 10th consecutive year of losses after in 2009 it received a £45 billion (US$59 billion) U.K. taxpayer bailout. In 2017, RBS faced a US Department of Justice US$9 billion penalty over bond fraud dating back to the 2008 banking crisis.

N M Rothschild & Sons, (known as Rothschild), is a private investment banking company owned by the Rothschild family. It was founded in the City of London in 1811 and is now a global firm with 50 offices around the world.

Contact: http://www.rothschild.com/contactus
Web: http://www.rothschild.com

In truth, these small, exclusive British private banks neither need nor want many customers, so applicants are screened with care. To gain entry, it helps to have an existing relationship with a U.S. bank that's affiliated with an international private bank network (such as Harriman, J.P. Morgan, or the oldest privately-owned bank in America, Brown Brothers). Making the necessary connections might take some time and effort, but the rewards are worth it.

Non-Doms Lose Tax Haven

Nearly one in 10 people living in the U.K. in 2016 were foreigners, nearly 6 million people. Until 2008, as resident foreigners, many were able to escape most of the high income and other taxes that U.K. citizens suffer. Although the tax law was tightened, in 2017 a reported 134 billionaires lived in the U.K., a record number and 14 more than in 2016. The wealthiest 1,000 people and families had a record total wealth of £658 billion (US$869 billion), a rise of 14% over 2016.

The British tax system has an interesting quirk. Dating back to the early 19th century, the British established a "non-domicile" status, which are foreigners who reside in Britain or "hereditary" non-doms who were born in Britain but who have parents or grandparents that have another country they consider their permanent home, yet claimed they want the option to return to their ancestral land. These "non-dom" residents have special tax benefits available to them. This shielded foreigners who benefitted from the "non-dom" income tax exemption, a major tax break for wealthy foreigners there. Under U.K. tax law (until a 2008 change) anyone living in Britain, but not born there and who qualified, could choose "non-domiciled" tax status.

In effect, they claimed a foreign country as their "tax domicile." The non-dom law made London a tax haven for many thousands of rich folks, from Russian oil tycoons to international investment bankers and Saudi princes.

Until 2008 this law allowed thousands of wealthy foreigners to live and work in the U.K. but pay taxes on the relatively small amount of money they brought into the U.K. each year, known as "remittances," and on what they earned within the U.K. They paid no taxes on much larger offshore earnings. It was argued, these foreigners enriched the U.K. by spending billions on real estate, goods and services and investments.

The British political Left repeatedly attacked this non-dom tax arrangement. When Labor gained power in 1994, then-Chancellor of the Exchequer, Gordon Brown, pledged to close the "non-dom loophole," but did nothing.

Finally, in 2008, with the economy sinking, Brown, by then prime minister, adopted tough tax proposals on high-earning non-domiciled resident; an annual minimum levy of £30,000 (US$42,000) on those who had lived in Britain for at least seven years. Foreign non-doms now pay an annual tax of up to £90,000 (US$125,000) for the privileged tax status. This tax provoked a storm of criticism from business leaders who claimed it would drive well-paid foreign workers out of Britain, which appears to have happened.

The government also closed the loophole that allowed non-doms to bring assets purchased with foreign earnings into Britain without paying tax on them. Goods worth more than £1,000 (US$1,400) kept in the U.K. for more than nine months became liable to tax. U.K. tax law still does not require payment of income taxes by non-doms on much foreign-source income, or estate taxes on foreign assets.

Income from U.K. sources generally is subject to U.K. taxation without regard to the citizenship or the place of residence of the individual or the place of registration of a company. For individuals who are neither resident nor ordinarily resident in the U.K., this means they are liable for U.K. income tax liability in the form of taxes deducted by a U.K. income source, together with tax on income from a trade or profession carried on through a permanent establishment in the U.K. and tax on rental income from U.K. real estate.

Individuals who are both resident and domiciled in the U.K. (versus those who are a resident but not domiciled) are additionally liable to taxation on their "worldwide" income and gains.

Under the U.K. CDOT reporting law, discussed earlier in this chapter, the British version of the U.S. FATCA, U.K. resident non-doms who have interests in accounts or structures in the U.K.'s offshore financial centers currently are not required to provide any information about the offshore funds to HMRC, provided they claim the remittance basis of taxation in the U.K. and nothing is remitted to the U.K. from the offshore account/structure.

In 2014 the government doubled the minimum for a U.K. investor visa to £2 million (US$2.8 million) for high net worth individuals willing to invest in British companies in exchange for the right to apply for citizenship after five years. Previously, an investment of £1 million could lead to permanent residence after six years, reduced to three years when investing £5 million and two years when investing £10 million. Physical presence in the country is required. But why spend all this cash when a wealthy person may qualify for the non-dom status?

If you are considering becoming a resident of the U.K. and think you can qualify legally as a "non-domiciled," be sure to check the current tax law status and what benefits may still be available, if any.

Taxes on Former Residents

In the past, the U.K. might have been generous tax-wise to resident foreigners, but it is not kind to its own citizens who live offshore (known as "expats"), many to avoid high U.K. taxes.

Until 1998, U.K. citizens who lived and worked outside the U.K. for more than a year were exempt from taxes on their earnings, if they were not physically in the U.K. longer than 62 days each year. The Labor government abolished this "foreign earnings deduction" in what it called "tax fairness." Currently any U.K. citizen who earns any amount of U.K. source income while in the U.K. must pay taxes on their entire year's earnings, regardless of where in the world the rest of the income was earned.

The results were predictable and swift. Nonresident U.K. athletes and entertainers modified business and travel schedules to avoid earning even a single shilling of U.K. source income.

Case in Point: The Rolling Stones canceled the U.K. leg of their 1998 world tour as a direct result of tax law. The world's leading rock band claimed it would have lost more than £12 million (US$16.7 million) if they played four 1998 U.K. concerts. Labor government spokespersons were quick to respond to the announcement of the cancellation as being driven by "greed." But when the Stones offered to play the concerts for charity in return for a tax exemption, the government turned down the offer. The bottom line: Great Britain is a great place to live, but a bad place to be tax domiciled. Just ask Mick Jagger.

Avoid U.K. Withholding Taxes

British bankers do not deduct withholding taxes on interest paid to nonresident accounts because the law imposes no taxes on a foreigner's account. When opening an account, a foreigner must state that he is a nonresident and show proof with a passport. What are by now traditional "know your customer" rules in most countries and in the U.K. impose broad information requirements on all persons opening new accounts.

If you decide to make a long-term home in the U.K., very careful tax plans must be made to avoid the possibility of U.K. estate taxes being imposed. British law treats a foreigner who is resident in the U.K. during 17 out of the 20 years prior to death for estate tax purposes, as having been domiciled in the U.K.

These U.K. death taxes can be avoided with the creation of a trust or international business corporation (IBC). When a foreigner purchases shares in a U.K. company, capital transfer taxes (estate taxes) may be payable to Customs and Revenue when the purchaser dies.

But purchasing U.K. shares in the name of an IBC completely avoids U.K. death taxes.

I'll say it again: check with your tax professional before you do anything. For tax and other legal information for foreign persons establishing residence in the U.K. contact solicitor:

James McNeile Esq.
Royds Withy King Law Firm
Midland Bridge House
Midland Bridge Road
Bath BA2 3FP
Tel.: 01225 730 100 / 01225 730 235
Contact: https://www.roydswithyking.com/contact
Email: james.mcneile@roydswithyking.com
Web: https://www.roydswithyking.com

For Assistance in Obtaining U.K. Residence:

Immigration Advice Service
Tel.: 0844 887 0111 / 0333 305 9375
Email: info@iasservices.org.uk
Web: http://www.iasservices.org.uk

U.K. Investment Trusts

In the U.K. an entity known is an "investment trust" is a closed end financial fund that sells shares to individuals and invests insecurities issued by other companies.

Initial purchase of British investment trust shares must be made through a brokerage house or bank. The shares are publicly traded on the London Stock Exchange, frequently at a 10% to 12% discount to net asset value. When you sell or switch between funds, you may face an even bigger discount. In the interim, you can have more money working for you than you are investing.

The accounts of investment trusts also are subject to regulation by the government. That means these funds are audited periodically by major international accounting firms, but even so, check the facts carefully before you buy.

The British and the Scots pioneered the development of investment trusts and the total number trading in London far exceeds closed-end funds trading in New York. Many specialize in investments in non-British markets, a painless indirect route into European equities for Americans operating offshore.

Unlike a U.S. fund, a U.K. investment trust's total investments may exceed 100% of the value of invested shares. Borrowing to buy additional shares is allowed, increasing both leverage and risk. U.K. investment trusts do not pay tax on capital gains realized within the portfolio and most dividends are distributed to the trust shareholders.

Management fee are low compared to those of "unit trusts," as mutual funds are called in Britain. For investment trusts, smaller is not necessarily better. It is difficult to withdraw money from smaller trusts that may require written withdrawal notices or impose "no withdrawal" time periods. A good source for up-to-date information is the Financial Times of London (www.ft.com), the respected journal that publishes weekly net asset value figures for all funds. Check before you invest.

City of London Investment Management Company Ltd. was founded in 1991 by Barry Olliff, the current CIO. City of London (CoL) is an active emerging markets equity manager with offices in London, U.S., Singapore and Dubai.

U.K. Office:
77 Gracechurch Street
London EC3V 0AS
Tel.: + 44 (0) 207 711 1566
Email: ukclientservicing@citlon.co.uk
Web: http://www.citlon.com

U.S. Offices:
The Barn
1125 Airport Road
Coatesville, PA 19320
Tel.: 610-380-2110
Email: client.servicing@citlon.com
Web: http://www.citlon.com

Seattle Office:
Plaza Center Suite 1519
10900 NE 8th Street
Bellevue, WA 98004
Tel: + 1 206 505 2587
Email: oliver.marschner@citlon.co.uk

U.K. Unit Trusts

In the United Kingdom, the "unit trust" is the equivalent of an open-ended mutual fund in the United States. Because of adverse U.S. tax consequences from such investments, check with your American tax advisor before investing in a unit trust.

British banks will hold stocks, bonds and unit trust shares and collect dividends and interest for foreign clients, with no withholding taxes levied on investment accounts. There is even a reimbursement of the 40% tax on corporate dividends when you file for relief from the U.K. Customs and Revenue. This unusual tax credit is payable to U.K. company shareholders as reimbursement for corporate taxes already paid by the company in which they own shares of stock. Customs and Revenue routinely informs U.S. authorities about U.K. tax payments made by Americans.

Communicating with Shareholders

British banks usually communicate well with unit trust shareholders on behalf of companies. In the U.K., official rolls of corporate shareholders are maintained either by the corporation, the unit trusts, or the bank that holds shares for nominee share purchasers. These institutions routinely keep shareholders up-to-date on any important developments.

Generally, U.K. investment and unit trust managers are more accessible than their American counterparts. In the U.S., heavy institutional investor involvement in the mutual funds market leaves fund managers with little time for small investors. In the U.K., firms customarily deal with masses of small investors and are significantly more forthcoming with information and help.

Profits from Interest Rate Differentials

Some British and continental banks allow overseas investors simultaneously to deposit assets in a high-yield currency then borrow the equivalent value or more in a low-yield currency, such as the dollar or the euro. The lending bank requires the borrower to deposit the loan with them.

The remaining difference between the yield and the fee the bank charges for the loan is credited to your account, which opens another possibility for high interest returns. Of course, the risk is yours; the interest rate is higher on the second currency precisely because there is a devaluation risk.

Gamblers who cover the exchange risk by buying currency "futures" may lose the interest advantage as well. That's because the price of futures reflects interest rate differentials and because significant transaction fees are charged for small sums. To beat the odds, you must predict currency trends more successfully than even the market can.

Another popular U.K. bank plan (also available in other offshore financial centers) enables business customers in good standing to borrow against their own deposits, effectively lowering taxable earnings and enabling a build-up in foreign exchange assets, even as loans are repaid. As a foreigner unfamiliar with local bank plans, get a second opinion from a U.S. accountant or tax attorney before you proceed with any plans offered.

CHAPTER SEVEN

United Kingdom's Offshore Financial Centers

Many of the world's offshore financial centers (OFCs) long have been (and still are) associated politically with the UK, including the 14 British Overseas Territories (BOTs). These include seven OFCs: Anguilla, Bermuda, the British Virgin Islands, the Cayman Islands, Gibraltar, Montserrat and the Turks & Caicos. (We will discuss these OTs individually later in this text, especially in Chapter Ten.) Also included among these OFCs are the UK "Crown dependencies," the Channel Islands and the Isle of Man, which we explain in this chapter.

In Chapter Five, we described London as an important financial center for your possible use.

London also is the global hub of a network of offshore financial centers that grew out of Britain's imperial, trading and naval history, dating back more than 500 years. In 1571, the Royal Exchange in the City of London was founded by merchants as a center of commerce for England. In subsequent centuries, with expansion of trade in goods, especially banking and financial services into Asia, Africa and elsewhere, the City of London became what has been described as "governor of the imperial engine."

British colonial expansion and financial power also was enhanced by significant legal developments, such as the British common law origins of offshore companies and of asset protection and other trusts.

Another important development was the legal principle of "residence without taxation" which was applied in the British Empire and extended to the U.K. territories, now including some of the world's leading OFCs. Late 19th century British court rulings distinguished for tax purposes between a company's place of formal registration, and the place from where control was exercised. Courts held that a company should be taxed in the country where control is exercised, even if registered in the U.K., thus avoiding U.K. taxes. That meant that if control was exercised in a tax haven, no taxes would be due at all, giving rise to beneficial international tax competition.

Another major legal development for valuable offshore use was the British common law of trusts, where ownership is separated from control of assets, allowing maximum privacy for ownership of assets held in trust. Trust creation and management are major services in the U.K. and its dependencies and OTs. There have been major targets of the U.S. IRS, and the OECD and other anti-privacy advocates.

The Crown Dependencies

Here we focus on the U.K. "Crown dependencies," the two Channel Islands and the Isle of Man.

They are separate from the OTs and governed under different constitutional arrangements. These unique jurisdictions have a well-developed regime of law that offers strong asset protection, solid investments and tax savings, including banking, and some life insurance and annuity products that may have the advantage of being U.S. tax-deferred investment vehicles.

Located off the southeast coast of the United Kingdom a group of two islands offers even more sophisticated financial services than those found in the fabled City of London. Located in the Bay of Saint-Malo in the English Channel, about 30 miles from the north coast of France and 70 miles from the south coast of England are the Channel Islands of Jersey, Guernsey, Sark and Alderney. Off the west coast of the United Kingdom, between the U.K. and Ireland in the Irish Sea, is the Isle of Man.

So unique are these financial centers that tens of thousands of investors and businesspersons worldwide use the professional services of their specialized investment houses, accountants, lawyers, insurance brokers and trust and corporation services located there.

While each of these semi-independent islands is associated constitutionally with the U.K. in their status as Crown dependencies, until recently each remained free of most of the U.K.'s tax and other financial restrictions. In the past, that broad financial freedom, coupled with determined self-promotion, made these islands important world business centers in miniature and they remain so.

After the end of World War II in 1945, the British government tolerated the offshore finance industry in these Crown dependencies because on balance it brought more expatriate and foreign wealth into the U.K. than was lost from the attractive tax avoidance mechanisms the islands offered.

When the Labor Party government gained a parliamentary majority in 1997, that tolerance turned into antagonism and attacks. Over the next decade various restrictions were imposed and by 2009, during the worst British recession in 30 years, Labor Prime Minister Gordon Brown demanded "the end of tax havens." He demagogically blamed these islands for the British economic downturn, which had root causes in the City of London, Wall Street and elsewhere. The Conservative-Liberal Party coalition government elected in 2009 was more sympathetic to the British offshore financial centers.

Second Dissolution of the British Empire

"I have not become the King's First Minister in order to preside over the liquidation of the British Empire." Winston Churchill's famous statement in November 1942, just as the tide of the Second World War was beginning to turn towards victory, pugnaciously affirmed that great British leader's loyalty to the global colonial institution he served during his lifetime.

Britain fought and sacrificed on a world scale to defeat Hitler and his allies — and won. Yet less than five years after Churchill's defiant speech, the British Empire effectively ended with India's 1947 independence and the 1948 termination of the British Mandate of Palestine.

Gordon Brown, Britain's most recent Labor prime minister (2007-2010), seemed bent on causing another major setting of the sun on what little then remained of Britain's truncated empire in 2009.

Under pressure from British labor unions and a nose-diving economy, in an election year Brown began attacking Her Majesty's Crown dependencies, as well as the U.K. overseas territories, that had been nurtured London during the 20th century.

Under heavy fire for deficit spending and £1.2 trillion (US$1.7 trillion) in bailouts for the Royal Bank of Scotland, HBOS, Lloyds, and Northern Rock, Brown thought blaming offshore tax havens for alleged lost tax revenues was good politics. One British newspaper headlined: "Brown does a U-turn on tax havens."

Brown's blacklist included most of the U.K. overseas territories, including the Cayman Islands, Bermuda, the British Virgin Islands and the Turk and Caicos Islands. The Labor government also turned hostile to the Crown dependencies, Jersey, Guernsey and the Isle of Man — all the major offshore financial hubs closely tied to the City of London.

His move was also a crude political attempt to counter international criticism and pressure from high-tax governments in the U.S., France and Germany who complained that the U.K. tax havens, comparable to the villainous Switzerland, were obstacles to a global "transparent financial system" — meaning an end to financial privacy to collect more taxes.

OFCs Self-Regulate

Her Majesty's Labor government's attacks on the British offshore tax havens produced an ironic result. Over a decade, as Labor governments in London demanded substantial reforms in U.K. offshore financial centers, and they got that and more. Reforms included statutory transparency, tax information sharing, and anti-money laundering laws, all important reforms Brown conveniently ignored when he attacked the overseas territories.

These offshore reforms are written into local laws in these semi-independent islands and include:

- Much stricter anti-money laundering and foreign tax evasion criminal statutes;

- Extensive banking client surveillance;

- Cooperation with foreign officials seeking tax and other information about persons and legal entities based on the islands;

- Major weakening of previously strict financial privacy laws;

As part of the campaign to curb tax havens, the U.K. Labor government acted to curtail the strict financial privacy and bank secrecy formerly offered by these islands.

Of course, an honest foreign taxpayer who is active financially offshore, and who knows and abides by his own country's reporting rules, has little to fear from the reduced degree of privacy now available in the U.K. havens. The Isle of Man, Jersey and Guernsey each have existing tax information exchange agreements (TIEAs) with the U.S. and adhere to OECD-inspired Common Reporting Standard (CRS), and the U.K.'s Crown Dependencies and Overseas Territories (CDOTs) rules.

When the anti-tax haven pressure from London began 25 years ago, the Labor government warned it would precipitate a constitutional crisis by forcing these changes into local law without the approval of the OFCs' governing bodies. No further threats were needed. One by one, each island's politicians adopted the changes demanded with minimal protests. They realistically concluded that since offshore finance was their major product, reforms were a matter of protecting their considerable income.

Unique Status

These self-ruling British Crown dependencies have the power to make their own laws and to set their own corporate and personal income tax rates. Through their constitutional association with the U.K., although they are not considered European Union members, the islands enjoyed some selected benefits of EU membership, such as the direct access to continental financial activities within all 28 EU countries. Those access privileges at this writing are in serious question, the eventual outcome dependent on UK-EU Brexit negotiations.

The Channel Islands are the preferred place for offshore money market funds sold to the British expatriate market. Because of a legal quirk, this once was the only place where a single corporate entity could offer money market funds in a variety of currencies, making it easier to offer free switching between currencies to customers investing only modest sums. Other offshore havens now offer streamlined transactions, but the Channel Islands remain the center for multi-currency money market and bond funds.

The range of business being conducted on the Channel Islands and the Isle of Man is highly diverse. Mutual funds offer shares that literally span the globe. Major corporate employee pension and benefits programs are headquartered in the islands.

Few Brits now use these islands because of determined anti-tax avoidance campaigns by HM Customs and Revenue and the broad investigative powers they now have.

Multiple Financial Services

For the potential foreign banking client or investor, the Channel Islands (Jersey and Guernsey) and the Isle of Man have a great deal to offer in the way of investments, banking, insurance and useful legal entities. The International Stock Exchange, headquarters located in Guernsey, lists more than 2,000 securities, and receives international recognition.

The Channel Islands is highly regarded among international financial centers. In fact, Jersey is ranked among the top 20 of all world financial centers by a survey for the City of London Corporation. Furthermore, *Banker* magazine listed Jersey and Guernsey within the top five. The islands' level of financial regulation and anti-money laundering measures have earned them widespread international respectability.

The Channel Islands are the last remnants of the medieval Dukedom of Normandy founded in 911 AD, which famously conquered Great Britain at the Battle of Hastings in 1066. Her Majesty, Queen Elizabeth II, is the official head of state, not as Queen, but in her separate role and title as "Duchess of Normandy." These islands were the only British soil occupied by German troops in World War II.

For the most part, both Jersey and Guernsey base their legal systems on the ancient customs and laws of the French province of Normandy, their near neighbor on the eastern shore of the English Channel. The Channel Islands have also incorporated many British common law features into their commercial code and legal activities, although with a French flavor.

In theory, the British Parliament lacks power to enact laws for these islands. Technically, they are not considered a part of the United Kingdom. The special status of the Channel Islands and the Isle of Man in relation to the United Kingdom means that while they are not technically part of the U.K., the U.K. is responsible for their foreign relations and military defense.

In their internal domestic affairs, the islands govern themselves, although laws enacted by their legislative assemblies must be validated by "Royal Assent," in the past a pro-forma procedure common to all British territories.

Bailiwick of Jersey

*Fourteen miles off the coast of Normandy in northern France,
lies the Bailiwick of Jersey, (population 98,840 — July 2017
est.). This largest of the Channel Islands has developed into
one of the world's leading offshore finance jurisdictions in the
last half century. In volume of business and assets, it is much
larger than Guernsey, its smaller neighbor.*

Jersey draws on its political and economic stability, product innovation and the quality of its regulation and legal system to support the successful development of its offshore finance industry. It has attracted many of the world's leading financial groups to its shores and its workers have the experience to cater to the diverse needs of global investors. Jersey has thriving banking, mutual funds and trust sectors. While it is a leading center for private clients who want a safe, well-regulated home for their assets, its diversity has made it a preferred jurisdiction for worldwide corporate and institutional business as well.

In 2017, *Fortune* magazine recalled that Jersey's status as a tax haven rose in the mid-20th century, when many rich British citizens moved their wealth to the island. At that time, Britain's inheritance tax on amounts over 1 million pounds (US$1.4 million) was 80%, and Jersey, then and now had no inheritance tax. The island now houses and estimated $5 billion worth of assets per square mile.

Jersey's economy is based on international financial services which represents 50% of GDP, followed by agriculture, and tourism. Low taxes (20% on income and 5% on goods and services) and no death duties make the island a popular tax haven. What might be termed the gross island income (GDP) in 2015 was US$6 billion and US$49,500 per capita.

Jersey is innovative. It has financial alliances with the Gulf States, the United Arab Emirates and China. The finance industries in Jersey and the Gulf region jointly work to deliver financial services, including Muslim Sharia law compliant products. There are firms in Jersey incorporating Islamic investment vehicles such as Sukuks, Islamic asset-backed investment certificates, certified as complying with the requirement of Sharia law governed by the Islamic religion.

Other sectors that account for Jersey's outputs also includes tourism, which represents approximately 25% of the GDP, agriculture such as potatoes, tomatoes, flowers, and dairy cattle, and more recently, electronics through the government's encouragement in the development of the light industry.

Any currency can be used to incorporate Jersey companies. In addition, investments in or out of Jersey company can be done without restrictions as well as the repatriation of dividends, interest and profits. Bank interest on deposits, payable to a nonresident, is exempt from Jersey income tax. Royalties are treated for the purposes of tax in the same way as interest.

Authorities welcome "passive" investment, such as the purchase of real estate for the purpose of investing, or investing in existing business assets. However, "active" foreign investment is not welcome. This include new businesses and permanent immigration. The goal is this policy is to safeguard the islands resources. The island offers no domestic investment incentives beyond its low-tax regime.

Banking

In 2016, there were 54 banks licensed in the Channel Islands; 29 in Jersey and 25 in Guernsey. In recent years, there has been a consolidation of banks and banking staffs on the islands, reflecting world banking trends. Nevertheless, total assets under management in each of these islands have continued to increase to record levels, a testament to their standing among global investors. Very few companies operate on the Channel Islands of Alderney and Sark, both have very sparse populations.

Because of the economic and political stability of Jersey, it is a highly regarded — and safe — location to bank, invest, and establish a trust.

Jersey's financial institutions are home to an astonishing amount of wealth. In 2016, there were 29 banks operating in Jersey including branches and subsidiaries of British clearing banks and international banks, offering a full range of services with total deposits of US$150 billion. In 2017, Jersey reformed and consolidated its fund laws with a total of 1,141 registered funds valued at US$345.6 million. (It's impossible to quantify the value of trust assets exactly since they don't have to be reported to authorities.)

Individuals must be professionally qualified or have years of direct, hands-on experience to be licensed to set up and manage trust companies. Jersey provides financial services to customers worldwide with over 13,000 people employed fulltime in this sector.

As do most offshore jurisdictions, Jersey's banking law traditionally established the confidentiality of a bank account, but other laws provide routes by which that confidentiality can be breached on application from other countries with a demonstrable legal case against an individual or company. In theory, fishing expeditions are not entertained.

The history of the last 17 years concerning Jersey's banking secrecy is mainly a story of attempts by the OECD and the EU to impose extensive information-sharing requirements on the island's financial institutions. Jersey has now signed 18 TIEAs, including one with the United States.

Advantages of banking on the Island include confidentiality, freedom of currency exchange, tax deferral, tax reduction and low commercial and political risk. There are no exchange controls. In the event of a bank failure the government of both Jersey and Guernsey will pay up to £50,000 (US$70,500) per individual customer.

Banking operations in Jersey are governed by the Banking Business Law and the Banking Business Order both of 1991. The laws provide for the protection of Jersey as a financial center and for depositors. Operations are supervised by the Jersey Financial Commission (http://www.jerseyfsc.org) which also issues banking licenses.

Opening an offshore bank account in Jersey is much the same as in any well-run jurisdiction with anti-money laundering and "know your customer" due diligence rules. Basic requirements are completion of an application form, with notarized copies of identification, proof of current address and citizenship and proof of fund sources presented in person.

Trusts, Corporations, Funds

The Trusts Law of 1984 succeeded in clearing up many uncertainties and raised protecting for beneficiaries. Amendments that followed included one in 1996 that recognized the purpose of trust even though the usual Jersey trust form is discretionary. Not surprisingly, this created a jump in corporate use of Jersey trusts.

The Companies Law 1991 governs companies incorporated in Jersey. This law is very similar to the English 1984 Companies Act, which was updated in 2014. Beneficial ownership for private companies must be disclosed, but it is not a part of public record. Shelf companies, while not available, are quick and inexpensive to form assuming that the new company will not operate on Jersey itself.

A company must have a registered office in Jersey. Accounts need not be audited but must be filed with the Jersey revenue authorities. Partnerships of all types also are available, and foundations are also recognized.

Americans enjoy specific benefits when doing business through these islands, such as purchasing non-U.S. mutual funds that typically cannot sell shares in the United States because of SEC regulations. U.S. investors can invest in these funds by using an accommodation address on the islands, thus legally skirting the SEC rules that forbid offshore funds from sending materials or having direct contact with investors when physically located in America. Check with a U.S. tax attorney before purchasing offshore funds; the American tax consequences can be brutal without careful planning.

Taxes

The islands' tax systems have been remarkably free of political manipulation for many years. Successive legislatures have preserved the standard income tax rate at about 20% for more than half a century. In 2017 it was 20% on the first $820,000, another 1% tax on amounts above that.

In answer to OECD complaints about the two-tax system formerly in place that exempted foreign-owned business but not locals, corporate taxes were reduced to zero for all businesses, except for some banks and financial firms. There is no inheritance tax, gift tax, or other wealth taxes. The possibility of any increase in the income tax or the enactment of new taxes is remote because the islands want to continue to attract corporate business.

Nonresidents are subject to income tax only on locally earned income, and bank interest is exempt. A local trust is treated as a nonresident for tax purposes, provided none of the beneficiaries is an island resident.

Immigration

Jersey, the largest of the Channel Islands, is attractive for private residence or to establish an international business. The government of Jersey closely controls long-term residence and allows only rare exceptions for those who do own a residence. Very few wealthy new immigrants are accepted annually by Jersey — only about seven a year. The government favors those purchasing luxury and high-end real estate because these individuals add to local tax coffers.

There are no corporate taxes other than a 10% tax on some trust and banking operations. The Jersey government usually grants residence to persons who qualify to purchase property. Applicants for residence permits are required to prove a net worth of at least US$29 million and an income sufficient to produce an annual tax liability of at least US$220,000 at an income tax rate of 20% and to buy local real estate worth at least US$1.5 million.

Guernsey is far less restrictive on newcomers who want to establish residence, but requires work permits for those who start any form of business. Establishing residence on the Isle of Man is simpler, mainly because it is comparatively spacious, with a land area more than seven times larger than Jersey and more than ten times the size of Guernsey.

One of the lesser Channel Islands, Alderney, has a small number of financial service companies and places few restrictions on immigration by wealthy foreigners. Sark, an even smaller island, has few residents and very tight property ownership restrictions, but no taxes.

Contacts:

States of Jersey Government: http://www.gov.je

Jersey Evening Post: https://jerseyeveningpost.com

Mourant Ozannes
Daniel Birtwistle
22 Grenville Street
St. Helier, Jersey JE4 8PX Channel Islands
Tel.:+44 (0) 1534 676 000 / +44 (0) 1534 676 333
Email: daniel.birtwistle@mourantozannes.com
Web: http://www.mourantozannes.com

One of the leading Jersey attorneys is **Mourant Ozannes**, reportedly the world's third-largest offshore law firm with 250 attorneys and offices in the BVI, Cayman Islands, Guernsey, Jersey, Hong Kong, and London.

Atlas Trust Co. Ltd.
Ian R. Swindal, Managing Director
17 Queen Street, Suite 1
St. Helier, Jersey JE4 5PP Channel Islands
Tel.: +44 (0) 1534 608 878
Email: ian.swindale@atlastrust.co.uk

There are so many trust, banking, and investment companies in Jersey that it is difficult to know where to start. There are 76 trust companies alone. **Atlas Trust Company (Jersey), Limited** is a small trust company founded by professionals, all of whom have considerable experience in the financial field. Atlas will put you in contact with other professionals on the island who might also be able to accommodate your financial goals.

Quilter Cheviot Investment Management
Tim Childe, Head of Office
P.O. Box 276
4th Floor, 28/30 The Parade
St. Helier, Jersey JE4 8TE Channel Islands
Tel.: +44 (0) 1534 506 070
Email: jersey@quiltercheviot.com or tim.childe@quiltercheviot.com
Web: http://www.quiltercheviot.com

Leading & Investment Banks:

Coutts
Locations: https://www.coutts.com/locations
Tel.: +44 020 7753 1000 / 020 7957 2424
Web: https://www.coutts.com

Royal Bank of Jersey
Gaspé House
66-72 Esplanade
St. Helier, Jersey, JE2 3QT
Tel.: +44 (0) 1534 283 000
Web: https://www.rbcwealthmanagement.com/gb/en

Appleby Trust (Jersey) Ltd.
13-14 Esplanade
St. Helier, Jersey JE1 1BD
Tel.: +44 (0) 1534 888 777
Email: jersey@applebyglobal.com
Web: https://www.applebyglobal.com

Bailiwick of Guernsey

Guernsey, (population 66,502, July 2017 est.), embraces not only 10 parishes on the Island of Guernsey, but also the smaller islands of Herm, Jethou, and Lihou, as well as Alderney and Sark, the latter two each with its own parliament.

Guernsey has a strong economy dominated by its financial sector. Financial services, banking, private equity fund management, and insurance, account for about 55% of total income and 40% of employment. 2016 GDP was estimated to be nearly US$3.5 billion which averages at about US$52,500 GDP per capita in this tiny, prosperous Channel Island economy.

Political stability and a history of low taxes and a respected international reputation as an important financial center make it an attractive place for foreign investors to conduct business. To protect the island's limited resources, the government discourages labor-intensive local investment by non-residents. Other than low taxes, there are no investment grants or incentives.

Guernsey has Europe's largest captive insurance sector, and has strong banking, investment fund and trusts sectors, with very well-developed advisory and financial professionals. The International Stock Exchange is based here. Most corporations are tax exempt except for certain finance companies taxed at 10%.

Modern Guernsey business emphasizes tailored structures, with clients considering private trust companies, managed trust companies, and private trust foundations. Generally, these trusts include very specific provisions drafted purposefully to suit a family; off the-shelf trust structures are a thing of the past. Clients range from Russia and China to Latin America.

As with Jersey, Guernsey is not an EU member per se, but both islands have come under much EU and OECD pressure in opposition to their low- or no-tax policies. Both islands formerly exempted only foreign-owned corporations from taxes, which the OECD attacked as discriminatory. Both islands responded by abolishing all corporate taxes other than those on selected finance companies, known as the Zero-Ten corporate tax system.

The Guernsey government followed the example of the Isle of Man and switched from a withholding tax system to the automatic exchange of tax information. Guernsey signed a TIEA with the United States in 2006 and now has over 35 TIEAs with other jurisdictions including most major countries.

An independent survey found Guernsey to be the most popular place for fund management in the U.K. Banker magazine ranked Guernsey as the No. 1 specialist finance center in Europe and second in the world. For banks in Guernsey see https://thebanks.eu/banks-by-country/Guernsey.

Contacts:

States of Guernsey Government: https://www.gov.gg

Home Guernsey News: http://guernseypress.com

Banks:

Royal Bank of Canada
PO Box 48, Canada Court
St. Peter Port, Guernsey
Channel Islands, GY1 3BQ
Tel.: +44 (0) 1481 744 000
Web: http://www.rbcwealthmanagement.com/gb/en

Rothschild Bank International Limited
St. Julian's Court
St. Peter Port, Guernsey, GY1 3BP

Tel.: +44 (0) 1481 713 713
Web: http://www.rothschild.com

Investments:

Investec Asset Management
P.O. Box 250
St. Peter Port, Guernsey, GY1 3QH
Tel.: +44 (0) 1481 710 404
Email: offshore.investor@investecmail.com
Web: http://www.investecassetmanagement.com/en

Attorney:

Appleby
Regency Court
Glategny Esplanade
St. Peter Port, Guernsey, GY1 1WW
Tel.: +44 (0) 1481 755 600
Email: guernsey@applebyglobal.com
Web: http://www.applebyglobal.com

Captive Insurance:

Callum Beaton (Insurance Consulting) Limited
Le Moigne, Val au Bourg
St. Martin's, Guernsey, GY4 6EP
Tel.: +44 (0) 1481 238 537
Email: callum@callumbeaton.com
Web: www.callumbeaton.com

The Isle of Man

The Isle of Man's history and legal system differ from those of the Channel Islands, but its offshore financial advantages are similar.

Located in the Irish Sea just 30 miles from the U.K. mainland, the island firmly is established as an important international offshore financial center. Historically, it has never been part of the U.K. Its independent parliament, the Tynwald, claims to be the oldest in the world tracing its origins back over a thousand years. The Tynwald is responsible for all domestic legislation, including taxation for its 88,815 residents, the July 2017 estimate.

Unlike the Channel Islands and their French civil law influence, the legal system is based on English common law, the currency is the Manx pound sterling and social and economic links with the U.K. are strong; the island defense and foreign affairs are conducted by the United Kingdom.

Although Brexit will change this, the island was a member of the EU single market trade area and the value added tax (VAT) area, but otherwise not part of the EU fiscal area. There are no exchange controls. The economy has averaged over 6% growth in real terms over the past 30 years. The unemployment rate has remained around approximately 2% compared to the OECD average of 6%. The island's GDP value has exceeded US$7 billion and the per capita GDP has been around $85,000.

Taxes

As with Jersey and Guernsey, under EU and OECD pressure over a period of years, the government gradually abolished corporate income tax altogether, and now a 10% tax applies only to financial institutions. The Island has a zero rate of corporate tax and a higher 10% rate which is applied to banking and retail businesses with annual taxable profits of £500,000 or more.

The standard individual income tax rate of 10% is payable on the first £10,500 of income above the personal allowance, with a top marginal rate of 20%. Anything above that is tax exempt. That means no tax on capital transfer or capital gains, surtax, wealth, death duty, or gift. A value added tax is collect, but by the Isle of Man Customs and Excise at the same rate that is applied to all of the United Kingdom.

Opportunities

Strong banking, well-developed advisory and financial infrastructure, investment fund and captive insurance sectors are hallmarks of the Isle of Man. It has an active trusts sector and even offers licenses for online gambling. There are a significant number of legal business formats such as limited liability companies (LLCs), corporations and limited partnerships. In fact, there were more than 30,000 registered corporations on the Isle of Man in 2016. The Isle of Man offers tailored annuities and life insurance, international banking, trust and incorporation services, global investment funds, and pension funds.

And all this activity is carefully regulated. The government fully supports the island's financial sector, yet maintains strict control through the Insurance and Pension Authority and a Financial Supervision Commission that licenses banks, trusts and investment advisors. Strict laws govern financial managers, investors' rights, money laundering and excludes undesirable elements.

This high level of compliance with global financial standards was confirmed by an investigation and report from the International Monetary Fund (IMF). This tough supervision assures financial integrity and has earned the Isle of Man a reputation for what The Economist condescendingly described as "stuffed shirt probity."

The Isle of Man offers an excellent communications network, modern business facilities and a highly skilled work force. The financial sector is the largest single contributor to GDP at 45%, employing more than 20% of the total work force of nearly 40,000.

Banking

The 18 licensed banks (including international banks) offer comprehensive, discreet and confidential services that compare favorably with the banks in Switzerland or Liechtenstein. In addition to banking, high-caliber legal, accounting, insurance and other financial services are available on the island. Among 18 banks in 2017, only one bank (Conister Bank Ltd), operated with Manx capital. The rest were controlled branches and subsidiaries from U.K. banks.

The Isle of Man in 2017 won the award for International Finance Centre of the Year at the International Adviser Product and Service Awards, besting Dublin, Ireland and Dubai. The Awards celebrate companies that offer cross-border products and services for advisers with international and/or expatriate clients.

Banking on the Isle of Man can take many forms, but often accounts opened by foreigners are associated with the trusts, corporations, insurance or pension plans they have set up on the island.

Under the Isle of Man Banking Act of 1975 as amended, all banks must be licensed by the government. Banks on the Isle of Man are not directly supervised by the Bank of England, but they do apply its standards in practice.

Investor and depositor protection is strong and on a par with the U.K. Individual depositors are protected up to a maximum of £50,000 (US$70,000) per depositor. Interest on deposits paid to nonresidents is free from withholding tax.

In spite of its ancient history, banking on the island is modern, sophisticated and user-friendly. Total deposits in the 18 banks in 2017 exceeded US$51 billion. There are more than 200 licensed corporate and 125 trust service providers on the Isle of Man. There are also registered 40,000 companies and partnerships and about 40,000 trusts under the administration of these local service providers.

Life Insurance and Annuities

One way to obtain maximum financial privacy is to purchase the products for which the Isle of Man is known worldwide — excellent insurance and annuity products carefully tailored to individual needs. In 2017, there were 151 captive insurance companies, 15 offshore life companies, 9 general insurers, and 7 reinsurers.

The minimum premium for these policies is US$250,000, but most are purchased for US$1 million or more. These policies were popular with Americans because, under U.S. tax law, this is one of the last investment areas that permit legal tax deferral. Because of the regulatory and cost impacts of the U.S. Foreign Account Tax Compliance Act (FATCA), life insurance and annuity companies on the island are reluctant to accept U.S. persons as clients.

The Isle of Man also offers great benefits for pensions. Asset protection and the option to claim benefit starting from the age of 50 are two of the main reasons that many international companies have their employee pension plans hold their account there. However, just employer-sponsored retirement accounts enjoy the lax tax code. International mutual funds held by individuals are taxed heavily under U.S. tax law.

(For a more detailed explanation of the many benefits of offshore life insurance and annuities, see Chapter Three.)

Privacy

In 2014, the U.K. adopted CDOT (informally called the U.K. FATCA). Starting in 2016, it requires the Isle of Man and all other British OFCs to make FATCA-like disclosures about all U.K. account holders to U.K. tax authorities, as does the U.S. FATCA for American account holders.

The Manx government has signed TIEAs with 41 countries, including the U.S. and the U.K. As has become the international norm, the government here applies the OECD Article 26 standard for exchange of tax information among governments.

The Isle of Man has signed a tax information exchange agreement with Guernsey and Jersey, to enable the three islands' authorities to curb tax evasion. All three Crown Dependencies each have negotiated an intergovernmental agreement (IGA) with the U.S. to implement the U.S. Foreign Account Tax Compliance Act (FATCA).

Contacts:

Bank:

IsleofMan.com: http://www.isleofman.com/directory/category/33927/Banks-Financial-Institutions

Trusts:

IOMA Fiduciary
IOMA House
Hope Street
Douglas, Isle of Man IM1 1AP
Tel.: +44 (0) 1624 681200
Email: info@iomagroup.co.im
Web: http://www.iomagroup.co.im

Insurance & Annuities:

Isle of Man Assurance
IOMA House
Hope Street
Douglas, Isle of Man IM1 1AP
Tel.: +44 (0) 1624 681200
Email: info@iomagroup.co.im
Web: http://www.iomagroup.co.im

Americans Investing Offshore

Access to investment and mutual funds on the Channel Islands and the Isle of Man is certainly not limited to major corporations, insurance companies and wealthy investors.

Middle-class, small-share investors are also welcome, certainly including foreigners, because volume makes profits. These funds typically allow free worldwide switching between funds that invest in the U.K., or in money market instruments denominated in sterling or foreign currencies.

Unless they are registered with the U.S. SEC, U.K. unit trust (mutual fund) groups will not respond to inquiries from a United States address. One way in which U.S. persons can avoid legally these restrictions is by investing in the name of your own offshore trust, private foundation, LLC or international business corporation.

Traditionally, Americans have used domestic brokers to invest in foreign markets, if the brokers offered these services. It required broker contact with a U.S.-based "market maker" or an affiliate firm located in the country where you wanted to buy shares. This was a slow, cumbersome route that didn't always guarantee timely access.

As an alternative, as explained in Chapter Three, you can open an investment account with an offshore broker in London or on any of these islands in your own name and then purchase individual stocks in many offshore markets. Better still, the easiest route is to open your own brokerage account at any of the numerous foreign brokers that now offer online services worldwide.

SEC rules do limit sharply the ability of foreign brokers to solicit business inside the U.S., unless they are registered with the SEC, a lengthy and costly procedure. However, the SEC does not prohibit U.S. citizens from opening offshore brokerage accounts to buy and sell foreign stocks so long as you, the investor, approach the foreign firm and the offshore firm doesn't approach you.

CHAPTER EIGHT

Special Offshore Financial Centers in Europe

While Europe has no monopoly on jurisdictions that qualify as low-tax or asset protection havens, economic and political history combined to make continental Europe a financial center beginning in the Middle Ages. In Chapter Five, we described two European countries, Switzerland and Liechtenstein, which count among the leading offshore financial centers.

Here some of the lesser-known European OFCs are described. Some are best for tax-free residence, others for banking, investment funds or as an international business base.

In considering European venues for your cash and investments, keep in mind the continuing pressure from high tax EU countries, the EU bureaucracy in Brussels and the OECD. They want to end financial privacy and to impose uniform high income and corporate taxes on all EU member states, a trend these OFCs continue to resist.

Republic of Austria

The Austrian Republic is not a haven in the sense of low taxes, but it is a "banking haven." That's because this nation still has some of the strongest financial privacy laws in the world, although they have somewhat weakened. The basic privacy guarantee has constitutional protection that can be changed only by a national referendum of all voters.

For a very few select of the foreign wealthy, Austria also offers low-tax residence for those who can qualify. The Austrian Republic has long been a bastion of banking privacy strategically located on what was once the eastern European border of countries dominated by Communist Russia, the Soviet Bloc. From the end of World War II in 1945 to the collapse of Soviet Communism in 1992, with the Soviet Union and the United States locked in armed confrontation, Austria served as a willing Cold War financial and political go-between for both West and East.

With a population of 8.8 million in 2017, Austria covers 62% of the eastern Alps. It borders on Germany, Liechtenstein, Switzerland, Italy, Slovenia, Hungary, Slovakia and the Czech Republic. German is the official language, but most people, especially the younger generations, speak English.

Vienna was once the center of power for the multinational Austro-Hungarian Empire created out of the realms of the Habsburgs by proclamation in 1804. It was the second-largest country in Europe, after the Russian Empire, and one of the world's great powers.

But the country's loss in World War I resulted in Austria shrinking in size, after Nazi Germany's seizure in 1938 and the 1945 occupation by World War II Allies. For nearly a decade, Austria's standing was murky. Austria regained its independence with the 1955 treaty. Austria joined the European Union in 1995.

Since World War II, two parties usually dominated Austrian political life: the conservative Austrian People's Party (ÖVP) and the center-left Social Democratic Party of Austria (SPÖ).

The SPÖ was the largest party after the 2013 elections and had led the government since 2007. Known as the "Grand Coalition," these parties formed successive governments, but divisions grew due to issues of an aging population, an influx of illegal immigrants, and global and EU economic problems.

In 2017, the Austrian People's Party (ÖVP) won as the largest party in the National Council, and the Social Democratic Party (SPÖ) finished second, slightly ahead of the Freedom Party (FPÖ). The leader of the strongest party in a coalition became Chancellor Sebastian Kurz, the leader of the ÖVP and an avowed conservative. The leftist press called the OVP "an anti-immigrant, anti-Muslim party" but it was clear Austrians wanted change and a move to the right. Kurz pledged support for the EU but was critical of its policies.

Austria is a gem within the EU thanks to its high standard of living, developed market economy and skilled labor force. It remains tied to other EU economies, particularly Germany. Austria's economic is composed of a substantial service sector, a solid industrial sector, and a small agricultural sector.

In term of GDP per capita, Austria ranked in the top 10 wealthiest countries in the world. Its 2017 GDP topped US$434 billion, with US$49,200 GDP per capita. The country enjoyed a number of years of high foreign demand for exports and strong employment growth. However, the 2008 financial collapse and global economic downturn resulted in a painful but brief recession. The GDP shrank by 3.8% in 2009 and bounced back to 2% growth in 2010 and 2.7% in 2011.

Austria's bank also ran into problems during the 2008 collapse, logging significant losses. To stabilize the banking system, the government provided some support as well as some nationalization. Austria continues to have high banking exposure to central and Eastern Europe.

The country maintains close ties to Eastern Europe and has grown thanks to these ties following the 1992 fall of the Soviet Union. Business within Eastern Europe have moved to Austria over the past several years, including Swarovski crystal and the maker of Red Bull drinks.

Overall, Austria has the honor of stating that it has the highest number of graduates from secondary education. Furthermore, its people are incredibly reliable and motivated. The country has nearly no industrial labor issues.

Secrecy: It Is the Law

When Austrian national banking laws were officially re-codified in 1979, the well-established tradition of bank secrecy was already two centuries old. During that time, Austrian bank secrecy and privacy produced two major types of so-called "anonymous accounts."

These accounts usually required no account holder identification, no mailing address and no personal references. Just deposit funds and use the account as you pleased, all done anonymously. Both the *Sparbuch* bank account and the *Wertpapierbuch* securities account have been abolished, victims of the European Union's fixation with destroying financial privacy wherever possible.

Notwithstanding the demands of the EU, current Austrian bank secrecy laws forbid banks to "disclose secrets which have been entrusted to them solely due to business relationships with customers." This prohibition is waived only in criminal court proceedings involving fiscal crimes, except for petty offenses. The prohibition does not apply "if the customer expressly and in writing consents to the disclosure of the secret."

The Austrian Federal Constitutional itself does not recognize explicitly the right of privacy, but section 1(1) of the 2000 Austrian Data Protection Act does have constitutional status recognizing protection of personal data as an individual fundamental right. This special law guarantees and raises banking and financial privacy to a constitutional level and it can be changed only by a majority vote in a national referendum, an unlikely event. The Data Protection Commission (*Datenschutzkommission*) is responsible for enforcing the DP Act and decides complaints.

All major political parties support financial privacy as a longstanding national policy. As a member EU country, until 2009 Austria strongly opposed EU demands for compulsory withholding taxes and financial information sharing. The government refused to share personal bank account information with other countries until similar rules were applied to financial centers such as Switzerland, that are not part of the 28-nation EU bloc. It was the first time that Austria, long known for its strict banking secrecy, had made such a commitment, after refusing for a decade.

As discussed in Chapter Three, OECD Article 26 recognizes "tax evasion" as a valid basis for foreign tax agency inquiries concerning their citizens with offshore accounts. Under the former OECD procedure, foreign tax authorities wishing to take advantage of tax information exchange agreements had to supply evidence of suspicions (e.g., names, facts, alleged tax crimes) to the requested government. If there was sufficient probable cause of tax evasion, the requested government had to supply the information.

Austria finally yielded to EU and OECD pressure and starting 2018 it applied automatic tax exchange information rules as established in the OECD common reporting standard.

Stocks and Bonds

Until the 2008 world recession began, the Austrian stock market had one of the world's best performance records. It benefited in part from the eastern European expansion boom that began in the 1990s after the East-West Iron Curtain disintegrated and its formerly Communist-dominated eastern European neighbors turned to free market polices.

Nonresidents are not subject to restrictions on securities purchased in Austria and they can be transferred freely abroad without reporting. Nonresidents can purchase an unlimited amount of bonds and/or stocks on the condition that the money used for purchase is in either foreign currency or euros. When securities are sold, the cash proceeds can be freely converted and exported without restrictions.

Taxes

Taxes are relatively low with corporate income tax coming in at 25%. Personal income tax tops out at 50%. The corporate income tax applies to all resident companies and permanent establishments of non-resident companies. Furthermore, resident companies must pay taxes on their worldwide income, while non-resident companies pay taxes on their Austrian-sourced income only. An interim tax of 12.5% is levied on income from interest and capital gains from the selling of shares. Dividend income is not hit with a corporate income tax if it's held by a private foundation.

Austrian tax authorities found a way to profit from their attractive banking haven status — the government levies a 25% tax on the total bank interest earned. Foreigners can avoid the 25% tax on bond interest if a declared nonresident is the bank account holder. Interest paid on investments held in non-bearer form in banks, such as certificates of deposit, is also exempt from the withholding tax. Interest on convertible bonds, however, is subject to a withholding tax of 20% at the payment source.

Unfortunately, an American citizen bondholder is subject to capital gains tax in the U.S. on the full capital gain, despite the Austrian tax. A double taxation treaty between the U.S. and Austria eases this hardship. If you file a request with the IRS, the Austrian tax will be partly repaid, diminishing the net tax burden to 10%. The remaining 10% tax can offset part of the U.S. capital gains tax ordinarily imposed. The double taxation agreement does not apply to Austrian interest and dividends, which remain fully taxable in the U.S.

The Austrian government's decision to reduce the corporate tax rate from 34% to 25% in 2005 led to a 30% increase in new investment projects. In addition to cutting corporate taxes to one of the lowest levels in the EU, the reforms also reduced the tax burden on multinational firms using Austria as regional headquarters.

Austria also offers significant tax concessions to holding companies, foundations and certain other investment incentives, all successfully designed to attract foreign capital."

My longtime colleague, Mark Nestmann, who lived in Vienna for three years, offers this first-hand observation: *"Austria offers major advantages including a stable economy, safe banks and, for foreign investors, virtually no taxes. Austria is also a popular expatriate haven. If you have sufficient wealth to support yourself, it is one of the world's top havens for residence — although unfortunately it is difficult to obtain a residence permit. Austria welcomes foreigners, but it doesn't promote itself as an investment or residential haven, so you'll have to take the first step if you are interested in investing or living here.*

Live Income Tax-Free

Austria is also a desirable place to reside. Mercer's, a human resources consultancy, rates Austria's historic capital of Vienna as the most desirable city in the world in which to live.

Because of its diminutive geographic size, Austria does not accept many new resident aliens. Indeed, limiting immigration was a major political issue in the 2017 election, when the Austrian Peoples Party (ÖVP) coopted the issue from the conservative Freedom Party that opposes all further immigration. In response to an influx of immigrants from Eastern Europe, Turkey, and Africa, Austria enacted legislation in 2005 significantly restricting immigration. The country admits only about 8,000 immigrants annually, with the majority being foreigners married to Austrian nationals. In practice, it is difficult for non-EU nationals to obtain legal residence in Austria without an expensive and time-consuming application process.

An Austrian passport is one of the world's most desirable travel documents. It not only permits you to live or work in any of the 28 EU countries without obtaining a visa, but it ranks fourth among 100 countries allowing visa-free travel to more countries.

It is not widely known, but a wealthy foreigner who can qualify to become a resident of Austria also may qualify for a unique tax break — 100% of annual income completely free of taxes! This preferential tax treatment, called a *Zuzugsbegünstigung*, used to be ready and waiting at the obliging Ministry of Finance.

A foreigner who is a new Austrian resident can qualify if the person meets all the following requirements:

- Had no residence in Austria during 10 years prior to application.

- Doesn't engage in any business activity within Austria.

- Can prove sufficient income from outside sources.

- Agrees to spend a minimum of US$70,000 in Austria each year.

- Has a residence and intends to stay in Austria for at least six months (183 days) each year.

When all those conditions are met, a foreigner may be able to live tax-free in Austria. All income from foreign pension or retirement funds, dividends and interest from foreign investments and securities or any offshore businesses outside Austria are tax exempt.

In most cases, officials grant a tax break of at least 75% of potential tax liability — but a good local lawyer may be able to negotiate a 100% reduction. If you have foreign income taxable in your home country and there is no double taxation agreement between Austria and your country, the Ministry of Finance may grant you a zero-tax base, or a special circumstance ruling, but only after you establish your residence in Austria.

Although Austria does not have an economic citizenship program per se, statutory law does allow the granting of citizenship to a foreign person if he or she is judged to contribute in some extraordinary way, including economic, to the interests of Austria. However, this is a very difficult way to acquire citizenship and may require a year to process at a minimum.

Applicants are approved on a case-by-case basis and must be willing to invest or make a charitable contribution of at least US$2 million in an approved project in Austria. Investment proposals are submitted to the Office of Economic Development. Those that provide export stimulation or local employment receive preference. Representation by a knowledgeable Austrian lawyer is essential and is likely to cost considerably more than US$50,000. Fees of €250,000 (US$308,000) or more apply, depending on the case and the number of persons in an application, as each case is handled on an individual basis. The Nestmann Group and Henley and Partners can provide details on these possibilities.

Is Austrian residence status for sale to the very rich?

To be frank, yes. If you are a reputable and wealthy foreigner, there will be few obstacles to becoming a resident. Residency gives you the best of both worlds — life in an extremely desirable location, but without the high taxes Austrian citizens must pay.

Once in residence, you could apply for citizenship, but that would defeat the purpose. As an Austrian citizen, you'd be liable for full taxation. The only additional advantages would be having an Austrian passport and the right to purchase as much real property as you wish, which is otherwise very difficult for a foreigner merely residing in Austria.

Even with its agreement to share tax information using the OECD standard, Austria's financial and banking privacy laws provide much great security than most other countries. As a result, it's wise to keep Austria near the top of your potential banking list, especially if your major area of business interest lies in Eastern Europe or Russia.

Contacts:

Embassy of Austria
3524 International Court NW
Washington, D.C. 20008
Tel.: 202-895-6700
Email: austroinfo@austria.org or consularsection@austria.org
Web: http://www.austria.org

United States Embassy
Boltzmanngasse 16
1090 Vienna, Austria
Tel.: +43-1 31339-0
Email: ViennaUSEmbassy@state.gov
Web: https://at.usembassy.gov

BMF, Federal Ministry of Finance
Johannesgasse 5
1010 Vienna, Austria
Tel.: +43 1 51433-500000
Email: Hans-Joerg.Schelling@bmf.gv.at
Web: https://english.bmf.gv.at

Recommended Banks:

Wiener Privatbank
Parkring 12, 1010
Vienna, Austria
Tel: +43 1 534 31-0
Email: institutional@wienerprivatbank.com
Web: https://www.wienerprivatbank.com/en

Bank Winter & Co. AG
Singerstrasse 10
A-1010 Vienna
Postfach 878
Tel: +43/1/51504-0
Email: contact@bankwinter.com
Web: https://www.bankwinter.com/en

Because of FATCA restrictions, Wiener Privatbank and Bank Winter do not accept applications for bank investment accounts directly from U.S. persons. The Banyan Hill associates listed below work closely with these banks and you can contact them for that purpose.

WHVP: Weber, Hartmann, Vrijhof & Partners
Robert Vrijhof, President
Contact: Julia Fernandez
Schaffhauserstrasse 418
CH-8050 Zürich, Switzerland
Tel.: 01141 44 315 77 77 (USA/Canada) / +41 44 315 77 77
(International)
Email: info@whvp.ch
Web: http://www.whvp.ch

ENR Asset Management, Inc.
Eric N. Roseman, Founder, President & Chief Investment Officer
1 Westmount Square, Suite 1400
Westmount Quebec
H3Z 2P9 Canada
Tel.: 1-514-989-8027
Toll-free: 1-877-989-8027
Email: eric@enrasset.com
Web: www.enrassetmanagement.com

Recommended Offshore Vault for Storage of Precious Metals and Valuables:

DAS SAFE
Auerspergstrasse 1
A-1080 Wien, Austria
Tel.: +43 1 406 61 74
Email: info@dassafe.com
Web: http://www.dassafe.com

Residence & Citizenship Services:

The Nestmann Group, Ltd.
c/o AVENTA Consulting Services Ltd.
Representative Office
Hertha Firnbergstrasse 9/311
1100 Vienna, Austria

Tel.: + 43 1 587 57 95 60
Email: service@nestmann.com
Web: http://www.nestmann.com and https://www.nestmann.com/
nestmann-group-opens-representative-office-in-austria

Henley & Partners
Linke Wienzeile 8/14
1060 Vienna
Tel.: +43 1 361 6110
Web: https://www.henleyglobal.com/citizenship-austria-overview

Principality of Andorra

*The Principality of Andorra, nestled high in the Pyrenees,
between Spain and France, is a low-tax jurisdiction for very
wealthy foreigners who enjoy winter sports. It is difficult to
become a citizen, but establishing residence is easy. Strict
banking privacy no longer exists after international siege due
to charges of money laundering.*

High and Jagged

This tiny, mountainous country has few taxes, no military and
little poverty. It has been accessible from its neighbors, France or
Spain, only by motor vehicles over mountainous roads, depending
on weather conditions. The country's standard of living is high, the
cost of living relatively low, but growing, and the scenery delightful.

According to legend, Charlemagne, Emperor of the Holy Roman
Empire, in 748AD gave Andorra its name and its independence.
Gazing over the mountain region newly wrested from the Moors of
Spain, the Bible-quoting emperor is said to have exclaimed, "Wild
valley of hell, I name you Endor!" (The valley of Endor, at the foot of

Mount Thabor in the Holy Land, was the campsite of the Israelites during the war against the Canaanites. Old Testament: 1 Sam. 28:20.)

With political and economic stability, no labor strikes, virtually no unemployment and the lowest crime rate in Europe, and banking secrecy that was too strict for its own good, remote Andorra could be a haven to escape the modern world.

Although Spanish, French and English are spoken there, Andorra is the only country in the world with Catalan as its official language. As the world knows because of Catalonian demands for independence from Spain, Catalan is spoken in Spain, and in parts of southern France and a small part of Sardinia.

Bargain Isolation

Until the end of World War II, Andorra was a time capsule of traditional European mountain life. Napoleon, who was busy elsewhere, declined to invade the diminutive joint principality, is quoted as saying: "Andorra is too amazing. Let it remain as a museum piece."

In the last half century, the country has been transformed from a pastoral and farming economy to one of tourism and commerce. Andorra has an amazing 11.6 million visitors annually, mainly skiers, but many more bargain hunters for low tax discount goods and cigarettes.

The population has increased from 5,500 in 1945, (the same as in the 1880s), to an estimated 76,965 in 2017. Only about 14,000 are citizens, the rest resident foreigners. Most of the latter have moved here for work opportunities or to escape onerous taxes in their home countries.

Geography, Government

Andorra consists of 185 square miles, about one-fifth the size of the smallest American state, Rhode Island. Andorra's rugged terrain consists of gorges and narrow valleys surrounded by mountain peaks that rise higher than 9,500 feet above sea level.

It is an independent nation-state and is governed by 28 elected members of the General Council. Until 1993, the President of France and the Bishop of Seo d'Urgel (Spain), as co-princes, were responsible for Andorra's foreign affairs and judicial system. These "co-princes" could veto decisions by the General Council. They controlled the judiciary and police, but did not intrude into Andorra's affairs, except in 1933, when French gendarmes were sent in to maintain order after the judiciary dissolved the General Council. For the next 60 years, demands for independence were a repeated political refrain.

In 1993, Andorrans voted to sever their feudal links with both France and Spain. The country subsequently gained a seat in the United Nations as the third-smallest member-state.

While citizenship is a daunting prospect (it can only be attained by marrying an Andorran or 25 years as a resident), the large number of resident foreigners demonstrates how attractive the country is as a tax haven. Seventy percent of the people who live in Andorra are resident foreigners and these immigrants have been demanding more political rights.

Andorra established formal links with the European Union in 1991. After two years of tough negotiations, Andorra signed its first ever international treaty by joining the EU customs union, the first non-EU member country to do so. Andorra now applies the common EU external tariff and trade policy. This allows free transit of its goods (except for farm products) within the EU market. Andorra adopted the euro and signed a monetary agreement with the EU making it subject effectively to the monetary policy of the European Central Bank.

Duty Free

Andorra's simple, pastoral life of a half century ago is gone. Instead, it has become the shopping mall of the Pyrenees because of its duty-free tax status. The country is exempt from the EU's value added taxes, making it a sort of "Mall of Europe." More than 11 million visitors a year, mostly day-trippers from Spain, invade Andorra. They pour over the border and head for shops along the central valley road. On weekends, traffic jams are a prelude to the jostling, shopping, crowd-packed streets of Andorra la Vella, the capital city.

Until recently, Andorra's citizens and residents paid no taxes on personal income, capital gains, capital transfers, inheritance or profits. There is no sales tax or value-added tax (VAT). Until 2011, there were also minimal taxes for resident companies, which included modest annual registration fees, municipal rates, property transaction taxes, some minor sales taxes and a sliding scale capital gains tax. Then from 2011-2015, the parliament approved direct taxes on resident and non-resident individuals and corporations on capital gains, savings, and economic activities.

A corporate income tax of 10% was adopted, along with a 10% tax for non-residents on local-sourced income, (so much for encouraging foreign investment). This tax covers resident individuals with annual incomes of €30,000 (US$37,000) or more. Since 84% of Andorrans earn less than that each year, this was a popular "soak-the-rich" measure affecting only a wealthy minority. Nominal local property taxes pay for municipal services; average annual rental property tax varies from around US$120 for an apartment to US$240 for a house of any size.

Little known outside of the skiing and financial communities, this small European tax haven saw some startling, double-digit rises in real property values in recent years. Buyers come from an active local market, second homebuyers looking for ski condos and international buyers who want to establish residence in a leading tax haven. A two and three-bedroom condo here can sell for US$500,000, approximately half the cost of similar digs in Monaco.

Since 2009, for the first time in seven centuries, the government of Andorra has allowed limited investment in resorts and businesses by foreigners. The government paid lip service of wanting to be an "investment haven" and not a "tax haven."

Residents

A second residence in Andorra won't alter your domicile of origin for the purposes of home nation inheritance or estate taxes. But if you're granted a "passive" residence in Andorra, you have the right to protection under local law, certain benefits from the health and social security systems, the right to a driver's license and to own and register resident-plate vehicles. Resident status does not confer the right to vote, nor does it allow local commercial activity, such as owning or running a business.

If you're looking for residence status, there are two categories of permits, both difficult to obtain; those that give the right to work in Andorra and those that don't allow employment.

To encourage immigration of high-net-worth individuals, often retired persons, the government grants "Passive Residence Permits" called *residencias* that are subject to a quota determined periodically according to the "economic and social needs of the Principality of Andorra."

Otherwise, long term residence is only possible for those with work permits, which are controlled by quotas. It is possible to get around this system by owning a local nominee company, which is relatively expensive, but government watches closely, and suspicious activity or competition against locals can bring expulsion.

Because of the high ratio of foreigners to Andorrans, the government selectively admits new residents. Residence permits, *residencias*, are available to applicants, retired or otherwise, who have an address in the principality and who wish to reside in Andorra and become an active community member.

The annual quota for non-work permits in recent years has ranged from 200 to 500. The earlier you apply, the better chance of success. Applicants must also show sufficient economic means to live without having to work during the period of passive residence.

Applicants must prove private income sufficient that he/she need not seek local employment. Once the applicant is accepted, a *residencia* is issued for one year, renewable after the first year for a period of three years. Applying for a *residencia* is a lengthy procedure and must be conducted in the official language, Catalan. Applications are handled by the Immigration Department of the Police.

Tel.: +376 836255
Email: residcncy@livinginandorra.com
Web: http://www.livinginandorra.com/applications.html

Anyone in Andorra not a resident is considered a tourist, but there's no legal limit on the period of stay. Tourists can even rent or purchase a property for personal use for as long as they wish. So, it's easy to live in Andorra without an official residence permit.

Bank Secrecy

Andorra has no exchange controls and bank secrecy used to be very strict, but that's gone now, with transparency the official mantra. The principality has four banks with combined assets of about 16 billion euros, or US$17 billion, an integral part of the economy of Andorra. A fifth new bank, Vallbanc, replaced the defunct BPA and is the only foreign owned bank.

"*Very strict*" bank secrecy ended in 2015 when a major money laundering scandal erupted.

Criminal investigators for the U.S. Treasury Department Financial Crimes Enforcement Network (FinCEN) then published a report accusing Banca Privada d'Andorra (BPA) of laundering hundreds of millions of dollars on behalf of powerful criminal gangs from Russia, China, Mexico and elsewhere. The bank president was arrested, board member ousted, with suspect funds impounded and others "semi-frozen." Soon after the report was presented, foreign correspondent banks ended their links to BPA and regulators sold the bank's remaining assets to a U.S. investment firm. All this came as a shock for the small country, which was trying to shed its reputation as a tax haven.

Beginning in 2018, Andorra will apply the OECD common reporting standard allowing automatic exchange of tax and financial information among governments. Andorra also has 18 TIEAs with other countries, including neighboring France and Spain, as well as Monaco, Liechtenstein, Austria and the Netherlands, although none with the United States or the United Kingdom.

A leading Andorran website warns: "Gone are the days when you could walk in with a passport and be given a numbered account. The golden rule now is 100% transparency, and if they have any doubt, no matter how remote they will say 'no' rather than risking the wrath of the USA and other institutional blacklists." The http://www.livinginandorra.com site says opening an account now is "…a major headache. Expect a financial rape; if you have anything to hide or are unwilling to disclose any of your banking history then do not apply."

Under pressure from the OECD, France and Spain, before the BPA scandal Andorra already had adopted a broad definition of the crime of "money laundering." That includes any account here that has not been declared to the tax authorities of the country where the account owner lives and is taxed. If an official foreign tax authority, such as the U.S. IRS, tells the Andorran government that one of its nationals is suspected of foreign tax evasion in Andorra, banking secrecy is automatically suspended.

Interestingly, Andorra's two major banks, Andorra Credit Bank and Andbank now have offices in Miami, Panama, and Brazil, and are actively seeking foreign clients and funds, a trend that an Andbank official confirmed to us back in 2015.

Andorra has been home to thousands of bank accounts belonging to prudent Spaniards. Annually, an estimated 10% of the billions of euros that escape Spanish regulation and taxes are thought to be funneled through Andorran accounts. Perhaps 1,500 tax exiles from the U.K. have residences here also.

The four main local banks have a worldwide network of foreign correspondents and some foreign branches. With no exchange controls, accounts can be held in 20 or more foreign currencies and traded in any quantity at the rate quoted in Zurich. Exchange rates for clients are some of the best in Europe.

Banks:

Andbank: http://www.andbank.com/en
MoraBanc: https://www.morabanc.ad/en
BancSabadell d'Andorra: https://www.bsandorra.com/en
Crèdit Andorrà: http://comercial.creditandorragroup.ad/en
Vallbanc: https://www.vallbanc.ad/eng

Economy

Andorra has a developed free market economy with a per capita income of over $50,000, above both the European average and its neighbors, Spain and France. The country has a sophisticated infrastructure including a micro-fiber-optic national network. Tourism, retail sales, and finance are the core of Andorra's small economy, accounting for more than three-quarters of GDP, estimated about US$4 billion in 2017. The inflation rate in 2017 was a deflation rate of -0.9%.

The country has well-developed summer and winter tourist resorts, with more than 250 restaurants and over a thousand retail and wholesale shops. There are about 300 hotels, ranging from elegant to simple. Some have double rooms available for as low as US$50 per night. Tourism employs a large portion of the labor force.

During the winter, skiers flock to Andorra's slopes. High peaks separate six deep valleys and though the Pyrenees lack the famous Alpine altitudes, they are breathtakingly steep and far less expensive to visit. The Andorran government encourages upscale tourism at its popular ski resorts, attractive because of comparatively low prices. Ski areas are state of the art and bountiful snowfall guarantees weekend visitors from throughout Europe. Hikers use the lifts in the summer.

In the past, Andorra's thriving tourist industry hastened the country's economic transformation. Former shepherds, now wealthy investors, imported cheap Spanish and Portuguese labor to support the building boom, which transformed Andorra's central valley into a string of shops and condominiums. Don't get the idea, however, that all the land is developed. Only 8% of Andorra's land is both suitable and zoned for development. One can still find small villages in which to live with less than 100 inhabitants offering peace and quiet.

Contacts:

Andorran Tourism Board: http://visitandorra.com/en/home

Embassy of Andorra
Two United Nations Plaza, 25th Floor
New York, NY 10017
Tel.: 212-750-8064
Email: contact@andorraun.org
Web: http://www.embassy.org/embassies/ad.html

The Andorran Permanent Representative to the United Nations is accredited as Andorra's ambassador to the United States. The U.S. Ambassador to Spain is also accredited as ambassador to Andorra. U.S. Consulate General officials in Barcelona are responsible for the conduct of relations with Andorra.

United States Embassy
Calle de Serrano, 75
28006 Madrid, Spain
Tel.: +34 91 587 2200
Email: askACS@state.gov
Web: https://es.usembassy.gov

U.S. Consulate General Barcelona
Paseo Reina Elisenda de Montcada 23

08034 Barcelona, España
Tel.: +34 93 280 22 27
Email: Barcelonaacs@state.gov
Web: https://es.usembassy.gov/u-s-citizen-services/citizenship-services

Servissim
(Private client services / residence permits / property sales / rentals)
Avinguda Sant Antoni, 26, edifici Rossell, baixos, local 2
AD400 La Massana
Principality of Andorra
Tel.: +376 737900
Email: maite.servissim@andorra.ad or http://www.servissim.com/contacto.cfm
Web: http://www.servissim.com

Grand Duchy of Luxembourg

Relatively unfamiliar to Americans, Luxembourg is an established international financial and banking center of great importance. It offers a no-nonsense EU base for business operations with excellent private banking services. Although this tiny country lacks the lure of Swiss ski slopes or the white sands at Grand Cayman, it more than compensates for lack of tourist attractions by offering possible special tax-free operations and definite banking privacy.

Luxembourg is primarily a business and banking center, rather than a personal tax haven. It is also a world hub for international holding companies and investment funds. A leading lawyer says that when it comes to investment funds, Luxembourg is the "Delaware of Europe,'" is the entry point for international capital into Europe.

Its financial privacy laws have a long history, but in 2017 it began following the OECD common reporting standard that allows automatic exchange of tax and financial information among governments.

Luxembourg's conservative nature is revealed in a still popular 19th century patriotic song lyric, *"Mir wëlle bleiwe wat wir sin"* ("We want to remain as we are"), a sentiment that could be the national motto. This attitude has special meaning as the European Union, especially neighboring Germany, constantly pressures this tiny grand duchy for reforms of their banking, tax and financial privacy laws.

Under Pressure

In 2015, the government of Luxembourg joined a Europe-wide effort to share records on bank accounts held by foreigners. Then Prime Minister Jean-Claude Juncker explained that, after years of resistance, Luxembourg would start automatic exchange of information with foreign tax authorities. In 2017 the country adopted the OECD common reporting standard that allows automatic exchange of tax and financial information among governments.

Juncker was elected in 2014 as president of the European Commission, the executive branch of the EU. But for 19 years Juncker was prime minister of the Grand Duchy, when many tax deals now under EU scrutiny were arranged. Juncker now supports a tax-law overhaul that could threaten Luxembourg's livelihood. Unlike the OECD, the EU commission has the power to order governments to claw back subsidies given to companies deemed to be unfairly granted tax breaks.

Earlier in the section on Panama we explained about the dishonest activities of the so-called International Consortium of Investigative Journalists (ICIJ). Luxembourg also received unwanted attention because of the media-dubbed "LuxLeaks," a scandal where thousands of stolen documents with tax deal details were published in 2014 by the far left, anti-offshore ICIJ. The charge was that companies, such as Amazon, eBay and automaker Fiat, effectively lowered their tax burden to less than 1% of profit by making deals with Luxembourg tax authorities. The stolen documents suggested 35 major companies, including Walt Disney Co. and Koch Industries used complex financial structures to funnel profits through subsidiaries in Luxembourg, legally avoiding taxes in other jurisdictions.

In 2015, the EU Commission responded with proposed rules that would make mandatory automatic exchange of information on advance cross-border rulings on taxes and advance pricing arrangements. High tax members of the EU Commission demanded prior automatic exchange of information about tax deals that member-governments offer to companies. Such a radical change to EU rules requires unanimous approval from all 28 EU nations.

But there are many reasons why the grand duchy has attracted so much business. "What Luxembourg has shown in the last 30 to 40 years is that it continuously redefined itself, reinvented itself, to remain top," said Yves Kuhn, chief investment officer of *Banque Internationale a Luxembourg.*

Right in the Middle

Little Luxembourg (51 miles long by 34 miles wide) is a constitutional hereditary Grand Duchy.

The House of Orange-Nassau and its branches have ruled since 1815. The reign of the present ruler, Grand Duke Henri, began in 2000 and the Heir Apparent is Prince Guillaume, his son. Locals commonly speak French, German, English and their own peculiar version of German called *Letzebürgesch* or Luxemburgish. That's a dialect said to be incomprehensible even to those who have spoken "normal" German since birth.

Hidden in a river valley is the fortress of Luxembourg City. Built in 963, the castle was constructed on a rocky peak, giving it a strategic advantage while control of the area shifted from Burgundian, French, Spanish, Austrian and Prussian officials. Over the centuries, each new occupant added to the location, until its defenses included 24 forts, three fortified rings, a 14-mile network of underground tunnels and a secret network of chambers for soldiers, animals and supplies totaling more than 400,000 square feet.

An 1867 peace treaty between Austria and Prussia that ended their "Seven Weeks' War" decreed that this "Gibraltar of the North" be destroyed. Luxembourg survived, and you can still see plenty of intriguing remains. In fact, the old town and the fortress walls constitute a UNESCO World Heritage Site.

The pie-shaped country, with a 2017 population of 594,130, shares borders with Germany to the east, Belgium to the west and France to the south. A charter member of the EU, Luxembourg is also a part of the Benelux group along with Belgium and the Netherlands, a three-country union that was a precursor to the EU.

Since 1922, Luxembourg has had a fully integrated monetary and economic union with its larger neighbor, Belgium. The local currency was the Belgium-Luxembourg franc, now replaced by the euro. Today, Luxembourg City is the home of the European Court of Justice, the secretariat of the European Parliament, the European Investment Bank and European Court of Auditors.

Luxembourg was listed as the second-richest country in the world in 2017, with a GDP per capita of $109,100 and national GDP of US$64.39 billion. The country continues to enjoy an extraordinarily high standard of living, the highest in the euro zone. The economy has evolved and flourished, reporting a projected GDP growth rate of 4.5% between 2017 and 2018, which far out paces the European average of 1.8%.

Luxembourg's economy was once dominated by steel production, but since World War II the government successfully has encouraged development of a diversified financial sector. Tourism is also important.

Luxembourg is also the world's second-largest investment fund asset domicile, after the U.S., with $4 trillion of assets held in financial institutions. In Europe, it has the second-most extensive banking industry, after London, with 144 banks employing over 26,000 people and holding over US$980 billion in assets. More than 20% of Luxembourg-based banks come from non-European countries and most are foreign-owned with extensive foreign dealings.

The Stock Exchange specializes in collective investment funds and many of the several thousand Luxembourg-registered funds are listed there. The Grand Duchy's stock exchange is used extensively for issues of EU bonds, demonstrating Luxembourg's international importance. Luxembourg has also passed a series of new laws aimed at attracting mutual fund investment companies.

Offshore Haven

Although the nation's international banking activity dates to the late 19th century, Luxembourg did not hit its stride as an offshore financial center until the 1980s. It was then that greatly increased activity in the Eurobond markets based there put Luxembourg on the global financial map.

Luxembourg is comfortably in the world's top 10 financial centers with a large accumulation of cash and a commanding presence in key areas such as holding companies, private banking, investment funds and reinsurance.

This growth process developed from historic forces over which Luxembourg had no control. Rather, growth came from foreign nationals seeking better profits and escape from their own governments' anti-free market policies. Major factors were:

- Expanded foreign investment in the European Common Market in the mid-1960s.

- Imposition by the U.S. Congress of a domestic interest equalization tax in the 1980s that drove American corporations to borrow funds abroad rather than at home.

- German domestic capital flow restrictions and mandatory lending ratios.

- The 35% Swiss withholding tax on bank account and other interest.

- Currency exchange controls in France.

- Stiff bank account reporting rules in neighboring Holland.

To avoid these restrictive circumstances and taxes, astute western Europeans and Americans searched for a safe place to invest. They also needed a convenient place to conduct business with maximum freedom and lower taxes. In the middle of Europe, Luxembourg and its banks beckoned. Microsoft, FedEx, AOL, iTunes and Skype are among companies with global or European headquarters, and big tax savings, in Luxembourg.

Business Banking a National Passion

About 60% of all Luxembourg bank activity is now denominated in euros, another one-third is in U.S. dollars. Roughly 24,000 people, 11% of the workforce, are employed directly or indirectly in the Grand Duchy's nearly 150 banks and financial groups and nearly 30% of the GDP flows from financial business.

German banks operate here to escape domestic withholding taxes on interest and dividend loan limitations on corporate customers, accounting for more than 50% of all banking business. They also use the nation to deal in gold, as Luxembourg imposes no VAT.

Luxembourg's authorities closely watch bank solvency and reserves. Bank accounts are insured against loss in an amount equivalent to about US$15,000 each. Until 2009, the government did not accept that it had a duty to ensure that a bank's foreign clients paid home country taxes. Tax evasion is not a crime here, although the government maintains tax treaties with many nations, including the U.S. and U.K.

The government also began negotiating a round of tax information exchange treaties with other nations, including France and Germany, two major past antagonists on the issue of bank secrecy and it concluded a revised TIEA with the U.S. allowing information exchange in cases of alleged tax evasion. As of 2017, Luxembourg had double taxation treaties with 70 jurisdictions, including the United States.

Bank assets, liabilities and other operations must be reported to the Banking Commission. This enables the commission to maintain strict controls on the solidity and honesty of Luxembourg banks.

Taxes

Keep in mind that Luxembourg is not a tax haven — it's an investment and banking center.

The effective corporate rate tops 30% while personal income taxes can reach 38%. Resident companies must pay taxes on their worldwide income. A business qualifies as resident if its main establishment is located within Luxembourg and has its general meetings and carries out central administrative functions within Luxembourg. On the other hand, non-resident companies that have a "permanent establishment" in Luxembourg pay taxes on just Luxembourg-sourced income.

If income is below €15,000 (US$18,000), the tax rate is 9%. Income above €15,000 has a tax rate from 10% to 42%. Depending on location, there is a charge of between 6% and 10.5% for municipal services, and a 5% employment fund surcharge.

World Connections

Luxembourg's financial picture depends on more than the solvency of its banks.

The nation is a major transaction center and clearinghouse for international currency and bond markets. It is home to Clearstream Banking S.A., the electronic clearing and settlement division of *Deutsche Börse*, based in Luxembourg and Frankfurt. It functions as

International Central Securities Depository and clearing house for securities. As such it is one of the major custodians and clearers of the Eurobonds market.

This links Luxembourg's financial health to the state of the entire international banking system, especially the German and U.S. economies. Most banking clients in Luxembourg are multinational corporations, not individuals and their collective fortunes directly affect Luxembourg's financial stability. Because of this close tie to the prosperity of others, those seeking shockproof banking might do better with an account in Switzerland.

This is particularly true if you possess sufficiently large deposit sums to command the personal attention of Swiss bankers. For those with less cash but who still desire privacy every bit as good as (or better) than Switzerland, try Luxembourg.

Virtual Tax Freedom for Holding Companies

Since 1929, Luxembourg has been a tax-free haven for holding companies and investment funds. Both are tax exempt except for a relatively small fee at initial registration (1% of subscribed capital) and an annual *taxe d'abonnement*, computed at about 0.2% of actual share value for holding companies and 0.06% for investment funds. Holding companies, with their special status, escape most taxes, but a minimum tax of US$1,678 is levied. Holding companies are suited to holding international investments but are not allowed to trade themselves.

Holding companies typically own foreign company shares or bonds. They can manage these interests but cannot engage in local business beyond operational maintenance and staffing. Holding companies are exempt from taxes on dividends, interest and royalties, bond interest, profits from securities sales, or purchases and capital gains taxes. Luxembourg is home to approximately 2,000 holding companies (including many major multinational holding and finance corporations) and that number is growing. Holding companies are exempt from taxes on dividends, interest, royalties, profits from securities sales and purchases and capital gains taxes.

Collective investment funds (UCIs) are also taxed on a low basis. Thanks for the EU Savings Tax Directive, Luxembourg employs a withholding tax to non-residents' investment returns. A nearly 30% marginal corporation tax rate comes from income tax and municipal business tax on profits; rates for individuals are higher, and they pay a wealth tax in addition.

SICAV Investing

Luxembourg has its own mutual funds, known as *Sociétés d'Investissement Collective à Capital Variable*, (SICAVs). Each Luxembourg bank encourages clients to enroll in its SICAV, unless the investor has an unusually large sum to invest. Banks earn fees of between 1.5% to 3% annually for managing client mutual fund investments, plus commissions on sales of bonds or stocks in the fund. The Luxembourg government also gets its slice from fees and taxes on the funds. There are more than 8,000 funds collectively, in 2016 with US$3.2 trillion in assets.

Luxembourg is the center of ready-made offshore private banking. Your banker alternates as broker and mutual fund salesperson. He or she can help you select one or more SICAV funds to meet your investment objectives, then complete all the necessary paperwork. SICAVs accept relatively modest initial deposits starting at a US$25,000 minimum at most local banks.

Contacts:

Government of Luxembourg: http://www.gouvernement.lu

Embassy of the Grand-Duchy of Luxembourg
2200 Massachusetts Avenue NW
Washington, D.C. 20008
Tel.: 202-265-4171

Email: luxembassy.was@mae.etat.lu or
http://washington.mae.lu/en/Contact
Web: http://washington.mae.lu/en

United States Embassy
22 Boulevard Emmanuel Servais
L-2535 Luxembourg
Grand Duchy of Luxembourg
Tel.: +352 46 01 23 00
Email: Luxembourgconsular@state.gov
Web: https://lu.usembassy.gov

Commission de Surveillance du Secteur Financier
283, route d'Arlon
L-1150 Luxembourg
Tel.: +352 26 25 1 - 1
Email: direction@cssf.lu
Web: http://www.cssf.lu/en

OCRA (Luxembourg) S.A.
Parc d'Activité Syrdall 2
18-20 rue Gabriel Lippmann
L-5365 Munsbach
Grand Duchy of Luxembourg
Tel.: +352 224 286
Email: luxembourg@ocra.com
Web: http://www.ocra.com/group_offices/luxembourg.asp

OCRA Worldwide is a leading independent corporate and trust
service provider.

Principality of Monaco

Monaco is a tax haven for the exceedingly wealthy — great wealth is what it takes to afford living here. It is home to more millionaires and billionaires per capita than any place in the world, many retired and enjoying the exceedingly good life.

This unique and ancient principality is not suitable for everyone. If you want to make this your permanent home, it helps to have more than a modest amount of money and an assured income for life. And it doesn't hurt to know Prince Albert II and members of the royal family.

The 1.08 square miles of Monaco's territory on the French Riviera was home to about 30,645 people in 2017. An impressive 60% of Monaco's residents are not Monégasque citizens, but resident foreigners.

Many residents are wealthy retired people, drawn to the pleasant atmosphere, Mediterranean climate and leisure. It is also a popular resort, attracting tourists to its casino and beaches. Monaco has the facilities that wealthy people consider necessary: country clubs, health spas, golf and tennis clubs. The second-smallest country in the world in area also boasts the world's greatest longevity for its citizens. Residents can expect to live to an average age of 89.4 years, a measure of what well-spent wealth can achieve.

Monaco is for individuals who already have money — people who want to practice the art of living, while others mind affaires for them; people who want to spend time on the Riviera. If tax avoidance is the only goal, there are cheaper places to achieve that.

Monaco is small in population and area, but it enjoys all the services and cultural activities of a city the size of San Francisco. Prices are expensive, but no worse than London, Paris or Geneva. Long before the euro, cash of any kind was the European common currency in this principality. Monaco has wealthy families of many nationalities with complex affairs, so estate and inheritance planning is among the areas of local professional expertise.

Some people may find Monaco's police presence a little severe. The principality has the lowest crime rate of any highly urbanized area in the world. This physical security is, of course, one of its great advantages.

Monaco is certainly what can be called "high profile." The Grimaldi dynasty's sun-blessed, fiscally enhanced slice of the Cote d'Azur is home to the famous Monaco Formula One Grand Prix auto race that draws a crowd of 200,000 annually. The late Grace Kelly, the Hollywood film star, put Monaco on the map in 1956 when she married its ruler, Prince Rainier III. The international spotlight followed her until she died there in a tragic car accident in 1982.

During his long rule, her husband, the Prince, worked to expand the economic and professional scope of the country. Few modern monarchs can claim credit for extending their territorial dominions by one-fifth without conquest. But, by land filling the sea, the Prince managed to expand the territory of his tiny principality by 23% in his long reign that began in 1949. This land expansion mirrored the Prince Rainier's determination to make this a dynamic modern mini-state.

In 1997, the Principality celebrated the 700th anniversary of the hereditary rule of the Grimaldi family. On April 6, 2005, just three months after the death of his father Prince Rainier III, Prince Albert II formally accepted the throne.

The Grimaldi children have earned wild personal reputations, the details of their private lives constantly appearing in the gossip columns of the European tabloid press. As they aged, things calmed down, although years ago Prince Albert acknowledged paternity of a child born to an African airline hostess and another to a California woman.

In 2011, Prince Albert, then 53, and Princess Charlene, 33, the former Charlene Wittstock of South Africa, were married in an elaborate wedding costing a reported US$70 million. In 2015 twins were born to the royal parents; Jacques, the heir to the throne, and Gabriella.

Economy

Customs, postal services, telecommunications, and banking in Monaco are governed by an economic and customs union with France. Monaco has an economy primarily geared toward finance, commerce and tourism.

Low taxes have drawn many foreign companies and their production accounts for about 50% of the annual government income. If more than 25% of a company's revenue is generated abroad, it pay 33.3% tax. Monaco corporations are in the form of a *société anonyme monegasque* (SAM) and are taxed on a territorial basis. Monaco does not allow "brass plate" companies and requires that a SAM have an office and staff and a minimum paid in capital of about US$150,000.

Until the 2008 world recession, Monaco had experienced a remarkable economic development based on trading, tourism and financial services in a tax-friendly environment. Until then Monaco generated annually more than US$8 billion worth of business. Reliance on tourism and banking caused it to suffer from a downturn in France and other EU economies, the principality's main trade partners. It has rebounded since. In 2016, GDP grew by 6%, once again an estimated US$8 billion, with per capita GDP at around US$116,000.

Monaco's famed Monte Carlo Casino opened in 1856, and ever since has been an important draw for tourists. The gambling and entertainment complex includes a casino, the Grand Théâtre de Monte Carlo, and the office of Les Ballets de Monte Carlo. It currently accounts for nearly 25% of annual revenue. The principality may appear to be a frivolous playground for the rich, but they fund its government through casino gambling proceeds.

Resident's Tax Benefits

Undeniably, there are tax benefits to be gained from residence in Monaco. Authorities no longer want the principality to be known as a tax haven, but since 1869, there have been no income taxes for Monegasque nationals and resident foreigners, one of the main attractions for high net worth individuals. There are no direct withholding or capital gains taxes for foreign nationals, except for the French, who because of a bilateral tax treaty with Paris, cannot escape the clutches of the French tax collectors. There are first-time residential registration fees, but no ongoing real estate taxes, although foreign-owned real property is taxable when sold at 4.5% of the market value.

With no income tax and low business taxes, Monaco thrives as a tax haven both for individuals with an established residence and for foreign companies that set up businesses and offices. Monaco, however, is not a tax-free shelter. It charges an average 20% value-added tax, 33% tax on worldwide profits, unless they can show that three-quarters of profits are generated within the principality, and duties on such things as stamps and precious metals.

Banking

The principality is a major banking center that successfully has diversified with services and small, high-value, nonpolluting industries. There are corporate and banking advantages too. The official currency is the euro.

The Bank of France is responsible for the Monegasque banking system and carries out regular inspections. There is a strong anti-money laundering law. Banking services are not as comprehensive as they could be and the normal minimum for opening an account is €300,000, about US$369,000.

Confidentiality and privacy are good for business records and banking services. Banking secrecy is strict, but the government exchanges information about French citizens with neighboring France. In 2018, the country begins applying the OECD common reporting standard that allows automatic exchange of tax and financial information among governments. There are 21 TIEAs with other countries, including France, Germany, Liechtenstein, the Netherlands, and the United States.

Residence and Citizenship

It is much easier to obtain a residence permit here than many might suppose. A clean record, solid bank references and a net worth of US$500,000 should do it. Fees for establishing residence are in the US$10,000 to $20,000 range.

The principality has offered financial and fiscal concessions to foreign nationals for a long time. These were restricted by 1963 Conventions and more recent agreements with France.

And herein is a major concern. Monaco isn't likely to initiate changes in its tax haven status. But the rest of Europe, especially France, which always has exhibited a jealous, dog-in-the-manger attitude toward the principality, might pressure it to become less low tax attractive.

If you're a world traveler, place stability may not be that important. However, if you're looking for a new base you would do well to consider Monaco. The lifestyle is appealing but it's not for everybody. If you are contemplating a move purely for financial or fiscal reasons, depending on your specific requirements, you might do better elsewhere.

Once there, keep a low profile. Smart foreign residents do not criticize the country or government publicly. If the authorities consider a resident a troublemaker, they can issue a 24-hour notice of expulsion. There's no appeal and out they go.

Can we make any predictions about Monaco?

It's not going to become a ghost town. It is stable, and any major changes are unlikely to come from inside. After 718 years under the rule of the Grimaldi family, Prince Albert, now in charge, in many ways is far more liberal than his late father. He even has made noises about cleaning up Monaco's reputation for alleged money laundering and tax evasion. But the Monegasque financial and social establishment is not going to allow anything that hurts their financial bottom line.

Contacts:

Embassy of Monaco

888 17th Street NW
Suite 500
Washington, D.C. 20006
Tel.: 202-234-1530
Email: info@monacodc.org
Web: http://www.monacodc.org

U.S. diplomatic representation to Monaco is conducted by the U.S. Embassy in Paris, France.

United States Embassy

2 Avenue Gabriel
75008 Paris, France
Tel.: +33 1-4312-2222
Web: https://fr.usembassy.gov

U.S. Consulate General

Place Varian Fry
13286 Marseille Cedex 6, France
Tel.: 01-43-12-48-85
Email: CitizeninfoMarseille@state.gov
Web: http://marseille.usconsulate.gov

Consulate General is also located in Strasbourg, and U.S. Consulates in Bordeaux, Lyon, Rennes, and Toulous.

Principality of Monaco: http://en.gouv.mc

Monaco Government Tourist and Convention Bureau
565 Fifth Avenue - 23rd Floor
New York, NY 10017
Tel.: 212-286-3330
Toll free: 800-753-9696
Email: info@visitmonaco.com
Web: http://www.visitmonaco.com/us

Department of Tourism and Conferences:
http://visitmonaco.com/us

Monaco Real Estate Board:
http://www.chambre-immo.monte-carlo.mc/en

Banks:

Banks in Monaco: https://thebanks.eu/banks-by-country/Monaco

Residence & Citizenship Services:

Henley & Partners
Dr. Christian H. Kälin TEP, IMCM, Group Chairman
Henley Haus, Klosbachstrasse 110
8024 Zürich, Switzerland
Tel.: +41 44 266 22 22
Email: christian.kalin@henleyglobal.com
Web: https://www.henleyglobal.com

Henley & Partners
Jon Green, Partner
906 — 1112 West Pender Street
Vancouver, BC
V6E 2S1, Canada
Tel.: +1-604-239-2170
Email: jon.green@henleyglobal.com
Web: https://www.henleyglobal.com

Legal Assistance:

Carey Group
Gildo Pastor Center
7 rue Du Gabian
98000 Monaco
Tel.: +377 97 77 28 60
Email: monaco@careygroup.eu
Web: http://www.careygroup.gg/locations/monaco

Campione d'Italia

This little bit of northern Italy is an enclave surrounded by Switzerland and it's one of the least-known residential tax havens in the world. To become a resident, you must buy or rent a condo or home. In the past, foreigners who could afford to live here and foreign-owned businesses paid few taxes. It is Italian territory, but everything here is Swiss — auto license plates, currency, postage, communications and banking, but the taxes are Italian.

"Comune di Campione," as the Italians call it, on the shores of beautiful Lake Lugano, is distinguished by its uniqueness; a little plot of Italian soil, surrounded by the southern Swiss canton of Ticino. Although in the middle of Swiss territory, it is an Italian commune (municipality) of the Province of Como, an enclave separated from the rest of Italy by Lake Lugano and mountains; eleven miles north of the Swiss/Italian border town of Chiasso, and five miles by road from Lugano, Switzerland, a beautiful scenic drive around the lake.

We have visited Campione and recommend its beauty. It is a pleasant place to live, located in the heart of one of the best Swiss and nearby Italian tourist areas of Lombardy. The region boasts lakes, winter sports, and the cultural activities of Milan, Italy, are only one hour south by auto.

Until his death in 777 A.D., Campione was the private land of one Sr. Totone Campione, for whom it is named. He willed it to the Archbishop of the Milan Archdiocese. Over ensuing centuries his testamentary bequest endured a tug of war for control between Italy and Switzerland. At one point it was part of the Austrian empire. After the fall of Napoleon, the 1815 Congress of Vienna rejected the Swiss claim and it remained part of the "Kingdom of Lombardy" (Northern Italy) until 1861, when it was awarded to the Kingdom of Italy. It has remained Italian soil ever since.

There are no border controls and complete freedom of travel. Home to less than 3,000 people (including about a thousand foreign residents), this mountainside village uses Swiss banks, currency, postal service, and telephone system. Even automobile license plates are Swiss. All that's needed to become an official resident is to rent or buy property here, although formal registration is required. However, living here is very expensive; you might have to pay US$750,000 for a very small townhouse. Foreigners may buy real estate without restrictions, unlike in Switzerland.

Real estate prices are well above those in surrounding Ticino. Condominiums range from US$5,500 to $6,500 per square meter, and broker fees add a 3% commission. The real estate market is very small, hence the extremely high prices. It is also served by a handful of local real estate agents, some who don't necessarily operate professionally, including possibly without a license. A foreign buyer must be very careful. If you are interested in establishing your residence and purchasing real estate, you should be represented by a competent lawyer. (See pg. 374 for recommended professional contacts.)

Corporations

Corporations registered in Campione have some advantages over Swiss companies. They use Swiss banking facilities and have a mailing address that appears to be Swiss, while escaping Switzerland's income and withholding taxes. Corporations are governed by Italian corporate law and can be formed with a minimum capitalization of about US$1,000.

Corporations can be owned and directed entirely by foreigners, a status Swiss law limits to some degree. Corporate registrations are usually handled by Italian lawyers in nearby Milan, and fees are modest. As part of Italy, EU business regulations apply to businesses, as do Italian corporate taxes, which can be high.

While the Swiss franc is the official currency, the euro is also accepted. Swiss bank handle all bank, giving residents additional financial privacy.

Taxes

A famous casino does generate substantial revenue, which is among the reasons residents enjoyed special tax concessions. Until 2006, there were clear tax advantages to living here. But when gambling was made legal in Switzerland, the casino, the only major income source, declined. It is still active for gambling and entertainment. To make up the deficit some Italian personal income and corporate taxes were levied, but Campione is still exempt from the Italian VAT.

Tax advantages only apply to resident private persons but not to companies domiciled or managed from there. Residents do not pay the full Italian income tax. Based on a special provision in Italian law, the first CHF200,000 (US$214,000) of income is exchanged into euro, the official currency in Italy, at a special exchange rate. This results in a lower effective income and consequently a lower tax rate is applied. Other than this special concession, the Italian tax laws and tax rates apply.

Taxation of an individual's income in Italy is progressive. In 2017, the tax rate for an individual was between 23% and 43%. In addition to direct taxation there is also a regional tax of 0.7% to 3.33% and a municipal tax of 0% to 0.9%. The standard rate of Italian corporate tax in 2017 was 24%. In addition, local tax is imposed at a rate of 3.9%, bringing the effective tax rate to 27.9%.

There is no local inheritance or gift taxes, but inheritances of spouses and direct descendants are subject to an Italian inheritance tax at a rate of 4% on the amount exceeding €1,000,000 per beneficiary (US$1.2 million). Transfers to brothers or sisters are taxed at 6% on the amount exceeding €100,000. Income from interest of foreign bonds paid through an Italian bank is taxed at a special, reduced rate of 12.5%. Capital gains taxes range from 12.5% to 27.5%

To say that the Italian authorities are less than zealous in collecting taxes in Campione is an understatement. Unlike Switzerland or Italy, at this writing, Campione has no tax treaties, but Italy has signed 97 double taxation treaties, and exchanges tax information under OECD common reporting standard.

Residence

To obtain a residence permit, you most likely will need to buy an apartment or a house because rentals are very difficult to find. You will also need approval from local authorities, and clearance from the Italian police.

All that said, while residence permits are issued by Italian authorities, access to the territory is governed by Swiss visa regulations. This means you should be able to enter Switzerland without a visa using your passport. If you would need a visa, however, you would apply for a Swiss one beforehand. A passport is required for entry into Switzerland, but a visa is not required for U.S. citizens for stays of up to 90 days.

Obtaining facts about Campione is more difficult than for other tax havens because the enclave does not promote itself. There is no central office of information. Outsiders are not unwelcomed, but no one readily volunteers news about this secret haven. A personal visit is mandatory for anyone seriously interested in making this their home.

Contacts:

Amministrazione Comunale, Comune di Campione d'Italia
Piazza Maestri Campionesi
22060 Campione D'Italia
Como, Italy
Tel.: +39 031 272463
Email: protocollo@comunecampione.ch
Web: http://www.comune.campione-d-italia.co.it

Tourist Guide:

Azienda Turistica
Corso Italia n. 2
22060 Campione d'Italia
Tel.: +41 91 649 50 51
Email: aptcampione@pec.it
Web: http://www.campioneitalia.com/wordpress/en/3640-2

Residence & Citizenship Services:

Henley & Partners
Dr. Christian H. Kälin TEP, IMCM, Group Chairman
Henley Haus, Klosbachstrasse 110
8024 Zürich, Switzerland
Tel.: +41 44 266 22 22
Email: christian.kalin@henleyglobal.com
Web: https://www.henleyglobal.com

Henley & Partners
Jon Green, Partner
906 — 1112 West Pender Street
Vancouver, BC
V6E 2S1, Canada
Tel.: +1-604-239-2170
Email: jon.green@henleyglobal.com
Web: https://www.henleyglobal.com

Republic of Cyprus

This sunny island in the eastern Mediterranean Sea,
politically divided between Greek and Turkish Cypriots, was
once proud of its designation as a "tax haven." Since joining
the EU in 2004, Cyprus has changed, raising corporate and
individual taxes and sharing financial and tax information
with other governments.

Crisis

In 2013, the government of Cyprus was nearing bankruptcy because of huge losses by their banks on their Greek investments. Rescued came in a US$13.8 billion bailout loan from EU nations and the International Monetary Fund (IMF) worried about the possible collapse of the euro. To meet the loan terms, Cyprus and its EU creditors introduced the world to a dangerous new term — "*bail in.*"

The parliament approved what amounted to confiscation of vast sums from the island's personal and corporate bank accounts, much of it deposits of wealthy Russians who used the island as their international banking center. Because part of the money seized was converted into bank shares in the bail-in wealthy Russians became some of the largest shareholders in the remaining Cypriot banks. The raid on deposits, known as "a haircut" in international financial circles, was described by Russian Prime Minister Dmitry Medvedev as "stealing," and Russian president Vladimir V. Putin "denounced the move as 'dangerous' and 'unfair,' warning of a 'sharp chill in relations.'"

Cyprus is still in trouble. The economy contracted by an accumulated 11% between 2009 and 2014, but in 2015 and it grew 1.5% and 2.8% in 2016. The reported GDP for 2017 was $31.19 billion. Unemployment did fall from 13% in 2016 to 11.8% in 2017, but the rate of non-performing bank loans was still very high at 49%.

The island's economic prospects did rise after discovery of large reserves of natural gas, which eventually may bring a large injection of needed revenue.

Tangled in restrictions imposed by the EU as part of the 2013 bailout for the country's ailing banks, a euro in Cyprus was no longer seen as the same as a euro in France, Germany or Greece. In Cyprus created a "second-class euro" when the island became the first euro zone nation to impose capital controls, severely restricting the movement of cash in and out of the country. These ended in 2015.

Colorful History

Cyprus, a developed island nation south of Turkey, is the third-largest island in the Mediterranean Sea, (after Sicily and Sardinia). It once billed itself as a "tax haven" but its membership in the EU has caused it to alter many of its low tax and financial privacy laws.

Over a 40-year period the government intentionally created a favorable offshore tax system while maintaining a normal domestic economy, although taxes were low by international standards. The success of this program was confirmed by tens of thousands of offshore companies registered in Cyprus since 1975.

After the island joined the EU in 2004, the offshore tax system was restructured. One result was that both domestic and offshore companies alike now pay a corporate tax of 12.5%, one of the lowest rates in the EU, along with Ireland, also 12.5%. (The Isle of Man, Jersey and Guernsey have a zero rate). Cyprus has double-tax treaties with 54 other countries, including the U.S., making Cyprus a prime location for holding and investment companies targeting emerging markets.

One active business is incorporation of new companies for foreigners. The registration of what are mostly shell companies created to shelter income, was 215,702 companies in late 2017, an amazing figure in the Republic whose population is only about 839,000 in its southern area of the island. Taking no chances on a repeat bank bail-in most of these companies wisely do their banking anywhere.

Split Nation

With mild winters and dry summers (an average of 300 sunny days per year), Cyprus enjoys one of best climates in the Mediterranean. The population was 1,221,549 (July 2017 est.), 77% Christian Greek Cypriots, 18% Turkish Cypriots and 9% foreign workers. Of these there are over 200,000 displaced persons, both Turkish and Greek Cypriots, many refugees for more than 30 years.

Cyprus became an independent state in 1960, after 82 years of British rule. It has a system of democratic government based on human rights, political pluralism and respect for private property. Cyprus is a member of the United Nations and the British Commonwealth.

After decades of conflict between Greek and Turkish Cypriots, violent hostilities in 1974 divided the island into two independent entities: The Republic of Cypriot government in the south and a Turkish-Cypriot community in the north (that governs about 37% of the land area).

Repeated UN-backed rounds of negotiations for 43 years have failed to reunite the island country. Yet another UN effort at reunification failed in 2017, when the Greek Cypriots rejected the plan. The main issues were power-sharing in a unified government and security guarantees for the island's ethnically Turkish north, where 30,000 Turkish troops are currently stationed. Cyprus for years has had a United Nations peacekeeping force on its territory.

Russian Connection

With the fall of Communism in Soviet Russia in 1992, Cyprus became a financial (and literal) home away from home for Russian tycoons, bankers and businesspersons thanks to a communist-era treaty that removed double taxation. Most of the country's thousands of offshore companies are Russian-owned. An estimated 50,000 Russians and Ukrainians lived in the country in 2017. About 25,000 ex-Soviet citizens will be eligible to vote in a presidential election in 2018.

The "double-tax" treaty with Russia grants Cyprus-registered firms tax breaks on revenue earned in Russia. The use of Cypriot holding companies brings large amounts of foreign investment into Russia and facilitates investment worldwide by successful Russian businesses. Cyprus and Russia share the Eastern Orthodox faith and the Cyrillic alphabet.

In spite past criticism of the Cyprus bank bailout, Putin received Cyprus's president, Nicos Anastasiades, in Moscow. Putin hailed relations with the Mediterranean nation as "always being truly friendly and mutually beneficial" and agreed to extend, on greatly improved terms for Cyprus, a US$3.5 billion 2011 Russian loan.

The New York Times observed: "Tugged in different directions by outside powers, Cyprus hosts British military bases and vast eavesdropping facilities, allows the U.S. Navy to use its ports…Yet it still looks to Russia as a vitally important diplomatic protector, particularly in relation to Turkey's military occupation of the north of the country."

In 2018, incumbent Cyprus President Nicos Anastasiades defeated leftist challenger Stavros Malas and won another five-year term. The island in the Mediterranean has been divided since 1974, when Turkish troops invaded following a Greek-backed coup. The Turkish Cypriot and Greek Cypriot communities are separated by a U.N. buffer zone, and many attempts to reunite the island have failed. The vote took place barely seven months after the latest round of peace talks ended abruptly. Anastasiades steered the Cyprus' economy to recovery after a 2013 financial crisis and has pledged to seek the resumption of U.N.-mediated peace talks.

Island Changes

Formerly part of the Byzantine Empire, historically Cyprus was a great place to make things and people disappear.

The nation long has been a way station for international rogues and scoundrels, with officials traditionally willing to look the other way. Just 150 miles from Beirut, closer to the Middle East than to Europe, Cyprus has been a Mecca for cigarette smuggling, money laundering, arms trading and the like. The site of secret meetings between Israelis and Palestinians, it has also been a refuge for the Russian mafia transporting wealth of immense size and dubious provenance.

In the past, Cyprus' attraction was low taxes and lax government oversight of the financial sector, which contributed to its 2013 financial crisis. This history made the island a hotspot for shady personal deals and "brass plate" firms, offshore entities that did no real work but served as a tax-free conduit for income earned abroad.

Cyprus is possibly the most pro-U.K. jurisdiction within the EU. Outside of the British Isles, it is the only EU member state that imposes English common law as binding in cases not governed by local legislation. The reason for closeness with the U.K. is historical: Cyprus was itself a U.K. Crown dependency until independence in 1960 and continues close association with the U.K. especially in matters involving financial services.

Cyprus is also a popular low-tax haven for publicly traded companies, which can find significant advantages in the double taxation treaties network available to offshore companies. It is otherwise expensive and subject to significant disclosure requirements.

After joining the EU in 2004, it rapidly increased financial information sharing with other governments. The tax environment also became decidedly less friendly. The former 4.25% flat tax on offshore firms that attracted so many Russians in the 1990s has risen to 12.5%.

The offshore regime in Cyprus has also changed as part of the island's accession to the EU and because of agreements with the OECD. A residence-based system of personal taxation is now in place, exempting offshore income.

Even before the G-20 and OECD attacks on offshore financial centers, Cyprus changed its laws to allow the exchange of tax and finance information. It now applies the OECD common reporting standard rules and has many double tax treaties. The island also now boasts one of the world's toughest anti-money laundering laws.

Cyprus plans to maintain its company and trust management regime, although the identity of the beneficiaries must be disclosed to the tax authorities when a company is registered or when a change of ownership takes place.

Retirement Tax Benefits

Cyprus does not usually offer citizenship to foreign nationals, but it may be a good place for a retirement home for some. Residence is straightforward if you can demonstrate an annual income of as little as US$7,500 for one person or US$19,000 for a family of four.

Cyprus offers interesting tax benefits for non-domiciled residents, from a retired investor to an author, musician, inventor, or even someone receiving a royalty income, so long as they come from the right nation.

There are also certain residence programs for foreign nationals willing to make substantial investment in the island's economy. Foreigners who become residents are not allowed to carry on any local business without permission, but they can conduct their business anywhere in the world from their Cyprus base.

Cyprus is a perennially popular location for international consultants and independent contractors, groups that in the once burgeoning offshore sector accounted for the greatest percentage of expatriate workers. It is also a popular destination for active retirees, attracted not just by the lifestyle, but also by the 54 double taxation treaties in place that exempt foreign retirement income from local taxes.

Residence and Taxes

Although residence for the purposes of taxation in Cyprus is defined as the "presence in the country for more than 183 days," calculation of tax liabilities is complex, because the country has several different levels of taxation for the various categories of residents.

Except for foreign nationals working for offshore entities (for whom the rate of income tax is reduced), all groups are liable to pay the following taxes on income paid within Cyprus; income tax (at a progressive rate of up to 30%), capital gains tax (at a rate of 20%), estate duty (at between 20% and 45%) and real estate taxes.

A non-domiciled resident pays a flat tax of 5% on investment income received from abroad and remitted to Cyprus. The first US$4,000 of remitted investment income and all investment income that is not remitted to Cyprus is tax-free.

Royalties are treated as investment income. Foreign earned income can be remitted to Cyprus to reduce foreign withholding taxes and foreign withholding tax paid can be credited against any Cyprus tax owed. That can wipe out the 5% Cyprus tax obligation. Unfortunately, these benefits are not available under Cyprus tax treaties with the U.K. or U.S., but most other nationals can benefit. Cyprus imposes death taxes, but the estates of non-domiciled residents are taxed only on assets located in Cyprus at the time of death.

To qualify for local residence, an applicant must provide evidence of good character, show independent financial means and document income. The Cypriot Immigration Control Board also imposes minimum amounts of income that must be received by residents during a tax year. Foreigners allowed residence may purchase property in Cyprus, but only after obtaining a permit. Approval to buy real property usually is a formality for an owner-occupied house or apartment.

This may fall within the status of "Would you buy a used car from this man?" In 2013, during the Cyprus bankruptcy and bank crisis, the Cypriot Department of Immigration, seeking quick cash, began selling "economic citizenship" to gullible foreigners. Asking price at first was as much as €10 million (US$12.3 million), but was reduced after the government confiscated billions of euros in Cyprus bank accounts. A Cyprus passport does give the right to take up residence there or in any of the 28 EU countries.

A "fast track citizenship" law was adopted to attract much needed investors. The law guarantees for qualified applicants expedited residence within two months and citizenship within four years. Applicants must own a permanent residence worth at least €500,000 (US$615,000) and have substantial Cyprus investments of €2,500,000 (US$3 million) or more. It is worth noting that the amount asked for this program is 128 times the average annual income in Cyprus.

Alternately, a foreign person can invest €300,000 (US$369,000) in Cypriot real estate, maintain a deposit of €30,000 (US$37,000) in a Cypriot banking institution and demonstrate sufficient foreign funds for support.

Contacts:

Embassy of the Republic of Cyprus
2211 R Street NW
Washington, D.C. 20008
Tel.: 202-462-5772
Email: info@cyprusembassy.net
Web: http://www.cyprusembassy.net
Consulate offices are located in New York, NY and Washington, D.C.

United States Embassy
Metochiou & Ploutarchou Streets
2407, Engomi
Nicosia, Cyprus
Tel.: +357- 22-393939
Email: consularnicosia@state.gov
Web: https://cy.usembassy.gov

Cyprus Embassy Trade Center
13 East 40th Street
New York, NY 10016
Tel.: 212-213-9100

Email: ctcny@cyprustradeny.org

Web: http://www.cyprustradeny.org

Turkish Cypriots maintain offices in Washington, Tel.: 202-887-6198 and at the Republic of Turkey's Mission to the United Nations.

For Information on Residence Applications:

Chief Immigration Officer
Ministry of Foreign Affairs
Presidential Palace Avenue
1447, Nicosia Cyprus
Tel.: +357 22 651000
Email: info@mfa.gov.cy
Web: www.mfa.gov.cy

Attorney:

Christodoulos G. Vassiliades & Co LLC
Ledra House
15 Agiou Pavlou Street, Agios Andreas
1105 Nicosia, Cyprus
Tel.: + 357 22 55 66 77
Email: cgv@vasslaw.net
Web: www.vasslaw.com

Offices also in Greece, Malta, U.K., Hungary, Russia, Belize, and Seychelles

Kingdom of Denmark

The Danes are overwhelmingly a happy bunch. In fact, if you believe those contentment surveys that come out every couple of years, Denmark is one of the happiest nations on earth with some of the best quality of life. Denmark is not really an offshore financial center in the usual "tax haven" sense, but it does have and a low-tax holding company legal regime.

Located in Northern Europe, little Denmark (26,777 square miles, of which 410 square miles are water), borders on the Baltic Sea and the North Sea, on a peninsula north of Germany (Jutland) and includes several major islands (Sjaelland, Fyn, and Bornholm). It also includes the non-contiguous Faroe Islands and Greenland.

An EU member, its laws conform to the EU on most issues. While it qualified for the European Monetary Union (EMU), Denmark did not join, although the Danish kroner is pegged to the euro. It is a constitution monarchy with a unicameral legislature.

Danes enjoy one of the highest standards of living in the world with a 2017 per capita GDP of US$49,600. The economy is characterized by extensive government welfare measures and an equitable redistribution of income. Denmark's fiscal position remains among the strongest in the EU with debt at 35.1% of GDP and a 2017 GDP of US$285.5 billion.

The 2017 annual EU Social Justice Index that rates levels of poverty, social cohesion, job opportunities, education, discrimination and health issues in the EU member states rated Denmark as number one in Europe. That explain the Dane's high happiness level.

Holding Companies

A "holding company" is defined as a company that owns other companies' outstanding stock. The term usually refers to a company that does not produce goods or services itself; rather, its purpose is to own profitable shares of other companies. Holding companies allow the reduction of risk for the owners and allow the ownership and control of many different companies, (think Warren Buffet and his Berkshire Hathaway).

Under U.S. tax law 80% or more of stock in voting and value must be owned before tax consolidation benefits, such as tax-free dividends can be claimed as a holding company.

Denmark has high rates of personal income tax and is in the mid-range in terms of corporate tax and has never been considered an offshore financial center. However, since 1999 its holding company law has provided outstanding opportunities for the international investor and subsequent adjustments to the law have increased its low-tax attractiveness.

Historically, nine European countries (Austria, Belgium, France, Germany, Luxembourg, the Netherlands, Spain, Switzerland and the United Kingdom) have competed with changes in their fiscal laws in attempts to make themselves the most attractive in which to locate holding companies. This is another attractive form of international tax competition that benefits investors, companies and ultimately, consumers.

However, liberalized laws on Danish holding companies revolutionized the market and made it the most attractive location, with the result that the Netherlands' historic dominance of the holding company market was seriously threatened, and other holding company jurisdictions slipped.

Denmark has more than 70 double taxation treaties in place and this network of treaties offers greater leverage to reduce withholding taxes on incoming dividends. An elaborate network of double taxation treaties is a key factor for an attractive holding company jurisdiction and almost all dividend income received in Denmark is free of withholding tax.

Denmark's combined tax treaty network and holding company regime allows about 35 major countries with proper legal structuring to route dividends through Denmark and avoid any withholding taxes.

In about 40 countries withholding taxes can be reduced substantially, owing to this Danish double taxation treaty network. It's proven to be lucrative for Denmark given hundreds of holding companies have been set up by corporations Countries that benefit include Argentina, Austria, Belgium, Brazil, China, Cyprus, Finland, France, Germany, Greece, Iceland, India, Ireland, Italy, Luxembourg, Malaysia, Mexico, the Netherlands, Norway, Portugal, Singapore, Spain, Sweden, Switzerland, the U.K. and Malta.

Contacts:

Danish Government:
http://denmark.dk/en/society/government-and-politics

Embassy of Denmark
3200 Whitehaven Street NW
Washington, D.C. 20008
Tel.: 202-234-4300
Email: wasamb@um.dk
Web: http://usa.um.dk/en

United States Embassy
Dag Hammarskjolds Allé 24
2100 Copenhagen Ø, Denmark
Tel.: +45 33 41 71 00
Email: copenhagenacs@state.gov
Web: https://dk.usembassy.gov

Invest in Denmark: http://www.investindk.com

Danish Ministry of Taxation: http://www.skm.dk/english

Tourism: http://www.visitdenmark.com/denmark/tourist-frontpage

Law Firm:

Fabritius Tengnagel & Heine
Store Kongensgade 67C

1264 København K
Tel.: +45 33 13 69 20
Email: shl@dklaw.dk
Web: http://www.dklaw.dk/en

FT&H was established in 1865 and is one of the oldest law firms in Copenhagen. They provide legal advice on all areas of business, banking, commercial and international law.

Private Banking:

Jyske Bank
Vesterbrogade 9
DK-1780 Copenhagen V, Denmark
Tel.: +45 89 89 62 34
Email: privatebanking@jbpb.dk
Web: http://jyskebank.com/en

Jyske also has banks in Gibraltar and Germany.

Gibraltar

Looming like some great ship off southern Spain, Gibraltar is a fascinating compound of curiosities. Despite police Bobbies on the beat, red post boxes and other reminders of 1960s England, Gibraltar is a cultural cocktail with Genoese, Spanish, North African and other elements that have made it fantastically prosperous. Naturally, the main sight is the awesome Rock; a vast limestone ridge that rises to 1,400 feet, with sheer cliffs on its northern and eastern sides. For the ancient Greeks and Romans this was one of the two Pillars of Hercules, split from the other, Jebel Musa in Morocco, during Hercules' arduous Twelve Labors.

The Rock of Gibraltar, famously used for more than a century as the logo of the Prudential Insurance Company, is said to be one of the most recognized corporate symbols in the world. The Rock, as it is known locally, is the United Kingdom's only continental European colonial possession, although it is a territory forcefully and loudly claimed by neighboring Spain.

Gibraltar has fashioned itself into a dual-purpose residential tax haven for high-net-worth individuals from around the world, and as a professional base for tax-free international banking, business corporations and trusts.

But the government is careful about its image. In 2015 Gibraltar's government filed suit for defamation against the Spanish newspaper, ABC, because it called the Rock a "tax haven" which the government denies. Gibraltar has gone to great efforts to project a clean image and wants to be known as a respectable offshore financial center.

Colonial History

Gibraltar, a colonial possession of the United Kingdom, was ceded to England "forever" under the 1713 Treaty of Utrecht. Neighboring Spain's 305 years of efforts to recover this British overseas territory, located on Spain's southern flank, have been rejected repeatedly, by a large majority of the 29,336 citizens of Gibraltar, most recently by a 99% "no" vote in a 2002 referendum, and by successive British governments, both Conservative and Labor.

Constitutionally, Gibraltar is a British Overseas Territory with internal self-government under a 2006 constitution. The U.K. is responsible for defense, foreign affairs, financial stability and internal security. Gibraltar has its own House of Assembly with 15 elected members and two nominated members. There is a Council of Ministers, which consists of the Chief Minister and seven other Ministers.

Gibraltar residents have repeatedly voted overwhelmingly to reject any "shared sovereignty" arrangement with Spain and the government insists on equal participation in any talks between the U.K. and

Spain. Spain strongly opposed the U.K.'s plan to grant Gibraltar even greater autonomy. After the U.K.'s 2016 Brexit vote to leave the EU, Spain then renewed its demand for an eventual return of Gibraltar, but London dismissed any connection between the vote and its future commitment to Gibraltar.

The 2006 constitution grants local autonomy in many areas but reserves strategic decisions to London. Its legal system is based on English common law. Gibraltar has been part of the European Union by its association through the U.K. since 1973. It does not come under the EU's VAT, common agricultural policy or external tariff regimes. Gibraltar has implemented much EU financial legislation and applies common EU passport rules, including 2017 tougher Schengen border crossing rules, although it is not a Schengen member state.

Rock-Solid Economy

The famous Rock is tiny, only 2.5 square miles, but boasts a comprehensive banking and financial services industry. Gibraltar has no exchange controls and offers first-rate communications and infrastructure. The colony's financial services industry is the mainstay of the local economy, providing 30-35% of GDP, with 5,000 jobs that depend on the offshore finance center.

Gibraltar's GDP per capita for 2016/17 was claimed to be $92,843 by its Chief Minister, Fabian Picardo, ranking it third worldwide, behind only Qatar and Luxembourg and among the top 15 countries of the world, higher than Switzerland. The 2014 GDP was $2.044 billion, the latest available number from the *CIA World Factbook*.

Gibraltar generates revenue from a variety of sources. The financial sector, tourism, and the shipping sector contribute approximately 30%, 30%, and 25%, respectively, of the GDP. Telecommunications, e-commerce, and e-gaming account for the remaining 15%. The British military presence has been sharply reduced and now contributes about 7% to the local economy, compared with 60% in 1984.

The currency is the Gibraltar pound (£G) = 100 pence and is equivalent with the British pound sterling.

Offshore Leader

Gibraltar has the honor of being among the first British Overseas Territories to create tax-exempt corporate forms for offshore business. While domestic income taxes are high, the territory offers low-tax regimes to foreign resident and their registered companies. In addition, Gibraltar offers tax incentives for investment. Gibraltar is, in fact, the lowest cost European offshore jurisdiction in which to operate a business.

The territory offers an advanced business and professional infrastructure. Its offshore business sectors are composed of banking, insurance, investment fund management, trust management, shipping and investment holding companies. In an effort to avoid the U.K.'s high taxes while benefiting from strong digital telecom facilities, many British gaming operations have shifted to Gibraltar.

Under EU common passport legislation any branch of an authorized EU bank may establish itself in Gibraltar, subject only to notification procedures. Conversely, a Gibraltar-licensed bank may set up branches elsewhere in Europe. Most of the 13 fully operational banks established in 2017 were branches of major U.K., U.S., Swiss or other European banks.

Interestingly, Gibraltar has about 40 authorized banks entitled to accept deposits without establishing full branches in Gibraltar. At this writing, Gibraltar has 75 insurance companies, 43 trust companies and 551 licensed financial management companies managing nearly 4,000 registered trusts.

There are about 41,000 registered corporations. The banking sector is well established in both the offshore and local market with assets of more than £G9.3 billion (US$13 billion). Advantages of offshore banking in Gibraltar include its favorable tax status, lack of exchange controls, excellent communications, stable government, and EU membership.

Most Gibraltar banks offer wealthier private depositors a special interest rate that fall under a "private banking" headings. Minimums are as low as US$10,000 in some cases, although some firms still maintain more traditional entry levels of US$100,000 or higher before offering special treatment to clients.

Gibraltar imposes no capital gains, wealth or estate taxes. The reopening of the border with Spain in 1985 enabled Gibraltar to expand its role as a major international finance center, against a background of political stability and administrative and legal systems derived from English common law and traditions. The absence of any exchange control restrictions together with exemptions and concessions from domestic taxes for certain categories of companies, high net worth and non-resident individuals and trusts administered for non-residents has created many opportunities for offshore investors and led to substantial growth in financial sector services.

Gibraltar, as do all U.K. overseas territories, applies the OECD common reporting standards allowing automatic exchange of tax and financial information. It also has a TIEA (tax information exchange agreement) with the U.S. allowing information exchange in cases of alleged tax evasion. It has TIEAs with 20 countries including the U.K., France and Germany.

HNWI

Gibraltar is also home to "tax exiles" from many nations, wealthy individuals who enjoy the local tax-free regime for foreign residents. Under Gibraltar tax law, the category known as "high net worth individuals" (HNWI) receives the biggest concessions.

A major banking activity is asset management for high-net-worth individuals. That is because Gibraltar has a special program to attract wealthy people. Under the high-net-worth individual (HNWI) tax scheme the minimum tax payable per annum is £G18,000 (US$25,000) and the taxable income level is £G60,000 (US$83,000) and up.

Of special note is the fact that there is no capital gains tax or estate taxes in Gibraltar. Starting in 2011, the Gibraltar Deposit Protection Scheme covers 100% of a bank's total liability to a depositor to a maximum of €100,000 (US$123,000).

Autonomy Confirmed

Previously, when the OECD listed Gibraltar on its harmful tax competition "blacklist," the government countered with a cut in corporate tax rates across the board to zero. Both the OECD and the European Union attacked Gibraltar's tax haven status and Spain joined the critical chorus for its own political purposes. The EU had ruled that Gibraltar's offshore favorable tax status was incompatible with EU regulations that apply to the United Kingdom and its co-lonial dominions.

Gibraltar appealed the EU ruling and won a significant victory when the EU's highest court ruled that the Rock had "from a consti-tutional point of view, a political and administrative status separate from that of the central government of the United Kingdom." In effect, this affirmed the constitutional right of Gibraltar to set its own tax policies independent of the U.K., allowing its continuation as an offshore financial center.

Gibraltar's hopes of attaining special status following Brexit might have been dashed thanks to a 2017 case ruling. The EU high court decided that Gibraltar and the U.K. can be treated as a single EU member in regard to some aspects of EU law.

The Future

Because of the 2016 Brexit vote, the U.K.s and Gibraltar's EU membership will cease to exist by March 30, 2019, unless all parties to the negotiations agree on another date. Gibraltar voted strongly to remain in the EU, fearing loss of membership in the EU single market trading block.

U.K. PM Theresa May promised that "...the U.K. would seek the best possible deal for Gibraltar... and there would be no negotiation on the sovereignty of Gibraltar without the consent of its people." Spanish leaders said they would not make Gibraltar a pawn in Brexit discussions, saying they did not want to jeopardize a future deal by demanding a change in status to the British overseas territory as part of Brexit.

The fear is that, if Brexit talks turn nasty, Spain might again shut the border. The EU has been a buffer against these Spanish strong-arm politics. Gibraltar chief minister Fabian Picardo noted that in the negotiations for Spanish to access the European Economic Community Spain finally reopened the frontier. "We see the EU as a guarantor of the freedom of movement of people," he said.

What will happen to Gibraltar's status after U.K. membership in the EU ends depends on current negotiations. Many EU member states have important financial interests in Gibraltar they want to preserve and, as they say, money talks.

Contacts:

Government of Gibraltar: https://www.gibraltar.gov.gi/new

Affairs for Gibraltar, a British Crown colony, are handled through the U.S. Embassy in London.

United States Embassy London
24 Grosvenor Square
London, W1A 2LQ
United Kingdom
Tel.: + 44 (0)20 7499-9000
Web: https://uk.usembassy.gov

Gibraltar Financial Services Commission
P.O. Box 940, Suite 3, Ground Floor, Atlantic Suites
Europort Avenue, Gibraltar
Tel.: +350 200 40283
Email: info@fsc.gi or http://www.fsc.gi/contact
Web: www.fsc.gi

Gibraltar Tourists Board: http://www.gibraltar.gi/home

Official Gibraltar Tourist Board: http://www.visitgibraltar.gi

Gibraltar News: http://gibraltarpanorama.gi

Gibraltar Asset Management
World Trade Center
Suite 5.28
Gibraltar
Tel.: +350 200 75181
Email: gam@gam.gi
Web: http://www.gam.gi

Private Banking:

Licensed Banks:
http://listofbanksin.com/List-of-Banks-in-Gibraltar.htm

Jyske Bank
Vesterbrogade 9
DK-1780 Copenhagen V, Denmark
Tel.: +45 89 89 62 34
Email: privatebanking@jbpb.dk
Web: http://jyskebank.com/en

Jyske also has banks in Denmark and Germany.

Republic of Malta

*Malta is a microcosm of the Mediterranean. Few European
countries have such a concentrated history, architecture, such
an eclectic mix of influences and a roll-call of rulers over the
centuries. Malta offers an excellent deal in its special tax-free
status for foreign retirees. It courts international business and
financial firms with tax breaks and subsidies. When it joined
the EU, it revised its tax laws and does not want to be known
as the tax haven, even though it still is. Alleged government
corruption and selling citizenships was an issue.*

Malta is composed of a group of islands (Malta, Gozo and
Comino) in the center of the Mediterranean Sea, south of the continent of Europe and 50 miles directly south of the Italian island of
Sicily. Its geography and history has made it a cultural and political
stepping stone between Europe and North Africa.

About 95% of the nearly 416,388 islanders are natives, descendants of the ancient Carthaginians, Phoenicians, Greeks and Romans
that plied these waters. Malta offers an excellent climate and quality
of life, modern health care and educational systems.

In 1530, the Holy Roman Emperor, Charles V, ceded Malta to
the governance of the Knights of Malta, a Catholic lay religious order
dating from the Crusades. Their fortifications in the harbor of Valetta,
the capital, were so strong that in 1565 a Turkish siege was repelled by
these excellent defenses, still extant today. In 1798, Napoleon invaded
Malta and expelled the Knights.

At the Congress of Vienna in 1815, Britain got possession of
Malta. With the 1869 opening of the Suez Canal, Malta became an
important strategic British base. During World War II, Malta was
bombed heavily by the German Luftwaffe since it was a valuable

Allied convoy port. The island staunchly supported the U.K. through both world wars and remained in the British Commonwealth after independence. In 1947, Malta was granted self-government and in 1964, independence, after 149 years as a British colony. Malta joined the EU in 2005.

Malta's government has been controlled by the conservative Nationalist and the social-democratic Labor parties since 1964. The island's most powerful families have close ties to both parties. As a result, there are claims that the lines police, justice and business are frequently murky.

In 2017, the Labor Party called an early election and was re-elected by a landslide in despite charges of corruption.

Malta is dependent on imports due to its lack of natural resources and shortage of arable land. However, the government has focused its efforts on establishing a high tech manufacturing sector and creating processing and distribution facilities around its expanding Freeport.

To expand its role as a leading international financial center, the government has created extensive investment incentives and laws.

These provide a variety of tax and financial incentives to banks, insurance companies, fund management firms, trading companies, trusts and investment companies.

Law and Order

In 2017, the European parliament raised "serious concerns" about democracy and the rule of law in Malta after the assassination of a well-known investigative journalist, Daphne Caruana Galizia. By two thirds vote, the parliament adopted a sharply critical resolution directing EU authorities to send a formal mission to the government of Malta to discuss the rule of law.

The murdered reporter had crusaded against official corruption and opposed the sale of Maltese passports to wealthy foreigners under the IIP Program (which we discuss below). Ms. Caruana Galizia wrote about alleged corruption in Malta involving politicians, the mafia and business leaders.

The EU resolution said: "Developments in Malta in recent years have led to serious concerns about the rule of law, democracy and fundamental rights, including freedom of the media and the independence of the police and the judiciary." Parliament members also have also accused Maltese police of failing to investigate "several serious allegations of corruption and breach of anti-money laundering and banking supervision obligations", describing this as "a threat to the rule of law in this member state".

Economy

While it is not a tax haven for individuals as such, Malta's government actively courts foreign capital with attractive incentives aimed at investors and entrepreneurs. These include generous tax incentives, soft loans, training grants and customized facilities at subsidized costs. This pro-business policy seeks to build on Malta's many existing strengths: favorable trade relations with countries around the world; a strategic location on world shipping lanes; and a high quality, productive, English-speaking workforce.

Malta's free market economy, the smallest in the euro-zone, relies heavily on trade in both goods and services, principally with Europe. In 2014-2016, Malta led the euro zone in growth, expanding more than 4.5% per year. The nation has maintained a surplus balance of payments, stable currency and low inflation (less than 1%), all impressive numbers that reflect the overall strength and diversity of the economy. Figures for 2017 show GDP of US$18.53 billion and a per capita GDP of US$42,500, low on the European scale.

British military and naval bases once dominated Malta, but since 1979, when the last British forces departed, the excellent port facilities have been underutilized. Tourism is a major contributor to the economy, especially cruise ship visits. The Valletta airport has good connections to a wide range of European cities.

Traditionally, agriculture was important, but the economy has undergone major change. Manufacturing, especially high-tech industries, now accounts for more than a quarter of Malta's GDP. The 2016 est. from the *CIA World Factbook* states about 77.7% of the labor force works in services, 20.7% in industry/manufacturing, and 1.6% in agriculture. Major industries now include textiles, machinery, food and beverages, and high-tech products, especially electronics and online betting services.

Tourism is also a growing and increasingly important sector. Valletta, the capital city, was chosen by the European Commission as European Capital of Culture for 2018. Key sectors that provide exceptional investment opportunities include trade, tourism, manufacturing, maintenance services, and international financial services.

Malta real economy suffered during the 2008 global economic collapse and was made worse by high electricity and imported water prices. However, the territory rebounded as the rest of the globe recovered. Traditionally agriculture was important, but the economy has changed. Major industries now include high-tech manufacturing, food and beverages, tourism and international financial services. Malta is also one of world's preferred jurisdictions for tax-free private yacht registrations.

Two unique factors helped Malta's economy: online Internet gambling and generic pharmaceuticals. At a time when the U.S. and the U.K. both cracked down on online gaming, Malta welcomed the industry to its shores. Gaming companies are sanctioned by the government and courts. Leading online gaming companies have relocated to Malta, producing local jobs and bolstering the banking system. The generic pharmaceutical industry has taken advantage of Malta's liberal patent laws that protect companies that do research and testing of generic drugs before a patent expires.

Offshore Financial Center

The Maltese government enacted legislation to increase the islands' role as a leader in international finance services. It intentionally avoided the old tax haven model and refashioning itself as a modern international business center. EU conforming laws provide a variety of tax and financial incentives to banks, insurance companies, fund management firms, trading companies, trusts, and investment companies.

Malta's financial services industry has grown and escaped significant damage from the 2008 international financial crisis because of the stability of the Maltese banking system and its conservative risk-management practices. There are more than 600 investment funds with total net asset value under management that exceeds US$107 billion.

The International Monetary Fund 2015 annual report on Malta confirmed the stability of its financial services, praising the strengthening of regulatory and supervisory procedures. The financial reporting service, Fitch, said that banks enjoyed a loan/deposit ratio of only 66% and the Basil Tier 1 capital ratio was 11.08%, well above the regulatory minimum threshold of 8%.

The government actively seeks to attract foreign capital with generous tax breaks aimed at international investors. Malta is a good jurisdiction in which to establish low-tax international trading companies and treaty-protected international holding companies.

Taxes

Residences and individuals domiciled in Malta pay income tax on their world-wide income. A six-month test is usually the most effective in establishing residence. Those who are domiciled elsewhere and not ordinarily residents in Malta pay taxes on income earned in Malta or remitted there, but they do not pay capital gains, whether remitted or not. There are no property taxes.

Just Malta-sourced income is taxed for non-resident individuals, while local interest and royalty income escape taxation. Capital gains on holdings that are a part of collective investment schemes or on securities if the underlying asset is not Maltese immovable property are also tax exempt.

There's even a special tax benefit to returning migrants. If a person was born in Malta and return can choose to pain 15% income tax on local income only. However, there are some conditions. Highly qualified expatriate employees working in the financial services or online gaming industry are subject to a flat tax of 15%. The 15% flat tax incentive applies to highly skilled and qualified expatriates who are required for certain industrial sectors including those who do research or market an invention or technology in Malta, plus digital gaming professionals, such as game directors and game software designers.

Holders of Permanent Residence Permits issued under the Immigration Act 1970 pay tax at a reduced rate on income earned in Malta plus remittances of foreign income. Such individuals are considered non-resident for purposes of investments in offshore and non-resident companies.

Malta has three types of taxes: income, corporate and estate taxes — the latter applies only to property located on the island. Income tax rates for foreign residents range from 2% to 30%. A permanent resident is not taxed on capital gains paid from offshore, unless the person also is domiciled in Malta. Malta now has 65 double tax treaties with other nations.

Residence Status

A permanent resident in Malta can enjoy a privileged tax status, as well as the benefits from the country's wide network of double taxation treaties. A further advantage of this status is that if the resident abides by the rules, they do not need to spend any time physically in Malta.

Foreign nationals are not eligible for immediate Maltese citizenship, but they are welcomed as residents. Maltese residence is of three types:

- Visitors staying less than three months are counted as nonresidents.

- Those remaining over three months are temporary residents.

- Permanent residents are granted a permit entitling them to stay.

A residence permit can be inherited by a surviving spouse, but not by other surviving descendants. Any person may apply for naturalization as a citizen of Malta after having resided there for at least five years.

Maltese citizenship law now allows second generation Maltese born abroad to become citizens of the island by registration and proof of lineage. The applicant must provide documentary evidence showing direct descent from an ancestor or a parent who was born in Malta. Documents required include birth, marriage and death certificates. The registration procedure can occur at any Maltese Embassy, High Commission, Consulate, or at the Department for Citizenship and Expatriate Affairs in Malta. In this category physical residence in Malta is not required to qualify. A valid passport is required for entry into Malta.

Citizenship for Sale

Malta is an attractive location in Europe for tax advantaged private residence. Non-Maltese persons, may acquire permanent residence status through a program that makes persons of all nationalities eligible to apply for residence permits. These sunny Mediterranean islands especially cater to expatriates looking for a second or retirement home.

The Maltese Individual Investor Program (IIP) became law in 2013, a modern version of what in the past was known as an "economic citizenship" in which investments and/or cash buy citizenship. Malta IIP is one of the costliest of these programs that have multiplied in the EU. Other EU countries that sell residence leading to citizenship in return for investments now include Austria, Belgium, Cyprus, Portugal, Poland, Hungary, Bulgaria and Romania. Italy plans to begin its program in 2018.

The Maltese IIP program is aimed at the top of the citizenship-by-investment market. The fee structure and cost of compliance put the minimum cost of IIP citizenship at more than US$1 million. But the benefits are extraordinary: fast-track Maltese and therefore EU citizenship, with a short application process, and low non-resident tax rates.

Under the IIP successful applicants must contribute of €650,000 (US$800,000) to a National Development Fund (for social projects), plus €25,000 (US$31,000) each for spouse and minor children, and €50,000 (US$61,000) each for dependent children 18 to 25 years, or dependent parents above 55. For a family of four, the cost per person could be around €185,000 (US$228,000).

Regardless of an applicant's acceptance or rejection, the government also charges due diligence fees for the main applicant, spouses, adult children and parents and each for minor children; as well as passport fees and bank charges that can add another US$174,000.

Official records indicate that by the end of 2016 as many as 1,600 passports were issued to non-EU nationals generating at least US$235 million for Malta. The CEO of Henley & Partners, Eric Major, confirmed the main markets for the passports were from Russia, former Soviet republics and the Middle East.

To ward off domestic criticisms that it was "selling citizenship," and to block undesirables, the Maltese government stressed that "the due diligence to be applied to those applying for Maltese citizenship will be subjected to complete X-ray of applicants' and relatives' lives and the source of their riches." The government insisted that IIP candidates would have clean criminal records and must produce a medical certificate confirming that they and their dependents have no contagious diseases and are in good health.

As originally proposed, IIP foreign participants were not required to live in Malta. But that raised strong opposition from EU officials and other governments, since it amounted to granting successful applicants full EU citizenship, including freedom of movement and residence in all 28 countries, but without requiring actual residence. Now they are required to prove at least 12 months of prior residence in Malta before a grant of IIP citizenship. EU concerns forced Malta to cap the program at 1,800 new citizens in total.

In 2017, the EU Parliament again raise as alarm about the sale of Maltese passports concerned that any wealthy person could buy the right to free movement and protections of EU citizenship. It was confirmed that the European commission was investigating the "so-called sale of passports" across the EU and would publish a full report in 2018.

In 2018, it was revealed that the Maltese government was considering expanding their controversial passports-for-sale scheme and that Russia's business elite were snapping up Maltese passports amid EU and US anti-Russian economic sanctions.

In a Bloomberg News article headlined: "Why Russians Are Choosing Malta Over Putin," it was reported that the Maltese passport scheme was proving irresistible to Russian business elites and their families.

The newly-minted Maltese/Russian nationals were on a list of more than 2,000 names published in the country's legal gazette at the end of 2017. The names of wealthy foreign nationals stood out as the most likely to have paid the €1.1 million (US$1.4 million) in fees, Maltese bond, and Maltese real estate investments that it costs to buy nationality. The Russian roll-call for 2016 included millionaires from the sectors of media, energy, oil and gas, transport, mining, internet, real estate developers, retailers, agricultural land owners, bankers and investment brokers. In 2015, 40 % of new passport buyers were Russians. A co-founder of the suspect Russian cyber security firm Kaspersky Lab, was also listed.

Those interested in the IIP program can contact:

Henley & Partners
Aragon House
Dragonara Road
St. Julian's STJ 3140, Malta
Tel.: +356 2138 7400
Inquiry Form: https://www.henleyglobal.com/
contact/?chosenform=malta.php
Web: https://www.henleyglobal.com/citizenship-malta-citizenship

Contacts:

Government of Malta: https://gov.mt/en

Embassy of Malta
2017 Connecticut Avenue NW
Washington, D.C. 20008
Tel.: 202-462-3611
Email: maltaembassy.washington@gov.mt
Web: http://www.embassy.org/embassies/mt.html

Consulate of Malta: http://consulatewashington.tripod.com

United States Embassy
Ta' Qali National Park
Attard, ATD 4000
Tel.: +356 2561-4000
Email: usembmalta@state.gov
Web: https://mt.usembassy.gov

Ministry of Foreign Affairs
Palazzo Parisio
Merchants Street
Valletta. VLT 1170
Tel.: +21242191
Email: info.mfa@gov.mt
Web: http://foreignaffairs.gov.mt/en

Malta Tourism Board: http://www.visitmalta.com

Banks:

Central Bank of Malta: http://www.centralbankmalta.com

Banks in Malta: http://www.europebanks.info/malta.php

Law Firm:

Chetcuti Cauchi Advocates
120, St. Ursula Street
Valletta VLT 1236, Malta
Web: www.cc-advocates.com

CHAPTER NINE

Asia, Mid-East, Africa

The growth in national economies, in the Middle East, Africa and Asia has spawned new offshore financial centers (Dubai, Labuan and Samoa) and transformed existing low-tax jurisdictions (Hong Kong and Singapore, which were discussed in Chapter Five).

Here we describe the competition among these newer offshore centers and the struggle for acceptance in the offshore world.

The Cook Islands

Way out in the South Pacific (some say in the middle of nowhere) are the Cook Islands — home to a very modern code of offshore financial laws that may be just what you need: iron-clad asset protection trusts, international business companies (IBCs), limited liability partnerships, global banking and a very strict financial privacy law that really does protect your personal business. Some folks don't like too much distance between themselves and their assets, yet distance provides greater protection — especially here.

The islands are named after Captain James Cook, (1728—1779), British globe girdling seafaring explorer, navigator, cartographer, and captain in the Royal Navy, who sighted the islands in 1770. (Cook was also the first European to visit the Hawaiian Islands, where on his third trip there in 1779, he was killed by natives.) The Cook Islands became a British protectorate in 1888 and in 1900 administrative control was transferred to New Zealand. Hundreds of islanders fought alongside British troops in Europe in World War I.

In 1965 CI residents voted for self-government in free association with the country of New Zealand. The emigration of skilled CI workers to New Zealand, government deficits, and limited natural resources are continuing concerns here.

Independent but Dependent

If you're researching the more esoteric parts of the world of offshore asset protection, you'll soon learn about the Cook Islands. Since 1981, when the government there first began adopting (and updating) a series of wealth and asset-friendly laws, the Cook Islands, though small in population and geographically remote, have earned a definite role in offshore financial circles.

The Cook Islands are a self-governing parliamentary democracy in a loose constitutional association with New Zealand, 2009 miles to the southwest in the South Pacific. As a member of the Commonwealth, Queen Elizabeth II is Head of State and New Zealand has a CI High Commissioner there. The Prime Minister and cabinet are appointed from among elected members of a Westminster-style parliament elected every four years by universal suffrage. The legal system is based on British common law and closely reflects that of New Zealand and other Commonwealth jurisdictions.

The people are ethnically like New Zealand Maoris, living in widely scattered islands in the South Pacific halfway between New Zealand and Hawaii, southwest of Tahiti. The capital, Avarua, on Rarotonga Island, has direct flights to Los Angeles, Hawaii and New Zealand. The climate is tropical with typhoons in summer.

The Cook Islands are spread over 850,000 square miles, with 15 coral islands in the central heart of the South Pacific. The islands occupy an area the size of India, with a declining population (9,290 in 2017) no larger than an American small town. Local time is 10 hours behind GMT, with 9 a.m. in Hong Kong being 3 p.m. the previous day in the Cook Islands. When it is 9 a.m. in the islands, it is 2 p.m. EST the same day in the eastern United States. This geographic location and modern communications give the Cook Islands a strategic time advantage in dealing with both the Asian and American markets.

Indirectly, the islands are part of the British Commonwealth by their unique association with nearby New Zealand. From 1901 to 1965, the Cook Islands were a colony of New Zealand and NZ still subsidizes the CI government. This New Zealand subsidy has become a sore point for both nations. The islanders even have dual New Zealand and Cook Islands citizenship.

Like many other South Pacific island nations, Cook Island's economic development is hindered by isolation from foreign markets, limited domestic markets, lack of natural resources, periodic devastation from natural disasters and inadequate infrastructure. Agriculture, employing more than one-quarter of the working population, provides the economic base with major exports made up of copra and citrus fruit. Beautiful black pearls are the Cook Islands' leading export. The 2016 annual GDP is estimated at US$250 million with per capita GDP at less than US$15,000.

Planned Offshore Center

The Cook Islands' offshore financial industry resulted from the government's official collaboration with the local financial services industry. Financial services now rank second only to tourism in the economy.

Despite some 50,000 visitors a year to the capital island, Rarotonga, the islands have remained largely unspoiled. In 2017, *Forbes* and *Readers Digest* both cited Muri Beach as one of the best beaches in the world. Cook Islanders have their own language and enjoy a vigorous and diverse culture, though most speak English. The New Zealand dollar is the local currency, but most offshore transactions are in U.S. dollars.

This is a microstate with macro aspirations, but the grasp at times exceeds the reach. Their checkered history of high finance has been marked by some scandals, sponsored by fast-talking American, U.K. and New Zealand expatriates.

The CI government is in debt, much of it a result of past bad decisions. Two-thirds of the workforce is on the government payroll, financing an old-fashioned spoils and patronage system. In the 1980s and 1990s, the government had debt due to a significant amount of foreign debt and a bloated public service. To rebuild, it reformed by selling state assets, improving the economic management, restructuring its debt, and developing its tourism.

Local taxation includes a 20% corporation tax and resident personal income tax at rates up to 30%. There is a VAT of 12.5% and stamp duties. Withholding tax on payments including interest to non-residents is 15%. The Cook Islands have no double taxation treaties, but 21 TIEAs are in effect, none with the U.S. In 2016, the CI signed the OECD Multilateral Convention allowing automatic exchange of information in tax matters.

Companies can take advantage of low rates of taxation by locating their websites in the Cook Islands. These websites, which perform functions such as sales and marketing, supply of financial services, treasury management, and most of all, the supply of digital goods, operating in the Cook Islands now escape high-tax jurisdictions.

Tailored Wealth Protection

But don't let the deficits and the distance put you off. There is much here to cheer the hearts of knowledgeable offshore financial enthusiasts.

Existing statutes meticulously provide for the care and feeding of IBCs, limited liability companies (LLCs), as well as offshore banks, insurance companies and trusts. All offshore business conducted on the Cook Islands must be channeled through one of the six registered trustee companies. A comprehensive range of trustee and corporate services is offered for offshore investors. The government officially guarantees no taxes will be imposed on offshore entities.

Thousands of foreign trusts, corporations and partnerships are registered here, protected by an exceedingly strong financial privacy law, although that has been tempered somewhat by the adoption of OECD standards for the exchange of tax information among governments.

Strict Confidentiality

Notwithstanding this adherence to OECD tax information exchange rules, strong financial and banking secrecy applies in the offshore regime, requiring government officials as well as trustee company and bank employees to observe strict secrecy backed by criminal sanctions. The official registrar records of foreign companies and of international trusts are not open for general search, with defined exceptions under the Financial Transactions Reporting Act of 2004 and the Proceeds of Crimes Act of 2003.

According to Puai Wickman, a leading CI trust officer, when the CI government receives a request for tax information from a foreign government with which it has signed a tax information exchange treaty, the standard of proof required of the alleged tax evasion or tax fraud is "beyond a reasonable doubt." Approval for release of requested tax, or any other information concerning foreign holdings, must be approved by a court applying this standard. Few foreign government TIEA requests have been granted and few have been received.

The CI Development Investment Act requires all foreign enterprises (those with more than one-third foreign ownership) to first obtain approval and register their planned activities with the CI Development

Investment Board. There are various incentives and concessions for tariff protection: import duty and levy concessions; tax concessions by way of accelerated depreciation; allowance for counterpart training; and recruitment of Cook Islanders from overseas.

Updated Laws

The Cook Islands parliament systematically has adopted a series of anti-money laundering, financial reporting and anti-financial crime laws. These laws were sufficient to get them removed from the Financial Action Task Force blacklist, which was their stated objective.

The laws liberalize the extent to which local financial institutions are obligated to disclose information and override all other laws, making compliance with anti-money-laundering laws and standards paramount, but only with court approval, as stated above.

This law instituted a due process procedure before information can be released, including a formal request to the Financial Intelligence Unit showing reasonable grounds to believe that money laundering or criminal activities have occurred. This ensures that any disclosure is through proper channels with legal justification. This same procedure is also used for tax information exchange requests from foreign governments.

International companies incorporated here have a great deal of flexibility in corporate structure with provisions for ease of administration and maximum benefit in global commercial transactions. Incorporation can be completed within 24 hours.

Cook Islands APT

It's no secret that certain American asset protection attorneys played a large role in advising the government on asset protection issues, drafting statutes for the island's parliament. In 1989, by an amendment to the 1984 International Trusts Act, the Cook Islands introduced what experts judge to be the best modern asset protection trust (APT).

This legislation was considered cutting edge at the time and, because of its excellence, has since been copied and adopted in law by other offshore centers and by several American states. Both government and trust companies here constantly update this law and develop new products to meet the complexities of the offshore world.

As we explained in Chapter Three, Part 2, an offshore APT offers strong protection for personal and/or business assets, far greater than a domestic American trust can assure.

If a trust is registered in a non-U.S. jurisdiction that doesn't enforce foreign legal claims, the property held therein is safe, even if the existence of the trust is known to U.S. litigants and U.S. courts. Unlike foreigners who invest in U.S. real estate via LLCs because they provide privacy, offshore trusts protect by being untouchable according to the laws of the countries where they are located.

But remember, a foreign trust can hold title to U.S. real estate, but that won't protect it, because the property physically is in the U.S. and can therefore be attached by a U.S. court.

The best foreign jurisdictions have courts that are reliably refusing automatic enforcement of U.S. and other foreign judgments. That is why we have recommended the Cook Islands as a leading location for trust registration and operation.

Foreign court judgments are not enforced automatically in the Cook Islands. All foreign judgments must be retried and proven again in a CI court. Since the Cook Island's 1989 trust law was enacted, there has been only one case that challenged a Cook Islands trust — and the CI court upheld the trust and refused to enforce the U.S. judgment.

The value of Cook Islands trust assets is not disclosed publicly, and it is illegal to identify the beneficiary of a trust or to provide any information about them, unless by CI court order. The government officially guarantees that it will impose no taxes on trusts based here. CI trusts have other significant advantages relative to U.S. trusts. Majority decisions by co-trustees are permitted, rather than unanimous decisions. It is possible quickly to transfer a CI trust to another country and register it there, (a process known as "portability").

"Duress clauses" are permitted in trust deeds, which means a legal attack against the trust requires the trustee to shut down the trust operation and guard against any foreign court orders. A trust can be perpetual and can operate for multiple generations. CI trusts are full legally under U.S. tax and other laws and are reportable to the IRS.

In a major American legal case, the U.S. government tried to force the repatriation of funds under a CI trust and lost, even though the Americans who created the trust for a time were jailed in the U.S. for contempt of court. Not even a U.S. federal court could crack the Cook Island trust laws. (*FTC* vs. *Affordable Media LLC*,179 F. 3rd 1228, U.S. Ct. of Appeals, 9th Cir. 1999).

A CI trust can be specially designed for you, giving all the benefits described here with starting assets of $100,000 up to US$250,000. Origination fees are about US$10,000, a fraction of the cost of most U.S. trusts and many offshore trust options. Those with a higher net worth or numerous beneficiaries with special requirements will need a more complex trust at a higher cost, but our recommended U.S. and Cook Islands partners can assist with that, too.

If you are interested in creation of a Cook Islands APT, contact Puai T. Wichman listed below who provides CI trust services to U.S. persons.

Puai T. Wichman LLB, Managing Director
Ora Fiduciary (Cook Islands) Limited
Global House, P.O. Box 92
Avarua, Rarotonga, Cook Islands
Tel.: +682 27047
USA Direct Tel.: 734-402-7047
Mobile: +682 55418
Email: puai@oratrust.com or info@oratrust.com
Web: http://oratrust.com

With 20 years of trust and company management experience, Puai Wichman heads Ora Fiduciary (Cook Islands) Ltd., one of six registered trustee companies in the Cook Islands. A native Cook Islander, Puai is a qualified attorney in both the CI and New Zealand and is a former president of the Cook Islands Trustee Companies Association. He holds a law degree from the University of Auckland, New Zealand, and is a member of the Asia Offshore Association. He welcomes inquiries from Banyan Hill members and assists in trust and corporate creation and in opening local bank accounts.

Licensed Cook Islands Trust Companies:

Southpac Trust Limited
Tarita Hutchinson, Managing Director
ANZ House, P.O. Box 11
Maire Nui Road, Avarua, Rarotonga, Cook Islands
Skype: southpac-tarita
Tel.: +682 20 514
Email. THutchinson@southpactrust.com
Web: www.southpactrust.com

Asiaciti Trust Pacific Limited: http://www.asiacititrust.com

Cook Islands Trust Corporation Limited:
http://cookislandstrust.com

HSBC Trustee (Cook Islands) Limited:
http://www.hsbcprivatebank.com

Portcullis TrustNet (Cook Islands) Limited:
http://www.portcullis.co/expertise/trust-services

Domestic Banks:

ANZ Banking Group Limited:
http://www.anz.com/cookislands/en/personal

Bank of the Cook Islands Limited: http://www.bci.co.ck

Capital Security Bank Cook Islands Limited:
https://www.capitalsecuritybank.com

International Banks:

ANZ Banking Group Limited: https://www.anz.com.au/personal

Capital Security Bank Ltd:
https://www.capitalsecuritybank.com

Recommended Bank:

Capital Security Bank Limited
P.O. Box 906
Centrepoint, Avarua
Rarotonga, Cook Islands
Tel.: +682 22505
Email: info@capitalsecuritybank.com
Web: www.capitalsecuritybank.com

Government:

Cook Islands Financial Supervisory Commission
P.O. Box 594, Avarua
Rarotonga, Cook Islands
Tel.: +682 20798
Email: Inquire@fsc.gov.ck
Web: https://www.fsc.gov.ck/cookIslandsFscApp/content/home

Ministry of Finance & Economic Management:
http://mfem.gov.ck

Cook Islands Tourism: http://www.cookislands.travel

Malaysia (Labuan)

Malaysia is a pleasant, hassle-free country in Southeast Asia. It is wealthy, and pluralist based on a fusion of Malay, Chinese, Indian and indigenous cultures. Malaysia's love of Western-style industrialization is seen in its big cities. Aside from gleaming modern glass towers, Malaysia has some of the best beaches, mountains and national parks in Asia. It is also home to an officially planned and promoted offshore financial center, called "Labuan" which has tried to become the world's leading Islamic financial center.

Unwanted Notice

Many people had never heard of Malaysia until the fateful day of March 8, 2014. That was the date that a Malaysian Airlines Boeing 777, carrying 239 passengers and crew, became an aviation tragedy and mystery by vanishing during a flight from Kuala Lumpur to Beijing.

Years later, after authorities had combed about 60% of a 23,000-square-mile search area in the southern Indian Ocean, the mystery remained. Many were frustrated with the Malaysian government and its inept handling of the affair. In 2018, the government claimed it was still looking.

To add to their national woes, on July 17, 2014, Malaysia Airlines Flight MH17, flying from Amsterdam to Kuala Lumpur, was shot down in Ukraine by Vladimir Putin's thugs attempting to destabilize the Ukrainian government. All 283 passengers and 15 crew were killed by the Russian BUK ground-to-air missile.

Observers say the mishandling of the lost plane was a symptom of much larger problems, including political disunity and the uninterrupted 62-year rule by the country's largest political party, United

Malays National Organization (UMNO), which rules in a coalition government.

Starting in 2014, an investment scandal in the state investment firm, 1 Malaysia Development Berhad (1MDB), exposed US$12 billion in unexplained debts triggering investigations in six countries, including the U.S., Singapore and Switzerland.

History

Malaysia is a southeastern Asian peninsula bordering Thailand and the northern one-third of the island of Borneo. It borders Indonesia, Brunei and the South China Sea, south of Vietnam.

The country exists under many different influences. It was ruled by the Portuguese, Dutch and British over five centuries. During the late 18th and 19th centuries, Great Britain established colonies and protectorates in Malaysia, which were militarily occupied by Japan from 1942 to 1945. In 1948, the British-ruled territories on the Malay Peninsula formed the Federation of Malaya and gained independence in 1957.

Malaysia is really two countries in one, cut in half by the South China Sea. The peninsula is a multicultural mix of Malay, Chinese and Indian, while Borneo hosts a wild jungle of orangutans, granite peaks and remote native tribes. These two regions offer a stark contrast of state-of-the-art high rises in Kuala Lumpur, the capital, compared to Sarawak's remote villages or the serene beaches of the Perhentian Islands.

Malaysia is comprised of three federal territories and 13 states. It was first formed back in 1963 when former British colonies of Singapore, as well as Sabah and Sarawak (both East Malaysian states located on the northern tip of Borneo) joined the Federation. Two years later, in 1965, Singapore became independent.

In his 22-year tenure from 1981 to 2003, Prime Minister Mahathir bin Mohammad successfully helped diversify Malaysia's economy from its previous dependence on raw materials by expanding into tourism, manufacturing and services. His leadership converted the nation's plantation-based economy into what has been called an "Asian Tiger."

In 2017, Prime Minister Najib Razak launched huge infrastructure products, including the world's first Digital Free Trade Zone (DFTZ) in March together the Alibaba Group. National elections must be held before August 2018. Najib was said to have consolidated his power, leading to optimism within his UMNO party about the upcoming election.

The western half of Malaysia is bustling and commercial, with urban centers sprinkled throughout the tropical vegetation of the country. Much of this development in the west is driven by the energy of its Chinese business community. In the east, Malays constitute the majority and agriculture, fishing and cottage industries predominate. Life in the east is quiet and laid back where one experiences the traditional Malay culture.

Boosted by economic diversity and a move away from raw materials, Malaysia also found economic success in large part due to a boom in electronic exports. Additionally, the country has benefitted from oil and gas exports, with big profits rolling in from worldwide high energy prices. Healthy foreign exchange reserves have managed to keep Inflation and external debt low. The economy remains dependent on continued consumer growth in the U.S., China and Japan — all top export destinations and key sources of foreign investment.

The World Economic Forum named Malaysia as the region's top emerging economy in its Global Competitiveness Report for 2017-2018, listing it as 23rd out of 137 countries in Global Competitiveness Index, ahead of even China.

Planned Islamic Financial Center

In the mid-1980s, Malaysian leaders, with British-controlled Hong Kong about to be handed over to the Communist Chinese in 1997, decided to establish their own international offshore financial center. They located it on Labuan, a small island off the coast of Borneo; it was formally launched in 1990. Together with the enactment of a series of offshore-friendly laws, the Malaysian government created the Labuan International Business and Financial Center.

Labuan, a designated federal territory within Malaysia, is a group of islands located off the northwest coast of the island of Borneo facing the South China Sea. It is comprised of Pulau (a Malay word meaning "island"), Labuan and six smaller islands. Bahasa Melayu (Malay) is the native language, but English is widely spoken, as well as Chinese dialects and Tamil. Labuan is 35.5 square miles in size, with a population of about 97,000, with a good harbor and airport.

Islam is the official religion, but freedom of worship is guaranteed by law. Labuan, like the rest of Malaysia, has a local island parliamentary system of government based on the British common law.

Low Taxes, Legal Structures

Labuan offers low-tax/no-tax corporate structures and provides a modern banking system that in 2017 had US$10.4 billion in total assets held by 52 banks. In 2017, the Inland Revenue Board audited 15 banks with offshore dealings as part of anti-tax evasion enforcement aimed at Malaysian citizens.

There are two categories of companies, trading, and non-trading. A Labuan "trading" company is an operating business that sells products or services to customers. A Labuan "non-trading" company is a traditional holding company that owns assets or other companies that earns dividends, rents, and royalties. Labuan's offshore center offers services including banking, insurance, trust creation, international business corporations and investment fund management. China is Malaysia's largest trade partner.

Offshore income is tax-free and there is no withholding, capital gains, or dividend tax. For trading companies that operate a business, there is an option to either pay 3% of their profits, or simply pay a flat tax of 20,000 Malaysian ringgits (US$5,000). Since Malaysia has double taxation treaties with many countries, foreigners whose business qualify under a tax treaty can operate a Labuan company and pay the low Malaysian tax instead of paying higher taxes in their home country.

Labuan offshore companies can make good use of Malaysia's double tax treaty network. This has made the island the preferred conduit for foreign direct investment in neighboring Asian countries including Korea and Malaysia itself. A stock exchange established in 2000, aiming particularly at the listing of Islamic financial debt issues, has had considerable success. The main advantage Labuan enjoys is its role as a center for developing Islamic financial law.

Islamic financial practices follow *Shari'a*, Islamic law based on the Koran. The law specifically prohibits the receipt or payment of interest and any transaction that involves gambling or speculation, a category that includes futures contracts, interest rate hedging and other financial arrangements common in the West.

In lieu of the payment of interest, Islamic institutions pay investors a share of their profits. Making a profit is not prohibited, but Muslims believe that financial relationships should be equal rather than hierarchical. Thus, profit sharing is preferable to interest, which implies the unequal relation of debtor to creditor.

The amount of wealth estimated to be under professional management in the world Islamic financial sector is about US$400 billion, a small quantity in comparison with the global capital market, but still a significant and growing niche that Labuan seeks to serve. That wealth has produced competitors in other offshore financial centers such as Jersey, Guernsey and the Isle of Man that now cater to *Shari'a* law clients worldwide.

Contacts:

Embassy of Malaysia
3516 International Court NW
Washington, D.C. 20008
Tel.: 202-572-9700

Email: mwwashington@kln.gov.my
Web: http://www.kln.gov.my/web/usa_washington/home

Consulate General-Los Angeles
777 South Figueroa Street Suite 600
Los Angeles, CA 90071
Tel.: 213-892-1238
Email: lax.info@kln.gov.my
Web: http://www.kln.gov.my/web/usa_los-angeles/home

Consulate General-New York City
313 East 43rd Street
New York, NY 10017
Tel.: 212-490-2722 / 212-490-2723
Email: mwnewyorkcg@kln.gov.my
Web: http://www.kln.gov.my/web/usa_new-york/home

United States Embassy
376 Jalan Tun Razak
50400 Kuala Lumpur, Malaysia
Tel.: + 60-3-2168-5000
Email: klacs@state.gov
Web: https://my.usembassy.gov

Ministry of Foreign Affairs, Malaysia
Wisma Putra
No. 1, Jalan Wisma Putra, Precinct 2
62602 Putrajaya
Tel.: +603-8000-8000
Web: http://www.kln.gov.my/web/guest/home

Labuan International Business and Financial Center
Suite 3A-2, Level 2, Block 3A
Plaza Sentral
Jalan Stesen Sentral, KL Sentral
50470 Kuala Lumpur

Tel.: +603-2773-8977
Email: info@libfc.com
Web: http://www.labuanibfc.com

Tourism Malaysia: http://www.malaysia.travel/en/us

Republic of Mauritius

Mauritius is the most accessible island in the Indian Ocean, boasting a tropical paradise at bargain prices. Though geographically near South Africa, it's more influenced by its British and French ties and a predominantly Indian workforce. It is the offshore financial center of choice for wealthy Indians - and a favorite target of India's tax collectors. A stable democracy with regular free elections and a positive human rights record, the country has attracted considerable foreign investment and has one of Africa's highest per capita incomes.

Mauritius is a volcanic island of lagoons and palm-fringed beaches in the middle of the Indian Ocean off the coast of Southern Africa and approximately 500 miles east of the island of Madagascar. It is strategically located between India, Africa and Asia. The tiny island country is praised as being one of Africa's success stories.

It has a reputation for stability and racial harmony among its mixed population of 1.3 million Asians, Europeans and Africans. The island has maintained one of the developing world's most successful democracies and has usually enjoyed continued constitutional order. But are some disturbing clouds on the political horizon that could affect the country's standing as a major African offshore financial center.

One troubling development is the recent emersion of jihadi recruits influenced by a small network of radical Muslim ideologues.

The group, Abu Faaris, has links with two other Islamist social groups, both sympathizers with Islamic State ideology. Their public calls for Shariah law have become more prominent. Some think the group has some support among the people, especially with young Mauritians, converts to Islam and those swayed by economic complaints.

This raises the risk of attacks against Western targets on the island's international tourism, and against the government itself, which follows progressive, pro-Western policies. No terrorist violence has occurred, but it could undermine tourism a main source of income and create political instability.

An independent member of the Commonwealth since 1968, Mauritius officially became a republic in 1992. The country's official language is English and its people are predominantly Indo-Mauritian. The dominant religion of the country is Hindu. The government of Mauritius is presidential. It has a single elected National Assembly as well as a Council of Ministers, which is headed by a Prime Minister. The region's mixed French and British ancestry shines through in its legal system, while administration can be bureaucratic with a French influence.

Mauritius first explorers hailed from Portugal in the early 1500s, not counting Arab and Malay sailors in the 10th century. It was later claimed by the Dutch, French and then British in the 1800s, before achieving independence from the U.K. in 1968. The Republic boasts a stable democracy with free elections and a laudable human rights record. As a result, it has attracted considerable foreign investment and garnered one of Africa's highest per capita incomes.

Since breaking free from the U.K. 50 years ago, Mauritius has evolved from a low-income, agrarian economy to a highly diversified industrial, financial and tourism base. The country, with green sugar cane fields, blue lagoons and jagged volcanic mountains, is known for its palm-fringed beaches and cobalt blue seas, attracting nearly a million tourists annually. This has brought more equitable income distribution, greater life expectancy, lower infant mortality and better infrastructure. Mauritius' sound economic policies and banking practices countered negative effects of the 2008 global financial crises.

GDP grew 3 to 4% per year between 2010 and 2017. It continues to expand its global trade and investment outreach, boosted by major public infrastructure projects. The unemployment rate was 6.9% in 2017. Global businesses based in Mauritius have assets valued at US$630 billion, almost 25 times the tax haven's GDP of US$27.44 billion in 2017. Most of this is investment in real estate, hotels and restaurants. France is the main source of investment.

Africa's Offshore Financial Center

The economic development policy of the Mauritian government has focused on nurturing offshore financial services through the expansion of local financial institutions, as well as supporting the domestic information telecommunications industry. At latest count Mauritius claims more than 32,000 offshore entities (IBCs, trusts), most of which are focused on Indian, Chinese and South African commerce, with a banking sector exceeding US$1 billion. Financial Services account for 10.3% of GDP with 4% from cross-border transactions. Mauritius ranks first in sub-Saharan Africa in the World Bank's Doing Business Report.

The Mauritius offshore sector takes a cautious course. Until 1998, offshore laws allowed zero taxation across a range of offshore activities, including international business corporations (IBCs), banking, shipping, insurance and fund management, as well as in free trade zones. The legal system is a hybrid combination of both civil and common law practices.

Mauritius has decided to be a "respectable" offshore financial center. Thus "tax free" is gone and there is now a tax rate of 15% in most areas, although corporate exemptions can reduce the tax to as low as 3%. Mauritius has tax treaties with 30 countries that can be combined with offshore laws to produce profitable trade and investment, especially for the many thousands of wealthy Indian investors. According to the World Bank, it ranks first in Africa for ease of doing business, surpassing even South Africa to become the continent's most competitive economy.

IBCs are known here as "Global Business Licenses Categories 1 and 2." A GBL-1 is used for international tax planning and structuring and is appropriate for investment funds or mutual funds seeking relief under double taxation agreements. A GBL-2 is not considered as resident in Mauritius and is therefore exempt from local taxation, but it cannot access the benefits of the network of double tax agreements. It is primarily used for non-financial consultancy, trading, logistics, marketing or invoicing.

With a strong anti-money laundering law, it has managed to avoid both the OECD and Financial Action Task Force (FATF) blacklists. Offshore laws are continually modernized, kept up to date and competitive. Mauritius's African neighbors have complained that the island's gains have come at their expense and have taken their case to the international community. As a result, in 2015, the European Commission placed Mauritius on a Top 30 blacklist of tax havens. However. The government is committed to adopt in 2018 the OECD automatic exchange of tax information program.

Tax Conflict with India

Mauritius has been one of the largest sources for foreign direct investment in India. According to the *Financial Times*, the country accounted for 43% of all foreign direct investment flows into India, thanks to a favorable Mauritian tax agreement with New Delhi.

Mauritius had been criticized by the government of India because of its role as a tax haven for wealthy Indians. Of the total US$81 billion foreign direct investment (FDI) that came into India during since 2005, almost half (US$35.18 billion) was routed through Mauritius. By comparison, Singapore, with a far larger economy than Mauritius, sent only $2 billion in FDI to India in the same period.

Mauritius became a favorite of the Indian financial elite and a prime target of the Indian government seeking tax evaders because of the island's double tax avoidance treaty that allowed investors to take advantage of much lower tax rates in Mauritius, compared to India's higher taxes. Foreign institutional investors had invested more than US$100 billion in Indian equities sent to India through Mauritius holding companies.

In 2012, India's high court ruled that India's tax collectors had no power to collect taxes on transactions in Mauritius, saving the Indian Vodafone Company many millions. The Indian government promptly proposed a set of general anti-avoidance rules (GAAR) that empowered revenue authorities to deny tax benefits to arrangements that had no commercial substance, but implementation was delayed until 2017.

The debate on whether treaty shopping is tax planning or tax avoidance, largely has ended. Re-negotiation of the 1983 India-Mauritius tax treaty confirmed India's taxing rights on capital gain income arising on shares of an Indian company acquired on or after April 1, 2017. Investments made before that date were grandfathered exempting all existing investments from Indian capital gains tax. This allowed past tax breaks for Indians using Mauritius but ended future benefits.

In 2015, India's "pro-business" Prime Minister, Narendra Modi, visited the island nation and Mauritius leaders expressed appreciation for India's revision of the treaty.

Contacts:

Government of Mauritius: http://www.mauritiusgovernment.com

Embassy of Mauritius
1709 N Street NW
Washington, D.C. 20036
Tel.: 202-244-1491
Email: mauritius.embassy@verizon.net
Web: http://www.maurinet.com/tourist_information/mauritius_embassies

United States Embassy in Mauritius & Seychelles
4th Floor, Rogers House
John Kennedy Avenue
Port Louis, Republic of Mauritius
Tel.: +230-202-4400
Email: usembass@intnet.mu
Web: https://mu.usembassy.gov

Mauritius Mission to the United Nations
211 East 43rd Street, 22nd Floor
New York, NY 10017
Tel.: 212-949-0190 / 0191
Email: mauritiusmissionnyc@gmail.com
Web: www.newyork.mauritius.govmu.org

Tourism Mauritius: http://www.mauritius.net

Mauritius Business and Travel Directory:
https://mauritiusdirectory.org

Samoa

If you're looking for a tax haven that has an inside track with the People's Republic of China, or if you need to form a trust or corporation yesterday, this small Pacific island nation that sits on the other side of the International Dateline may be your best bet.

Writing in *The National Forum*, an Australian e-journal, former Australian diplomat, David Morris tells us: "Samoa is a world of beautiful beaches, waterfalls and sumptuous seafood and abundant fruit, with an easy-going people whose welcome ("*Talofa!*") is as warmly offered as it is meant. It's a place, and a state of mind, that's hard to leave. And in a sense Samoans never leave. Even when they live and work in New Zealand or Australia, Samoans retain strong links to their villages, their families and, indeed, support the Samoan economy with their remittances."

The few professionals who really know offshore financial centers realize the relative importance of The Independent State of Samoa, a group of seven islands in the heart of the South Pacific Ocean, about halfway between Hawaii and New Zealand. The islands include Upolu, home to most of Samoa's population, and Savai'i, one of the largest islands in the South Pacific.

In 1914, at the outbreak of World War I, New Zealand occupied this former German protectorate then known as "Western Samoa." In 1997 it dropped "Western" from its name. New Zealand administered the islands as a UN mandate and then as a trust territory until 1962, when the islands became the first Polynesian nation to reestablish independence in the 20th century. This small seven-island country had an estimated population of 200,108 in 2017. Rugby is the fervently followed but financially troubled national sport.

In 1975, Samoa became one of the first countries in the South Pacific to grant diplomatic recognition to the People's Republic of China. That led in Samoa to the creation of an Asian niche market for its offshore financial center servicing business in mainland China and the Far East. Because of massive amounts of aid from China, Samoa tends to be an offshore financial center especially for Chinese investors and it caters to them.

China has a major presence here with a long-standing Chinese community in the capital, Apia. The Chinese government provides in-kind assistance, grants and soft loans. Beijing paid for a US$100 million hospital in Apia, a new office complex for the Prime Minister and another government building nearby. Chinese agricultural experts guide a rice-growing project and other cash crops in Samoa.

The economy of Samoa traditionally depends on development aid and loans from other countries (China, Japan, Australia and New

Zealand), family remittances from more than 100,000 Samoans who live abroad, and agriculture and fishing. The country is vulnerable to devastating cyclones. In 2009, an earthquake and the resulting tsunami severely damaged Samoa, and nearby American Samoa, disrupting transportation and power generation, resulting in nearly 200 deaths.

Agriculture, including fishing, employs two-thirds of the labor force and furnishes 90% of exports, featuring fish, coconut oil, and taro. The manufacturing sector mainly processes agricultural products. Tourism is an expanding sector, accounting for 25% of GDP. The country had approximately 145,000 tourists in 2016. The island nation's luxurious Return to Paradise Resort opened in 2014 and has received international praise. In 2017, the GDP was US$1.13 billion, and per capita GDP $5,700.

Offshore Financial Center

For those looking for legal entities to be used in the Asia in general or especially in China, Samoa is an interesting alternative to Hong Kong and Singapore. Along with the Cook Islands, the strategic location of Samoa, just east of the International Date Line in the South Pacific, allows an Asian investor the unusual ability to register a company "yesterday."

The Samoan government supports maximum deregulation of the financial sector, encourages investment and continued fiscal discipline. This is reflected in healthy foreign reserves, low inflation, and manageable external debt. The government mixes tribal leadership with parliamentary democracy under a British common law legal system.

There are five major laws enabling Samoa's role as an international finance center:

1. The International Companies Act of 1987 is the business corporation law.

2. The International Banking Act of 2005 allows three types of bank licenses subject to the Basel international banking standards. All holders of international banking licenses must establish an office in Samoa, have at least two directors who must be individuals and employ at least one person.

3. The International Trusts Act of 1987 governs the creation and registration of offshore asset protection trusts.

4. The Trustee Companies Act of 1987 is the licensing law for trustee companies, which include corporate service providers, those who deal directly with clients. Only established professionals with international connections are accepted.

5. The International Insurance Act of 1988 allows four categories of insurance licenses, general, long term, reinsurance and captive.

All entities established under the offshore laws, except for licensed trustee companies, are exempt from all local taxation, currency and exchange controls and stamp duties.

Fortunately for Samoa, out of concern for its offshore finance center it enacted the Money Laundering Prevention Act of 2000. Thus, the islands never appeared on the OECD and FATF blacklists. Samoa was among the first countries to commit to the OECD principles of transparency and tax exchange of information. In 2018 it began applying the OECD common reporting standards allowing official automatic exchange of tax information.

Contacts:

Government of Samoa: http://www.govt.ws
Embassy of the Independent State of Samoa
800 Second Avenue, Suite 400D
New York, NY 10017
Tel.: 212-599-6196
Email: samoa@un.int
Web: http://www.embassy.org/embassies/ws.html

United States Embassy
5th Floor, ACC Building
Matafele Apia, Samoa
Tel.: +685 21436 or +685 21452
Email: AmEmbApia@state.gov or Apiaconsular@state.gov
Web: https://ws.usembassy.gov

Samoa International Finance Authority
Level 6, Development Bank of Samoa Building
Apia, Samoa, South Pacific
Tel.: +685 66400 / +685 24071
Email: offshore@lesamoa.net
Web: http://www.sifa.ws

Republic of Seychelles

The islands of the Seychelles form an oceanic tropical paradise. However seductive the travel brochure images, they simply can't compete with the real-life dazzling beaches and crystal-clear waters. All this and a fledgling offshore financial center that wants to serve your offshore needs quickly, efficiently and at a lower cost.

The Seychelles is a collection of 115 islands in the Indian Ocean off the east coast of Africa about five degrees south of the Equator. It gained independence from the United Kingdom in 1976. Most Seychellois are descendants of early French settlers and the African slaves brought to the islands in the 19th century by the British, who freed them from slave ships on the East African coast. Indians and Chinese (1.1%) account for other permanent inhabitants. About 4,000 expatriates live and work in Seychelles among the 93,920 people in the islands in 2017. The capital, Victoria, is located on the island of Mahe.

Seychelles culture is a mixture of French and African (Creole) influences. Creole is the native language of 94% of the people; however, English and French are commonly used. English remains the language of government and commerce.

When we consider recommending a country we consider its suitability as a place to live, the attractiveness of its tax and banking systems, the respect for the rule of law, individual freedom and the level at which it operates free market economic principles. In many of these areas of concern the Seychelles has had a struggle to meet acceptable standards.

History

After independence from the United Kingdom in 1976, socialist one-party rule bankrupted this tiny country. The economy was saddled with price, trade and foreign exchange controls, government-owned companies, and uncontrolled state debt-funded development spending.

This caused rapid economic development, but also serious problems: large fiscal and external deficits and debts, persistent foreign exchange shortages and slow growth. Press reports indicated that high-level official corruption contributed substantially to these problems.

In 2008, facing the near-depletion of official foreign exchange reserves, Seychelles defaulted on interest payments due on a US$230 million Eurobond issued two years previously, severely damaging its credibility as a borrower.

Since 1976, the country has had a checkered history of coups and counter-coups by the military and rival parties, although it appears currently stable. James Alix Michel resigned the presidency in 2016 and was succeeded by Danny Faure who serves as both chief of state and head of government. The next election is in 2020.

Economy

In 2008, the government signed a standby arrangement with the IMF that mandated floating the exchange rate, removing foreign exchange controls, cutting government spending, and tightening monetary policy. When this was done successfully, the IMF upgraded its assistance to Seychelles by US$31 million for three years. In 2014, the IMF declared that Seychelles had successfully transitioned to a market-based economy with full employment and a fiscal surplus.

The economy recovered in 2010 to 2011 after the reforms took hold and tourism increased; the islands are home to 61 hotels and resorts. Seychelles is said to be trying to implement further reforms with a new tax system, reorganizing state-owned enterprises, and deregulating finance and communications. In 2017, Seychelles became ineligible for trade benefits under the US African Growth and Opportunities Act since it gained developed country status.

Seychelles grew at 4.1% in 2017 because of a strong tourist sector and low commodity prices; its fiscal surplus reached 3% of GDP. The Seychellois government met the IMF's performance criteria for 2016, but there is a need to combat high poverty levels, estimated at 39%. In 2017, the country's estimated GDP was US$2.712 billion with a per capita GDP of US$28,900.

One bright spot has been the arrival of the Eastern Africa Submarine Cable System, an undersea fiber optic cable system connecting eastern Africa countries to the rest of the world. The system replaced an existing satellite connection. The increased bandwidth and stability significantly has enhanced the Seychelles offshore financial services and brought in an influx of other businesses.

European Union (EU) Naval Force officials have praised the support of Seychelles in deterring pirate attacks in the region, and the government assists anti-piracy activities on a continuing basis. Tourism is important and during 2017 more than 30cruise ships docked at Port Victoria. In 2017, Anse Lazio beach, in the Seychelles, came in third among the world's best beaches chosen by Flight Network, a leading Canadian online travel agency.

Offshore Financial Center

As with some other former British colonies, the Seychelles has made an increasingly successful effort at becoming an offshore financial center, with official encouragement of foreign investment in real estate and resort properties, and with much needed help from the World Bank.

Seychelles has adopted comprehensive and modern international financial services laws within the last decade. The legal system is based on a mixture of the English common law and French civil code. The company, banking, trust and other financial services laws based on English law are patterned after successful British Caribbean offshore jurisdictions.

This centerpiece has been the establishment of the Seychelles International Business Authority (SIBA) together with legislation to encourage the development of offshore companies. For a time, there was an "economic citizenship" program aimed at enticing foreigners, but that initiative died in 1997. SIBA regulates the offshore industry, registers offshore companies and also supervises the Seychelles International Trade Zone (SITZ), a development to encourage direct foreign investment, which so far has been limited.

Seychelles' offshore financial services sector has grown from 650 international business companies in 1996 to more than 145,000 in 2017. In addition, there are nearly 1,000 registered trusts and more than 300 private foundations. These increased numbers are attributed to lower, competitive pricing, fast and efficient processing and turnaround for incorporation, acceptability to international banks, tax-free foreign investments, a high degree of privacy and asset protection and ease of administration. The typical Seychelles IBC is a limited liability company which conducts its trading and business outside the islands.

Confidentiality is guaranteed by law and all civil proceedings concerning offshore entities may be held in closed session rather than in public. However, the government fully complies with the OECD common reporting standards allowing official automatic tax information exchange.

The currency is the Seychelles Rupee, set at a fixed rate with the U.S. dollar at 10 Rupees=0.78 USD, and dollars and euros are used. The commercial banking sector includes Barclays Bank PLC, Mauritius Commercial Bank, Bank of Baroda, Habib Bank and Seychelles International Mercantile Credit Banking Corporation (SIMBC). The first four are branches of foreign banks and the last is a joint venture between the Seychelles government and the Standard Chartered Bank Africa PLC. Commercial banks offer the full range of services.

Contacts:

The Seychelles ambassador resident in New York is accredited to the United Nations, to the United States and to Canada. The U.S. Embassy in Mauritius also serves the Seychelles.

Embassy and Mission of Seychelles
685 Third Avenue, Suite 1107
New York, NY 10017
Tel.: 212-972-1785
Email: seychellesmissionun@gmail.com or seychelles@un.int

United States Embassy in Mauritius & Seychelles
4th Floor, Rogers House
John Kennedy Avenue
Port Louis, Republic of Mauritius
Tel.: +230-202-4400
Email: usembass@intnet.mu
Web: https://mu.usembassy.gov

Permanent Mission of Seychelles to the United Nations
800 Second Avenue, Suite 400C
New York, N.Y. 10017
Tel.: 212-972-1785
Email: seychelles@un.int
Web: http://www.un.int/seychelles

Financial Services Authority Seychelles (FSA)
P.O. Box 991
Bois de Rose Avenue
Roche Caiman, Victoria
Mahe, Republic of Seychelles
Tel.: +248 438 08 00
Email: siba@seychelles.net
Web: http://www.fsaseychelles.sc

Trust, Incorporation Services:

Omega International Agents Ltd.
Salamat House
La Poudriere Lane, Victoria
Mahe, Republic of Seychelles
Tel.: +248 4225356
Email: info@omega-worldwide.com
Web: www.omega-worldwide.com

United Arab Emirates: Dubai

Even though the UAE and Dubai are absolute monarchies
that greatly limit personal and political freedom, their
impressive achievements are envied in the Arab world. Dubai
has become the Arab Manhattan. Here young Arabs can come
to enjoy the arts, business, media, education and technology
start-ups with world-class companies, all this in their own
culture, language, and religious milieu, with added the
pleasures of their own preferences in food, music fashion and
the high life.

Dubai proves that Arabs can build and realize their own
potential. Dubai is one of the world's newest international
financial centers. It aims to rival New York, London and
Hong Kong, seeking to serve the vast, oil-rich region between
Europe and Asia. When Dubai began as an offshore financial
center it attracted leading Fortune 500 and regional firms,
but the global financial recession and its aftermath slowed
down Dubai — but by no means stopped its progress.

The United Arab Emirates (UAE) are in the Middle East, bordering the Gulf of Oman and the Persian Gulf, between Oman and
Saudi Arabia.

The Trucial States of the Persian Gulf coast granted the United
Kingdom control of their defense and foreign affairs in 19th century
treaties. In 1971, six of these states, Abu Zaby, 'Ajman, Al Fujayrah,
Ash Shariqah, Dubai, and Umm al-Quwain, merged to form the
United Arab Emirates (UAE). They were joined in 1972 by Ras al-
Khaimah.

The UAE union of seven sovereign sheikdoms formed when the
British withdrew from the Arabian Gulf in 1971. Strategically lo-

cated Dubai, has become the leading of the seven emirates and the UAE commercial gateway to nearly two billion consumers in Asia, Africa, Europe, India and the Middle East. Dubai is located on the Eastern coast of the Arabian Peninsula, in the southwest corner of the Arabian Gulf. It boasts mountains, beaches, deserts, oases, camel racing, markets and the renowned duty-free shopping, all packed into a relatively small area.

The United Arab Emirates extend along the Arabian Gulf coast bordering the Gulf of Oman and the Persian Gulf, between Oman and Saudi Arabia with an area of 32.2 thousand square miles.

The U.N. estimates the country's total population to be 6,072,475 as of mid-2017; immigrants account for more than 80% of the total population, according to U.N. data. Only 11.6% are UAE citizens (Emirati) with full political rights. The rest are South Asian 59.4% (Indian, Bangladeshi, Pakistani), Egyptian 10.2%, Philippine 6.1%, and others, 12.8%. Arabic and English are the dominant languages.

Jebel Ali, site of a huge man-made port, has the largest free trade zone in Arabia, home to a list of international corporations that use this zone for manufacturing and as a redistribution point. Dubai's harbor is the most important port in the Middle East and is ranked among the world's top 10 in terms of container traffic.

In 2014, Dubai's International Airport surpassed London's Heathrow to become the world's busiest air transit hub with nearly 70 million international passengers. Its second major airport, Al-Maktoum International, opened for passengers in 2013, will be capable of handling 120 million travelers annually when completed in 2022 at a cost of US$32 billion. Dubai aims to become the world's leading aviation hub, linking North America, with Asia with an over the North Pole route that skips Europe altogether.

The UAE's per capita GDP US$68,200 (2017 est.) is on par with those of leading Western European nations. It has a significant role in the broader affairs of the region because of its generosity of oil revenues and moderate stance on foreign policy.

Petroleum has dominated the UAE economy. Once being an underdeveloped area, by 1985 it became one of the highest per capita income nations in the world. That wealth allowed for investments in capital improvements and social services, spread across all of seven emirates. Petroleum production is centered in Abu Dhabi and Dubai. As oil prices and production levels lowered, tourism, aviation, real estate, and financial services now drive the UAE economy.

The Jebel Ali Free Trade Zone is home to 5,500 companies from 120 countries. Restrictions are relatively simple, with no foreign controls, trade barriers, or quotas, plus low import duties, many products even being exempt from them. The UAE currency, the dirham, is freely convertible and is linked to the U.S. dollar.

Dubai Investment Park (a.k.a. Dubai Internet City) has a highly developed technical infrastructure. More than 1,400 companies had established themselves in the DIC, including many of the big names in IT such as Microsoft, Oracle, HP, IBM, Compaq, Dell, Siemens, Canon, Sony Ericsson and Cisco with over 12,000 knowledge workers. The DIC occupies over 12 square miles south of Dubai and offers state of the art facilities for anything from manufacturing, distribution, and logistics to offices, housing, academics and research.

Of the many national economies that incurred huge debts in the boom years, Dubai stood out. In just a few years the emirate's investment arm, Dubai World, ran up US$59 billion in debt, borrowing to build glitzy real estate developments including a giant island shaped like a palm tree aimed at upscale celebrities, and investing in properties like the MGM Grand Casino in Las Vegas.

The global financial crisis, tight international credit, and deflated asset prices constricted the economy. UAE authorities tried to blunt the crisis by increasing spending and boosting liquidity in the banking sector. The crisis hit Dubai hardest, heavily exposed to depressed real estate prices. Dubai lacked cash to meet its debt obligations, prompting global concern about its solvency. A $20 billion bailout from the UAE Central Bank and the neighboring Abu Dhabi-emirate government allowed refinancing and creditors agreed to extend payment on outstanding debts through 2022.

Offshore Financial Center

The UAE is not considered a tax haven in the conventional sense, but it comes within the type of country G-20 governments oppose because of its no-tax regime. When the U.S. corporate giant Halliburton relocated its offices to tax-free Dubai there was a political outcry from the U.S. political left even though it was the company's legal right to do so.

Jebel Ali and Dubai offshore centers have positioned themselves as Middle East offshore financial centers comparable to the Cayman Islands or Liechtenstein. Observers predict the UAE is becoming the world center for Islamic finance. With a GDP per capita in 2017 of US$68,200, the UAE ranks with the U.S. and Liechtenstein in personal income. The estimated UAE GDP for 2017 was US$691.9 billion.

Dubai's government has pursued plans to make the emirate a center for an "Islamic economy" with *sharia*-compliant businesses. This includes banking, asset management, trade, food preparation and certification, fashion, education and tourism.

Dubai is home to close to three million people, most them foreigners, especially south Asians. The city was also home to some 100,000 British and other Western expatriates, with Brits as leaders in the offshore financial sector, many of whom moved here from banks and investment firms in the City of London. The 2009 global recession caused a major exodus of expats.

More than 14 million international tourists visited the country during 2016, up from over eight million in 2010. It is estimated that that number will reach 39 million by 2024, generating visitor spending to more than US$28.5 billion. Dubai is the world's second most popular destination for shopping after the U.S. The city boasts 95 shopping malls, including the world's most visited, The Dubai Mall.

Human Rights in Dubai

For foreigners considering doing business or living in the United Arab Emirates should know that the constitution and laws supposedly promise human rights and equitable treatment of all people, regardless of race, nationality or social status. However, that seems to be a false promise.

After it began in 2010, the world watched the so-called "Arab Spring" that began in in Tunisia. Within 14 months, rulers were forced from power in Tunisia, Egypt, Libya, and Yemen. Civil uprisings and major protests erupted in seven other Arab countries. The UAE escaped the Arab Spring, but that may be because more than 100 Emirati activists were jailed and allegedly tortured because they sought reforms.

Homosexuality is a crime in the UAE. Individual rights are limited by criminal and family Sharia law, which discriminates against women. Extreme sentences have been imposed for any form of alleged drug use. In 2017, an American citizen upon arrival was arrested for possession of legal codeine prescribed for a back condition. He was held for months as U.S. diplomats tried to free him. He was released only after court proceedings that cost his family thousands of dollars.

Freedom House has stated: "Extreme forms of self-censorship are widely practiced, particularly regarding issues such as local politics, culture, religion, or any other subject the government deems politically or culturally sensitive. The Dubai Media Free Zone, an area in which foreign media outlets produce print and broadcast material intended for foreign audiences, is the only arena in which the press operates with relative freedom."

Dubai continues to be in the news as human rights organization has raised concerns regarding human rights violations. The biggest black eye is the approximately 250,000 foreign laborers who live in conditions that are "less than humane" according to Human Rights Watch. The documentary, *Slaves of Dubai*, and an expose on CBS *60 Minutes* examines these violations.

The UAE government does not offer naturalization or permanent residence to expatriates. Foreigners are permitted to purchase and own specifically designated property without a local partner or sponsor ("freeholds," as they are called).

Zero Taxes

Dubai also has one of the world's largest free trade zones and first-class Internet, media and communications infrastructure, all this and zero taxes. And Dubai has no Mutual Legal Assistance Treaties (MLATs) or tax information exchange agreements with the United States. Dubai resisted the Organization for Economic and Community Development's "harmful tax competition" initiative, defending its zero-tax regime. However, in 2018 Dubai will begin applying the OECD common reporting standards for tax information exchange.

Dubai is a good choice for companies setting up distribution channels in Europe, the Middle East, Africa and Asia. It's worth considering for a bank account, although the banks tend to cater to rich Arabs and Dubai's large expatriate community. Residence permits are easy to acquire, especially if you're hired by a local company.

Dubai seems to have limitless ambition, with plans, such for the Middle East's largest shopping mall, the new airport at Jebel Ali and the world's tallest skyscraper Burj Khalifa, known as Burj Dubai, (2,717 feet) and 164 floors.

DIFC

The Dubai International Financial Centre (DIFC) is an international financial center with an announced aim of rivaling New York, London and Hong Kong. It primarily serves the vast region of the Middle East between Western Europe and East Asia.

Since it opened in 2004, the DIFC has attracted leading global firms as well as regional firms. A world-class stock exchange, the Dubai International Financial Exchange (DIFX), opened in 2005.

The DIFC is a 110-acre free zone, part of the larger government vision of a free environment for progress and economic development in the UAE. DIFC has a total of 813 active companies located in the center.

The DIFC focuses on sectors of financial activity: 1) banking services, including investment, corporate and private banking; 2) capital markets, equity, debt instruments, derivatives and commodity trading; 3) asset management and fund registration; 4) insurance and reinsurance; 5) Islamic finance; 6) business processing operations and ancillary services. Financial institutions may apply for licenses in these sectors.

Firms operating in the DIFC are eligible for benefits such as a zero-tax rate on profits, 100% foreign ownership, no restrictions on foreign exchange or repatriation of capital and full modern operational support and business facilities.

Contacts:

Dubai Government: http://www.dubai.ae/en

Embassy of the United Arab Emirates
3522 International Court NW, Suite 400
Washington, D.C. 20008
Tel.: 202-243-2400
Email: http://www.uae-embassy.org/contact-embassy
Web: http://www.uae-embassy.org

Mission of the U.A.E. to the United Nations
3 Dag Hammarskjöld Plaza 305 East
47th Street, 7th Floor
New York, NY 10017
Tel.: 212-371-0480
Email: NYUNPRM@mofaic.gov.ae
Web: https://www.un.int/uae

United States Embassy

P.O. Box 4009
Abu Dhabi, UAE
Tel.: +971 2 414 2200
Email: AbuDhabiACS@state.gov (in Abu Dhabi) or
DubaiWarden@state.gov (in Dubai)
Web: https://ae.usembassy.gov

U.S. Consul General

Corner of Al Seef Rd. and Sheikh Khalifa bin Zayed Rd
Dubai, U.A.E
Tel.: +971-4-309-4000
Commercial Office Tel.: +971 4 311 6149
Web: https://ae.usembassy.gov/embassy-consulates/dubai

Dubai International Financial Center Authority

The Gate, Level 14
P.O. Box 74777
Dubai, UAE
Tel.: +971 (0)4 362 2222
Email: https://www.difc.ae/make-enquiry
Web: https://www.difc.ae

Department of Tourism: http://www.dubaitourism.ae

Residence & Citizenship Services:

Henley & Partners AG

Reef Tower, JLT, Suite #1301
P.O. Box 213757
Dubai, UAE
Tel.: +971 56 474 12 23
Web: https://www.henleyglobal.com

CHAPTER TEN

Atlantic/Caribbean OFCs

The wide arc from Bermuda in the mid-Atlantic to Panama in Central America and the adjacent Caribbean is home to several historic and very useful offshore financial centers. In the past, these small jurisdictions built a reputation for protecting the wealth of persons from many nations. But times are changing still, so be certain you understand the current status of any of these OFCs before you decide to do business there.

Some of these jurisdictions are British Overseas Territories and, as such, have yielded to pressure from London to restrict their tax haven status, especially curtailing what was once strict financial privacy and banking secrecy. High finance generates far more money than agriculture, tourism and fisheries combined — especially among the Atlantic and Caribbean OFCs. Bananas don't outweigh billions in cash earnings.

After World War II ended in 1945, many of the sunny islands of the Caribbean realized this economic fact and purposefully transformed themselves into international tax and asset protection centers. Some of them, as British colonies, took these steps with encouragement from their colonial masters in London. At the time, the U.K. Foreign Office saw this transformation as a way to reduce the need for colonial cash subsidies from the British Treasury. In a far freer international atmosphere decades ago, London was not much bothered by far-off colonies where foreigners paid no taxes, arrived with briefcases full of cash and bank accounts could be opened in fictitious names.

The written constitutions that govern the overseas territories pursuant to the U.K.'s Statute of Westminster (1931) allow the British Crown (i.e., the government of the moment) to bypass local legislatures by declaring an emergency and imposing its own rules. The U.K. overseas territories live with this threat as a possible limitation and temper their actions accordingly.

Historic Policy Change

In the last decades of the 20th century, British politicians and the tax collectors at the Her Majesty's Revenue and Customs began to imagine that vast sums of unpaid taxes were hidden in what London now officially calls "British Overseas Territories" ("BOTs" for short).

The socialist welfare states of Europe, joined by the United States, began to see "*tax havens*" (as they were then called) in general, as a vast sink hole of tax evasion and lost revenues. As explained in Chapter Four, tax havens came under siege from a diverse group of big government, big spending, high tax, leftist antagonists, including the European Union, the Organization for Economic Cooperation and Development (OECD), its Financial Action Task Force (FATF), and even the United Nations.

The U.S. "war on drugs" was a big boost for the U.S. Internal Revenue Service and other national tax collectors, since much of the illegal drug traffic originated in Latin America. Caribbean jurisdictions where banking secrecy ("financial privacy") had always been a positive selling point for customers now were accused of hiding millions in illicit drug money.

The term "money laundering," is defined by the *Oxford English Dictionary* as "the process of concealing the origins of money obtained illegally by passing it through a complex sequence of banking transfers or commercial transactions." While organized crime has long been associated with "laundering" dirty money, but "money laundering" as a figurative term means "sanitize, render acceptable."

In the 1970s, anti-money laundering laws became the new government imposed standard for international banking and finance. The major nations, especially the U.S. and the U.K., associated dirty money with tax havens, ignoring the fact that their own domestic onshore banks in Manhattan and the City of London laundered most of the world's criminal cash. Fighting the drug war became a useful public relations ploy and an easy, shorthand way for politicians to accuse tax havens of being criminal cash conduits.

In most cases, a lazy news media cooperated in this tax haven smear with little concern for the truth. Besides, it made for a good story — drug kingpins stashing millions in illicit cash in secret bank accounts in little-known places with unfamiliar names just looked shady. Pot-boiler novels and sensational movies picked up this questionable theme.

This anti-tax haven campaign only intensified after the terrorist attacks in New York and Washington, D.C. on September 11, 2001. In the confused aftermath of these 9/11 events, leftist politicians falsely accused offshore financial centers as serving as hiding places for the terrorist cash that financed the deaths of thousands of innocent Americans.

After an extensive investigation this assertion proved totally untrue, but that mattered little to the major nations who saw an opportunity to push their anti-tax evasion plans as "fighting terrorism." They demanded an end to financial privacy, automatic tax information exchange among all nations and abolition of the low or no taxes breaks for foreigners who did business in offshore financial centers.

The high-tax, big spending Labor Party government that took over in London in 1997 was among the strongest proponents of this new onslaught against tax havens, even though many of the leading offshore financial centers were under British jurisdiction.

Labor had strong allies in the City of London, where many financial firms viewed far off Caribbean tax havens as a drain on their business, preferring the familiar Isle of Man or the Channel Islands as business partners (see Chapter Seven). This sharp reversal of U.K. offshore policy for a time set back the British Overseas Territories in the Atlantic and Caribbean, but ultimately brought about needed reforms, much better regulation and net business gains in these jurisdictions.

The British Labor Party that viewed the U.K.'s colonial offshore tax havens with such disfavor was defeated in the 2010 general election. Since then Conservative Party dominated governments have steered a course more sympathetic to the U.K. offshore financial centers.

This history review means you must be knowledgeable when doing business with any of BOTs. In each of these jurisdictions, financial privacy and banking secrecy has been diminished but still exists, far stronger than in the U.S. All U.K. BOTs now apply the OECD Article 26 standard for tax information exchange. Importantly, in British Overseas Territories" where tax evasion by foreigners formerly was not considered a crime, it is now. The jurisdictions all have Tax Information Exchange Agreements (TIEAs) with the United States and many other countries.

What anti-tax haven London did not expect were the major "clean house" policy changes these U.K. offshore havens adopted on their own. As did the U.K. havens in the Channel Islands and the Isle of Man, the Caribbean havens adopted strict anti-money laundering, tough "know-your-customer" rules and much stronger criminal investigation units aimed at financial fraud and terrorist cash. Indeed, these jurisdictions now have tougher laws and better financial law enforcement than the U.K. or the U.S.

In our opinion, several of these Atlantic, Caribbean and Central American OFCs are examples of well-developed offshore financial centers that offer good professional, legal, banking, trust and corporate services. Insurance and annuities are also specialties. As an added attraction, some, such as Panama and Belize, offer attractive, tax-free residential retirement programs for foreigners. But if maximum financial privacy is your major concern, proceed carefully in this area.

These definite pluses must be weighed against the rapidly changing political and legal climate in these OFCs, but we again remind you to obtain the current facts before you make decisions.

Richard W. Rahn, a senior fellow at the Cato Institute, provides a good summary of the importance of OFCs: *"The fact is the world would be poorer with even less growth if the offshore financial centers did not exist — because the amount of productive investment and its efficient allocation would be less. The offshore centers are merely a response to bad tax, regulatory and spending policies in most of the major, rich countries. The major countries could conquer the offshore centers, but as the smart people know, that would make the rich countries poorer, and without a convenient scapegoat. Or, the rich countries could reduce the size of their own governments, cut tax rates on capital, and make their regulatory systems cost-efficient. Such actions would reignite growth and job creation, but reduce the power of the political and international bureaucratic classes, so they continue the big lie".*

Traditional OFCS

In a broad arc stretching southward from Bermuda in the mid-Atlantic through Central America are independent countries and some British Overseas Territories that specialize in offshore banking and finance. Each offers varying degrees of financial privacy and friendly, no-tax or low-tax special programs designed for foreigners.

Each of the sovereign nations in this group is a member of the United Nations and the more-or-less toothless Organization of American States (OAS). Some, as former British colonies, are members of the British Commonwealth and others, by their U.K. association, enjoy special participation rights in the European Union.

Most are members of the Caribbean Community (CARICOM), an area-wide economic and trade group of 16 nations. Created in 1973, the CARICOM group includes Anguilla, Antigua and Barbuda, The Bahamas, Barbados, Belize, Dominica, Grenada, Guyana, Haiti, Jamaica, Montserrat, Saint Kitts and Nevis, Saint Lucia, Saint Vincent and the Grenadines, Suriname and Trinidad and Tobago. Bermuda, the British Virgin Islands, the Cayman Islands and the Turks and Caicos Islands are associate members of CARICOM.

CARICOM members have developed the "Single Market and Economy," a space within the community that exempts most goods and services from export and import duties and that applies a common external tariff. Revenues are shared among member states. It has free trade agreements with Cuba, the Dominican Republic, Costa Rica, the European Union, and is discussing further agreements with Canada, the Mercosur bloc (Argentina, Brazil, Paraguay, Uruguay, Venezuela) and the United States.

These islands still offer superior financial services and investments in which you can have confidence without worrying about U.K. government intervention. What this U.K. history means to the average offshore investor is less financial privacy. For those trying to hide funds abroad, it means, as it should, an increased probability of discovery and prosecution.

The danger lies in a middle area in which foreign tax collectors try to conduct "fishing expeditions." They're looking for possible tax evasion simply because their citizens are financially active offshore. The TIEAs with the United States could lend themselves to just this sort of tax overreaching. But, so far, the way in which the island governments have administered the TIEAs with Washington has shown no evidence of allowing IRS fishing expeditions.

As we explained in Chapter Six, the U.K. government has adopted CDOT (informally called the "U.K. FATCA" because it is patterned after the U.S. law). "CDOT" is an acronym for the constitutional status of the 10 British offshore financial centers to which it applies; the Crown Dependencies of Jersey, Guernsey and Isle of Man, and the Overseas Territories of Gibraltar, the Cayman Islands, Bermuda, Montserrat, the Turks and Caicos Islands, the British Virgin Islands and Anguilla.

Starting in 2016, CDOT requires British OFCs to make FATCA-like disclosures about all U.K. account holders to U.K. tax authorities. Under CDOT rules, information will be provided automatically to Her Majesty's Revenue and Customs about offshore bank accounts and non-U.K. structures with U.K. resident owners, or U.K. resident settlors, beneficiaries or protectors of trust structures.

Anguilla

This luxury tourist destination offers high-priced villas and upscale resorts. The most northerly of the British Leeward Islands, it retains the laid-back character of a sleepy backwater. Goats still wander the streets and reggae music blares from cars passing luxury hotels frequented by Hollywood movie stars and Wall Street bigwigs. However, Anguilla offers a unique electronic Internet system (ACORN) for instant online registration of IBCs, trusts and other legal entities.

Anguilla (2017 est. population of 17,087) located in the Caribbean Sea between the Caribbean and North Atlantic Ocean is the northern-most island in the Leeward Islands chain, what used to be known as the British West Indies (BWI). It lies east of Puerto Rico and the British Virgin Islands.

The ubiquitous Christopher Columbus named the island after a sleek reptile Anguilla, which means eel. It was first colonized by English settlers from Saint Kitts, beginning in 1650. The island was administered by England until the early 19th century when, against the wishes of the inhabitants, it was incorporated into a single British dependency along with Saint Kitts and Nevis. After a 1967 rebellion and brief period as a self-declared independent republic, it became a separate British "dependency" (now known as a "British overseas territory") in 1980.

Located on the northernmost tip of the Leeward Islands, Anguilla is only 16 miles long and three miles wide, making it easy to get to any of its 33 public beaches. The ocean water is well-suited for wind and kite surfers and visitors with money. Tourism makes up 25% of a GDP of only around US$200 million, with a weak per capital GDP around $12,000.

The island long has been a sanctuary for celebrities in search of a secluded retreat. Recently, it has been discovered by Wall Street's jet set. Unbothered by cruise ships, the island's location off the beaten path makes the difference. In 2013, it was invaded for the filming of three episodes of Bravo-TV's *"The Real Housewives of Atlanta."*

With limited natural resources, Anguilla is dependent on luxury tourism, lobster fishing, offshore banking and remittances from emigrants. Growth in tourism sparked new construction, which led to economic growth. In addition, government officials have pushed for the development of Anguilla's offshore financial sector.

Affected by the world recession, the economy of Anguilla contracted an average 5.5% from 2008 to 2013. The impact was felt from everywhere, from tourism, which the numbers fell by the tens of thousands, to the halt of construction projects, loss of fortunes and legal actions against investors. A major airline service even left the country. The Caribbean nation's economy "virtually collapsed," according to the Eastern Caribbean Central Bank, that took control of two of Anguilla's largest banks after they exceeded limits on non-performing loans. However, reports in 2015 saw Anguilla on the comeback road as tourism markedly increased.

Electronic Offshore

Since 1998, Anguilla's Commercial Online Registration Network (ACORN) has allowed for the filing of documents and signatures in electronic form. Today, 95% of all documents, including new registrations, are filed electronically by locally licensed service providers and their approved overseas agents, who are given direct access to

ACORN. This allows the Director of Financial Services, to control and identify users. ACORN uses VeriSign digital signatures and provides the ability to encrypt transactions.

Using the latest technology, ACORN enables instant and secure electronic incorporation and registration of Anguillan domestic companies, IBCs, limited liability companies (LLCs), limited partnerships and trust companies. In addition to English, ACORN has been able electronically to incorporate companies with Chinese characters and in French, Spanish and Russian (Cyrillic). (In 2007, the government of Latvia also began offering an online digital e-business register for company formation.)

Anguilla has enacted numerous laws authorizing offshore insurance, mutual funds, trusts and private interest foundations, but with a small professional sector and limited personnel it will be a while before the island can compete fully with the established offshore "big boys."

There is no income tax, capital gains, estate, profit or other forms of direct taxation on either individuals or corporations, whether resident or not, making it attractive for financial services. There are no exchange controls. And while the official currency for Anguilla is the Eastern Caribbean dollar, the U.S. dollar is commonly used.

Anguilla is a U.K. common law jurisdiction. Its judicial system is administered by the Eastern Caribbean Supreme Court and the appeal process culminates with the Privy Council in London. There are several firms with experienced lawyers. In 2013, it adopted a statute bringing its financial activities into FATCA reporting compliance.

Contacts:

Government of Anguilla: http://www.gov.ai

There is no U.S. Embassy in Anguilla. Relations are conducted through the U.S. Embassy in London and the Embassy of the United Kingdom:

British Embassy
3100 Massachusetts Avenue NW
Washington, D.C. 20008
Tel.: 202-588-6500
Email: britishembassyenquiries@gmail.com
Web: https://www.gov.uk/government/world/organisations/british-embassy-washington

United States Embassy
24 Grosvenor Square
London, W1A 2LQ
United Kingdom
Tel.: + 44 (0)20 7499-9000
Web: https://uk.usembassy.gov

Anguilla Financial Services Commission
MAICO Building
P.O. Box 1575, The Valley
AI-2640, Anguilla, BWI
Tel.: + 1-264-497-5881
Email: info@afsc.ai
Web: http://www.fsc.org.ai

ACORN (Anguilla Commercial Online Registration Network)
P.O. Box 60, The Valley
AI-2640, Anguilla, BWI
Tel.: 1-264-497-3881/2451
Web: http://commercialregistry.ai/acorn-welcome.html

Anguilla Bar Association
First Floor, Hannah Waver House
Caribbean Commercial Centre
A1-2640, Anguilla, BWI
(Mailing: P.O. Box 147, The Valley, A1-2640, Anguilla, BWI)
Tel.: +1+ 264-461-2227
Email: info@anguillabar.com
Web: http://www.anguillabar.com

Commonwealth of The Bahamas

During the 20th century, these islands off the southeast coast of the U.S. blossomed into a major tax and asset protection haven, especially for nearby Americans and Canadians seeking tax exemption and well-crafted laws allowing IBCs, trusts, offshore banking and insurance — all wrapped in maximum financial privacy protected by law.

Because so many Americans used The Bahamas as their favorite offshore tax haven, the islands came under heavy pressure from the U.S. government and the IRS because of suspected tax evasion, drug smuggling and money laundering. In 2000, the government adopted U.S.-demanded laws that disrupted past cozy arrangements with Americans, but also diminished the islands role as an offshore financial center. The final nail in the tax evasion coffin was a Tax Information Exchange Agreement with the United States.

It's still a nice place to retire, vacation, or to have a second home, but more secure and batter banking, investment, tax and asset havens can be found elsewhere.

Geography Determines History

Geography has always played a major role in determining Bahamian history. Located at the northern edge of the Caribbean, this chain of hundreds of islands lies in the North Atlantic Ocean, south and east of Florida and northeast of Cuba. The Bahamas archipelago at its nearest point is about 50 miles and a couple of hours' boat ride east of the United States.

Arawak Indians inhabited the islands in 1492 when Christopher Columbus made his first landfall in the New World on the island of San Salvador in the eastern Bahamas. After observing the shallow sea around the islands, it is reported that he mumbled, "*Baja mar!*" (low water or sea) and thus named the area "The Bahamas," or The Islands of the Shallow Sea.

English settlement began in 1647 and the islands became a British colony in 1783. Its population in 2014 was about 321,834. Since attaining independence from the U.K. in 1973, The Bahamas have prospered through tourism, international banking and investment management. The island chain had a foreign-born population of more than 18% in 2015. While the exact number of illegal immigrants is unclear, the islands long have drawn migrants sailing from nearby Haiti. Census figures from 2010 showed more than 10% of people in The Bahamas were Haitian, up from 3.6% in 1970.

Having the United States as your next-door neighbor has not been easy for the government and the people of The Bahamas. (By the way, the proper name is not "*Bahamas*" but "*The Bahamas*" always used with a capitalized "The" by both the official Bahamian government and unofficial sources such as the BBC and the U.S. CIA.)

Offshore Powerhouse No More

The Bahamas grew from a tiny offshore tax haven comprising a few branches of foreign banks in the mid-1960s to a world banking powerhouse by the year 2000. The country's legislation and regulatory structure, comparatively highly skilled workforce and its friendly, pro-business government attracted some of the world's most prestigious financial institutions.

The Bahamas is, and has been for several decades, home to a well-developed but shrinking offshore financial center. Until a few years ago, it had more than 400 banks and trust companies, 580 mutual funds and 60 insurance companies operating here. It also had registered about 100,000 IBCs, mostly for nonresidents.

The asset base of The Bahamas' banking center was in excess of US$200 billion, positioning it among the top 10 countries in the world, behind Switzerland, the U.S., the U.K., Japan and the Cayman Islands, among others. Private banking, portfolio management and mutual fund administration are important. In those days, banks from 36 countries were licensed to conduct business within or from The Bahamas. Licensees included about 100-euro currency branches of international banks and trusts, as well as 168 Bahamian incorporated banking institutions. Sixty percent of all licensed banks offered trust services in addition to their regular banking operations.

The Bahamas is still one of the wealthiest Caribbean countries with an economy heavily dependent on tourism and offshore banking. The 2017 GDP was US$9.339 billion, and the per capita GDP was US$25,100, both down from prior years. Tourism, manufacturing, and tourism-driven construction, such as new hotels, resorts, and residences, account for close to 70 to 80% of GDP. These are also the key industries — whether directly or indirectly — that employ half of the archipelago's labor force. Even so, since the global recession, not only has tourism been affected, but so has the budget deficit. Fortunately, in recent years, The Bahamas have experienced growth. The Bahamian dollar is pegged to the U.S. dollar on a one-to-one basis.

Manufacturing and agriculture contribute to about one-tenth of GDP, and despite government incentives, doesn't look like it will be improving. Growth, at least in the short run, rest more so on tourism and foreign investments in tourism infrastructure projects.

After tourism, financial services represents the second-most important sector of the Bahamian economy. It, along with other business services, account for approximately 15% of the GDP. However, since 2000, when the government enacted new and stricter regulations on the financial sector, many international businesses abandoned The Bahamas and went elsewhere. Nevertheless, largely due to increased offshore financial activity, the GDP has grown consistently, with drops primarily between 2007 and 2013, when pillars such as financial services, tourism and construction remained weak.

Growing public debt, increases in government expenditures, a narrow revenue base, and heavy dependence on customs and property taxes have led to limited growth for The Bahamas. Previously tax free, in 2013 for the first time a graduated series of taxes was imposed on all businesses located here with an annual volume of US$5 million or more. The taxes ranged from one half of one percent to 1 and ½ percent on the total annual revenue of the business without any deductions. A 5% stamp tax also was imposed on transfers out of The Bahamas of funds greater than US$500,000 per year that represent dividends, profits or payments for services rendered by a related party. In 2015, a 7.5% value-added tax (VAT) was imposed on all goods or services supplied to a resident.

After 2000 and the adoption of new, stricter laws, 200 of the 223 private banks in The Bahamas closed and more than 30,000 international business companies were stricken from the official register. The local news media attributed these departures, at least in part, to stricter money laundering legislation and a weakening of banking and financial secrecy. Since 2013 the remaining commercial banks have been taxed 3% on their gross annual business volume.

Drastic Changes

Until 2000, The Bahamas was one of the world's premier asset and tax haven nations. But the former Free National Movement (FNM) government (later defeated for re-election) systematically began to "reform" and weaken the islands' offshore legal framework that carefully had been designed to protect financial privacy and offshore wealth brought into the islands.

This signaled retreat from tax haven status by the FNM government was a defeatist response to the double "honor" of being listed on two tax haven blacklists issued by the FATF and the OECD. These outsiders charged The Bahamas with damaging "international financial stability," being uncooperative in combating money laundering and engaging in "harmful tax competition," meaning levying no taxes on foreigners. The Bahamas were threatened with undefined "stern countermeasures" if they failed to open bank and other financial records to foreign tax and criminal investigators and to make numerous other changes in their offshore laws.

Pressure From Washington

Instead of fighting back and telling these outsiders to "buzz off," the FNM government rapidly pushed through Parliament, over strong PLP minority opposition, a host of statutory changes that substantially weakened the very financial privacy and asset protection that had attracted to the islands tens of thousands of offshore bank accounts, international business companies and asset protection trusts.

These new laws admittedly were drafted with the direct assistance of "financial experts" from London and Washington, D.C. The government also said it had accepted "a generous offer" of technical drafting assistance from the U.S. Treasury Department, no doubt including IRS agents. Indeed, the PLP signed a U.S. Tax Information Exchange Agreement initiated by the defeated FNM government. The Bahamas already had in force mutual legal assistance treaties with the U.S., U.K. and Canada.

This capitulation to Washington's demands echoed a crisis in the early 1980s when the late Prime Minister, Lynden O. Pindling, accused of drug dealing, was confronted by an angry U.S. government that threatened sanctions against The Bahamas. Although Pindling was cleared of wrongdoing, he was forced to grant U.S. FBI and DEA enforcement officers' diplomatic immunity and free passage through the archipelago, plus limited access to secret offshore bank accounts of some accused criminals.

The Progressive Labor Party (PLP) parliamentary opposition at first argued that weakening the offshore laws that brought huge investments to The Bahamas would result in capital flight and that is what happened. Many private banks and offshore financial firms departed, citing the new laws as reason for the exodus.

PLP opposition members of parliament called on the government to resign over the OECD and FATF debacle, claiming that the blacklisting was directly related to the government's prolonged inability to deal with drug trafficking. Privately, Bahamian sources said government figures were implicated in numerous questionable, but highly profitable, financial activities, a situation the U.S. was holding over their heads unless they acted as Washington demanded.

Since 2002, whether one party or the other has been in control, neither has changed the laws at issue. Both Bahamian parties caved in to the pressure from the U.S. government that had re-written the laws as Washington wanted them. The PLP Prime Minister, Perry Christie, who first took office in 2002, was returned to power in 2012, but in the 2017 election FNM won a landslide 57% victory and Hubert Minnis became Prime Minister.

Reform Laws

Among the many laws, the "Evidence Act 2000" removed the requirement that foreign government requested evidence could not be released to another country until a court proceeding had begun in the requesting nation. Evidence can now be released for foreign preliminary investigations.

This Bahamian law permits: 1) enforcement of U.S. civil forfeiture orders; 2) confiscation of cash and assets under a U.S.-style civil forfeiture procedure that permits freezing of bank and other accounts; 3) courts to extradite criminal suspects during investigations before trial. Because of its location, the country is a major transshipment point for illegal drugs, particularly shipments to the U.S. and Europe, and its territory is smuggling route for illegal migrants into the U.S.

Dirty Money

Tough anti-money laundering laws were make violations punishable by a possible sentence of 20 years in jail and/or a US$100,000 fine for each instance. A "Currency Declaration Act" requires reporting of all cash or investment transfers, in or out of the islands more than US$10,000. The Central Bank has also broad powers to regulate offshore banks, their registration, operation and reporting. The law allows foreign bank inspectors to conduct on-site and offsite examinations of the accounts in bank branches or subsidiaries located in The Bahamas.

The Bahamas' "Financial Intelligence Unit" is modeled after the U.S. Treasury Financial Crimes Enforcement Network (FinCEN). Opposition members of parliament criticized the financial intelligence unit's (FIU's) powers as far too broad, charging there are no provisions to prevent political "fishing trips" or "witch hunts" by government police. This unit can request ("order" might be a better word) a bank to freeze any funds suspected of being part of criminal activity for up to 72 hours, while a secret "monitoring order" is sought by police to confiscate money or block transactions. In such cases, all other financial confidentiality laws are waived. The FIU issued U.S.-style rules requiring "suspicious activity reporting" by all financial institutions.

Still other laws require all banks to verify the true identity of customers for whom Bahamian intermediaries open accounts. Bahamian banks now use special U.S. cash flow analysis software ("fishing expeditions") to detect possible money laundering. Offshore financial trustees and attorneys are required to maintain records of beneficial owners of offshore trusts and international business corporations. Previously, professional attorney-client privilege rules prevented revealing such information.

Uncle Sam Is Listening: Watch what you say on your cellphone if you visit The Bahamas. In 2014, it was revealed that the U.S. National Security Agency (NSA) is secretly intercepting, recording, and archiving the audio of every cellphone conversation on The Bahamas. According to the story shared by Glenn Greenwald, "Documents provided by NSA whistleblower Edward Snowden show the surveillance is part of a top-secret system, code-named SOMALGET that was implemented without the knowledge or consent of the Bahamian government. NSA used access legally obtained in cooperation with the U.S. Drug Enforcement Administration to open a backdoor to the country's cellular telephone network, enabling it to covertly record and store the "full-take audio" of every mobile call made to, from and within The Bahamas." NSA

documents indicate that SOMALGET has been deployed in The
Bahamas to locate "international narcotics traffickers and special-
interest alien smugglers," traditional law-enforcement concerns,
but that is a far cry from derailing terrorist plots or intercepting
weapons of mass destruction. No doubt the IRS has been listening
regarding some tax matters as well. In 2015, a year after The
Bahamas government protested, the NSA promised in the future it
would only act legally!

IBCs Under Fire

Previously beneficial owners of IBCs were required to disclose
the identities of shareholders or other detailed business information
unless under a court order. Now, the right of IBCs to issue and use
bearer shares has been repealed and all IBCs are required to submit to
the government the true identities and addresses of directors. There
are currently more than 100,000 international business corporations
in The Bahamas, with about 16,000 added each year.

Even though The Bahamas is still an offshore tax haven, it remains
in considerable internal government and political turmoil. The mass
exodus of so many Bahamian financial professionals a decade ago
speaks volumes the state of affairs. The best financial and investment
climates are those that enjoy some degree of predictability; that's not
The Bahamas.

My advice is to scratch The Bahamas off your list of offshore financial centers. Things may change someday, but if you were thinking
of using the islands as a base of offshore operations, there are more
reliable places.

Contacts:

Government of The Bahamas: http://www.bahamas.gov.bs

Embassy of The Commonwealth of The Bahamas
2220 Massachusetts Avenue NW
Washington, D.C. 20008

Tel.: 202-319-2660
Email: embassy@bahamasembdc.org
Web: http://www.bahamasembdc.org

Consulate Generals are located in Washington, D.C., New York, Miami, and Atlanta.

Web: http://www.bahamasembdc.org/contact/locations-consulate-information

United States Embassy
42 Queen Street
Nassau, The Bahamas
Tel.: + 242 322-1181
Email: acsnassau@state.gove
Web: https://bs.usembassy.gov

Securities Commission of The Bahamas
3rd Floor, Charlotte House
Shirley and Charlotte Streets
P.O. Box N-8347
Nassau, Bahamas
Tel.: +242 397-4100 / 1-360-450-0981
Email: info@scb.gov.bs
Web: http://www.scb.gov.bs

Bahamas Tourism: https://thebahamas.com

Bank:

The Central Bank of The Bahamas
P.O. Box N-4868
Nassau, N.P., The Bahamas
Tel.: +242 302 2600
Web: http://www.centralbankbahamas.com

Barbados

*This Caribbean island is not a full-fledged tax haven, but its
low business and professional taxes, combined with a network
of bilateral double tax treaties with major nations makes it a
favorite for foreign investment, especially among Canadians.*

Barbados is the most easterly of the Caribbean islands, northeast of
Venezuela, 166 square miles in area, located 1,200 miles southeast of
Miami, about four and a half hours by air from New York and eight
hours from London. It is in the U.S. Eastern Time zone.

Although it only achieved independence in 1966, the country has
one of the oldest Westminster-style parliaments in the western hemisphere in existence for 362 years. Ninety percent of the population
of 289,680 is of African descent and more than 80% of the people
live in urban areas.

Barbados is a politically stable parliamentary democracy. The education system is excellent with a literacy rate of almost 100% providing a highly trained workforce for both professional and skilled workers. English is the official language, which helps to make Barbados a
good place to do business.

The island was uninhabited until the British settled in 1627.
Sugar plantations then became the main crop of the land, which were
worked by slaves until 1834, when slavery was abolished. The economy remained heavily dependent on sugar, rum and molasses production through most of the 20th century. The gradual introduction of
social and political reforms in the 1940s and 1950s led to complete
independence from the U.K. in 1966. In the 1990s, tourism and
manufacturing surpassed the sugar industry in economic importance.

Barbados' closest neighbor is nearly 100 miles away, allowing it to escape the fighting of the Spanish, French, and Danish during the era of exploration, keeping it firmly in the hands of the British. In fact, Barbados is seen as the "Little England" of the Caribbean. In 2007, the island even hosted the finals of the Cricket World Cup. Called "Banjans," the islanders are as West Indian as any of their Caribbean neighbors but have selectively borrowed over time some English customs.

Economy

Barbados is the wealthiest and most developed country in the Eastern Caribbean and enjoys one of the highest per capita incomes in Latin America, US$17,500 in 2017. Historically, the Barbadian economy was dependent on sugarcane cultivation and related activities, but in more recent years, the economy has thrived more in tourism. The economy remained heavily dependent on sugar, rum and molasses production through most of the 20th century.

Governments of Barbados have made a habit of deficit spending, depending too much on high debt. Favoring an aggressive offshore financial sector has meant low tax rates for high-net-worth investors, foreign companies, and banks, and high tax rates for everyone else. At 94%, in 2013 Barbados' ratio of public debt to GDP was the Caribbean's second highest, more than the 93% that forced Cyprus to seek an EU bailout. The public debt-to-GDP in 2017 was a reported 108.3%.

After an IMF 2013 survey, 3,000 public sector workers were let go and wages frozen. This brought back painful memories of an IMF 1991 intervention, when 4,000 government layoffs and sharp real wage cuts were also imposed. It took more than six years to recovery.

Barbados is one of the more prosperous of the Caribbean's island states. In early 2015, the government announced it had achieved a turnaround from the deficit of $385 million to a surplus of $56 million. But tourism, which accounts for more than half of economic output, has struggled since the 2008 financial crisis. In 2018, the Barbados Central Bank warned about the dwindling amount of foreign exchange reserves in the system, noting that the tourism and financial services-dependent economy has lost US$1 billion in the past five years. As a result, government debts and unemployment have risen and even crime is becoming a concern in the normally peaceful island. In 2017, unemployment in Barbados stood at nearly 10%.

Offshore Financial Center

Powerful foreign exchange earners include offshore finance and information services. These sectors further benefit from the fact that the island is in the same Eastern Time zone as U.S. and Canadian financial centers and offers a highly educated workforce. Unfortunately, the 2008 global financial collapse hit the island's tourism, financial services, and construction industries hard.

Even with the impeding economic crisis, Barbados still represents a strong international business and financial service industry, employing over 3,000 locals, and by some unofficial estimates, contribute 7.5% to the country's GDP. The major appeal as an offshore financial center is the country's low corporate and business taxes, plus a network of bilateral double tax treaties with major nations that allow tax credit for foreign taxes paid. There are nearly 4,000 registered international businesses.

Double taxation treaties exist with Canada, CARICOM, China, Cuba, Finland, Norway, Malta, Mauritius, Sweden, Switzerland, U.S., U.K., Venezuela and Botswana. The court system is based on British common law and is generally unbiased and efficient. The protection of property rights is strong, and the rule of law is respected.

Barbados has avoided OECD and FATF blacklists by having low tax rates, double taxation agreements and exchange of information treaties to attract business. It has a strict anti-money laundering law and is serious about applying "know your customer" and suspicious activity rules. Barbados and the U.S. signed an inter-governmental agreement to comply with FATCA. In 2017, an OECD review of the island's tax laws produced the usual criticism that the island's financing and leasing regimes had "potentially harmful features" that allowed tax avoidance.

Its no-nonsense, clean business image undoubtedly accounts for its popularity among foreign investors and businesses who choose to locate here. Another advantage is sharing the same time zone as the eastern U.S. and Canadian financial centers and a highly educated workforce.

The Barbados dollar has been pegged to the U.S. dollar since 1975 at a rate of two Barbados dollars to one US dollar and this stability has proven attractive to foreign business. The country has some exchange control regulations but international business corporations and financial services, including insurance companies, international banks and international trusts are exempted. There are 57 international banks; qualifying insurance companies and exempt insurance companies can make payments free of Barbadian income tax and in any foreign currency.

The government has established a separate ministry to facilitate the development of the international business sector. Some of the incentives include reduced tax rates between 1% and 2.5%, exemption from withholding tax on dividends, interest, royalties or other income paid to non-residents and freedom from exchange controls. The top individual income tax rate is 33.5%, and the top corporate tax rate is 25%. Other taxes include a value-added tax and a property tax. A special tax break exempts from tax 35% of the paychecks of qualified foreign employees working in IBCs.

Canadian Connection

Canada's influence in Barbados is based on a strong commercial relationship with Canada for well over a century. The legal and financial system and banking standards on the island are like Canada's, making it familiar to Canadian companies. There was a deliberate attempt in the 1990s to copy Canadian corporate law because of its special 1987 tax treaty with Barbados.

Government officials always have made efforts to attract Canadian investors. Investment by Canadian companies looking to avoid paying Canadian tax on income derived from foreign earnings has grown from US$500 million in 1987 to US$30 billion in 2015. Nearly 9% of all Canadian direct investment offshore is done here. Canadian subsidiaries, which include many mining, oil and gas and financial services companies, account for one-third of the 3,750 corporate structures registered here. Barbados is promoting its expanding network of bilateral double taxation treaties and appealing to Canadian companies to invest in order to take advantage of them.

Of the 57 international banks; 78% are Canadian; of the 144 mining companies 41% are Canadian and of the 230 oil and gas companies, 30% are Canadian. Barbados 25% corporate tax rate has attracted Canadian investors since Canada signed its own double taxation treaty with the country in 1987. Under the treaty, Canadian companies can set up a subsidiary in Barbados to conduct international business. If the company has five employees in Barbados and maintains a management presence there, it can repatriate profits to Canada without paying Canadian tax.

Contacts:

Barbadian Embassy
2144 Wyoming Avenue NW
Washington, D.C. 20008
Tel.: 202-939-9200
Email: washington@foreign.gov.bb
Web: http://www.embassy.org/embassies/bb.html

Consulate of Barbados in New York
820 2nd Avenue, 5th Floor
New York, NY 10017
Tel.: 212-867-8435
Web: http://consulate-new-york.com/barbados.html or
http://www.embassy.org/embassies/bb-other.html

Consulate of Barbados in Miami
150 Alhambra Circle, Suite 100
Coral Gables, FL 33134
Tel.: 305-442-1994
Email: miami@foreign.gov.bb
Web: http://www.consulate-miami.com/barbados.html or
http://www.embassy.org/embassies/bb-other.html

United States Embassy in Bridgetown
Wildey Business Park
St. Michael BB 14006
Tel.: +246 227-4000
Email: bridgetownacs@state.gov
Website: https://bb.usembassy.gov

Barbados Tourism: http://www.barbados.org/index.html

Barbados Investment & Development Corp. (BIDC)
P.O. Box 1250
Pelican Huis
Prinses Alice snelweg
Bridgetown, St Michael
Barbados, BB 11000
Tel.: +246 427-5350
Email: bidc@bidc.org
Web: www.bidc.com

Central Bank of Barbados
Tom Adams Financial Center, Spry Street
P. O. Box 1016
Bridgetown, Barbados
West Indies, BB11126
Tel.: +246 436-6870
Email: info@centralbank.org.bb
Web: http://www.centralbank.org.bb

Invest Barbados
Trident Insurance Financial Center
Hastings, Christ Church, BB15156
Tel. (Local): +246 626-2000
Tel. (From the U.S.): 1-347-433-8942
Email: info@investbarbados.org
Web: http://www.investbarbados.org
(Offices also in the U.S. and Canada)

Belize

Belize, the only officially English-speaking nation in Central America, has had in place for more than two decades a series of offshore laws allowing asset protection trusts, IBCs, maritime registration, insurance and banking — plus financial privacy. The law welcomes foreigners as residents with special concessions.

Its parliament, courts and government support this offshore financial center and welcome foreign business and investment. An unusual feature is a special, tax-free retirement residence program for foreigners. But this definitely is a Third World country with all the problems that can present.

In the Caribbean region in third place, right after Panama and Nevis, stands Belize — offering banking privacy, low or no taxes and a business-friendly government. It should be on everyone's list of possible offshore financial bases, but its limitations need to be understood also.

Having visited Belize more than once we can attest that it's definitely "Third World," but people are very friendly, and oceanfront real estate is still relatively cheap. Belize is one of the few remaining independent nations that holds itself out as a tax and asset protection haven.

Independent since 1981, its language came from its colonial days when it was known as "British Honduras." So, while officially an English-speaking country, Spanish is rapidly becoming the majority language due to immigration.

The country borders on the Caribbean Sea, and lies east of Guatemala and south and east of Mexico, with which it has a continuing border dispute. Its mixed population of 340,844 includes descendants of native Mayans, Chinese, East Indians, and Caucasians. An influx of Central American immigrants, mainly Guatemalans, Salvadorans, and Hondurans, has changed Belize's ethnic composition.

It is home to the largest barrier reef in the Western Hemisphere and enjoys great deep-sea diving. To the east in the Caribbean there's a sprinkle of tropical islands included within its national borders. A few years ago, American television viewers discovered Belize as the locale for one of the first reality TV shows, *Temptation Island*.

Belize retains many of the colonial customs and features familiar in places such as the Cayman Islands and Bermuda, although it is far less developed. The first settlers were probably British woodcutters, who in 1638, found the valuable commodity known as "Honduran mahogany." Bananas, sugar cane and citrus fruit are the principal crops. Like many small countries dependent on primary commodities, Belize recognized the benefits of introducing offshore financial services to boost its income.

Clean Money

American government officials have had a well-deserved case of nerves over Belize. Some feared that the sleepy little capital town of Belmopan would become a prime site for U.S. tax evasion and money laundering. But the Belizean government has cooperated with the

U.S. in drug and money laundering cases, although extradition from Belize is still difficult. The nation's clean money reputation was aided by adoption of a strong anti-money laundering law.

The conservative Heritage Foundation rated Belize's economic 2018 freedom score as 57.1, making its economy 116th freest out of 185 countries. In recent years it says there has been deterioration in economic freedoms because of official and judicial corruption, disregard for the rule of law, and an increase in money laundering and drug transit activity.

Despite a high level of trade freedom, gains from trade are undercut by a need for investment and financial sector reforms. Heritage faulted Prime Minister Dean Barrow of the United Democratic Party, re-elected for a third and final five-year term in 2015, saying he has undermined investments by government exportation of the leading private telecommunications, electricity companies and the water company.

In 1992, the Belize National Assembly enacted modern legislation seeking to make the country a competitive offshore financial center. Drafters combed tax haven laws worldwide and came up with a series of minimal corporate and tax requirements that could well fit your business needs.

The new laws include the Trust Act, which allows a high level of asset protection, great freedom of action by the trustee and no taxes on income earned outside Belize. There is also a statute allowing the creation of international business companies that can be formed in less than a day for less than US$1,000. You only need one shareholder and/or director, whose name can be shielded from public view.

There are no local income taxes, personal or corporate, and no currency exchange controls. Since 1990 when the International Business Companies Act became law, foreigners have registered about 5,000 IBCs. That's a small number compared to a place like the British Virgin Islands with over 400,000 IBCs, but the number is growing. Belize is also witnessing major growth in the shipping registry business. Other laws favor offshore insurance companies, limited liability partnerships and banking.

Over the last decade, the government of Belize has carefully and systematically established the nation as an offshore haven that welcomes foreign investment and foreign nationals. It has enacted a series of laws crafted to protect financial privacy and promote creation of offshore trusts and international business corporations (IBCs). It has an attractive special residence program aimed at retirement-bound foreign citizens.

London Pressures

A member of the Commonwealth and a former British colony, but independent since 1981, Belize still has strong ties with London and is thus susceptible to U.K. Foreign Office pressures. In 2000, shortly after the OECD "harmful tax competition" blacklisting of Belize, London made known that future aid of all kinds, including debt forgiveness, would depend in part on Belize's willingness to cooperate in modifying some of its tax-haven attractions. At one point, London suspended debt relief to Belize in response to alleged tax breaks for favored offshore investors in Belize.

Belize bowed to the pressure by promising to tighten its offshore regulations. This subsequently included repeal of the Belize instant economic citizenship for sale program and limitations on the issuance and use of bearer shares.

The nation's cabinet officially ended the Belize economic citizenship program in 2002. A constitutional reform commission had urged the change, but pressure from the U.S. and Canadian governments undoubtedly was a factor. Even after the law was repealed, it appeared that some of the economic citizenship passports were still being sold under the table. Periodic rumors circulate claiming the economic citizenship program might be revived.

Despite the OECD's and London's carping, Belize's small offshore industry continues to struggle, providing financial services to a largely nonresident clientele. These services include international business company and offshore trust formation and administration; international banking services, including foreign currency bank accounts and international VISA cards; fund management, accounting and secretarial services; captive insurance; and ship registration.

A sympathetic government continues to work closely with the Belize Offshore Practitioners Association in drafting future legislation covering offshore banking, captive insurance, limited duration companies, protected cell companies and limited partnerships. All professional trust providers now must register with, and be licensed by, the government.

Banking Problems

The Belize banking sector is tiny and those with firsthand experience complain that the local banks are less than competent and careless with account information. Indeed, Belize is most definitely a third-world country. Visa credit cards are issued by Belize Bank International, Ltd., owned by BHI Corporation, a holding company with banking and financial services in Belize. BHI also has major stakes in many local Belizean businesses and industries. Belize Bank is the largest commercial banking operation and formerly was a correspondent of the Bank of America.

In 2016, Bank of Belize closed a large number of customer accounts and suffered a wave of withdrawal requests after also being caught up in a US tax-evasion crackdown and the withdrawal of foreign correspondent banking services. The value of deposits at Belize Bank International (BBI) shrank by almost three-quarters in just six months, and some BBI customers struggled to recover their cash.

In 2015, U.S. authorities filed civil and criminal charges against a major Belize-based fraud operation that allegedly allowed 100 or more U.S. investors knowingly to manipulate penny stocks, launder hundreds of millions of dollars back into the U.S., and evade U.S. taxes. Six men (none citizens of Belize) and related companies were indicted in U.S. federal court, charged with running the alleged $500 million scheme over five years. The U.S. SEC also filed civil charges for federal securities law violations. The indictment came after a two-year undercover investigation by the US Federal Bureau of Investigation. Court-approved wiretaps led them to over 100 U.S. clients.

The U.S. Department of Justice's tax division also obtained a court order forcing Bank of America and Citibank to disclose information about all U.S. taxpayers who held offshore accounts at Belize Bank International Limited (BBIL) or Belize Bank Limited (BBL), for which the two American banks provided correspondent banking services.

The investigation was aimed at concealed assets and tax-evasion schemes in Belize. In probable anticipation of the order, BoA and Citi in 2015 shut off their correspondent services to BBL and BBIL, ending their ability to execute international transfers in U.S. dollars. (Belize's other domestic banks, ScotiaBank Belize and Heritage, were not affected.) This court action probably was caused by voluntary disclosures made to the IRS by U.S. BBL and BBIL customers who admitted their undisclosed foreign accounts through the IRS's off-shore amnesty programs. An example: in 2016 a Spanish court found Barcelona football star Lionel Messi and his father guilty of tax fraud, including hiding funds in a Belize bank.

As a result of all this illegal activity, the remaining banks in Belize began a "de-risking" program, refusing new accounts and closing accounts of U.S. persons and other foreigners.

Belize's investment policy is explained in the *Belize Investment Guide*, which outlines the development priorities for the country. A country "Commercial Guide" for Belize is available at https://bz.usembassy.gov/wp-content/uploads/sites/279/2017/07/Belize-2016-CCG-final.pdf.

Tax Free Residence

Expats have been coming to Belize to live and retire for decades, especially Americans and Brits. Newcomers are welcome whether buying a home, getting a bank account, or just looking for anything needed.

A good example of a Belize welcome of foreign persons is the Retired Persons Incentive Act that is implemented by the Belize Tourism Board. The program, which resembles the popular *pensionado* program in Panama, is designed to attract foreign retirees and foreign capital.

Known as the "qualified retired persons" (QRP) program, the law offers significant tax incentives to those willing to become permanent residents, but not full citizens. The program is aimed primarily at residents of the U.S., Canada and the U.K., but is open to all.

A "qualified retired person" is exempted from all taxes on income from sources outside Belize. QRPs can own and operate their own international business based in Belize exempt from all local taxes.

Local income earned within Belize is taxed at a graduated rate of 15% to 45% and QRPs need a work permit in order to engage in purely domestic business activities. For QRPs, import duties are waived for personal effects, household goods and for a motor vehicle, airplane or boat. There is no minimum time that must be spent in Belize and QRPs can maintain their status so long as they maintain a permanent local residence, such as a small apartment or condominium.

To qualify for the QRP Program, an applicant must be 45 years of age or older and prove personal financial ability to support oneself and any dependents. A spouse and dependents (children under the age of eighteen or a child in college up to the age of twenty-three) qualify along with the head of household at no extra fee. Initial fees for the program are US$150, plus US$200 for an ID card upon application approval. Minimum financial requirements include an annual income of at least US$24,000 (US$2,000 monthly) proven from a bank statement from a bank with a pension, annuity or other sources outside of Belize.

For information about the QRP Program, contact the following agencies:

Government of Belize
Ministry of National Security and Immigration
Curl Thompson Building
Belmopan City, Belize
Tel.: +501-822-2231 / +501-822-2817
Email: minofnatsec@mns.gov.bz
Web: http://www.belize.gov.bz/index.php/ministry-of-national-security

Belize Tourism Board
P.O. Box 325, 64 Regent Street, Belize City, Belize
Tel.: +501-227-2420
Toll-free: 1-800-624-0686
Email: info@travelbelize.org
Web: http://www.travelbelize.org

Economy

Tourism is the primary foreign exchange earner in what is considered a small economy. Exports of marine products, citrus, cane sugar, bananas, garments, and oil are also big contributors. In 2017, the Belize Tourism Board (BTB) indicated a record of over 1.2 million visitors, a 13% increase in tourism, stating "The year 2016 culminated with another significant achievement for the tourism industry, boasting the highest overnight arrivals in twenty years."

The government spending boosted GDP growth. The 2017 GDP grew by 2.5% to US$3.23 billion with a per capita GDP of US$8,300. Although Belize has the third highest per capita income in Central America, the average income figure masks a huge income disparity between rich and poor. A major government goal is to reduce poverty and inequality through the help of international donors.

Although Belize has the second highest per capita income in Central America, the average income figure masks a huge income disparity between rich and poor.

Contacts:

Government of Belize: http://www.belize.gov.bz

Embassy of Belize in Washington, D.C.
2535 Massachusetts Avenue NW
Washington, D.C. 20008
Tel.: 202-332-9636
Email: reception@embassyofbelize.org
Web: https://www.belizeembassyusa.mfa.gov.bz

United States Embassy
Floral Park Road
Belmopan, Cayo, Belize
Tel.: +501-822-4011
Email: ACSBelize@state.gov
Web: https://bz.usembassy.gov

Recommended Bank:

The Belize Bank International Ltd.
The Matalon Business Center
Coney Drive, 2nd Floor
Belize City, Belize CA
Tel.: +501-227-0697 / +501-227-1548
Email: services@belizebankinternational.com
Website: http://www.belizebankinternational.com

Recommended Law Firm:

Barrow & Williams, Attorneys-at-Law
Equity House, 84 Albert Street
P.O. Box 617

Belize City, Belize CA
Tel.: +501-227-5280
Email: attorneys@barrowandwilliams.com
Web: http://www.barrowandwilliams.com

Bermuda

This mid-Atlantic island is the world's leading place for
"captive" self-insurance companies used by businesses and
for re-insurance companies; it offers excellent asset protection
trusts and IBCs. Its respected banks have worldwide branches
and investment services. But as a U.K. overseas territory,
ultimately Bermuda is forced to take orders from London.

The "crown jewel of the Atlantic" and a world-class offshore center, Bermuda is in the mid-Atlantic, 750 miles southeast of New York City and 3,445 miles from London. The island (69,839 people, 21 square miles) has a long history as a low-tax and banking haven. In the past, this has been a world-class financial outpost, not to mention a very pleasant place to visit or live in any season. But recently the government has experienced enough budget deficit problems that Fitch Rating Service reduced its bond rating.

The islands were first settled in 1609 by shipwrecked English colonists heading for Virginia. Bermuda has remained in British hands ever since and today is a British overseas territory with internal self-government.

The British Westminster system confers an immensely important constitutional right on each U.K. overseas territory, that of the right to declare independence. Until 2004, most local political leaders avoided the issue of Bermuda's possible independence from the

United Kingdom. But then-Prime Minister Alex Scott called for a national debate on the subject, looking towards the possibility of ending London's control over the island. A referendum on independence was defeated in 1995 but sporadic independence talk continues. Independence is a possibility, but a remote one.

With a GDP of over US$5 billion, despite four years of recession and a public debt that's 43% of the GDP, Bermuda enjoys the fourth highest per capita income in the world (approximately US$86,000), about 70% higher than that of the U.S. Its economy is primarily based on international business financial services and, due to the large number of tourists, luxury facilities.

Because of its liberal regulatory laws, many U.S. re-insurance companies relocated to the island following the September 11, 2001, U.S. terror attacks and again after Hurricanes, like Katrina, Rita, Wilma, and Irma, contributing to the expansion of a growing international business sector.

Tax-Free Business, Expensive Real Estate

Bermuda imposes no corporate income, gift, capital gains, or sales taxes. The income tax is extremely low — 11% on income earned from employment in Bermuda. More than 13,000 international business corporations call Bermuda home. They are drawn by the island's friendly, tax neutral environment, established business integrity and minimal regulation.

More than 60% of these companies operate as "exempted," meaning their business is conducted outside Bermuda (except for the minimal contacts needed to sustain an office on the island). Since Bermuda does not levy direct taxes, there are no double tax treaties with other jurisdictions. There is a tax treaty with the U.S. which exempts insurance premium payments from U.S. franchise taxes, and grants tax breaks to U.S. companies holding conventions in Bermuda.

Bermuda is also home to more than 600 "collective investment schemes" (mutual funds), unit trusts and limited partnerships. Under the strong protective umbrella of the U.K. Copyright Act of 1965, also applicable in Bermuda, many collective investment schemes with intellectual property and software interests use the island as a legal home port. With a statutory structure for protection, Bermuda has also become a center for offshore trust creation and management. The island offers a wide variety of trusts to meet every need, including offshore asset protection.

The "jewel of the Atlantic" is also a great place to live but be aware of tough real estate restrictions. Demand for homes is high and supply short. In general, non-Bermudians are permitted to own only one local property. Acquisition is allowed only after careful background checks, (at least one bank reference and two or more personal references). Out of 20,000 residential units on the island, only 250 detached homes and 480 condominiums qualify for non-Bermudian purchasers based on government set values.

The average 2017 cost was $1.2 million for a single-family house and $681,000 for a condo. These prices were lower than 2015 when they were $1.65 million for a modest two-bedroom, single-family house without water views and the average price of a condominium was above US$1 million. The overall living cost in Bermuda is four times that of US, three times of the UK and two times that of Canada.

In addition to the purchase price of a home or condominium qualified for sale to non-Bermudians, there is a 25% government upfront purchase tax on homes and 18% on condominiums. Purchase licenses are granted by the Department of Immigration and require six months or more for approval.

The buyers tend to be rich and famous. The late rock star David Bowie owns property on the island, while former Italian Prime Minister Silvio Berlusconi and Texan Ross Perot, the one-time U.S. presidential candidate, are neighbors. International celebrities such as former New York mayor Michael Bloomberg, a local land owner, can pass almost unnoticed on the island, a luxury unavailable on the streets of Manhattan or London.

Canadians currently have a special interest in buying on the island because Canadian tax laws make living abroad particularly attractive. The Immigration Department reports that citizens of more than 80 different countries work on the island, with the U.K. providing the most, followed by Canada, Portugal, the U.S., the Philippines, and workers from the Caribbean.

There are about 8,000 work permit holders on the island, a large number out of so small a population. Employers must apply to the Department of Immigration when they want to hire a non-Bermudian, showing proof that no suitably qualified islander is available. An estimated 8,000 registered U.S. citizens live in Bermuda, many of them employed in the international business community.

In recent years, friction has grown between native Bermudians and expatriates who come here for employment in the financial sector, the argument mainly based on disparities between wages. This has led to restrictions on the total number of expatriates allowed and their length of stay, and it is a continuing local political issue.

Bermuda Business and Banking

Over many decades, Bermuda has achieved a global reputation as a world-class business center. It has set high standards with the best laws and infrastructure with continuing improvements based on experience. There is a spirit of cooperation between business and government in support of the offshore sector. Bermuda as an offshore financial center dates to the 1930s, but began to grow significantly after 1960, initially concentrating on Canada, the U.K. and countries in the sterling area. When Bermuda moved to the Bermuda dollar on a par with the U.S. dollar in 1970, focus shifted from the U.K. to the United States.

Such extensive worldwide finance and insurance activity requires a highly sophisticated banking system. Bermuda provides this with up-to-date services and fiber-optic connections to the world. The four local banks clear more than US$3 billion daily. Under the Banking Act of 1969, no new banks can be formed or operate in Bermuda unless authorized by the legislature. The chances of that happening are slim. However, international banks may form exempted companies engaged in non-banking activities and many have done so.

Bermuda's three banks follow very conservative, risk averse policies. They hold an average of 85% of customer liabilities in cash and cash equivalents. The Bank of Bermuda, founded in 1889, has assets exceeding US$5 billion and offices in George Town, the Cayman Islands, Guernsey, Hong Kong, the Isle of Man, Luxembourg, and an affiliate in New York City. The Bank of Bermuda is owned by HSBC. Butterfield Bank (founded in 1859) also has offices in all of those tax havens, except the Caymans.

Perhaps the biggest local banking news in years occurred in 2003 when the world's second largest bank, HSBC, purchased control of the Bank of Bermuda for US$1.3 billion. Many Bermudans opposed the sale. Since then several national divisions of HSBC have been charged with money laundering and paid billions in fines, none involving the Bank of Bermuda.

The Bermuda dollar circulates on par with the U.S. dollar. U.S. currency is accepted everywhere. There are no exchange controls on foreigners or on exempt companies, which operate freely in any currency, except the Bermuda dollar.

Unlike Panama, the Cayman Islands or The Bahamas, Bermuda has no bank secrecy laws officially protecting privacy, but bank and government policies make it difficult to obtain information in most cases. To do so requires judicial process.

A 1988 tax treaty with the U.S. allowed for governmental exchange of limited information in certain cases, but a more recent Tax Information Exchange Agreement (TIEA) with Washington opened the door to free exchange of information with the IRS. Bermuda also has signed a FATCA agreement with the U.S. The island has a total of 80 treaty partners, including 41 bilateral TIEAs and is one of 76 co-signatories of the EU Multilateral Convention on Mutual Administrative Assistance in Tax Matters.

For your personal and business purposes, a Bermuda bank account can offer a tax-free means for global financial activity and vast investment possibilities. If you have need for an offshore-based business locale, Bermuda, with its IBC creation laws and its modern digital Internet connections, is a very good choice.

Foreign Tax Evasion a Crime

Bermuda has toughened the provisions of the 1998 U.S.-Bermuda tax treaty. It also upgraded anti-money laundering laws, as well as financial management laws governing the chartering and operation of banks and trust companies. These laws were Bermuda's calculated response to demands from the Foreign Office in London, the OECD and FATF.

The rewrite of the 1986 U.S.-Bermuda tax agreement in 1998 toughened the existing agreement at Washington's request. It clarified and expanded the types of information that Bermuda can now give the IRS "relevant to the determination of the liability of the [U.S.] taxpayer." For the first time, Bermuda also permitted on-site inspections of records by foreign tax authorities.

The Proceeds of Crime Act fiscal offenses list was broadened to include tax fraud. In effect, this meant that by proxy, American tax laws and their enforcement mechanisms were adopted by Bermuda.

Most importantly, the fraudulent evasion of foreign taxes was made a crime, a major reversal of prior Bermuda policy and law. This made Bermuda the first major offshore financial center (and the first British overseas territory) to adopt such legislation. Together, these laws allow the U.S. IRS and the U.K.'s Inland Revenue (as well as other nations' tax collectors) to pursue their alleged tax-evading citizens with the assistance of Bermuda prosecutors and courts.

Bermuda is an "approved jurisdiction" of the U.S. IRS for tax reporting purposes under the IRS Qualified Intermediary (QI) program. That means that the island's banks, investment advisors and other financial services that deal in U.S. securities agree to disclose to the IRS the names of their U.S. clients, or to impose a 30%

withholding tax on investment income paid to such U.S. persons. This agreement was said to show IRS approval of Bermuda's stricter know-your-customer and suspicious activity reporting rules.

Business

Because of the large number of international companies that conduct insurance operations from Bermuda, the island does not rely as heavily on personal offshore services and banking as do most other havens. In 2014, more than 15,000 international businesses maintained registration in Bermuda and more than 4,000 of these were local.

Total income generated by international companies exceeded US$2 billion. In the past the number of business permits surged as the island promoted itself as an e-commerce haven and opened its shores to licensed investment services providers for the first time. There is no income tax in Bermuda and international companies pay vastly reduced corporate taxes compared to the United States and Europe.

The Bermuda Stock Exchange, established in 1971, was intended as a domestic equities market. With the growth in international financial business, the exchange was restructured into a for-profit entity owned by the Bermuda banking institutions. It offers fully electronic clearing, settlement and depository services. The BSX has become the world's largest offshore fully electronic securities market offering a full range of listing and trading opportunities for global and domestic issuers of debt, equity, depository receipts, insurance securitization and derivative warrants.

Perhaps as a badge of its international merit, Bermuda was among the several offshore financial centers subjected to attack by the thieves at the bogus "International Consortium of Investigative Journalists." In 2017, in what was called the "Paradise Papers", the ICIJ trumpeted the theft and publication of more than 13.4 million documents stolen from the respected, 119-year-old Bermuda law firm, Appleby, which specializes in serving corporations and wealthy people. (For more about this, see *The Panama Papers* in Chapter Five in the section on the Republic of Panama.)

Politics

Its strict laws have led the Bermuda government to claim that the island is "the business leader among the British Overseas Territories," ready to meet and exceed international financial standards and regulation, but its international popularity has made it a target.

Even before Barack Obama became the U.S. president, Bermuda was made the target of anti-tax haven American politicians led by former U.S. Senator Carl Levin (D-MI). Barack Obama as an Illinois senator joined Levin in sponsoring anti-tax haven legislation that would have revoked long-standing U.S. offshore corporate tax breaks. As a presidential candidate, Obama repeatedly denounced tax havens as places where he claimed rich Americans engaged in tax evasion. U.S. companies that re-incorporated in Bermuda were Obama's special target.

The reason companies did this is easy to understand. Under the then current U.S. tax law, a corporation paid 40% or more in federal and state taxes, one of the two highest corporate taxes in the world. Once that company changes its corporate registration to Bermuda, its profits from foreign operations were tax-free if the funds were kept offshore outside the U.S. It was easy for U.S. politicians to demagogue this issue, rather than do the hard work of reforming tax laws and lowering U.S. corporate taxes.

Finally, in the 2017 Tax Cuts and Jobs Act, the U.S. Congress changed all these numbers. This law cut the U.S. corporate income tax rate permanently to 21% from 35%. The old offshore U.S. "worldwide" tax system was converted into a "territorial" system. Under the worldwide system, multinationals were taxed on foreign income they earned, but didn't pay the U.S. tax until they brought profits home to the U.S. As a result, many corporations left untaxed billions parked overseas. Under the new territorial system, they are taxed on foreign profits, but encourage to reinvesting in the United States. The 2017 Act allows U.S. companies to repatriate the $2.6 trillion they held in foreign cash stockpiles in 2018. They pay a one-time repatriation tax rate of 15.5% on cash and 8% on equipment.

Despite all the American political noise Bermuda remains a good, basic, no-tax asset protection jurisdiction for the location of offshore trusts, IBCs and it is a leader for all types of insurance. Its banks are first-class.

Contacts:

Bermuda's interests in the U.S. are represented by the Embassy of the United Kingdom:

British Embassy
3100 Massachusetts Avenue NW
Washington, D.C. 20008
Tel.: 202-588-6500
Email: britishembassyenquiries@gmail.com
Web: https://www.gov.uk/government/world/organisations/british-embassy-washington

U.S. Consulate General
16 Middle Road
Devonshire, DV 03, Bermuda
Tel.: +441-295-1342
Web: https://bm.usconsulate.gov

Bermuda Tourism: http://www.gotobermuda.com

Bermuda Corporation Registry: www.roc.gov.bm

Bermuda Monetary Authority
BMA House
43 Victoria Street, Hamilton
P.O. Box 2447
Hamilton HMJX, Bermuda
Tel.: +441-295-5278
Email: enquiries@bma.bm
Web: http://www.bma.bm

British Virgin Islands

"BVI" as it is known, has a little more than 31,000 people
— but more than 400,000 registered IBCs, second only to
Hong Kong in total number. That's because the BVI specializes
in creating, servicing and promoting offshore corporations
for every purpose. The BVI can truthfully say, "IBCs R Us."
And don't overlook their asset protection trusts, international
limited partnerships and insurance. But remember: they take
orders from London.

The British Virgin Islands consists of more than 60 islands, only 16 inhabited, at the eastern end of the Greater Antilles in the Caribbean, 25 minutes flying time east of Puerto Rico. Its economy is closely integrated with the nearby (to the west) U.S. Virgin Islands.

First occupied by Arawak and then the Carib Indians, the Virgin Islands were settled by the Dutch in 1648 and then captured by the English in 1672. Then in 1960, the islands became its own separate colony, and in 1960 became autonomous.

The capital, Road Town, located on Tortola, is the financial center and the seat of government and courts. As a British overseas territory, the BVI has a long history of political stability with a measure of self-government, but London calls the shots. There is a ministerial system of government headed by a chief minister, with an executive council chaired by the U.K. appointed governor and a legislative council.

The BVI is one of the world's most popular offshore jurisdictions for registering international companies and is a growing, but much lesser force in offshore hedge funds (currently about 2000), trust administration and captive insurance markets. The currency, since 1959, has been the U.S. dollar and there are no exchange controls.

The economy, which is one of the most stable and prosperous in the Caribbean, is highly dependent on tourism, generating an estimated 45% of the national income. Almost one million estimated tourists, mainly from the U.S., visit the islands each year. International financial services produce 50% of the GDP.

IBCs R Us

The BVI adopted its successful International Business Company (IBC) Act in 1984. The Act was superseded by the BVI Business Companies Act 2004, which removed the distinction between 'offshore' and 'onshore' companies. More than 500,000 have registered by 2015, the government said. That figures out to be more than 17 companies for every one of the BVI's 32,600 people.

Hong Kong and Latin America have been the main sources of clients, which is ironic, since Hong Kong leads all jurisdictions in registration of offshore corporations. (Many of BVI's Hong Kong clients are newly rich Chinese seeking to avoid taxes on the mainland.)

The IBC Act allows quick and cheap formation of tax-free corporations to hold assets and execute offshore transactions. The IBCs are used as holding companies, for consultancies, royalty income, foreign real estate, equipment leasing and ownership of moveable assets, such as airplanes and yachts.

The BVI has significant mutual fund and captive insurance sectors. Banking activity is, by design, minor. The BVI has tried hard to exclude money laundering, mostly with success, and has a relatively good reputation.

In 2013, the BVI received $92 billion in foreign direct investment, the fourth largest world amount, more than that which Brazil and India received combined. That was up 40% compared to 2012, continuing a trend that began after the 2008 economic crisis began. Unlike most countries where FDI is used by companies on new acquisitions and projects, most of the BVI money was transferred quickly in and out of the country or moved through the treasury accounts of large firms incorporated there.

The adoption of a comprehensive insurance law in 1994, which provides a blanket of confidentiality with regulated statutory process for investigation of criminal offenses, made the BVI even more attractive to international business. Since 1959, it also uses the US dollar as its currency due to its proximity to the U.S. Virgin Islands and the ties to that archipelago.

Ultimately, the financial industry here is under indirect control of the British government in London. The Labor Party during its control that ended in 2010 forced changes relaxing financial privacy and permitting international exchange of tax information. The islands now have in place a Tax Information Exchange Treaty (TIEA) with the United States and 24 other countries. In 2013, the BVI Premier announced the decision to negotiate an intergovernmental agreement with the U. S. to implement FATCA.

There is no statutory duty of confidentiality or privacy under BVI laws. However, confidentiality is imposed under the British common law and also may be imposed by contract. A breach, or threatened breach, of confidence is actionable in court, which may grant an injunction or award damages for an actual breach. Several laws waive confidentiality for criminal investigations.

In the past, one of the major attractions for BVI corporate registration was that true beneficial ownership was not a matter of public record. That has now changed. Under pressure from the Labour government in London, the BVI colonial government enacted numerous laws that compromised this former strict corporate privacy. In 2002, the BVI signed a tax information exchange agreement with the United States. The BVI has adopted the Article 26 OECD guidelines for tax information exchange.

Anti-money laundering laws cover reporting of suspicious activities and apply know-your-customer rules. The use of bearer shares (freely transferable corporate shares with the owner designated only as "bearer") has been so restricted that they remain "bearer shares" in name only.

In 2015, the BVI government again refused to establish a public central registry of beneficial corporate owners — in spite of pressure from London to adopt this as an anti-money laundering and tax evasion measure. It argued that BVI judicial procedures are adequate to discover ownership in cases where that is required. The only corporation documents on public record are the Memorandum and Articles of Association of each company. Names of directors are not public, much like the incorporation privacy laws of the State of Delaware after which they are patterned.

In 2014, as in the case of Luxembourg (see Chapter Eight), BVI bank records stolen by the far left, anti-tax haven International Consortium of Investigative Journalists revealed that two BVI companies had 21,000 clients from mainland China and Hong Kong who were using the BVI as a tax haven, many of them relatives of, or members of the Communist Chinese ruling elite. In response, the BVI proposed a new law holding a person who publishes in any media unauthorized information on BVI companies may be fined up to US$1 million or jailed for up to 20 years.

BVI companies are not subject to withholding tax on receipts of interest and dividends earned from U.S. sources. There are no capital gains or asset taxes. Use of a standard domestic BVI corporation can be more profitable than an IBC, particularly if one wants to take advantage of the BVI double tax treaties in effect with Japan and Switzerland. The U.S. canceled a similar BVI tax treaty more than a decade ago.

The BVI hobbled somewhat as an offshore center because of its status as a U.K. offshore territory under the control of the government in London. That's where its orders come from and it follows them. But the colonials are growing restless. With the past attacks on tax havens coming from London, BVI folks fear their economic lifeline could disappear. The revenue from registering foreign companies has paid for a community college and a hospital. But if you need an IBC to conduct your worldwide business, the British Virgin Islands will provide it efficiently — and all the service and maintenance you will ever need. They also offer trusts and limited partnerships.

Contacts:

Government of the BVI: http://inotes.bvi.gov.vg/portal/home.nsf

BVI is represented in the United States by the Embassy of the United Kingdom:

British Embassy
3100 Massachusetts Avenue NW
Washington, D.C. 20008
Tel.: 202-588-6500
Email: britishembassyenquiries@gmail.com
Web: https://www.gov.uk/government/world/organisations/british-embassy-washington

The U.S. has no embassy in the BVI. The nearest U.S. Embassy is located in Bridgetown, Barbados:

United States Embassy in Barbados, the Eastern Caribbean, and the OECS
Wildey Business Park
St. Michael BB 14006
Barbados, W.I.
Tel.: 246-227-4000
Email: bridgetownacs@state.gov
Web: https://bb.usembassy.gov

The U.S. Consular Agent in Antigua is closest to the BVI and can also assist in some limited, non-emergency cases.

U.S. Consular Agency
Jasmine Court, Suite #2
Friars Hill Road, St. John's, Antigua
P.O. Box W-1562
St. John's, Antigua
Tel.: +268-463-6531

Email: BridgetownACS@state.gov
Web: https://bb.usembassy.gov/u-s-citizen-services/consular-assistance-antigua-barbuda-french-west-indies

Ministry of Finance
33 Admin Drive, Wickhams Cay 1, Road Town
Tortola, BVI
Tel.: +284-494-3701 ext. 2144
Email: finance@gov.vg or gis@gov.vg
Web: http://bvi.gov.vg

BVI Finance
Cutlass Tower, 4th Floor Road Town
Tortola VG1110 BVI
Tel.: +1 284-468-4335
Email: info@bvifinance.vg
Web: http://www.bvifinance.vg

Cayman Islands

The Cayman Islands, described famously as "a sunny place for shady people," is the world's sixth largest international banking center in terms of liabilities and asset. For decades it was the jurisdiction of choice for tax free international banks and businesses that wanted ironclad secrecy guaranteed by law. But a sea change in international rules on tax evasion and reporting of foreign accounts has ended Cayman's absolute secrecy.

Under extreme pressure from London and Washington, this British overseas territory weakened, but did not end, its still-formidable financial secrecy laws. The Caymans remain an efficient, tax-free OFC for offshore bank accounts, trusts, international business corporations, hedge and mutual funds, captive and other insurance.

Its name may be a red flag for foreign tax collectors and anti-tax haven politicians everywhere, but it has weathered the political storm, as well as the occasional hurricane.

Let's face it: the major reason the Cayman Islands originally became a world-renowned tax-free haven was its strict bank and financial privacy — not just privacy, but near absolute secrecy. Guaranteed by law and zealously enforced by local courts, foreigners of all sorts doing business here were shielded from scrutiny — unless it was shown that they were engaged in overtly criminal acts. Even then, a lengthy judicial process often was needed to pierce this wall of secrecy.

Secrecy was for sale and the Caymans sold it well. But that was the old Cayman Islands before it was forced, under orders from its colonial masters in London, to compromise its bank and financial secrecy, and instead to become a potential proxy tax collector for other nations.

Many of Caymans' 54,000 residents do not agree with what has been forced upon them. Michael Alberga, a leading senior Caymans lawyer sees the world as practicing "economic terrorism" against the Caymans. He says, "We were simply practicing pure capitalism; few or no taxes and little regulation and asking to be left alone."

Government and History

The Cayman Islands is a parliamentary democracy, like the U.K. and U.S., with judicial, executive and legislative branches. The present 1972 constitution provides for governance as a British Dependent Overseas Territories, meaning ultimate power rests with London.

From his discovery of The Bahamas, Christopher Columbus's voyages continued and led him to these islands in 1503. He named them Las Tortugas, after the giant turtles that he sighted in the surrounding seas. The islands were later renamed *Caymanas*, from the Carib Indian word for a crocodile.

Consisting of three islands (Grand Cayman, Little Cayman, and Cayman Brac), the territory is located south of Cuba and about 500 miles south of Miami, Florida. While administered by Jamaica from 1863, the Caymans remained a British dependency after Jamaica became independent in 1962. The capital of Grand Cayman, called George Town, is the center for business and finance.

Prince Philip, Duke of Edinburgh, the husband of Queen Elizabeth II, who rules the British Commonwealth and is Cayman Islands Head of State, is known for his off-the-cuff remarks. During a 1994 royal visit to the Cayman Islands Philip asked one of hosts whether he was "descended from pirates."

Until the mid-1960s there were less than 8,000 Caymanians with most engaged in farming, fishing, turtling, and boat building. Many men served as merchant seamen on ocean-going ships. It was a place where everyone knew each other. In 1952, an aircraft runway was built and the next year Barclays Bank opened a branch on Grand Cayman. Cayman's status as an international offshore financial center grew out of the foresight of the island's early legal practitioners and a friendly government. Together they drafted and enacted laws to take advantage of the absence direct taxation on the income or wealth of individuals and corporations.

The Cayman Islands is an English-speaking, common-law jurisdiction with no direct taxation on income, profits, wealth, capital gains, sales, estates or inheritances.

The Cayman Islands was once described as "one of the more mature jurisdictions … in terms of regulatory structure and culture." But its long history of strict confidentiality ended abruptly when it signed a tax information exchange treaty with the U.S. As a result, the IRS now has the permission to look into the accounts of Cayman financial institutions.

World Leader by the Numbers

Banks: The Cayman Islands a few years ago was ranked as the eighth largest offshore banking center in the world, after New York, London, Tokyo, Singapore and Hong Kong. According to the *Global*

Financial Centers Index in 2017, the islands had slipped to 31st in banking, Regulated by the Cayman Islands Monetary Authority (CIMA), there were 150 banks in 2018, (24 of them U.S. branches), including 40 of the world's 50 largest banks. Assets and liabilities were reported respectively in June 2017 as US$1.026 trillion and US$1.027 trillion.

Captive Insurance: Cayman is the second largest captive insurance base, after Bermuda, with assets worth US$60 billion and a total of 724 companies licensed; it is the No. 1 jurisdiction for health care captives. Medical malpractice liability represents 34% of captive licenses, largest business area within the insurance sector. The second largest line of insurance is workers compensation, which accounts for 167 companies. Most captives were from North America, with 90% originating there.

Trusts, Mutual and Hedge Funds: In 2018 there were 147 active trust licenses managing more than US$500 billion. With 10,586 mutual funds with a net asset value of $3.575 trillion in 2016, this has been a growth sector since the 1997 opening of the Cayman Islands Stock Exchange. With 85% of the world market, the islands predominate in world registration for hedge funds in 2016 there were 10,586 with assets of $435 billion.

Companies: In 2018, there were 12,101 registered companies operating through the islands. Thousands of closed-end funds exist here, plus the latest financial schemes or special purpose vehicles for structured finance dreamed up by cutting-edge lawyers and investors.

The Caymanian dollar is fixed against the US dollar at CI$1 to US$1.20. There are no exchange controls. Cayman is an expensive jurisdiction with an established commercial and professional infrastructure in place and a flexible approach to regulation, within a strong desire to maintain respectability. It has excellent communications facilities and extensive professional services.

Companies Law

Until recently, a business could only be conducted in the Cayman Islands by: 1) a CI citizen or a resident foreigner who had a Residence Certificate, or; 2) a company licensed to do business or to trade within the Cayman Islands. The law now allows exempted companies and limited partnerships that locate in a "special economic zone," if they are registered with the Registrar of Companies for this purpose.

According to the former CI law, "exempted" CI companies or exempted limited partnerships could not engage in trade other than business outside the Cayman Islands. Under the 2011 "SEZ Law" this restriction remains but now, even if a business has a physical presence in the CI, it is legally deemed to be outside the CI for tax purposes. The SEZ law also ends in certain cases the requirement that local companies had to have 60% CI share control; beneficial ownership and at least 60% of its directors were Caymanians.

Offshore business accounts for roughly 30% of the territory's gross domestic product of nearly US$3.5 billion. Many of the world's most reputable companies, including many American companies, do business through subsidiaries registered in the islands, to take advantage of the favorable, tax-free laws. The Caymanians enjoy a standard of living comparable to that of Switzerland with a per capita GDP of US$49,902 a year. Comparing GDP, Cayman held foreign assets are 1,500 times the size of its domestic economy.

Politics as Usual

The Caymans, even more than Bermuda, became a major punching bag for U.S. politicians, especially after it was revealed that the defunct Enron Corporation used the islands for its numerous tax avoiding subsidiaries. Hollywood movies, such as the 1993 film *The Firm*, adopted form a John Grisham novel, falsely depicted the islands as a sinkhole of fetid corruption awash in billions of illicit cash.

Many U.S. firms have fully legal tax-saving subsidiaries registered in the Cayman Islands, including big energy companies such as El

Paso Corp., Transocean Inc. and GlobalSantaFe Corp. Most U.S. companies have corporate units offshore for strategic, financial and tax reasons and they make no attempt to hide them because they are a fully legal means of avoiding U.S. taxes.

In both the 2008 and 2012 presidential campaigns, candidate Barack Obama made his hostility toward offshore jurisdictions clear. He repeatedly scored points with crowds when he said: "There's a building in the Cayman Islands that houses supposedly 12,000 U.S.-based corporations. That's either the biggest building in the world or the biggest tax scam in the world, and we know which one it is."

It made no difference to Obama that a similar corporate registration building in Wilmington, Delaware, home of his running mate, U.S. Vice President, Joe Biden, houses more than 50,000 American corporations as a means legally to escape state taxes in other American states.

Ugland House, on South Church Street near the center of George Town, is indeed home to Cayman's largest law firm, Maples and Calder that serves as registered agent for all the 12,000 legal corporations that it represents.

The issue was also used in the 2012 presidential campaign when Democrats attacked Republican nominee, Mitt Romney, who had legal tax-reducing investments based in the Cayman Islands. This sort of unwanted publicity has made the Caymans the stereotypical media "tax haven" — but objective reality denies that false image.

Money Laundering Crackdown

The truth is that the Caymans has adopted many modern laws in response to the international pressure. But, fortunately for the islands clients, the prevailing attitude in Cayman remains highly protective of strict financial confidentiality in the absence of demonstrated criminality.

As far back as 2001, the Cayman Islands was praised by the OECD Financial Action Task Force for its efforts to conform to 40 FATF recommendations in a code of good practice governing money laundering. The islands adopted anti-money laundering regulations and amendments to laws governing the Monetary Authority, Proceeds of Criminal Conduct, Banks and Trust Companies, Companies Management and it required compulsory licensing for financial firms.

The Cayman Islands now has tax information exchange relationships with 81 jurisdictions, including 35 TIEAs, one with Washington. There is a separate tax agreement with the U.S., implementing FATCA. In 2015, with the approval of the U.S. IRS, the government opened a unique online Automatic Exchange of Information Portal that allows CI financial institutions to file required FATCA Notifications and Reports with the CI tax Information Authority. Cayman happens to be the jurisdiction with the highest number of financial institutions registered with the IRS under FATCA.

Anthony Travers, one of the Cayman Island's most respected senior attorneys and former Chairman of the Cayman Islands Stock Exchange, exposed the lie in arguments that exalt increased tax transparency at the expense of financial privacy. Calling them "the purest nonsense" he points out that Tax Information Exchange Agreements have failed to generate any discernable revenue but that any tax revenues generated by FATCA for the benefit of the U.S. and U.K. treasuries will not even cover the huge cost of enforcement.

The Cayman Islands rightfully view themselves at the forefront of the fight against money laundering in the Caribbean. Drug money laundering was made a serious crime in 1989 and so-called "all crimes" anti-money laundering legislation took effect in 1996 that encouraged reporting of suspicious transactions by providing a safe harbor from liability for those who report suspected crimes.

In 2000, the government announced what its politicians repeatedly had said they would never do. They reached an agreement with the OECD on the issue of future "transparency." The government officially embraced the OECD's demand for an end to the Caymans' traditional bank and financial secrecy, guaranteeing it would provide financial information about Caymans' clients to foreign tax collecting authorities when warranted by evidence. In return for this major change, the OECD did not include the Caymans on the OECD blacklist of tax havens allegedly engaged in "harmful tax practices."

Within three weeks of the OECD deal, all the primary legislation necessary to address every one of the FATF's concerns was on the CI statute books. A few weeks more, and additional anti-money laundering rules were introduced to complete the legislative framework.

The Cayman Islands now has a legal regime considerably tougher than that in many of the FATF's 29-member countries. The laws allow the Cayman Islands Monetary Authority to obtain information on bank deposits and bank clients without a court order and also allow sharing tax information with foreign investigators.

It is now a crime for bankers to fail to disclose knowledge or suspicion of money laundering. Previously, it had been a crime for financial sector workers to disclose any private financial information without a court order. The Caymans government even went so far as to guarantee that it would stop island financial services providers from "the use of aggressive marketing policies based primarily on confidentiality or secrecy."

But there are limits. As with the British Virgin Islands, the Caymans are one of a group of British Overseas Territories that have resisted demands from London that they implement more transparency reforms in the form of a public registry of beneficial corporate and trust ownership. The Caymans has judicial procedures that allow discovery of ownership in cases where that is required.

Recommendation

We have visited the Cayman Islands and met with financial and legal experts. We came away greatly impressed by what we heard and saw.

Regardless of the end of financial secrecy, enormous amounts of money have flowed through these islands for many years. That has created an impressive financial and professional community from which you and your businesses can benefit. These professionals can provide first-class investment advice, a variety of offshore legal entities, trusts and IBCs, annuities and insurance, mutual and hedge funds in which to invest.

If you value financial privacy and are considering or have financial dealings in the Cayman Islands, as with any British overseas territory haven, plan accordingly. But focus on what the Caymans have to offer — even if everything these days is public knowledge.

Contacts:

The Cayman Islands are represented in the United States by the Embassy of the United Kingdom:

British Embassy
3100 Massachusetts Avenue NW
Washington, D.C. 20008
Tel.: 202-588-6500
Email: britishembassyenquiries@gmail.com
Web: https://www.gov.uk/government/world/organisations/british-embassy-washington

U.S. Consular Agent in the Cayman Islands
202B Smith Road Centre
150 Smith Road
George Town, Grand Cayman
Cayman Islands
Tel.: +345-945-8173
Email: caymanacs@state.gov or usconsagency@gmail.com
Web: https://jm.usembassy.gov/u-s-citizen-services/consular-agencies

The Cayman Islands are part of the consular district administered by the U.S. Embassy in Kingston, Jamaica:

United States Embassy
142 Old Hope Road
Kingston 6
Jamaica, West Indies
Tel.: +876 702-6000
Email: kingstonacs@state.gov
Web: https://jm.usembassy.gov

Cayman Islands Monetary Authority
P.O. Box 10052
80 Shedden Road
Elizabethan Square
Grand Cayman KY1 - 1001
Cayman Islands
Tel.: +345-949-7089
Web: http://www.cimoney.com.ky

Cayman Islands Department of Tourism:
http://www.caymanislands.ky

Cayman Islands Immigration Department
94A Elgin Avenue
George Town, Grand Cayman
P.O. Box 1098
Grand Cayman KY1-1102
Cayman Islands
Tel.: +345-949-8344 or 1-800-534-2546
Web: http://www.immigration.gov.ky

Recommended Law Firm:

Travers Thorp Alberga, Attorneys at Law
Contact: Michael Alberga, Managing Partner
Harbour Place, 2nd Floor
P.O. Box 472
103 South Church Street
Grand Cayman KY1-1106, Cayman Islands

Tel.: +1 345-949-0699
Email: malberga@traversthorpalberga.com
Web: www.traversthorpalberga.com

Recommended Bank:

Royal Bank of Canada (Cayman) Ltd.: http://www.rbcroyalbank.com/caribbean/cayman/index.html

Recommended Real Estate Contact for General Questions, Agents, and Listings:

Cayman Islands Real Estate Brokers Association (CIREBA)
P.O. Box 1977
Grand Cayman, KY1-1104, Cayman Islands
Tel.: +345 949-7099
Email: info@cireba.com
Web: www.cireba.com

Curaçao

Not many Americans know that the Kingdom of the Netherlands (a.k.a. Holland) historically had a six-island Dutch colonial possession in the eastern Caribbean off the northern coast of Latin America. These semi-independent tropical islands, (formerly known as the Netherlands Antilles), are still associated with the Kingdom of the Netherlands with the motherland way off in Europe. One of these islands qualifies as an offshore financial center.

The Dutch Caribbean islands are in two groups; (ABC) Aruba, Bonaire, and Curaçao, 55 miles off the Venezuelan coast, and (SSS) Saint Eustatius, Saba and Saint Maarten, located southeast of the U.S. Virgin Islands and Puerto Rico. While still associated with the

Netherlands, the former Netherlands Antilles as a confederation was dissolved as a unified political entity in 2008 and each island is autonomous and self-governing. Holland manages matters of defense, foreign policy, final judicial review, human rights, and good governance.

Originally settled by Arawak Indians, Curaçao was seized by the Dutch in 1634 along with the neighboring island of Bonaire. The island was the center of the Caribbean slave trade but eventually suffered economically by the abolition of slavery in 1863. Prosperity restored in the early 20th century with the construction of the Isla Refineria, which serviced the newly discovered Venezuelan oil fields.

With a population of 146,836, Curaçao (along with Aruba) speaks a unique language, *Papiamentu*, a Spanish-Portuguese-Dutch-English dialect, reflecting the islands history and ethnic makeup; 81.2% Dutch; 8% Spanish, and 4% English.

Economy

Tourism, petroleum refining, offshore finance, and trade and transport are primary foundation for the economy of this small, yet closely tied to the outside world, country. Services make up more than 80% of the GDP of $3.1 billion. Although GDP grew slightly during the past decade, to the island enjoys a high per capita income of $16,000 and a well-developed infrastructure compared with other countries in the region.

Curaçao has two tax free economic free zones for transshipment and manufacturing. It also has a modern "e-commerce zone" which provides a state-of-the-art telecommunication infrastructure with high-speed Internet access. This Internet connectivity allows server hosting together with a variety of tax saving opportunities. Curaçao is located at the crossroads of the latest high capacity Caribbean submarine fiber-cable networks like Arcos-1, PanAm and Americas II, providing ample bandwidth while maintaining redundant connectivity options to/from the island.

Curaçao has been in the online gaming business since 1996. They offer only one type of license which covers operators and software providers of games of skill, chance and sports betting. The government offers gaming companies a low tax rate and master licensees often offer new entrants a single gaming package which includes a license and hosting.

Offshore Financial Center

Curaçao's history in financial services dates back to the period after World War I when the island's first private commercial banks were established. The Dutch Caribbean Securities Exchange is located in the capital of Willemstad, as is the Central Bank of Curaçao and Sint Maarten. The latter bank was founded in 1828, making it the oldest central bank in the Western Hemisphere. Its well-developed financial services sector is home to more than 50 of the world's leading financial institutions. For a list see https://thebanks.eu/banks-by-country/Curacao.

On the oldest is associated with ScotiaBank of Canada:

Maduro & Curiel's Bank
Plasa Jojo Correa 2-4
P.O. Box 305
Willemstad, Curaçao
Tel.: (+599-9) 466-1111
Email: info@mcb-bank.com
Web: www.mcb-bank.com

The corporate tax rate is a low 2% on net profits, excluding import duties, and there is no sales tax or currency controls.

The island is a corporate haven. Its legal system supports a variety of corporate structures Entities available include the usual limited liability companies or a unique form of private LLC.

There are special tax incentives for enterprises operating in the Free Zones. These are part of a wide range of legal and financial benefits which include asset protection, tax minimization, privacy and investment diversification. Since 1998 it has offered private interest foundations modeled after Panama and Liechtenstein.

Curaçao's offshore financial sector consists of trust service companies providing financial and administrative services to international clients, including offshore companies, mutual funds, and international finance companies.

Transparency

According to the OECD, a jurisdiction that qualifies as a "tax haven" can be identified by: 1) no or only nominal taxes; 2) laws protecting personal financial information; 3) a lack of transparency.

Curaçao qualifies on the first two counts, but it is certainly transparent by current international standards.

U.S. State Department claims that several international financial services companies have relocated their businesses elsewhere because of what it calls "a negative international perception as a tax haven." Several years ago, the Netherlands Antilles were cited repeatedly by the OECD FATF for alleged money laundering of drug monies. This did not prevent international financier George Soros from moving his corporate headquarters here. More recently, opposition members of the island's parliament have accused the Central Bank of being lax on money laundering.

Even though Curaçao is considered a tax haven, it adheres to the EU Code of Conduct against harmful tax practices and accepts the jurisdiction of the OECD and Caribbean Financial Action Task Force on Money Laundering. It has signed the OECD Multilateral Convention on Mutual Administrative Assistance in Tax Matters that imposes a global standard for the automatic exchange of tax information. Curaçao has TIEAs with 83 jurisdictions, including with the United States since 2002.

Dutch Treat for Americans

As a place that U.S. citizens can gain quick official residence, the Dutch islands, including Curaçao, are unique; upon arrival Americans are eligible for six months temporary residence under the terms of a 1956 "Treaty of Friendship, Commerce and Navigation between the Kingdom of the Netherlands and the United States of America" (DAFT).

Under this treaty, U.S. citizens can apply for a Dutch residence permit for self-employment in the Netherlands. Applicants can also sponsor their spouse and minor children for residence. All kinds of new business opportunities are available under the treaty, except the practice of law and medicine. Individuals can also invest in opening a branch or potential franchise of an existing U.S.-based business or invest in a share of an existing Dutch business. The minimum required business investment for a self-employed individual is US$6,000.

Based on the Netherland's immigration laws, "The first DAFT residence permit is issued for a period of two years. The minimum required business investment must be maintained throughout the entire period. There is no requirement to learn the Dutch language with a DAFT permit, although the language test (*inburgering*) is needed to apply for permanent residence or citizenship."

Some treaty provisions no longer apply to the Netherlands itself but still do apply to the Dutch Caribbean islands. In 2010, a Dutch court confirmed that the treaty guarantees U.S. citizens the same rights in the Netherlands Caribbean territories as those enjoyed by European Dutch citizens, including the right to stay for a continuous six months in the Caribbean territories.

Contacts:

Embassy of the Kingdom of the Netherlands
38 Hyde Park Gate
London SW7 5DP
United Kingdom
Tel.: 0044 207 590 3200
Email: lon@minbuza.nl (**NOT** for consular matters. For consular matters, please use website's contact form.)

Web: https://www.netherlandsworldwide.nl/countries/united-kingdom

U.S. Consulate General Curaçao
P.O. Box 158, J.B. Gorsiraweg 1
Curaçao, Netherlands Antilles
Tel.: +599-9-461-3066
Email: infocuracao@state.gov
Web: https://cw.usconsulate.gov

List of Curaçao Government Agencies:
http://curacaochronicle.com/goverment

Curaçao Chamber of Commerce:
http://www.curacao-chamber.cw

Federation of Saint Kitts & Nevis

Nevis, (pronounced KNEE-vis), is the other half of the two-island nation of Saint Kitts-Nevis, the smallest sovereign state in the Americas in both area and population. While it is not well known beyond international business circles, the island of Nevis is a leading tax-free offshore financial center. For more than three decades it has had in place asset protection-friendly laws that allow the creation of trusts, IBCs and limited liability companies. The government and courts have enviable records of support for offshore business.

The two-island "sovereign democratic federal state" of Saint Kitts and Nevis has a governmental form and name that is almost larger than its combined population and geography (52,175 and 261 sq. miles respectively). It is part of the chain of eastern Caribbean islands known in colonial days as the British West Indies (BWI), which has dropped the "British" part of that title. The British first settled the islands in 1623, but control was disputed with the French until 1783, when the British prevailed. Independence was achieved on September 19, 1983, and the two-island federation is a member of the British Commonwealth.

Nevis, the smaller of the two islands, has gained international fame for two well-known historical figures, one the subject of a hit Broadway musical, the birthplace of American patriot Alexander Hamilton, the first Secretary of the U.S. Treasury. It was also the setting in 1787 of the wedding to an island woman, Frances "Fanny" Nisbet, of Captain Horatio Nelson (1758—1805), the celebrated and much wounded British Royal Navy officer who led numerous victories at sea during the Napoleonic Wars, the most notable being the Battle of Trafalgar in which he died. You may have seen his impressive monument in Trafalgar Square, site of London's annual New Year's Eve celebration.

In the Federation of Saint Kitts and Nevis, it is the island of Nevis that stars as the offshore financial center. It has few banks, but you can bank elsewhere. And any legal entity you need can be set up in a matter of a few days, or even hours, at minimal cost. If there is any one financial center that has the requisites needed for smooth absentee offshore operations, it's the island of Nevis where financial services comprise 75.1% of GDP. Best of all, Nevis has a no-nonsense banking and business privacy law that even the U.S. government can't crack without showing cause.

Its pro-offshore laws have existed for three decades — so there is plenty of experience and precedent in the local courts — and the legislative assembly keeps the applicable laws current. There are well-established service companies that can do what you want, and several have U.S. branch offices for your convenience.

This tiny island of Nevis has earned its prominence in offshore financial circles. Like most other recommended countries, it imposes no taxes, has quick incorporation and trust laws, and has a genuine attitude of welcoming foreign offshore corporations and asset protection trusts.

The islands are located 225 miles east of Puerto Rico about 1,200 miles south of Miami. Until their 1983 declaration of independence, both islands were British colonies. They are still associate members of the British Commonwealth. Her Majesty, Queen Elizabeth II, as the titular head of state, appoints the Governor General. The elected unicameral parliament sits in the capital of Basseterre on Saint Kitts.

Saint Kitts and Nevis suffer under none of the restrictions inflicted by London on British Overseas Territories. Their national sovereignty allows them to enact their own laws and make their own policies, free from outside pressures.

In the 2015 election, the 20-year rule of President Denzil Douglas and his Labour Party was ended by the election of the Team Unity Party led by Dr. Timothy Harris, the new president. Douglas was accused of "creeping dictatorship" and disregarding parliament, running up a national debt of over US$3 billion, exceeding 100% of GDP, and failing to curb one of the highest per capita murder rates in the world.

Harris took office when the country's weak economy finally was on the upswing. After several years of no growth, real GDP growth in 2015 was 4.9%. The total GDP for 2017 was US$1.528 billion and the per capita GDP was US$26,800 in this impoverished country.

The economy of Saint Kitts-Nevis depends on tourism which has replaced sugar as the traditional mainstay of the economy. After a poor 2005 harvest, the government closed the sugar industry, ending decades of losses. To compensate for lost jobs, the government embarked on a program to diversify the agricultural sector and to stimulate other sectors of the economy, such as export-oriented manufacturing and offshore banking.

Roughly 200,000 tourists visit the islands each year, but reduced tourism arrivals and foreign investment led to a four-year economic that ended in 2013. As with other tourist destinations in the Caribbean, Saint Kitts-Nevis is vulnerable to natural disasters and shifts in tourism demand.

Very Independent

Unsuccessful moves by the Saint Kitts-based government to take over the Nevis financial sector have played a major role in spurring continuing calls for secession. In 1998, a vote in Nevis on a referendum to separate from Saint Kitts fell short of the two-thirds majority needed. Some in Nevis still continue efforts to separate from Saint Kitts.

Nevis owes much of its success as the business-friendly "Delaware of the Caribbean." During the last 30 years, the Nevis parliament has adopted and constantly updated excellent offshore corporation, trust and limited liability company laws, augmented by strong financial privacy.

The total 2017 population was 52,715, with about 40,000 on Saint Kitts and 10,000 on Nevis, the latter harboring a traditional inferiority complex.

Nevis also has its own Island Assembly and retains the constitutional right of secession from Saint Kitts. For years, there were heated demands for separation. Then, in 1998, defying international pleas, residents of the seven-mile-long island of Nevis voted on whether to secede from Saint Kitts and become the smallest nation in the Western Hemisphere. Approval of two-thirds of the island's voters was required for secession. The vote was 2,427 for secession and 1,418 against, falling just short of two-thirds.

The vote was the culmination of a struggle that began with Britain's colonization in 1628. In 1882, Britain stripped Nevis of its legislature and wed it to Saint Kitts. Then in 1983, when the islands became independent, Nevis joined in a federation with neighboring Saint Kitts reluctantly. Nevisians did insist on a constitutional clause allowing them to break away. After years of complaining that they are treated like second-class citizens by the federal government on Saint Kitts, they invoked that right with the failed referendum. Nevis retains the right to secede and proponents vow they will try again.

Under OECD Pressures

There are no exchange controls. In 2000, St Kitts- Nevis was named on the OECD and FATF blacklists but was removed from both after adopting anti-money laundering laws .

As a matter of official policy the government of Nevis did not exchange tax or other information with any other foreign government. However, in 2009, Saint Kitts-Nevis was placed in the G-20/OECD "gray list" of countries allegedly failing to meet international standards concerning tax information exchange.

Its officials took great offense at this listing and publicly denounced the OECD and larger nations for ganging up on small countries. Nevertheless, , it adopted a law containing the tax information exchange standard of OECD Article 26, allowing information to be provided in individual cases of alleged foreign tax evasion. There are no exchange controls and the country now has signed 34 TIEAs, including those with Canada and the United Kingdom, but none with the United States as yet.

Offshore Corporate Home

Nevis kicked off its efforts to meet the needs of offshore companies with its adoption of the Business Corporation Act of 1984. This statue includes elements of Delaware's liberal corporation laws as well as English commercial laws. Such a combination allows U.S. attorneys and U.K. solicitors ease in working through the provisions.

The statue does not require the public disclosure of ownership, management, or financial status of a business, offering complete confidentiality. International business corporations are exempt from taxes but must pay an annual fee of US$450. What's more, if the international business has no local business, individually negotiated, government guaranteed tax holidays can be attained.

Official corporate start-up costs can be less than US$1,000, and that includes a minimum capitalization tax of US$200 and company formation fees of US$600. These fees are attractive compared to those of other financial havens such as the Cayman Islands.

Nevis corporate law is unique in that it contains a very modern legal provision. It allows the international "portability," the transfer of an existing foreign company from its country of origin to the island, also known as "re-domiciling." This allows the smooth and instantaneous transfer of an existing corporation from any nation and retention of its original name and date of incorporation.

The main corporate records can be maintained by Nevis companies anywhere in the world. There is a requirement that a foreign-owned company must amend its existing rules, or "articles of incorporation" to conform to the local laws.

New company creation and registration is fast in Nevis. It's accomplished simply by paying the capitalization tax and fees mentioned earlier. Using Nevis corporate service offices in the U.S., your corporation or limited liability company (LLC) can be registered and ready to do business within 24 to 48 hours. You can do everything by phone, fax, wire and FedEx. Your confirmation papers can be sent to you overnight from Nevis. Formal incorporation documents must be filed within 10 days of receiving the confirmation papers. Corporate service firms will assist you with ready-made paperwork.

In the 33 years since the corporation law's original adoption, thousands of foreign corporate owners have registered companies in Charlestown, Nevis.

Corporate Contact:

Morning Star Holdings, Nevis Services Ltd.
545 Fifth Avenue, Suite 402
New York, NY 10017
Tel.: 212-575-0818
Email: nevisservices@nevisserv.com
Web: http://www.morningstarnev.com/nevis_services.htm

Asset Protection Trusts

Building on their reputation for corporate cordiality, in 1994, the Island Assembly adopted the Nevis International Trust Ordinance, a comprehensive and flexible asset protection trust (APT) law. This law is comparable, even considered superior, to that of the Cook Islands, which is already known as an APT world center. (See Chapter Nine sections on the Cook Islands.)

The Nevis law incorporates the best features of the Cook Islands law but is even more flexible. Its basic aim is to permit foreign citizens to obtain asset protection by transferring property titles to an APT established in Charlestown, Nevis.

Nevis is also leveraging the global surge in medical, professional and legal malpractice lawsuits. The legislative and judicial burden of no-fault personal liability on corporate officers and directors are now the norm, particularly within the United States. However, a Nevis trust protects personal assets from foreign governments, creditors, plaintiffs and contingency-fee lawyers.

Thanks to a 1994 law, non-domestic court orders aimed at its own domestic APTs. are not recognized by the Nevis judiciary. As a result, creditors must retry their case in Nevis courts with Nevis lawyers. In order to file suit against a Nevis APT, a plaintiff must first post a US$25,000 bond to cover court and other costs, Legal challenges to a Nevis APT must be filed prior to the two-year anniversary of its creation. The burden of proof in cases of alleged fraudulent intent falls to the foreign claimant.

All these factors combine to create an atmosphere in which a claimant confronted with a Nevis APT may settle for cents on the dollar, rather than attempt to fight an entire new battle in Nevis at great cost. This is especially useful to American doctors or other health providers who can shield their personal assets in an APT and may use the trust as a substitute for high cost malpractice insurance.

Nevis APT Formation

Nevis has a small international bar and local trust experts who understand and can assist in furthering APT objectives. The APT act has proven popular and a considerable number of trusts have been registered in Nevis.

Under the statute, the Nevis government does not require the filing of trust documents. They are not a matter of public record. The only public information needed to establish an APT is a standard form or letter naming the trustee, the date of trust creation, the date of the filing and the name of the local trust company representing the APT. The fee is US$200 upon filing and an equal annual fee to maintain the filing.

Broad Trust Powers

The Nevis International Trust Ordinance allows for the same person to be the APT grantor, beneficiary and protector, giving far more control over the assets and income than permitted by U.S. domestic law. American law, in general, doesn't allow the creation of a trust for one's own benefit. Overall, the basic structure of a foreign APT varies very little from an Anglo-American trust.

The trust is created when the grantor executes a formal declaration, laying out the purpose of the trust, then moves the assets that are to be overseen within the trust. Typically, there are three trustees: two in the grantor's country and one in Nevis. The Nevis trustee is also known as the "protector." Trust beneficiaries can vary based on the nature and purpose of the trust, but the grantor can also be a beneficiary.

A word of caution: from the point of view of American courts and law, it's far better that a grantor not serve as a protector or trustee. That's because U.S. law (and the IRS) view a grantor in that capacity as having such a large degree of control over the assets as to call into question the validity of the trust. In many such cases, U.S. courts have ruled the entity to be an invalid "sham trust."

A "trust protector" is required for a Nevis APT. This person supervises the trust operation and guarantees legal compliance. A protector doesn't manage the trust but has the power to occasionally vote against a trustee action. A beneficiary can also serve as a protector.

Tax and Legal Advantages for Americans

Foreign APTs and domestic trusts are tax neutral, according to U.S. tax law. The IRS treats the trust as the grantor's personal income. U.S. gift taxes can usually be avoided because the grantor holds some control over the transfer of assets to any foreign trust. U.S. estate taxes are brought down on the value of the Nevis trust assets. However, beneficiaries can use all existing exemptions for combined marital assets. There are no Nevis estate taxes.

To retain some control over trust assets, a grantor can create a limited partnership, then make the Nevis trust itself a limited partner. As such, the grantor keeps active control over the assets in the trust. This technique also adds another layer of protection from creditors and law suits.

Nevis, while a small nation, offers political stability, favorable local tax laws, excellent international communication and financial facilities, a highly reputable judicial system and no language barriers.

Nevis also has enacted comprehensive anti-money laundering laws, which are enforced. This has kept Nevis off the FATF blacklist of "dirty money" jurisdictions.

Fast Citizenship for Sale

Saint Kitts-Nevis offers citizenship for sale. Its economic passport is well-regarded internationally and the program has been managed carefully with very few passports issued.

Saint Kitts-Nevis citizens enjoy a passport with an excellent reputation and very good visa free travel to 139 nations. For visa-free travel throughout Europe, a Saint Kitts-Nevis passport can be combined with a residence permit in a European Union country.

Citizens of Saint Kitts-Nevis may hold dual citizenship, and the acquisition of citizenship is not reported to other countries. Saint Kitts-Nevis's citizenship program was established and is governed by the Citizenship Act of 1984.

The Citizenship-by-Investment Program was established in 1984 and requires applicants to make an economic contribution to the country. In exchange, they and their families are granted full citizenship. Under their current citizenship-by-investment rules, to qualify for Saint Kitts-Nevis citizenship, an investment of at least US$400,000 in designated real estate, plus additional government and due diligence fees are required.

Alternatively, a cash charitable contribution can be made to the Sugar Industry Diversification Foundation in the amount of US$250,000 (for a single applicant) or $300,000 for a spouse and two minor children.

Using the charitable contribution is an easier route for most applicants because it provides a set cost and avoids further expenses associated with owning real estate in a foreign country. Plus, you don't have to live in Saint Kitts-Nevis to secure citizenship, so buying real estate can be avoided if you're not interested in spending time there.

Both major parties support the 1984 Citizenship-by-Investment Program. After his inauguration, Prime Minister Harris imposed significant reforms including regaining visa-free access to Canada, which had ended in 2014. In 2015, Brazil restored visa-free access for Saint Kitts-Nevis citizens, a visa right not even U.S. citizens enjoy. Despite criticism in the local media, there is agreement that the country needs the millions of dollars in annual revenue the program earns.

If you are interested in obtaining this citizenship and a second passport contact:

The Nestmann Group, Ltd.
U.S Office:
2303 N. 44th Street #14-1025

Phoenix, AZ 85008
West Indies Office:
P.O. Box 1121
Charlestown, Nevis W.I.
Email: service@nestmann.com
Web: http://www.nestmann.com

Henley & Partners
Sugar Bay Club
Zenway Boulevard
Frigate Bay
St Kitts, West Indies
Tel.: +1 869 465-6220
Web: https://www.henleyglobal.com/citizenship-saint-kitts-nevis-citizenship/

Contacts:

Government of Saint Kitts and Nevis: http://www.gov.kn

Embassy of Saint Kitts and Nevis
1627 K Street NW, Suite 1200
Washington, D.C. 20006
Tel.: 202-686-2636
Email: stkittsnevis@embskn.com
Web: http://embassy.gov.kn

There is no American embassy in Saint Kitts and Nevis. The nearest U.S. Embassy is located in Bridgetown, Barbados:

United States Embassy in Barbados, the Eastern Caribbean, and the OECS
Wildey Business Park
St. Michael BB 14006
Tel.: 246-227-4000
Email: bridgetownacs@state.gov
Web: https://bb.usembassy.gov

Financial Services Regulatory Commission
P.O. Box 689, Main Street
Charlestown, Nevis
West Indies
Tel.: 869-469-1469
Email: info@nevisfsrc.com
Web: http://www.nevisfsrc.com

Saint Vincent & the Grenadines

As an offshore financial center, Saint Vincent and the Grenadines has unusual European origins and has had some questionable banking scandals. It's a great place for a vacation, but would you want to put your money here?

Saint Vincent and the Grenadines is a group of 18 small islands with 103,220 people that is part of the Windward Islands, located 1,600 miles east of Miami, between the Caribbean Sea and Atlantic Ocean, north of Trinidad and Tobago. Included are the popular holiday islands of Mustique and Bequia. The islands average more than 200,000 tourist arrivals annually mostly to the Grenadines.

Resistance by the native Caribs prevented foreign colonization on Saint Vincent until 1719. Disputed between France and the United Kingdom for most of the 18th century, the islands were ceded to the U.K. in 1783. The country gained independence from the U.K. in 1979 and has a parliamentary and common law system.

Most Vincentians are the descendants of African slaves brought to the island to work on plantations. There are also a few white descendants of English colonists, as well as some East Indians, native Carib Indians and a sizable minority of mixed race. The country's official language is English, but a French patois may be heard on some of the Grenadine Islands.

Recent years have seen important changes in the islands' precarious economy. Previously, St. Vincent and the Grenadines depended largely on agriculture, especially bananas that replaced the main sugar crop. The government has encouraged diversification, promoting other crops and supporting the development of tourism and financial services.

The islands are vulnerable to external shocks, both natural (weather changes, droughts or hurricanes) and economic, recession in the major tourism markets of the U.S. and U.K. In the late 1980s and 1990s, GDP growth variations ranged from a high of 13.2% to as low as -1.2%. In 2008 the economic climate drastically deteriorated in the global financial crisis. As world recession eased real GDP growth began to improve. In 2017, the GDP was reported at 2.2%.

With jobless rates as high as 20%, persistent high unemployment has prompted many to leave the islands. In 2017, GDP amounted to US$1.281 billion, with per capita GDP of US$11,600. On a poverty index of 184 countries, the country ranked No. 133, one of the poorest.

To put this in perspective, in 2003, the revenue from the local filming of the Walt Disney movie, Pirates of the Caribbean, starring Johnny Depp, surpassed that of the total income from the country's agriculture sector. Agricultural contributed 5.4% of GDP in 2013 and in the same year industry was 20.3% and services 74.4% of GDP. In 2017, those percentages were 7.1%, 17.4%, and 75.5% respectively.

Questionable Banking

The country has a long tradition of international banking and finance, but its banking reputation is questionable at best. Its first bank was set up in 1837 by Barclays out of London and the first domestic bank opened its doors in 1909. Kingstown, the capital, on the main island of St. Vincent, is the seat of the government and the business and finance center, including an ever-smaller offshore banking sector that claims to have adopted international banking and financial regulatory standards.

A major legislative overhaul of financial regulations was supposed to make financial services a focal point of the economy. The twin objectives of the legislation were said to protect the right to financial privacy and for maximum asset protection. The government stated then that it would not help other countries collect taxes under the guise of "fishing expeditions" or prosecuting tax offenses. However, the islands were soon embarrassed by banking scandals. Despite what was claimed to be careful vetting, the licenses of three banks were revoked in 2005.

In 2002, the U.S. Treasury issued a formal warning to U.S. banks that the islands' banks were suspected of money laundering and the OECD Financial Action Task Force (FATF) placed them on their "dirty money" blacklist. The response was official adoption of an anti-money laundering law that was said to be "on a par with the highest of international standards." In 2003, FATF removed the islands from its blacklist.

The head of government of St. Vincent & the Grenadines boasted in 2008 that he had closed 34 of 40 banks since 2001, hardly a major confidence builder.

In 2009, regulators took control of another island bank, Millennium Bank, which U.S. authorities linked to an alleged million Ponzi scheme. As it happens, for several years we had warned people who were attracted to this bank by promises of unrealistically high gains that the bank was questionable and should be avoided.

In 2015, Millennium Bank agreed to pay $75.5 million to resolve claims brought by the U.S. Securities and Exchange Commission in connection with a $130 million Ponzi scheme that bilked investors out of more than $75 million. Millennium owner William J. Wise in 2015 was sentenced to more than 21 years in federal prison for orchestrating the scheme which prosecutors say netted more than

$129.5 million in fraudulent certificates of deposit from more than 1,200 investors, causing losses more than $75 million. The bank attracted unwary investors through the Internet and other advertising luring investors by promising massive returns.

In 2009, questions were raised about another island bank that was accused of allowing two fraudsters based in Norway and New Zealand to use the bank to promote their Internet banking schemes.

International Offshore Center

The concept of an international financial services sector here was first introduced by Swiss and Liechtenstein lawyers in 1976, three years before independence, apparently looking for an out of the way jurisdiction where they could operate with greater freedom. A host of Swiss/Liechtenstein drafted offshore laws authorized various entities, including banks, business and limited duration companies, asset protection trusts, mutual funds and insurance companies.

Exempted companies and exempted limited partnerships receive a statutory guarantee of tax-free status for 20 years. At present, there are no corporate or individual income taxes or other taxes.

Until 2002, St. Vincent's law provided for strict financial privacy under the Confidential Relationships Preservation Act of 1996. It was repealed and replaced by an Act that allowed the disclosure of information between island regulators and foreign regulatory/government and tax officials.

In 2011, the government adopted a law to conform to the information exchange requirements of Article 26 of the OECD model act. The government now has signed 31 agreements, 10 double tax agreements and 21 tax information exchange agreements.

Contacts:

Embassy of St. Vincent and the Grenadines
1627 K Street NW, Suite 1202
Washington, D.C. 20006

Tel.: 202-364-6730
Web: http://wa.embassy.gov.vc/washington

The United States has no official presence in St. Vincent. The nearest U.S. Embassy is located in Bridgetown, Barbados:

United States Embassy in Barbados, the Eastern Caribbean, and the OECS
Wildey Business Park
St. Michael BB 14006
Tel.: 246-227-4000
Email: bridgetownacs@state.gov
Web: https://bb.usembassy.gov

Turks & Caicos Islands

The Turks and Caicos Islands are an English-speaking British overseas territory that combines tax-free status, an idyllic climate and proximity to the United States. There is no income, corporate or estate taxes nor any exchange controls. The U.S. dollar is the country's legal tender. There is a wide range of financial and other professional services readily available. Unfortunately, self-government here has not gone well in recent years, but that's history bow.

The Turks and Caicos Islands are a British self-governing territory, a chain of more than 40 islands, only eight inhabited. The inhabited islands of Providenciales, Grand Turk, North Caicos, Middle Caicos, South Caicos, Parrot Cay and Pine Cay, long have attracted those who love pristine beaches, and shrewd investors.

The Islands are in the Atlantic Ocean 575 miles southeast of Miami at the southern end of The Bahamas chain, north of eastern

Cuba. There is non-stop air service from Miami, New York, Boston, Charlotte, Atlanta, Philadelphia, Toronto and London.

In 2015, to gain an extra hour of winter daylight, the islands switched year-round from the U.S. Eastern Standard Time zone (EST) to Atlantic Standard Time (AST). That makes them one hour ahead of Miami, New York and Toronto, when the U.S. and Canada are on Eastern Standard Time, but in sync during Eastern Daylight Time (EDT) summer months.

The Turks and Caicos are called the "Isles of Perpetual June" because they enjoy a year-round comfortable climate cooled by trade winds, but with lots of sunshine. They have 230 miles of sandy beaches and have become a major stop for eco-tourists and divers who discover some of the finest coral reefs in the world.

In recent times, celebrities such as movie actor Bruce Willis, author Jay McInerney, designer Donna Karan and model Christie Brinkley have taken up residence. Vacationers include TV's Sarah Jessica Parker and her actor husband, Matthew Broderick and their children and the peripatetic Justin Bieber.

Providenciales was *TripAdvisor's* 2015 Travelers' Choice award for the world's top vacation island, based on quality and quantity of traveler reviews of hotels, attractions and restaurants. Indeed, in 2014 the Turks and Caicos Islands were the fastest-growing tourism destination in the Caribbean region, with a 50% increase in visitors during 2013, numbering nearly 450,000.

History

Europeans first visited these islands in 1512, but no settlement resulted. In the late 17th century British settlers from Bermuda came in search of salt. Gradually the area was settled by U.S. planters and their slaves, but with the local abolition of slavery in 1838, the planters left. Until 1848, the Islands were under the jurisdiction of The Bahamas. In 1873, they became a dependency of Jamaica and remained so until 1959. In 1962, Jamaica gained independence and the Turks and Caicos became a British Crown colony. Although independence was agreed upon for 1982, that policy was reversed, and the islands today remain a British overseas territory. Since 1976, it has had local autonomy, but that home rule was suspended from 2009 to 2012.

There has been a continuing political struggle between the islands on one hand and the colonial governors at the Foreign Office in London, on the other. This was partially due to a strong pro- independence movement, but also because of alleged drug smuggling and official corruption in the TCI.

The TCI legal system is based on both English common law and civil law, with a blend of laws from both Jamaica and The Bahamas.

Economy

The economy is based on tourism, fishing and offshore financial services. Most capital goods and food for domestic consumption are imported, which makes fees from customs receipts a major source of government revenue. Offshore financial activities provides another source of government revenue and tourism is a leading source of income.

U.S. citizens account for more than half of visitors per year. Most tourist facilities are located on Providenciales (known as "Provo") and Grand Turk islands. Provo is the tourist hub and scene of major developments including a Carnival Cruise ship dock, a Ritz-Carlton resort and numerous large condominium developments.

As in the case of some other British Overseas Territories, such as the Cayman Islands, creation of the T&C as an offshore financial center was an intentional legislative plan to broaden a small economy.

The offshore financial services sector began in 1981 with the adoption of the TCI Companies Ordinance, an innovative law that provides for formation of tax-exempt companies (IBCs), as well as for local domestic companies, foreign companies, non-profit organizations and limited life companies. Companies can be formed by a local agent within 24 hours at a low cost of between US$1,000 to $2,500, and an annual maintenance fee of US$300 for exempt companies. An attractive 20-year exemption from taxes is guaranteed.

Offshore activity contributes 7% of GDP and ranks second to tourism as the main source of income. For a decade the government has conducted a publicity campaign in the U.S., U.K. and other nations to attract offshore financial activities and investments.

The government encourages tourism with an agency, TCI (http://www.investturksandcaicos.tc), with direct foreign investment incentives.

Financial services developed rapidly in the 1990s, and there are more than 20,000 offshore enterprises, mostly using the International Business (Exempt) Company form. The key offshore sectors are banking, insurance and trust management. The islands have a popular yacht registry and a registry for aviation ownership. There is a reasonable level of professional expertise on the Islands and costs are low by comparison with many jurisdictions.

No Taxes

The Turks and Caicos is a zero-tax jurisdiction. Government revenues come from various user fees, levies and duties on imported goods and services. Investors in approved projects get duty concessions, which are more generous in the lesser developed islands.

The U.S. dollar is the local currency. There is no central bank or monetary authority and no restrictions on movement of funds in or out of the territory. The financial sector generates up to $20 million each year, or about 10% of all government income.

There are five licensed banks with combined assets of about $1 billion, 20 trust companies and about 3,000 insurance companies. The TCI has developed a niche market for captive insurance companies known as credit life or "producer owned reinsurance companies" (PORCs). These companies are typically owned by U.S. retailers and provide reinsurance for credit life and product warranty insurance.

If maximum financial privacy is important to you, keep in mind that the TCI are a British overseas territory. Ultimately they are under the policing and control of the U.K. government. The 1979 Confidential Relationships Ordinance oversees banking privacy and imposes penalties and imprisonment for professionals who reveal confidential information. Civil liability for breaches of professional privilege is covered under common law.

In 2009, the Turks and Caicos were on the G-20 OECD "gray list" of tax havens judged to be deficient in tax information exchange policies. Now the islands government applies Article 26 OECD guidelines for tax information exchange. In 2013, the TCI officially joined the OECD Convention on Mutual Administrative Assistance in Tax Matters "designed to combat tax avoidance and evasion."

Interim Colonialism

In 2009, the British government took control of the Turks and Caicos Islands after the revelation of widespread corruption in the territory by islands' then premier, Michael Misick. The House of Commons in London approved handing over control to the Queen's appointed Governor General of the islands, who ruled directly until 2013.

At the center of the corruption scandal were claims that Misick, who resigned as premier in 2009, had built a multi-million-dollar fortune by corrupt land deals. In 2011, Misick, and 13 others were charged with corruption after British investigators recovered about $12 million in assets and 900 acres of land. Scheduled to go on trial in 2013 along with four of his cabinet ministers, he fled the country but was arrested in Brazil and extradited. Their corruption trial began in 2015, and was still dragging on in 2018. The *T&C Weekly News* reported it would "not be coming to a close any time soon."

During the three-year British rule, a new constitution and numerous reforms were imposed, and the islands received a $417 million budget bailout from Britain. With London's approval in 2012, the Turks and Caicos Islands voters elected a new government The Progressive National Party won a four-year term and its leader, Dr. Rufus Ewing, became Prime Minister.

Last Word About London

This is an appropriate point to recall what was stated at the beginning of this chapter: all British Overseas Territories (BOTs) with significant offshore financial sectors exist under the 1931 Statute of Westminster, a constitutional status that gives each territory and the government of the United Kingdom certain rights. The BOTs are Anguilla, Bermuda, the British Virgin Islands, the Cayman Islands, the Turks and Caicos Islands and Gibraltar.

In all these territories, with some variations, the British government can and has, imposed its policies on the inhabitants surpassing the locally elected legislature. In recent years, Britain has "encouraged" its overseas territories to sign Tax Information Exchange Agreements with high-tax countries and all have done so. These agreements require the territories to release to tax officials in signatory countries financial information on clients of banks, trust companies and other financial institutions upon request.

For many investors there may be comfort in knowing that Her Majesty's Government stands behind its overseas territories. Yet this comes at a price of diminished democratic rule and financial privacy. Before you invest or do business in any of the BOT jurisdictions, be aware of the local internal political situation and policies so that there are no surprises.

Contacts:

For information on the Turks and Caicos, contact the Embassy of the United Kingdom:

British Embassy
3100 Massachusetts Avenue NW
Washington, D.C. 20008

Tel.: 202-588-6500
Email: britishembassyenquiries@gmail.com
Web: https://www.gov.uk/government/world/organisations/british-embassy-washington

There is no U.S. embassy or consular agency in the Turks and Caicos. The U.S. Embassy in Nassau, The Bahamas, has consular responsibilities over the territory.

United States Embassy
42 Queen Street
Nassau, The Bahamas
Tel.: +242-322-1181
Email: acsnassau@state.gov
Web: https://bs.usembassy.gov

The Government of the Turks and Caicos Islands
Hon. N.J.S. Francis Building
Grand Turk, Turks and Caicos Islands
Tel.: +649-946-2801
Web: http://www.gov.tc

Visit Turks and Caicos Islands:
https://www.visittci.com/government

Turks and Caicos Islands Tourist Board
Email: info@turksandcaicostourism.com
Web: http://www.turksandcaicostourism.com/contactus.html
Offices located in Turks & Caicos Islands; London, England; Toronto, Canada; and New York, NY.

TCI Mall Business Directory
Grace Bay Road in Le Vele Plaza
Providenciales, Turks & Caicos Islands
Tel.: +649 941-4634
Email: tcimall@tciway.tc
Web: http://tcimall.tc

United States Virgin Islands

*It's not well known, but under a unique special U.S. federal
income tax arrangement applying only to the U.S. Territory of
the Virgin Islands, it is possible for U.S. nationals and others
who make the islands their main residence to enjoy substantial
U.S. personal and business tax benefits. These lower taxes
make the islands an offshore tax haven option for very wealthy
U.S. citizens, entrepreneurs and foreign nationals seeking
U.S. citizenship.*

The Virgin Islands of the United States, as their name is officially
styled, constitutionally are "an unincorporated territory" of the U.S.
With the Caribbean Sea to the south and the Atlantic Ocean to the
north, the Virgin Islands offer a variety of deep sea and coastal fishing.
Their tropical climate and minimal industrial development assure an
abundance of unspoiled reefs for divers and snorkelers, with sandy
beaches ringing deep coves. The large number of isolated, secure
anchorages in the U.S. Virgin Islands and the British Virgin Islands
just to the east has made the chain a center for yachting. A thriving
charter-boat industry in the Virgin Islands draws tens of thousands
of visitors annually for crewed sailing adventures.

After their discovery by Columbus in 1493, the islands passed
through control by the Dutch, French, English, and ultimately the
U.S. Saint Thomas was occupied by Denmark in 1666 and five years
later, founded a Danish colony to supply the homeland country with
sugar, cotton, indigo, and other products. The Danes secured control
over the southern Virgin Islands of Saint Thomas, Saint John, and
Saint Croix during the 17th and early 18th centuries. Sugarcane, produced by African slave labor, drove the islands' economy during the
18th and early 19th centuries. That political status continued until
Denmark sold the islands to the U.S. for US$25 million in 1917.

The islands have a strategic value for the U.S. since they command the Anegada Passage from the Atlantic Ocean into the Caribbean Sea, as well as the approach to the Panama Canal.

U.S. citizenship status was conferred on the V.I. inhabitants in 1927. Although they do not vote in U.S. presidential elections, residents are represented by a non-voting delegate in the U.S. House of Representatives.

Little-Known U.S. Low-Tax Paradise

The United States Virgin Islands (USVI) lie 1,100 miles southeast of Miami, Florida — and it's one of the most impoverished jurisdictions under the American flag. But most Americans only know the islands as a vacation venue with beautiful resort hotels, white sandy beaches and blue lagoons.

The four principal islands — St. Croix, St. John, St. Thomas, and Water Island — have a population of about 107,268 (2017 est.). Per capita income in the territory is only US$14,500. That's less than half the average in the continental United States and $10,000 less than in Mississippi, the poorest American state. Island resident racial composition is black 76%, white 15.6%, Asian 1.4%, other 4.9%, mixed 2.1%; 17.4% self-identify as Latino.

In addition to poverty, the USVI has another unusual distinction. They have been, until now, America's very own "offshore" tax haven. So much so, that the low-tax hating OECD denounced the USVI as the U.S. version of "unfair tax competition."

What upset the OECD was the territory's prohibition against U.S. and local ownership of USVI "exempt companies," although this was required by the U.S. Congress in the U.S. Internal Revenue Code. The USVI was removed from the OECD "unfair tax" black list in 2002, but the OECD continued to criticize the islands for being America's own tax haven.

In 2009, when the G-20/OECD issued its list of tax havens allegedly deficient in tax information exchange, surprisingly, the USVI appeared on the "white list" of "good" offshore financial centers, even though the United States and President Barack Obama vocally, led the G-20 attack on all tax havens. But perhaps more importantly, the U.S. finances most of the budget of the OECD staff that authors the black list.

The islands have been territorial possessions of the United States since they were purchased from Denmark in 1917. They are overseen by the U.S. Department of the Interior. The Naval Service Appropriations Act of 1922 (Title 48 U.S.C. § 1397) provides in part: "The income tax laws in force in the United States of America … shall be held to be likewise in force in the Virgin Islands of the United States, except that the proceeds of such taxes shall be paid to the treasuries of said islands."

USVI residents and corporations pay their federal taxes on their worldwide income to the Virgin Islands Bureau of Internal Revenue (BIR), not the U.S. IRS. In the U.S. Virgin Islands, the average corporate tax rate is just 3.37%.

Persons who are born in the USVI or those who become naturalized U.S. citizens in the USVI, for purposes of U.S. federal gift and estate taxes, are treated as nonresidents of the U.S. Since the USVI has no estate or gift taxes, this means that upon death the estates of such persons owe zero U.S. or territorial estate or gift taxes as long as they are domiciled in the USVI at the time of death or at the time of making a gift and have no U.S. assets. (As with any other nonresidents of the U.S. for gift and estate tax purposes, assets located within the U.S. are subject to federal estate and gift tax.)

Generous Package

To attract outside investment, the USVI Economic Development Commission (EDC) grants generous tax relief packages that include a 90% credit against U.S. federal income taxes. This tax grant package, which is offered for a period of 10 to 30 years depending on the business location within the USVI (with possible 10-year and then five-year extensions), is available to USVI chartered corporations, partnerships and limited liability companies.

The tax credit applies to income from USVI sources including fees for services performed in the USVI, and certain related income, such as sales of inventory and dividends and interest from non-U.S. sources received by banking and finance companies based in the USVI.

For many years, a few U.S. investors with business activities ranging from petroleum production, aluminum processing, hotel and other tourism activities, to transportation, shopping centers, and financial services, have taken advantage of USVI tax laws and enjoyed income with very little taxes. Because of the EDC marketing campaign to attract corporations, about 100 companies qualified for the program in between 2002 and 2004, employing nearly 3,100 people.

The tax benefit program began paying dividends almost immediately after tax-wise hedge fund managers started moving to the USVI in 1995. The islands' tax revenue doubled from US$400 million to US$800 million in a five-year period ending in 2005. The increase effectively erased a US$287.6 million budget deficit for the territory. The EDC program was worth about US$100 million annually to the local economy. A USVI government spokesperson said that the EDC was crucial in lifting the territory from a dire financial crisis to a fiscal year surplus in excess of US$50 million.

Paradise Almost Lost

All went well until the early 2000s when the IRS noticed a rapid increase in the number of high-net-worth individuals moving to the USVI — based on the increasing amount of taxes that the BIR counted as tax-exempt income the USVI. The IRS discovered copies of what it perceived to be "marketing materials" from various EDC beneficiaries seeking additional investors; the federal and local statutes did not limit the number of investors to one beneficiary.

In 2003, the IRS raided a financial services firm, Kapok Management, in St. Croix, accusing the firm of sheltering income for dozens of partners who were living on the U.S. mainland, not in the USVI. In 2004, a Massachusetts life insurance executive who used this same fake resident ruse, pled guilty to federal tax evasion in St. Croix.

But in 2009, after a two-month trial in the USVI federal district court, the IRS lost a big case when a jury acquitted 99 Kapok defendants of conspiracy, attempted tax evasion and fraud charges. The original indictment accused Kapok of "fraudulently abusing the Virgin Islands' economic development program designed to promote local economic development and employment through the use of tax credits."

The IRS claimed authority to go back as far as it wants and examine tax years without regard to the usual three-year IRS statute of limitations. In the 2015 Sanders' case referenced below, the U.S. Tax Court expressly held that the IRS must abide by the three-year limitations statute in USVI cases.

But the U.S. IRS keeps on trying.

In 2015, the U.S. Tax Court ruled that the IRS could not assess alleged tax deficiencies against a deceased USVI man accused by the IRS of participating in a tax avoidance scheme. The Tax Court rejected the IRS argument, ruling that Travis L. Sanders, who paid taxes to the USVI Bureau of Internal Revenue from 2002 to 2004, was not a true resident and therefore was obligated to pay federal income tax. The case centered on IRS claims that Sanders was not a USVI resident, but the Tax Court disagreed, saying Sanders met his federal tax obligations through USVI Bureau of Internal Revenue filings and that the test of residence depends on an individual's intentions and length of stay. *Estate of Travis L. Sanders, Deceased et al. v. Commissioner of Internal Revenue*, case number 4614-11, U.S. Tax Court. 144 TC —, No. 5, Dec. 60,222.

The case is important also because the IRS has kept examinations of hundreds of USVI taxpayers in limbo since the early 2000s, ignoring the three-year limit. USVI observers fear now that *Sanders* has cut off IRS attacks on the transactions that qualified the income for the USVI 90% tax credit, the IRS will step up attacks on USVI residence, trying to define questionable residence as tax fraud. The islands' tax practitioners hoped that the IRS would drop its crusades against USVI taxpayers after the IRS resounding defeat in the 2009 Kapok case. Now they hope the Sanders case will cause the abandonment of hundreds of stale but never-decided-IRS examinations of USVI taxpayers from the early 2000s.

Strict Six-Month Residence Requirement

In 2004, U.S. Senator Charles Grassley (R-Iowa) drafted legislation to impose a strict six-month residency requirement and limited the territory's tax benefits only to income earned exclusively within the islands. (The 1986 legislation had provided that the territory's tax benefits applied to USVI and income connected with a USVI trade or business, but also directed the IRS to issue special regulations to define "source" and "effectively connected income" for this purpose. But the diligent IRS went 18 years without issuing these regulations.)

Grassley slipped his changes into a major tax bill without any hearings, and with no notice to the USVI delegate to Congress, the governor, or the U.S. Interior Department, all of whom were stunned to learn what had happened. This major change was imposed without any testimony, territorial input, and certainly without any consideration or understanding of the critical importance of the territory's Economic Development Program to its impoverished economy. The Congressional Joint Committee on Taxation estimated in a wild guess that Grassley's legislation would increase federal revenue by US$400 million over a 10-year period.

IRS Terror

In a reign of tax terror after the 2004 insurance executive case, the IRS opened about 250 audits on individuals who filed as USVI residents and on businesses that were beneficiaries of the economic development program. Many of these individual audits were of persons who had no economic development credits and made no tax exemption claims on their returns. The IRS and the U.S. Department of Justice also brought the Kapok case mentioned above. At that point everyone who lived in the USVI had to wrestle with the six-month residency requirements whether they were being audited or not.

After the 2004 residence changes were adopted, about 50 hedge funds managers and other financial services companies either halted activities temporarily or withdrew from the islands. The islands' finance sector boom withered, crushed by the IRS and Grassley with a combination punch of the law and subsequent IRS rules that are still unclear with regard to income eligible for tax credits.

Residence Rules

The old, pre-Grassley rules required a person to be a bona fide USVI resident on the last day of the tax year, "looking to all the facts and circumstances," similar to the "domicile" test for estate and gift tax purposes. There was no "number of days" test and no requirement that a person be a resident for all or most of the year to file as a resident for that year.

The rules now require a resident to be present physically in the USVI at least 183 days, or roughly six months, every year. The IRS did set up four alternative ways to meet the physical presence test of the new residency requirement: 1) spend no more than 90 days in the United States during a taxable year; 2) spend more days in the USVI than in the U.S. and don't have more than $3,000 in earned income from the U.S.; 3) average 183 days a year over a rolling three-year period, or; 4) meet a "no significant connection" test. This last test means no house, no spouse, no minor kids and no voting registration in the United States — and no number-of-days counting requirement.

The residence rules also require a "bona fide resident" to have a "closer connection" to the USVI than anywhere else — considering where you vote, what address you use, the location of the closet in which most of your clothes hang, where you have homes, where you bank and where your family lives. Finally, "a bona fide resident" must have a tax home in the USVI — which is usually your principal place of business.

The number of financial firms and other service businesses that once made the USVI their corporate home now has fallen by half from more than 80 several years ago.

The IRS also drafted an intrusive form for island residents it says is needed to prove valid residency. IRS Form 8898 requires those who stop filing tax returns with the IRS, in order to file them in the USVI, to list where their immediate family lives, where their cars are registered and where they hold driver's licenses.

The former chief executive officer of the EDC has said: "In the States, they definitely see that they are losing taxes when some of their taxpayers move elsewhere. All of the people everywhere are competing for the same business. What's wrong with the Virgin Islands attracting some of those people?"

In fact, the betrayal of the USVI by the federal government, assures only one thing — that Americans seeking legal tax breaks will instead find them in secure tax havens such as Panama, Belize, the Channel Islands, Singapore and Hong Kong.

Something for Everyone

Notwithstanding all the above, tax breaks could still be yours — but it is an absolute necessity that, to qualify, a person actually live and make their main residence in the USVI.

The USVI offers two types of benefit programs that are either fully or partially exempt from USVI taxes and U.S. federal income taxes as well.

One type is a USVI corporation (or partnership or LLC) that qualifies for the benefits of the Economic Development Program for its USVI business activities. Most beneficiaries of this program are in one of three areas — hotels, manufacturing, and service businesses serving clients outside the USVI. But benefits are also available for businesses engaged in transportation, marinas, large retail complexes, medical facilities and recreation businesses. Most of the service businesses that have obtained benefits are engaged in fund management, general management and financial services activities.

The beneficiaries that do qualify are fully exempt from most local taxes including the gross receipts tax (otherwise 4%), property taxes (otherwise 0.75%) and excise taxes on raw materials and building materials. Beneficiaries also get a 90% credit against their USVI income taxes (although for C corporations the credit is equal to 89% of taxes). Beneficiaries also enjoy a special customs duty rate of 1%. They are exempt from U.S. federal income taxes on their USVI operations. The 90% credit also applies to dividends or allocations to a beneficiary's USVI bona fide resident owners — which is why it is so critical to meet the residence requirements.

Strict Requirements

To qualify for these great benefits, a business must employ at least 10 people full-time (32 hours a week) and must make a minimum capital investment of $100,000 (or more). Beneficiaries must also provide health and life insurance and a retirement plan to employees and must purchase goods and services locally, if possible.

For non-U.S. foreign persons, generous exemptions are available by using a tax-free entity, a USVI exempt company. These exempt companies are used as holding companies for portfolio investments, for the ownership of aircraft that are registered with the U.S. Federal Aviation Administration, or as captive insurance companies. There are many other offshore tax-planning structures that can take advantage of USVI exempt companies. Up to 10% of the shares of an exempt company can be owned by U.S. residents and up to 10% can be owned by USVI residents.

The USVI also has a research and technology park at the University of the Virgin Islands, and technology businesses can also benefit from world-class connectivity through Global Crossing, AT&T's underwater cables on St. Croix.

Close By

Moving your residence to the USVI is no more difficult than moving from one U.S. state to another. The USVI has a well-developed infrastructure. The legal system is subject to the U.S. Constitution and is part of the Third Circuit U.S. Court of Appeals. The U.S. court system, postal service, currency, and customs and immigration agencies serve the islands. There is no restriction against maintaining a second home elsewhere inside or outside of the United States, so long as you maintain your principal residence in the USVI.

This unique American tax haven is limited, but certainly worth considering for any high net-worth foreign person considering U.S. naturalization, or any current U.S. citizen willing to relocate to a warmer climate legally to avoid burdensome taxes.

The benefits are particularly beneficial for businesses with a global, rather than a U.S., focus because certain foreign source (but not U.S.) dividends and interest are treated as effectively connected income for tax credit purposes and owners of such a business do not have to spend 183 days in the USVI as long as they are in the United States for no more than 90 days annually and have a closer connection to the USVI and a USVI tax home.

Obviously, the USVI tax exemptions are unique in that they require a foreign or U.S. person to reorder their personal and business lives in a major way. It means moving and establishing a personal residence and/or business headquarters in the USVI. However, this is a comparatively small price to pay to gain the substantial tax savings that can result from such a move.

Contacts:

Office of the Governor: http://governormapp.com

U.S. Virgin Islands Economic Development Authority:
http://www.usvieda.org

USVI Bureau of Internal Revenue
St. Thomas Office:
6115 Estate Smith Bay, Suite 225
St. Thomas, VI 00802
Tel.: 340-715-1040
St. Croix Office:
4008 Estate Diamond Plot 7-B
Chritiansted, VI 00820
Tel.: 340-773-1040
Web: http://bir.vi.gov

U.S. Virgin Islands Net: http://www.usvi.net/usvi

Recommended Attorney:

Marjorie Rawls Roberts, PC, LLB, JD, AB
One Hibiscus Alley
5093 Dronningens Gade, Ste. 1
St. Thomas, VI 00802
Mailing: P.O. Box 6347
St. Thomas, USVI 00804
Tel.: 340 776-7235
Email: jorie@marjorierobertspc.com
Web: http://marjorierobertspc.com

CHAPTER ELEVEN

The United States as an Offshore Tax Haven

Unbeknownst to most Americans, the complex tax laws of the United States make America one of the world's leading offshore tax havens — but not for Americans. Rather, almost exclusively, for foreign citizens who invest in America. There are ways that U.S. persons can also achieve reduced taxes and increased profits from U.S. tax laws that benefit foreigners, but those ways are highly complex, requiring costly professional advice and constant tax management.

I n this chapter, the intricacies of the U.S. Internal Revenue Code are explained briefly, so that you can judge whether you want to explore further these possibilities. Again, we urge you — get competent professional advice before you embark on any plans we may inspire you to attempt.

2017 TAX Cuts and Jobs Act

The 2017 Tax Cuts and Jobs Act, (Public Law No: 115-97), contains many tax related changes in its 185 pages. The law deals mainly with corporate and personal taxes, rather than the offshore tax provisions we discuss in this chapter. You should consult with your tax adviser to discuss how the law affects you and your business and to plan to take maximum advantage of these changes.

The law does make a major "offshore" change; the former corporate U.S. "worldwide" tax system is converted to a more "territorial" system.

Prior to this law under the former worldwide system, U.S. based multinationals were taxed on foreign income earned, but they paid the U.S. tax only when they transferred profits home to the U.S. As a result, many corporations left untaxed billions parked tax-free overseas.

Under the new territorial system, corporations are taxed on foreign profits at a new lower rate; the new flat corporate tax rate is 21%, a reduction from the old rates that ranged from 15% to 35%.

This was done to encourage business reinvestment in the United States. The 2017 Act allows U.S. companies to repatriate their estimated $2.6 trillion held in foreign cash stockpiles in 2018. They pay a one-time repatriation tax rate of 15.5% on cash and 8% on equipment.

Other important changes: pass-through entities: Many S-corporation shareholders, LLC members, partners, and sole proprietors will be able to deduct 20% of their pass-through income. But very complex rules apply, depending upon the individual's taxable income and whether the activity is a professional service or a real-estate business. The individual lifetime estate and gift tax exemption of $5.6 million is doubled to $11.2 million per individual and the exemption is indexed for inflation.

We repeat, consult with a qualified tax adviser to maximize your advantages. (See Appendix I: Recommended Contacts for suggested professionals.)

Tax Haven America

Few hard-pressed American taxpayers realize it, but the United States is considered a major tax haven for *foreign* investors.

There are a host of laws that provide liberal U.S. tax breaks and exemptions, but only for non-U.S. persons. While Americans struggle to pay combined taxes that can rob them of more than 50% of their total incomes, careful foreign investors can and do make profits in the United States — much of these tax-free. In 2016, for example, Chinese investment made up 29% of total foreign investment in U.S. commercial real estate, ahead of Canada, the second largest foreign investor, which invested $13.1 billion.

The fact that the United States itself is a major tax haven exposes the rank hypocrisy of American politicians who rail against "offshore tax havens," as we described in Chapter Four.

These demagogic attacks portray Americans' legal use of offshore financial centers as somehow unpatriotic and akin to tax evasion. But these same politicians have no problem when foreigners use the U.S. as their offshore tax haven — because the U.S. government badly needed billions of dollars foreign investors bring into the U.S. every year.

Foreigners had US$4.084 trillion in direct investment in the United States on January 1, 2018, according to U.S. Treasury figures. The U.S. government does not tax foreign persons on what the IRS calls "portfolio interest" income, or on passive capital gains earned in America. However, foreign corporations operating within the U.S. do pay corporate income taxes on some of U.S. earnings. A haphazard array of complex provisions in the U.S. Internal Revenue Code (IRC), coupled with a host of international tax treaties, provide rich opportunities for the astute foreign investor, and you may be able to join them.

Assisting these investors is an elite group of high-priced American tax lawyers and accountants known as "inbound specialists." Their specialty is structuring business transactions to minimize taxes and maximize profits for foreign clients.

The U.S. Treasury and the politicians need this foreign capital to bolster the national economy, to finance huge government deficit spending, and to refinance the enormous national debt — which as of this writing exceeds US$20 trillion, a figure greater than the gross domestic product of America in 2017 which was US$19.36 trillion. We owe more than we have.

With an estimated population of the United States at 318 million, each citizen's 2018 share of this debt exceeds US$64,400. Since more than 50% of U.S. people pay no income tax, those of us who do pay are stuck for a debt of over $170,000 each.

A large portion of foreign investment goes directly into short and long-term U.S. Treasury securities, called the "public debt" and in 2017 that was about $14.7 trillion. That's debt owed to individuals, businesses, and foreign central banks. Most (95%) is Treasury bills, notes, and bonds.

That public debt is owed to domestic and foreign lenders. Trillions of dollars are owed directly to European and Asian public and private investors. The Communist government of the People's Republic of China is one of America's largest individual creditors with $1.2 trillion investments in U.S. government debt securities at this writing.

Another scary fact: the annual interest paid on the total US$20 trillion government debt is now nearly three trillion dollars annually, a figure that exceeds all other federal budget program costs except that of the Department of Defense. Some 15% of the entire budget is for interest payments alone, and much of that goes to foreign investors. We're talking very big money here!

These foreign investors keep the government afloat, so they have a lot of influence over America. When the U.S. Congress imposed a 30% withholding tax on all interest payments to foreign residents and corporations doing business in the U.S., foreign investors bluntly let it be known they would take their money elsewhere if the withholding tax remained. Not surprisingly, the Internal Revenue Code (IRC) is now riddled with exceptions to the 30% tax.

The biggest U.S. tax break for many foreigners comes from a combined impact of domestic U.S. IRC provisions and the tax laws of the investor's own country. As Americans are painfully aware, especially since the adoption of the Foreign Account Tax Compliance Act (FATCA), the U.S. taxes its citizens and residents on their worldwide income.

But non-citizens and nonresidents are allowed by their own domestic laws to earn certain types of income from within the U.S. tax-free. As you can guess, smart foreign investors take advantage of these exemptions, also known as "loopholes."

Foreign direct investment (FDI) in the United States averaged $219 billion from 1994 until 2014. It reached $3.7 trillion through 2016 on a historical-cost basis. The U.S. defines foreign direct investment as the ownership or control, directly or indirectly, by a "foreign person" (individual, partnership, association, government, etc.) of 10% or more of the voting securities of an incorporated U.S. business enterprise, or an equivalent interest in an unincorporated U.S. business enterprise.

Where There's a Will

In a qualified, but highly circuitous way, and under the right circumstances, a U.S. citizen or resident alien (green card holder) also can benefit from this U.S. tax-free income for foreigners. The qualifying process is complex, but the IRC (tax code) offered real possibilities.

It is possible for an American to establish an offshore corporation that can invest tax-free in U.S. securities and other property. Nevertheless, unfortunate things can happen if that American doesn't structure these backdoor, offshore arrangements properly.

Offshore Corporation Loophole

Years ago, a U.S. person could pay a pleasant, tax-deductible business visit/vacation to a tax haven country, such as The Bahamas, and there form an international business company (IBC).

You could then transfer cash to the new Bahamian company and have it put cash into selected U.S. investments. If you picked right and this triangle shot paid off, all that corporate income was tax free. If your foreign corporation had no office in the U.S., the IRS treated it as a "nonresident foreign corporation" and most of its income was tax free.

As an owner, the offshore company could pay your legitimate business-related expenses. You paid no income tax unless and until you paid yourself dividends or a salary. Meanwhile, assuming good management, profits could be deferred, ploughed back, kept offshore and allowed to increase in value.

Part of that happy scenario remains true today.

So long as a foreign corporation does not maintain a U.S. office, or have sufficient contacts with the U.S. that would make it "effectively connected" to this country, the IRS considers it a "nonresident foreign corporation." Under the IRC, it can avoid taxes on certain U.S. source income as defined by law.

There is a big difference now: the U.S. shareholder in an offshore corporation is taxed as is a partner in a partnership. This means a controlling U.S. shareholder of a foreign corporation must pay annual income taxes on his or her pro-rata share of certain types of the foreign corporation's income when it is earned, even if that income is not distributed as dividends or in any other form, and even if the corporation retains these profits.

No longer can profits sit offshore outside the IRS tax collector's grasp. As you can guess, this has substantially reduced the incentive for Americans to create offshore corporations as a tax avoidance mechanism. If you abide by the law, most of the tax break is gone.

Except — and there's always an exception when it comes to U.S. tax laws — for two remaining loopholes that still allow tax-free investment possibilities for Americans using offshore corporations. These strategies must be executed carefully, with professional help, to be certain your actions are both legal and effective.

First, a little background and some definitions that hopefully will broaden your understanding of what's going on here.

Controlled Foreign Corporations (CFC)

The basic purpose of the complex rules governing "controlled foreign corporations" (CFCs) is to limit U.S. taxpayers benefitting from legally avoiding taxes by using offshore companies.

Keep in mind that to benefit from this tax exemption you must avoid your offshore corporation being ruled by the IRS as a CFC; that ruling means higher taxes. These rules can be found in IRC secs. 951 through 964.

Essentially, if a foreign corporation is controlled by U.S. taxpayers, those who own 10% or more of the corporation must report their respective share of the CFC income on their annual personal income tax return (IRS Form 1040). The effect is like the flow-through tax treatment of a domestic U.S. partnership or subchapter S corporation, but much more complicated.

The ingenuity of the "inbound" tax specialist U.S. lawyers has produced numerous loopholes used to circumvent the anti-CFC tax laws. Over time, the IRS and Congress repeatedly have tried to close these loopholes. The foreign tax area has become an ongoing battle of wits between the international tax experts and the IRS.

We tell you this because no prudent U.S. investor or businessperson should venture into this offshore tax arena without full understanding. You must cope with uncertainty and highly complex tax rules always in a state of flux. Considering the potential accounting and legal fees, unless the potential tax savings are significant, the cost of these arrangements may not be worth it.

Just so you understand how complex this area of tax law can be, we readily admit that most of what we explain in this chapter is an oversimplification, reviewed by two leading U.S. tax attorneys, but nevertheless still a crude condensation of thousands of pages of IRS regulations, rulings and tax court cases. But persevere, for there's a potential for big profits, along with light at the end of the tunnel.

The Investopedia website provides a basic explanation of the basics about controlled foreign corporations at https://www.investopedia. com/terms/c/cfc.asp.

Offshore Corporations Operating in the U.S.

Once your offshore corporation has done everything necessary to gain a favorable foreign business tax status under IRS rules, it is free to invest in the United States and reap the benefits of tax-free income just as a foreign citizen would.

But what you cannot do as a foreign corporation is "engage in a U.S. trade or business" as defined under U.S. tax law. Here are the guidelines to follow:

• No physical office or agent in the United States.

• Books and records must be maintained outside the U.S.

• Actual management and control must be exercised elsewhere.

• Directors' and shareholders' meetings must be held outside the U.S.

• The corporation cannot have a business located within the U.S.

Once your offshore corporation secures its status as a foreign business, some of the immediate big benefits include exemption from paying U.S. taxes on interest from U.S. Treasury securities or bank deposits, and no tax on capital gains earned on the sale of U.S. stocks and bonds.

Although there could be tax liability for some dividends paid by American stock shares, these taxes often can be reduced or avoided by locating the offshore corporation in a country with a favorable U.S. tax treaty. Some bilateral U.S.-foreign tax treaties provide for a greatly reduced U.S. withholding tax rate on dividends paid to foreign corporations. (For more about use of tax treaties see Chapter Three.)

U.S. Real Estate a Tax Bargain

Investing in U.S. real estate used to be an easy avenue to tax-free income and gains for foreign citizens. The real estate tax rules were changed, and profits earned by foreign owners are no longer tax-free. Still, investment in U.S. real estate through a controlled offshore corporation can result in lower taxes on profits, if the transaction is structured properly.

In the complicated and rapidly changing area of tax law, an off-shore company should be incorporated in a country that has a favorable tax treaty with the United States. The offshore company then creates a subsidiary U.S. corporation, which buys the real estate.

Remember that foreign investors can earn U.S. stock market trading profits entirely tax-free. This applies whether their home country has, or does not have, a double tax treaty with the U.S. The IRS periodically issues revenue rulings attacking current schemes, so obtain up-to-date advice from an experienced U.S. tax advisor. There is a 10% withholding tax imposed on the gross proceeds from the sale of a U.S. real estate property interest by a foreign person.

In this extremely complicated subject we have avoided going into in any depth, but we wanted you to know that this possibility for tax free profits does exist. Investigate more if this area interests you.

Summary

The major points to remember are those that apply to: 1) the off-shore ownership structure and 2) the type of income to be earned. In evaluating any offshore tax planning proposal, be especially wary of:

- Schemes involving chains of paper foreign entities, all of them ultimately controlled by the same person.

- Foreign-based agents who offer to act as accommodation agents to establish proxy control of a foreign entity.

- Any plan that depends on secrecy, non-reporting and hindrance of IRS oversight.

- Poorly capitalized, low asset corporations. The IRS and the courts often simply ignore such corporations when determining tax liabilities on a specific transaction. They view them as dummy or sham corporations with no continuing business purpose, set up mainly to avoid taxes.

This information is not meant to deter you, but to educate you about the risks of haphazard planning. The most disturbing aspect of studying offshore foreign corporations is the large number of Americans who are unaware of the tax-saving possibilities that do exist. If you take the next step and explore these strategies, you won't regret it if you are careful to play by the rules.

We repeat, have a qualified cost expert "run the numbers" before you decide to create a foreign corporation. A net profit of about US$100,000 in a foreign-based business is required to justify the added operating expenses that may produce tax savings. Each foreign venture involves different facts and costs; each must be vetted beforehand to determine whether potential tax savings are worth the cost and complexity of operating offshore.

If you do want to establish any offshore trust or corporation, financial success will be determined by attorneys and accountants and their professional abilities. It is vitally important that these professionals be qualified and experienced in practical offshore tax, business and legal operations. See Appendix I: Recommended Contacts.

In Conclusion

We are indebted for advice from that master investor, Warren Buffett, and to the inimitable Mae West, whom he quoted: "Too much of a good thing can be wonderful."

Persons of wealth can never have too much asset protection, but unfortunately many have too little — or have none at all.

As we advised in the Foreword, asset protection planning requires your action now, before potential threats arise endangering your wealth. Planning against the unexpected should have a new urgency considering events in the United States and across the world.

History teaches that things can and do change quickly, and too often, not for the better. No sensible person should believe they are immune from financial ruin and resulting personal harm.

That's what this book is all about — strictly legal ways for you to protect your wealth, invest and increase your money, save on taxes, to enjoy asset protection and financial privacy — and peace of mind — by "going offshore."

APPENDIX I

Recommended Contacts

Recommended Attorneys

Josh N. Bennett, Esq., P.A.
440 North Andrews Avenue
Fort Lauderdale, FL 33301
Tel.: 954-779-1661
Mobile: 786-202-5674
Email: josh@joshbennett.com
Web: http://www.joshbennett.com

Josh Bennett has more than 25 years' experience in law with extensive work in all aspects of international tax, estate, and gift tax planning for U.S. citizens, resident aliens, and non-resident aliens as well as citizenship and residence issues. He works with a network of legal, banking and other professional associates worldwide.

Michael Chatzky, JD
Chatzky & Associates
6540 Lusk Boulevard, Suite C121
San Diego, CA 92121
Tel.: 858-457-1000
Email: mgchatzky@aol.com
Web: http://www.chatzkyandassociates.com

Michael Chatzky specializes in U.S. and international taxation and wealth protection with an emphasis on business, estate and asset protection planning. For 36 years Michael has helped clients establish a variety of domestic and offshore wealth preservation structures.

Gideon Rothschild, JD, CPA, CFP
Partner, Moses & Singer LLP
405 Lexington Avenue, New York, NY 10174
Tel.: 212-554-7806
Email: grothschild@mosessinger.com
Web: www.mosessinger.com

Gideon Rothschild is a nationally recognized authority on offshore trusts and other planning techniques for wealth preservation. He is an Adjunct Professor at the University of Miami School of Law Graduate Program, and a Fellow of The American College of Trust and Estates Counsel.

William M. Sharp, Sr.
Sharp Kemm International Tax Law
1. 4890 W. Kennedy Blvd., Suite 900
Tampa, FL 33609-1850
Tel.: 813-286-4199
Email: wsharp@sharptaxlaw.com
Web: http://www.sharptaxlaw.com

2. 1750 K Street N.W., Suite 700
Washington, D.C. 20006
Tel.: 202-872-1800

3. Bahnhofstrasse 98
CH-8001 Zürich, Switzerland
Tel.: +41 (44) 218 12 81

4. 101 California Street, Suite 2940
San Francisco, CA 94111
Tel.: 415-677-9877

Sharp Partners P.A. is a specialized international tax law firm, with offices in Tampa, Florida, San Francisco, California, Washington D.C., and Zurich, Switzerland, that represents clients in international tax planning, tax controversies, foreign tax issues, joint ventures, special counsel and international business transactions.

Recommended Consultants on Residence and Citizenship

Mark Nestmann, LL.M., President
The Nestmann Group, Ltd.
2303 N. 44th Street #14-1025
Phoenix, AZ 85008
Tel.: 602-688-7552
Email: service@nestmann.com
Web: https://www.nestmann.com

Dr. Christian H. Kälin TEP, IMCM, Group Chairman
Henley & Partners
Henley Haus, Klosbachstrasse 110
8024 Zürich, Switzerland
Tel.: +41 44 266 22 22
Email: christian.kalin@henleyglobal.com
Web: https://www.henleyglobal.com

Jon Green, North America Partner
Henley & Partners
906 — 1112 West Pender Street
Vancouver, BC
V6E 2S1, Canada
Tel.: +1-604-239-2170
Email: jon.green@henleyglobal.com
Web: https://www.henleyglobal.com

Recommended SEC Registered Financial Advisors

Robert Vrijhof, President
WHVP: Weber, Hartmann, Vrijhof & Partners Ltd.
Schaffhauserstrasse 418
CH-8050 Zürich, Switzerland

Contact: Julia Fernandez
Tel.: 01141 44 315 77 77 (USA/Canada) / +41 44 315 77 77
(International)
Email: info@whvp.ch
Web: http://www.whvp.ch
Custodial banks: WHVP is associated with Swiss and other foreign
banks.

**Daniel Zurbruegg, CFA, Managing Partner & Chief Executive
Officer**
BFI Infinity Inc.
Bergstrasse 21
8044 Zürich, Switzerland
Tel.: + 41 58 806 2210
Email: idaniel.zurbruegg@bfiwealth.com
Web: https://www.bfiwealth.com
Minimum Balance: US$250,000 or equivalent

Dominique J. Spillmann, CEO & Partner
Swisspartners Advisors Ltd.
Am Schanzengraben 23
CH-8022 Zürich, Switzerland
Tel.: +41 58 200 0 801
Email: dominique.spillmann@swisspartners-advisors.com
Web: http://swisspartners-advisors.com
Custodial banks: Bank Julius Bär, Credit Suisse, LGT
Liechtensteinische Landesbank, Pictet & Cie, Sarasin, UBS,
Zürcher Kantonalbank

**Eric N. Roseman, Founder, President & Chief Investment
Officer**
ENR Asset Management, Inc.
1 Westmount Square, Suite 1400
Westmount Quebec
H3Z 2P9 Canada
Tel.: 1-514-989-8027

Toll-free: 1-877-989-8027
Email: eric@enrasset.com
Web: www.enrassetmanagement.com
Custodial banks: Valartis Vienna, Jyske Bank Private Banking,
Vontobel Private Banking Zürich, Royal Bank of Canada (RBC)

Thomas Fischer, Lead Investment Consultant
ENR Asset Management, Inc.
1 Westmount Square, Suite 1400
Westmount Quebec
H3Z 2P9 Canada
Tel.: 1-514-989-8027
Toll-free: 1-877-989-8027
Email: thomas@enrasset.com
Web: http://www.enrassetmanagement.com
Minimum Balance: $100,000

APPENDIX II

Legal and Investment Glossary

–A–

acceptance: unconditional agreement by one party (the offeree) to the terms of an offer made by a second party (the offeror). Agreement results in a valid, binding contract.

accredited investor: A term used by the U.S. SEC to define financially sophisticated investors that can purchase hedge funds and other exempt securities for lower minimums than other investors. In the U.S., individual accredited investors must have a liquid net worth of $1 million or earn income of $200,000 in each of the previous two years or earn a combined $300,000 income in conjunction with their spouse.

alternative asset class: non-traditional assets (versus traditional assets like stocks, bonds and cash) such as hedge funds, managed futures, real estate, private equity and collectibles (such as art, coins, wine, etc.). The diversification benefits of adding alternative investments to traditional portfolios are due to the low correlation of alternative investments to traditional investments.

arbitrage: the simultaneous buying and selling of a security or currency in different markets to take advantage of the price differential.

assets: items that have earning power or other value to their owner. Fixed assets (also known as long-term assets) are things that have a useful life of more than one year, for example buildings and machinery; there are also intangible fixed assets, like the good reputation ("goodwill") of a company or brand.

asset allocation: investment process whereby the total portfolio assets are divided among traditional assets (stocks, bonds and cash) and alternative assets (hedge funds, managed futures, real estate, private equity and collectibles) in an effort to reduce overall portfolio risk and improve risk-adjusted returns through portfolio diversification.

asset protection trust (APT): an offshore trust which holds title to, and protects the grantor's property from, claims, judgments, and creditors, especially because it is located in a country other than the grantor's home country.

attachment: the post-judicial civil procedure by which personal property is taken from its owner pursuant to a judgment or other court order.

–B–

bail-in: an official action by a national government whereby a set percentage of all a country's personal, corporate and other bank and financial accounts are confiscated, as in Cyprus in 2013.

balanced budget: particularly that of a government refers to a budget in which revenues are equal to expenditures.

basis: the original cost of an asset, later used to measure increased value for tax purposes at the time of sale or disposition.

basis point: one-hundredth of one percentage point, or 0.01%. Therefore 1.0% equals 100 basis points. Basis points are an easy way to state small differences in yield. For example, a return of 6.0% is 50 basis points greater than a return of 5.5%.

bear market: a prolonged decline in the prices in stocks, bonds, commodities or any other asset class usually brought on by declining or poor market fundamentals. In a bear market, prices trend downward and investors, anticipating losses, tend to sell. This creates a self-sustaining downward spiral.

bearer share/stocks: a negotiable stock certificate made out only to "Bearer" without designating the shareowner by name. Such shares are unregistered with the issuing company and dividends are claimed by "clipping coupons" attached to the shares and presenting them for payment. Bearer shares are illegal in most countries.

bench mark: a standard against which the performance of a fund or investment can be measured.

beneficiary: individual designated to receive income from a trust or estate; a person named in an insurance policy to receive proceeds or benefits.

bequest: a gift of personal property by will; also called a legacy.

bond: a debt security, or, more simply, an IOU. The bond states when a loan must be repaid and what interest the borrower (issuer) must pay to the holder. Banks and investors buy and trade bonds.

BOTs: British Overseas Territories. See also CDOT.

Brexit: a term that describes the potential formal departure of the United Kingdom from membership the European Union.

bull market: a sustained rise in the prices in stocks, bonds, commodities or any other asset class usually brought on by improving or positive market fundamentals when prices are generally rising and investor confidence is high.

–C–

CTA (commodities trading advisor): professional managed futures managers also referred to as CPOs (commodity pool operators).

call option: an option contract that gives its holder the right (but not the obligation) to purchase a specified number of shares of the underlying stock at the given strike price, on or before the expiration date of the contract.

capital: wealth (cash or other assets) used to fuel the creation of more wealth; within companies, often characterized as working capital or fixed capital.

capital gain: the amount of profit earned from the sale or exchange of property, measured against the original cost basis.

captive insurance company: a wholly owned subsidiary company established by a non-insurance parent company to spread insured risks among the parent and other associated companies. Bermuda is the leading jurisdiction where such entities are registered.

carry trade (currency): investment position involving the borrowing of funds or investments at a relatively low interest rate and the simultaneous purchase of an offsetting position earning a higher yield. Also, the borrowing of currency at a low interest rate, converting it to a currency with a high interest rate, and then lending it. The element of risk is in the fluctuations in the currency market.

CDOT: acronym for U.K. Crown Dependencies and Overseas Territories (together, the CDOTs), also the 2014 U.K. reporting law patterned after the U.S. FATCA that applies to 10 British offshore financial centers; the Crown Dependencies of Jersey, Guernsey and Isle of Man, and the Overseas Territories of Gibraltar, the Cayman Islands, Bermuda, Montserrat, the Turks and Caicos Islands, the British Virgin Islands and Anguilla.

civil suit: a non-criminal legal action between parties relating to a dispute or injury seeking remedies for a violation of contractual or other personal rights.

civil forfeiture: laws that allow the U.S. and state governments to seize private property allegedly involved with a crime without charging anyone with the crime; the burden is on the property owner to disprove the alleged criminal association.

Chapter 11: a term from U.S. bankruptcy law that describes court-supervised postponement of a company's obligations to its creditors, giving it time to reorganize its debts or sell parts of the business.

closed fund: a fund that is closed to new investments but may be available on a secondary market.

closed-end fund: a fund that issues a set number of shares and trades on a stock exchange with daily liquidity at market price. Unlike more traditional open-end funds, transactions in shares of closed-end funds are based on their market price as determined by the forces of supply and demand in the marketplace. The market price of a closed-end fund may be above (premium) or below (discount) the value of its underlying portfolio (or net asset value).

collateralized debt obligations (CDOs): financial structure that groups individual loans, bonds or assets in a portfolio, which can then be traded.

Common Reporting Standard (CRS): an information standard for the automatic exchange of tax and financial information on a global level, developed by the Organization for Economic Co-operation and Development (OECD).

commercial paper: unsecured, short-term loans issued by companies; funds that are typically used for working capital, rather than fixed assets, such as a new building.

commodities: products such as agricultural products or iron ore that, in their basic forms, have a market price and are bought, traded and sold. See also futures.

common law: the body of law developed in England from judicial decisions based on customs and precedent, constituting the basis of the present English, British Commonwealth, and U.S. legal systems. See also equity.

community property: in certain states in the U.S., property acquired during marriage jointly owned by both spouses, each with an undivided one-half interest.

contract: a binding agreement between two or more parties; also, the written or oral evidence of an agreement.

contrarian: investment strategy that invests contrary to prevailing market trends.

corporation: a business, professional or other entity recognized in law to act as a single legal person, although composed of one or more natural persons, endowed by law with various rights and duties including the right of succession.

corpus: property owned by a fund, trust or estate; also called the principal.

creator: See grantor.

credit default swap: a swap designed to transfer credit risk, in effect a form of financial insurance. The buyer of the swap makes period-ic payments to the seller in return for protection in the event of a default on a loan.

creditor: one to whom a debtor owes money or other valuable consideration.

currency: official, government issued paper and coined money; hard currency describes a national currency sufficiently sound so as to be generally acceptable in international dealings.

custodian: a person or institution entrusted with the safekeeping of a client's securities; one appointed to take charge of the affairs of another.

cyclicals: cyclical stocks rise and fall in sync with the economic cycle.

–D–

dead cat bounce: a phrase long used on trading floors to describe a short-lived recovery of share prices in a bear market.

debtor: one who owes another (the creditor) money or other valuable consideration, especially one who has neglected payments due.

decedent: a term used in estate and probate law to describe a deceased person.

declaration: a formal statement in writing of any kind, often signed and notarized, especially a document establishing a trust; also called an indenture or trust agreement.

deed: a formal written document signed by the owner conveying title to real estate, or other property, to another party.

deflation: the downward price movement of goods and services.

derivatives: investments that are short of full ownership but are "derived" from something else; options are derivatives because the option has an underlying stock, commodity or other asset on which its price is based. Futures, forwards and options are the most common types of derivatives, which are used to generate returns and/or hedge against certain risks.

distressed securities: debt, equity or "trade claims" of companies that are bankrupt or in financial trouble. Until these firms are restructured or other remedial action has been taken, their securities often trade significantly below par value and attract distressed securities managers anxious to benefit from a turn-around they expect can be realized.

dividends: a payment by a company to its shareholders, usually linked to its profits.

diversification: strategy that seeks to minimize overall portfolio volatility or risk by spreading investments across multiple securities and various asset classes; the basic premise behind Modern Portfolio Theory.

domicile: a person's permanent legal home, as compared to a place that may be only a temporary residence. Domicile determines what law applies to the person for purposes of marriage, divorce, succession of estate at death and taxation.

Dow Jones Industrial Average (DJIA): price-weighted average of 30 actively traded blue-chip stocks, primarily industrials including stocks that trade on the New York Stock Exchange. The Dow is a barometer of how shares of largest U.S. companies are performing.

due process: the regular administration of the law, according to which no citizen may be denied his or her legal rights and all laws must conform to fundamental, accepted legal principles.

due diligence: the quantitative and qualitative investigation process conducted prior to making an investment decision by a prudent person exercising reasonable care; investigation and background check into individuals prior to agreeing to do business.

–E–

emerging markets: strategy focused on investing in securities of companies from emerging or developing countries; may involve volatility, currency risk, political and liquidity risk.

equity: a body of judicial rules developed under the common law used to enlarge and protect legal rights and enforce duties while seeking to avoid unjust constraints and narrowness of statutory law; also, the unrealized property value of a person's investment or ownership, as in a trust beneficiary's equitable interest; also, the risk sharing part of a company's capital, referred to as ordinary shares.

equal protection: the guarantee under the 14th Amendment to the U.S. Constitution that a state must treat an individual or class of individuals the same as it treats other individuals or classes in like circumstances.

estate: any of various kinds or types of ownership a person may have in real or personal property; often used to describe all property of a deceased person, meaning the assets and liabilities remaining after death.

estate tax: taxes imposed at death by the U.S. on assets of a decedent. The 2017 estate tax rate is 40%, with an exemption of $5.45 million.

executor: a person who manages the estate of a decedent; also called an executrix if a female, personal representative, administrator or administratrix.

exemption: a tax law, a statutorily defined right to avoid imposition of part or all of certain taxes; also, the statutory right granted to a debtor in bankruptcy to retain a portion of his or her real or personal property free from creditors' claims.

expatriation: the transfer of one's legal residence and citizenship from one's home country to another country, often in anticipation of government financial restrictions or taxes.

–F–

family partnership (also, family limited partnership): a legal business relationship created by agreement among two or more family members for a common purpose, often used to transfer and/or equalize income and assets among family members so as to limit individual personal liability and taxes. See also partnership and limited partnership.

FATCA: "Foreign Account Tax Compliance Act," U.S. Public Law 111-147, seeks to require all foreign financial institutions to report to IRS information on U.S. clients.

FATF: Financial Action Task Force; a subgroup of the OECD that claims to establish international anti-money laundering standards. See also OECD and G-20.

FBAR: "Report of Foreign Bank and Financial Accounts," U.S. Treasury Form U.S. persons with offshore accounts with a value of $10,000 or more must file annually by June 30.

fee-based accounts: accounts with low and steady annual fees with little or no transaction costs; financial advisor compensation is related to the size of the assets rather than the level of trading activity; popular with fee-sensitive clients.

Federal Reserve: (informally called "The Fed") is the quasi-public, quasi-private central banking system of the United States created in 1913.

fiduciary: a person holding title to property in trust for the benefit of another, as does a trustee, guardian or executor of an estate.

FinCEN: Financial Crimes Enforcement Network: a law enforcement agency of the U.S. Treasury Department responsible for establishing and implementing policies to detect money laundering.

flight capital: movement of large sums of money across national borders, often in response to investment opportunities or to escape high taxes or pending political or social unrest; also called hot money.

front-end load: a charge levied on a fund at the time it is purchased.

FTSE-100: an index of the 100 companies listed on the London Stock Exchange with the largest market capitalization; the share price multiplied by the number of shares. The index is revised every three months.

fundamentals: a company's assets, debt, revenue, earnings and growth. Fundamentals determine a company, currency or security's value.

fund of hedge funds: a fund invested in a number of hedge funds and hedge fund strategies generally uncorrelated to each other usually with at least 20 separate funds.

futures: an agreement to buy or sell a commodity at a predetermined date and price. It could be used to hedge or to speculate on the price of the commodity.

future interest: an interest in property, usually real estate, possession and enjoyment of which is delayed until some future time or event; also, futures, securities or goods bought or sold for future delivery, often keyed to price changes before delivery.

–G–

G-20: a formal association of 19 of the world's largest national economies, plus the European Union (EU). Collectively, the G-20 economies comprise 85% of global gross national product, 80% of world trade and two-thirds of the world population. Member countries are Argentina, Australia, Brazil, Canada, China, France, Germany, India, Indonesia, Italy, Japan, Mexico, Russia, Saudi Arabia, South Africa, South Korea, Turkey, United Kingdom and United States.

GDP: gross domestic product. A measure of economic activity in a country of all the services and goods produced in a year. There are three main ways of calculating GDP — through output, through income and through expenditure.

gift tax: U.S. tax imposed on any gift made by one person to another person annually in excess of $14,000 (the 2017 exempted amount called the "exclusion."). Gifts to spouses who are a U.S. citizen are exempt from gift taxes due to the "unlimited marital deduction."

grantor: a person who conveys real property by deed; a person who creates a trust; also called a trust creator or settlor.

grantor trust: in U.S. tax law, an offshore trust, the income of which is taxed by the IRS as the personal income of the grantor.

gross estate: the total value for estate tax purposes of all a decedent's assets, as compared to net estate, the amount remaining after all permitted exemptions, deductions, taxes and debts owed.

growth stocks: stocks with higher-than-market earnings gains that are expected to continue to show high earnings growth; they typically have a higher price/earnings ratio and often pay no dividends.

guardianship: a power conferred on a person, the guardian, usually by judicial decree, giving them the right and duty to provide personal supervision, care, and control over another person who is unable to care for himself because of some physical or mental disability or because of minority age status.

–H–

haven or haven nation: a country where banking, tax, trust, and corporation laws are specially designed to attract foreign persons wishing to enjoy lower taxes or protect assets.

hedge fund: a private investment fund with a large, unregulated pool of capital said to be managed by experienced investors using a range of sophisticated strategies to maximize returns including hedging, leveraging and derivatives trading.

hedging: making an investment to reduce the risk of price fluctuations to the value of an asset; for example, when one owns a stock and then sells a futures contract agreeing to sell that stock on a particular date at a set price. A fall in price causes no loss nor would there be a benefit from any rise.

–I–

indices of ownership: factors indicating a person's control over, therefore ownership, especially of trust property, including the power of revocability.

income beneficiary: the life tenant in a trust.

income inequality: unequal distribution of household or individual income across the various participants in an economy.

incorporation: the official government registration and qualification process by which a corporation is formed under law.

indemnity: an agreement by which one promises to protect another from any loss or damage, usually describing the role of the insurer in insurance law.

inflation: the upward movement of the price of goods and services.

inheritance tax: a tax imposed by government on the amount a person receives from a decedent's estate, rather than on the estate itself; also known as death tax.

insider dealing: selling or purchasing corporate shares for personal benefit based on confidential information about a company's status unknown to the general public.

interest: a right, title, or legal property share; also, a charge for borrowed money, usually a percentage of the total amount borrowed.

international business corporation (IBC): a term used to describe a variety of offshore corporate structures, characterized by having all or most of its business activity outside the nation of incorporation, maximum privacy, flexibility, low or no taxes on operations, broad powers, and minimal filing and reporting requirements.

interbank rate of exchange: the interest rate which banks charge each other in their dealings. See also LIBOR.

insurance: a contract or policy under which a corporation (an insurer) undertakes to indemnify or pay a person (the insured) for a specified future loss in return for the insured's payment of an established sum of money (the premium).

IPOs (initial public offerings): initial public sale of stock by a private company usually smaller firms who need capital from external shareholders to expand operations; IPOs are risky because share value on first trading day can be extremely volatile.

irrevocable trust: a trust which, once established by the grantor, cannot be ended or terminated by the grantor.

–J–

junk bond: a bond (or loan to a company) with a high interest rate to reward the lender for a high risk of default.

joint tenancy: a form of property co-ownership in which parties hold equal title with the right of survivorship; a tenancy by the entireties is a similar tenancy reserved to husband and wife in some American states.

judgment: an official and authenticated decision of a court.

jurisdiction: the statutory authority a court exercises; also, the geographic area or subject matter over which a government or court has power.

–K–

Keynesian economics: economic theories of the late John Maynard Keynes; belief that government can directly stimulate demand in a stagnating economy by borrowing money to spend on public works projects such as roads, schools and hospitals (aka economic stimulus).

–L–

large-cap securities: stocks with a market capitalization of $1 billion or more.

last will and testament: a written document in which a person directs the post-mortem distribution of his or her property. In the U.S., state law governs the specific requirements for a valid will.

legal capacity: the competency or ability of parties to make a valid contract, including being of majority age (18 years old) and of sound mind.

leverage: borrowing money to invest in the hopes of earning a greater rate of return than the rate at which the money was borrowed.

liability: a financial obligation, debt or payment that must be made at a specific time to satisfy contractual terms of the obligation; also, an obligation arising out of damage to a person or property.

LIBOR: the London Inter-Bank Offered Rate; the rate at which banks in the U.K. and other countries lend money to each other. As a result of U.S. and U.K. government investigations of fixing of LIBOR rates to inflate fees for participating banks, proposed abolition of LIBOR is pending.

life insurance trust: an irrevocable living trust that holds title to a policy on the grantor's life, proceeds from which are not part of the grantor's estate.

life estate: the use and enjoyment of property granted by the owner to another during the owner's life, or during the life of another, at the termination of which, title passes to another known as the remainderman.

limited liability company (LLC): a flexible legal entity for conducting business that blends elements of partnership and corporate structures.

limited partnership: a partnership in which individuals known as limited partners have no management role, but receive periodic income and are personally liable for partnership debts only to the extent of their individual investment.

–M–

macroeconomics: analysis of big-picture trends in global markets and major currencies and other large-scale economic factors.

managed futures: globally oriented investment strategy that trades in listed financial, currency and commodity futures markets. A managed futures funds includes futures and forward contracts representing a wide range from agricultural products and livestock to gold, silver, interest rates and stock indices.

margin call: a demand for payment a brokerage firm makes when a client's position that was established using borrowed funds declines in value past a certain point; the client must either deposit additional funds into the account or sell part of the position.

market capitalization: total market value of a company or a stock calculated by multiplying the number of outstanding shares by their current market price. Investors generally divide equity markets into three basic market caps: large-cap, mid-cap and small-cap.

marital deduction: the right of the surviving spouse under U.S. law to inherit, free of estate taxes, all property owned at death by the deceased spouse.

mark-to-market: recording the value of an asset on a daily basis according to current market prices; also called marked-to-market.

marriage: the legal and religious institution whereby a man and woman join in a binding contract for founding and maintaining a family; a term also applied to same sex unions allowed by law or contract.

mid-cap securities: stocks with a market capitalization of approximately $250 million to $1 billion.

modern portfolio theory: portfolio management theory that seeks to maximize risk-adjusted returns and optimize worth through security valuation, diversification, and asset allocation strategies.

money laundering: the process of concealing the criminal origins or uses of cash so that it appears the funds involved are from legitimate sources; a crime in most nations.

MSCI (Morgan Stanley Capital International) World Index: index that tracks the stocks of approximately 1,300 companies representing stock markets of 22 countries.

mutual fund: a fund consisting of a group of investors pooled money with investments in a diversified portfolio of equities, bonds, or other securities. Each mutual fund has a specific stated investment objective and must operate within the investment parameters outlined in a legal offering document called a prospectus.

mutual legal assistance treaty (MLAT): bilateral treaties between nations governing cooperation in international investigations of alleged criminal conduct.

–N–

NASDAQ (National Association of Securities Dealers Automatic Quotation System): an indexed electronic system providing price quotations to market participants about leading companies in all areas of business including technology, retail, communications, financial services, transportation, media and biotechnology industries. About 3,300 companies trade on the NASDAQ.

numbered bank account: any account in a financial institution that is identified not by the account holder's name, but a number, supposedly concealing the beneficial owner. In the past, associated with Swiss banking, such accounts no longer exist since under current rules the true account owner must be known to the bank.

nationalization: the act of bringing an industry, banks or other private assets such as land and property under state control.

negative equity: a situation in which the current value of one's house or other mortgaged real estate is below the amount of the mortgage that remains unpaid.

negative interest: fees banks charge depositors to hold their money as payment for providing safety and protection.

–O–

OECD: The Organization for Economic Cooperation and Development, an international research and lobbying group financed by the G-20 that has led attacks on tax havens. See also FATF and G-20.

offer: a written or verbal promise by one person (the offeror) to another (the offeree), to do, or not to do, some future act, usually in exchange for a mutual promise or payment (consideration). See also acceptance and contract.

offshore: refers to jurisdictions that specialize in providing low taxes, guaranteed privacy, banking, finance, asset protection, insurance, annuities and investments.

offshore fund: a fund that is managed and domiciled in a foreign **country.**

offshore financial center (OFC): currently politically correct term to describe a jurisdiction that used to be called a "tax haven."

option: a contract provision allowing one to purchase property at a set price within a certain time period.

–P–

partnership: an association of two or more persons formed to conduct business for mutual profit. See also limited partnership.

passive foreign investment company (PFIC): A foreign-based corporation that has one of the following attributes: 1) at least 75% of the corporation's income is considered "passive", which is based on investments rather than standard operating business; 2) at least 50% of the company's assets are investments that produce interest, dividends and/or capital gains. PFICs include foreign-based mutual funds, partnerships and other pooled investment vehicles that have at least one U.S. shareholder.

policy: in insurance law, the contract between insurer and insured. See also insurance.

Ponzi scheme: similar to a pyramid scheme, an enterprise in which, instead of genuine profits, funds from new investors are used to pay high returns to current investors. Named after the Italian-American fraudster Charles Ponzi, such schemes are destined to collapse as soon as new investment decreases or significant numbers of investors simultaneously seek to withdraw funds.

power of attorney: a written instrument allowing one to act as agent on behalf of another, the scope of agency power indicated by the terms, known as general or limited powers.

preservation trust: any trust designed to limit a beneficiary's access to income and principal.

primary residence: especially in tax law, a home place, as compared to a vacation or second home. See also domicile.

prime rate: a term used in North America to describe the standard lending rate of banks to most customers. The prime rate is usually the same across all banks, and higher rates are often described as "x percentage points above prime."

private equity: equity capital offered to private investors rather than being offered publicly on an exchange.

probate: a series of judicial proceedings, usually in a special court, initially determining the validity of a last will and testament, then supervising the administration or execution of the terms of the will and the decedent's estate.

property: anything of value capable of being owned, including land (real property) and personal property, both tangible and intangible.

protector: under the laws of some offshore haven nations, an appointed person who has the duty of overseeing the activities of an offshore trust and its trustee.

put options: an option contract giving the owner the right, but not the obligation, to sell a specific amount of an underlying security at a certain price within a given time.

–Q–

quit claim deed: a deed transferring any interest a grantor may have in real property without guarantees of title, if in fact any interest does exist.

–R–

rate of return: percentage gain or loss of a security over a particular period.

real estate: land and anything growing or erected thereon or permanently attached thereto.

real estate investment trust (REIT): an investment fund in trust form that owns and operates real estate for shareholding investors who are the beneficiaries.

recession: a period of negative economic activity technically defined as two consecutive quarters of negative economic non-growth when real output falls. In the U.S., many factors are taken into account, such as job creation and manufacturing activity but this usually means that it can be defined only when it is well along or already over.

remainder: in testamentary law, the balance of an estate after payment of legacies; in property law, an interest in land or a trust estate distributed at the termination of a life estate. The person with a right to such an estate is the remainderman.

rescind: cancellation or annulment of an otherwise binding contract by one of the parties.

revocable trust: a living trust in which the grantor retains the power to revoke or terminate the trust during his or her lifetime, returning the assets to themselves.

right of survivorship: an attribute of a joint tenancy that automatically transfers ownership of the share of a deceased joint tenant to surviving joint tenants without the necessity of probate.

–S–

search and seizure: examination of a person's property by law enforcement officials investigating a crime and the taking of items as potential evidence; the Fourth Amendment to the U.S. Constitution forbids unreasonable searches and seizures but has been greatly weakened by court decisions and unconstitutional executive and police policies.

securitization: a process by which existing debt such as mortgages with their interest and principal payments are combined and converted into financial instruments backed by the cash flows from a portfolio or pool of mortgages or other assets. Securitization allows for an organization (such as a bank) to transfer risk from its own balance sheet to the debt capital markets through the sale of bonds. The cash raised is then used to issue new mortgages allowing the mortgage bank to increase its operational leverage. This type of securitization is known as a "mortgage backed security" (MBS). This type of activity was a major contributor to the global housing and banking melt down in 2008-2009 because buyers ultimately had no way of assessing the value of these debt instruments, which came to be known collectively as "toxic debt."

sequestration: 1) the act of taking legal possession of assets until a debt has been paid or claims have been met; 2) automatic spending cuts to US federal government spending in certain categories of outlays required by 2013 law.

settlor: the common law name for the person who creates a trust, also called grantor or creator.

short selling: a technique used by investors who think the price of an asset, such as shares, currencies or oil contracts, will fall. They borrow the asset from another investor and then sell it in the relevant market. The aim is to buy back the asset at a lower price and return it to its owner, pocketing the difference; also called shorting.

small cap securities: stocks with a market capitalization of less than $250 million.

spend thrift trust: a restricted trust created to pay income to a beneficiary judged by the trust grantor to be too improvident to handle his or her own personal economic affairs.

stagflation: the dreaded combination of inflation and stagnation; an economy that is not growing while prices continue to rise.

stop loss measures: a system designed to limit trading losses by automatically selling a position when a certain price is reached.

subchapter S corporation: under U.S. tax law, a small business corporation that elects to have the undistributed taxable income of the corporation taxed as personal income for the shareholders, thus avoiding payment of corporate income tax.

subprime mortgages: a mortgage with a higher risk to the lender (and therefore they tend to be at higher interest rates) because they are offered to people who have had financial problems or who have low or unpredictable incomes.

swap: an exchange of securities between two parties. For example, if a firm in one country has a lower fixed interest rate and one in another country has a lower floating interest rate, an interest rate swap could be mutually beneficial.

–T–

tax information exchange agreement: also known as a TIEA, a formal bilateral agreement between two countries governing tax treatment of its nationals by the other country; also providing methods of information exchange upon request or on a showing of probable cause of tax violations.

technical analysis (technicals): analysis and selection of stocks based on analyzing statistics generated by market activity, such as prices and volume. The security's intrinsic value is of no consequence to the technical trader.

territorial tax system: a national system of taxation that only taxes financial and economic activity within its borders and exempts such activities by its residents when conducted offshore.

toxic debt: debts that are unlikely to be recovered from borrowers. Most lenders expect that some customers cannot repay; toxic debt describes a package of loans that are unlikely to be repaid. See also securitization.

trust: a legal device allowing title to and possession of property to be held, used, and/or managed by one person, the trustee, for the benefit of others, the beneficiaries.

unit trust: in the U.K. and in Commonwealth nations, the equivalent of the investment fund known in the U.S. as a mutual fund.

–U–

"U.S. person:" for U.S. tax purposes, any individual who is a U.S. citizen or a U.S. resident alien (green card holder) deemed to be a permanent resident; also refers to a U.S. domiciled corporation, partnership, estate or trust.

–W–

warrants (plural): 1) documents entitling the bearer to receive shares, usually at a stated price; 2) a warrant (singular) is a judge-issued document based on probable cause directing police to arrest a named person or search a place or for named objects.

–Y–

yield: The percentage rate of return paid on a stock in the form of dividends, or the effective rate of interest paid on a bond.

–Z–

zero interest: the lowest percentage of owed principal that a central bank can set. In monetary policy, the use of a 0% nominal interest rate means that the central bank can no longer reduce the interest rate to encourage economic growth. As the interest rate approaches zero, the effectiveness of government monetary policy is reduced as a macroeconomic tool.

zero-tax haven: an offshore financial center that impose no taxes on foreign investments or business under a territorial tax system.